W9-APY-714

ANTHROPOLOGY

O F

Folk Religion

ANTHROPOLOGY

O F

Folk Religion

EDITED AND INTRODUCED BY

Charles Leslie

New York 1 9 6 0

VINTAGE BOOKS

A DIVISION OF RANDOM HOUSE

TO THE MEMORY OF

Robert Redfield

Soul clap its hands and sing . . .

W. B. YEATS

Introduction

ANTHROPOLOGISTS sometimes refer to field research as a *rite of passage* by which an individual becomes a fully qualified member of the profession. Like the youth in a tribal initiation who is ritually separated from his home and in the isolation of a "bush school" acquires the lore of adult society, the anthropologist cuts himself off from his own community to learn the "secrets" of his trade by living for an extended period in a folk society. What he does there and what he learns depends upon the community he chooses to study and upon the kinds of questions he asks. If he goes to India to study the economy of a peasant village, he does different things than he would do if he went to live among an African people to study personality development. But, in either case, he will devote a significant part of his field research to participant observation, which means simply that in whatever community he studies he will live on a day-to-day basis with its members. In so far as he can, he will eat and work, gossip and worship with them. And much of what he learns he will learn in the casual exchange of friendly relationships.

Because the study of religion in contemporary anthropology is firmly rooted in field research, I have brought together in this anthology essays and selections from monographs in which distinguished members of the profession report their own field observations. As an introduction to their work, I will describe the role of field research in the anthropology of folk religion.

In the first place, direct contacts with people in folk societies inform the analyses of anthropologists as well as provide them with original data. The informing principle of such contacts resides in part in the intimate quality of the knowledge of another culture gained by the field worker. Thus, the analogy between field research and a *rite of passage* indicates clearly that anthropologists consider the sheer "experience" of an exotic community a significant element in their training. In my opinion this *mystique* of field work is part of the romance of anthropology, and accounts for the willingness of many anthropologists to write in a literary manner. For example, the author of *Sons of the Shaking Earth,* a new book on Middle America, describes his purposes as follows: "Writing as a scientist, I here offer a general statement of what anthropologists have learned about one area of the world. . . . [But] Middle America has also been a personal experience; and in my writing I have attempted to convey something of the quality of this experience."

The authors of the selections in the present volume have, on occasion, declared the significance of their personal experiences of the communities that they have studied. Evans-Pritchard, who dedicates his book on Nuer religion to the Nuer people, recalls his field work as "an experience which has greatly influenced my life." He writes: "I was a *ger,* what they call a *rul,* an alien sojourner, among them for only a year, but it was a year's relationship of great intensity, and the quality of a relationship counts for more than its duration."

Similarly, Gregory Bateson, another of the authors in this anthology, after recording numerous incidents which illustrate what he calls the "mixture of pride and histrionic self-consciousness" of the men in the Iatmul tribe of New Guinea, cautions the reader as follows: "The pride of the men . . . may appear to my readers somewhat angular and uncomfortable. *I found it also splendid*" [my italics]. Yet, in common with most anthropologists who write from field experience, Bateson does not claim any nonempirical, intuitive knowledge of his subject. He explains in a footnote that he has used "terms which strictly should only be used by observers about their own introspections," because no other vocabulary would adequately "convey to the reader some impression of the behaviour of Iatmul natives."

In fact, the first-hand investigation of life in a folk

society is supposed to disabuse the anthropologist of whatever presuppositions he might otherwise make about various social institutions. A characteristic version of this notion can be found in the selection from *Nuer Religion*. Evans-Pritchard asserts that all comprehensive theories of primitive religion "suffered from a common weakness. The facts on which they were based were both inadequate and unreliable. Indeed, such wide generalizations could only have been put forward at a time when systematic studies of the religions of primitive peoples were lacking, *and by persons with no direct, however slight, experience of them*" [my italics]. Evans-Pritchard goes on to say that the earlier type of theorist, who "speculated" about religion in primitive societies, would have discovered the inadequacy of his theories about the nature of religion had he made direct studies of the meaning of religion to "ordinary people" in civilized societies, where reliable facts could be established more readily than in the second-hand study of remote and exotic communities.

It is an impressive fact in the history of the study of primitive religions that none of the most influential theorists (for instance, Tylor, Frazer, Durkheim, Lévy-Bruhl, Cassirer, Freud) had a direct knowledge of primitive societies. On the other hand, some field workers employed as ready-made hypotheses the theories of the more speculative students of religion. In this manner A. R. Radcliffe-Brown used Durkheim's theories, and Geza Roheim used Freud's theories, to give two disparate examples. The studies in the present collection improve upon those of earlier theorists and field workers, not merely because they are grounded in field work, or because field work that underlies them is of superior quality, but because they relate ethnological facts to general ideas in a more satisfactory manner.

This is not to say that the speculations and field research of earlier writers have completely lost their value. The reader who is familiar with recent advances in anthropological research will still find theorists like Durkheim and Freud instructive, as well as field researchers like Radcliffe-Brown and Geza Roheim. But he will be a critical reader, questioning the adequacy of their data, and challenging the validity of their generalizations. He will often learn more from their failures than from their positive contributions to the study of folk religions.

What I have called the *mystique* of field work would not alone be sufficient to make research based upon participant observation a touchstone of professional anthropology. In "Oedipus and Job in West African Religion," an essay reprinted in this volume, Meyer Fortes writes: "It is only by considering it, in Malinowski's words, as 'a mode of action as well as a system of belief, a sociological phenomenon as well as a personal experience' that the living meaning of ritual and belief becomes apparent. For this we must see religious ideas and rites in the context of the situation, the context of personal history and the context of social relationships: and these contexts can only be adequately supplied from one's own field observations." All of the authors represented in this anthology seek to understand religious beliefs and institutions by seeing them in the context of real-life situations: a young West African suffering the consequence of having defied the whim of his ancestors that he could not eat the grain which he had himself cultivated; the men in a New Guinea community expressing their contempt for the women's ceremonial dances and boasting that they made the women postpone a ceremony by breaking their taboos on sexual intercourse; a townsman in Yucatan reporting his reaction to a ceremony: "When I am with the others, poor creatures, my mouth is one way and my heart is another. They say the offering is for the *kunku* [great rain god], but they eat it all themselves! It is not true. The *zaztuns* [divining crystals] of the *h-mens* are just bottle tops."

Observations such as these have an important place in the selections in this volume, and in this they differ radically from ethnographic reports which ignore the complex meaning of lore and ceremony in the social life of real communities. Modern field work provides the variety and the kind of observation necessary for understanding religious phenomena, by presenting them in empirically valid and meaningful contexts.

But "meaningful contexts" do not present themselves to the field worker *in natura nascendi*; anthropologists bring a variety of ideas to their analyses of the contexts of religious belief and practice. This variety is illustrated in the essays reprinted in this volume; for example, it is assumed that the stories of Oedipus and Job can be used as paradigms for the notions of fate and supernatural justice among the Tallensi of West Africa; that a distinction between the Great Tradition of Hinduism and the Little Traditions of village India opens many avenues for understanding the religious life of Indian towns and cities; that the notion of a characteristic group ethos provides a useful way of describing the differences between men and women among the Iatmul of New Guinea.

These and other interpretive ideas used by contemporary anthropologists do not form a comprehensive theory of religion, nor do they lead to a single image of "primitive man." There is, however, a fashionable modern conception of "primitive man" as inhabiting a "mystical" world of "timeless," "cosmological," "metaphorical," and "magical" presences. Costumed in the "archetypal" masks of tribal art, and possessed of a special "primitive mentality," this phantasmagoria is said to perform "ritual dramas" of "mythic reality." This particular conception of primitive man enjoys greatest currency in artistic and literary circles, but a fascination with primitive culture is widespread in our society and has a respectable history. The approach of contemporary anthropologists to the study of folk religion needs to be seen within the context of this larger historical phenomenon.

"The 'noble savage,'" writes Professor Tinker, "was the offspring of the rationalism of the Deist philosophers, who, in their attack upon the Christian doctrine of the fall of man, had idealised the child of Nature." Philosophers, artists, and men of affairs from ancient times to the seventeenth century conceived of primitive society in various ways, and put their conceptions to many uses. But in the eighteenth and nineteenth centuries, naturalism in social philosophy, romanticism in the arts, and the ideas of evolution and progress in science, history, and politics, brought the contrast between civilization and savagery to the forefront of modern thought. To paraphrase André Malraux, primitive cultures are to modern culture what classical antiquity was to the Renaissance.

Even antiquity is now being reinterpreted in the perspective of comparative ethnology. For example, a recent book by E. R. Dodds, Regis Professor of Greek at Oxford University, borrows the language of anthropology to such an extent that chapters are entitled: "From Shame-Culture to Guilt-Culture," and "The Greek Shamans and the Origin of Puritanism." Professor Dodd's book is called *The Greeks and the Irrational*—the implications of this title will become apparent in the following paragraphs.

The fascination of modern culture with the primitive appears in many activities: connoisseurs collect American Indian, African, and Oceanic art, and artists themselves frequently turn to the arts of folk and primitive societies for instruction and pleasure. At the same time, poets and theologians allude to primitive cultures when they proclaim that there are "Truths" which can be expressed only by myths and rituals. Always imitative, popular culture reflects the influence of primitivism on *haute-culture*. Mail-order houses sell reproductions of primitive art. Folk songs become pop tunes. And the shelves of children's books in public libraries contain many volumes of American Indian, Polynesian, and African folklore. As one would expect, such widespread phenomena have commanded the attention of many gifted essayists. André Malraux's interpretation of primitivism in modern art is an excellent analysis for our purposes.

Malraux opposes genuine art to what he calls "the arts of delectation." Since both kinds of art use the same means to affect our sensibilities, they cannot be distinguished from each other on formal or material grounds. The distinction between them resides in the ends toward which they are directed, and these ends are determined to a considerable extent by the kinds of societies in which they are produced. In the past, at least, genuine art "nourished the best in man by the loftiest type of fiction," one based upon a religious communion. In contrast, the arts of delectation serve no "hierarchy oriented by the supernatural and a vision of the unseen world"; they seek only to satisfy impulses for diversion.

According to Malraux, our culture is the first in history to lose completely its religion. "Agnosticism is no new thing; what is new is an agnostic culture." In this situation the arts of delectation flourish. Worse, these arts do not simply differ from true art; they are anti-arts in the sense that they corrupt and destroy the values created by genuine art. Consequently, men of taste turn back to the arts of the most religious periods of the great civilizations, and discover much significance in the arts of folk and savage societies, which are or seem to be largely religious. "For the arts of religions in which we do not believe act more strongly on us than non-religious arts or those of religions which have lapsed into mere convention."

Although the forms of exotic arts appeal to our imagination as refreshing alternatives to the conventions of Western art, Malraux maintains that the aesthetic canons of men of taste are not eclectic; rather, "our modern pluralism stems from our discovery of the elements that even the most seemingly disparate works of art have in common." That is, with voices as multitudinous as their forms, all works of genuine art speak alike to our ultimate humanity. And in Malraux's view, this ultimate humanity is irrational and tragic. "What our anxiety-ridden age is trying to discern in the arts of savages is not only the expression of another world, but also that of those monsters of the abyss which the psychoanalyst fishes for with nets, and politics or war, with dynamite. . . . Every work that makes us feel its aesthetic value links up the dark compulsions it expresses with the world of men; it testifies to a victorious element in man, even though he be a man possessed."

The history of anthropology confirms Malraux's notion that the interest of modern society in primitive culture stems from an effort to grasp the full significance of human irrationality. As a special branch of learning, anthropology developed out of this interest, and one of the main themes of "the science of custom" is the power of uncritical tradition in society at large, and in molding our individual conceptions of reality. A. L. Kroeber, one of the grand figures of American anthropology, expressed this theme in a characteristic manner. "It has long since been recognized that the average man's convictions on social matters remote from him are not developed through examination of evidence and exercise of reason, but are taken over, by means of what used to be denominated the herd instinct and is now called social suggestion, from the society or period in which he happens to have been born and nurtured. His belief in democracy, in monotheism, in his right to charge profit and his freedom to change residence or occupation, have such origin."

The study of anthropology attracts to it individuals with personalities as varied as one is likely to find in any profession, and individual anthropologists maintain theories almost as various as their personalities. But it is not unfair to say of their work that they emphasize human irrationality when they consider man and culture in generic terms, while paradoxically emphasizing the rationality of people and institutions in particular folk societies.

Perhaps I have said enough about the theme of generic human irrationality. As for the anthropologists' attempt to show the rationality of actual folk societies, two arguments are used. The first argument makes an ironic comparison between modern and primitive societies. An excellent example is provided by F. E. Williams's comment on the cannibalism of a New Guinea tribe. "The reason for cannibalism itself has been given by the natives as the simple desire for good food. Indeed, we might profitably seek to explain why some people are not cannibals rather than why some people are. Anthropologically speaking, the fact that we ourselves should persist in a superstitious, or at least sentimental, prejudice against human flesh is more puzzling than the fact that the Orokaiva, a born hunter, should see fit to enjoy perfectly good meat when he gets it." This is a rather extreme example, and to tell the truth, I am not entirely certain that Williams intended these sentences to be ironic. But the anthropological literature contains many such passages.

The second kind of argument, which is more characteristic of the studies contained in the present volume, analyzes the ways institutions that seem exotic to us nonetheless constitute for the people who live under them a coherent and practical way of life. Thus, an elaborate system of divination by reading the cracks in burned scapula may be presented as an effective means for conducting and settling family disputes, and as a logical system of thought based upon the postulates about reality believed in that society. And though the postulates are erroneous, the anthropologist may explain their relationship to the experiences of members of the society in such a way that the reader can imagine himself reasonably making the same mistakes. This method of describing folk customs is called *functionalism*.

The point that I would make is that while the generic view of man in anthropology, as in modern culture in general, emphasizes human irrationality, contemporary anthropologists differ from nonanthropologists in attributing no special degree of irrationality to members of folk societies. In fact, anthropologists tend to find more irrationality in civilized than in primitive societies, while nonanthropologists like to posit an irrational "primitive mentality," or some pristine form of "mythopoeic thought" which is supposedly present in extraordinary degree in lore and arts of primitive communities.

Furthermore, when anthropologists make ironic comparisons between folk and civilized societies, they are obviously being rhetorical, but what is often overlooked is that their functional analyses are also rhetorical in that they are *apologia* for human rationality. Against the primitivism in modern culture which exalts the irrational, contemporary anthropologists set great store upon demonstrations of the logical quality and pragmatic value of the institutions of primitive communities.

The advantage of recognizing an element of rhetoric in functional analysis is that our attention is drawn to the inextricable mixture of judgments of fact and value in contemporary anthropology. For example, in the present volume Meyer Fortes asserts: "Not fear, ignorance or superstition but the moral bonds of the filio-parental relationship are the springs of Tale ancestor-worship." One may ask how different Fortes's interpretation of Tale ancestor worship would have been had he judged fear, ignorance, or superstition to be among its primary ingredients. As it is, his essay is written in a manner to persuade the reader of the accuracy of his judgment of the moral validity of Tale religion. And this persuasion is inseparable from his analysis, for without it he could not write: "What is of interest to us is *the deeper catharsis*, social as well as individual, made possible by the fusion in their religious system of Oedipal and Jobian notions" [my italics].

The reader will discover that compounded judgments of fact and value underlie all of the essays of this volume. Milton Singer's study of Madras is particularly interesting in this respect: he writes that he chose to make "a functional and contextural study of what happens to a Great Tradition and its literati in a metropolitan urban center" because he was suspicious of the usual view, which maintains that great traditions become decadent, fossilized, and secular in such a milieu. Rather than decadence, a sense of the vitality of Hinduism in the city of Madras is communicated by Singer's essay, and this sense of vitality is a necessary part of his analysis.

Few anthropologists limit themselves to strict analyses of the utility and logic of exotic institutions; they also try to communicate something of the way that those institutions express valid versions of the good life. In view of the tendency of contemporary research to follow the rhetorical mode of functionalism by emphasizing the positive side of religion, it is refreshing to read in Ralph Barton's *Ifugao Religion:* "The Ifugao religion is a distorted reflection of the Ifugao himself—distorted because it reflects his ignorance and not his knowledge, his slothfulness and not his industry, his fear and not his assurance, his wishful thinking and not his resourcefulness, his credulity and not his investigativeness, his helplessness and not his strength. Out of his weaknesses the Ifugao has created fantastic conceptions of refuge from harsh reality and has made them his gods." Fortunately Barton was an excellent field worker. He recorded abundant ethnographic materials with which the student can appraise his interpretation of Ifugao religion, and perhaps arrive at a better understanding of it. But Barton's statement stimulates the student's mind as the usual functionalist rhetoric does not, which would have argued that the Ifugao religion, however ignoble it may appear to the outsider, is meaningful and good for those who practice it.

Although this anthology does not contain a selection from Barton's monograph, the extreme judgment he makes of the spuriousness of Ifugao religion is a valuable reminder that the anthropological study of religion is not the study of something that is necessarily good. This fact can also be illustrated from the present collection. It may be necessary, if one is to grasp the historical reality of Iatmul religion, to speak as Gregory Bateson does of the "mass of fraudulent heraldry" that is their totemic system, or the "spirit of irresponsible bullying and swagger" with which they conduct their initiation ceremonies. Alfred Métraux tells us that we have to face the fact that in the Voodoo cults of Haiti the sacrament of communion is "a counterfeit." And Robert Redfield shows us a process of secularization in Yucatan in which pagan gods are reduced to the status of goblins. Fraudulent heraldry and irresponsible bullying, counterfeit sacraments and goblins, are not expressions of the good life, neither are they means for achieving such a life, and yet they are, in some situations, facts of religious experience.

Because I believe that the actual way of life of every human group is a mixture of the genuine and the spurious, just as it is a mixture of wisdom and folly, virtue and vice, it seems unlikely to me that any real community has achieved a religion that is completely genuine. If this is correct, then an anthropologist will severely limit his analysis if he restricts it to the genuine religion of a community. He may justify the adoption of this limitation by pointing to the impossibility of including all aspects of the religious life of a community within the bounds of a single essay or monograph. And his analysis may achieve great clarity by excluding the mélange of experienced reality. My purpose here is not to quarrel with any individual who concentrates upon the positive side of religious institutions, but simply to indicate this limitation to analysis.

The point to be made is that complex value judgments regarding the authenticity of religious beliefs and practices are necessary for the determination of all but the most formal and external facts about them. The distinction that Malraux makes between true art and the arts of delectation is parallel to the distinction that anthropologists require between genuine and spurious religion. Without such a distinction anthropologists cannot discriminate vital from decadent traditions, beliefs that are pious from those that are superstitious, rituals that dignify from those that degrade. Such discriminations recur throughout the selections in this volume, and the ways in which the authors make them are crucial to their conclusions.

Yet I doubt that many anthropologists would consider useful a collective effort to define genuine and spurious religion. The problems involved in coming to discriminations of genuine from spurious religion are not subject to resolution by definition; they can only be dealt with by the field researcher who brings the full power of his intellect and accumulated experience to the observation and analysis of the contexts of behavior in living communities. Thus we return to the role of field work in contemporary anthropology.

Contemporary anthropologists study the human condition from the perspective of actual primitive and folk societies. In doing so, they do not encounter individuals with a "primitive mentality" but come to know people who are alike in their common humanity, and different in the circumstances of its realization. The reader of the selections from their works reprinted in this volume will gain an understanding both of that common humanity and of its various realizations.

CHARLES LESLIE

Pomona College
Claremont, California

Contents

Maps

AFRICA

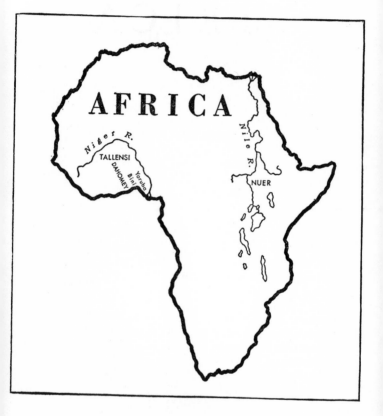

AFRICA showing the approximate locations of the
societies described by Meyer Fortes and E. E.
Evans-Pritchard in the following pages.

A NOTE ABOUT THE AUTHOR

Meyer Fortes

MEYER FORTES (1906–   ) conducted field research in the Northern Territories of the Gold Coast between 1934 and 1937. He spent most of that time among the Tallensi, whose conceptions of destiny and of supernatural justice he analyzes in the following essay. Along with the selections reprinted in the present collection from the works of E. E. Evans-Pritchard and Raymond Firth, this essay provides an excellent introduction to the British "school" of social anthropology.

The British "school" of social anthropology stems from the dual influence of Bronislaw Malinowski and A. R. Radcliffe-Brown. By exhortation and his own example, Malinowski set a very high standard of field research. He worked among the Trobriand Islanders before they were much influenced by contact with European society, and he made a great point of learning to speak the native language, and of living for an extended time in native communities. Trained by Malinowski at the London School of Economics, Meyer Fortes wrote of the field work he and his wife did among the Tallensi: "We were the only white people who had ever lived among the Tallensi for any length of time and the first to speak their dialect. After their initial suspicions had been allayed, we were quickly accepted and soon had many friends. . . . We remember with gratitude the patience, tolerance, tact, and friendliness of many dozens of Tale men, women, and children. They welcomed us to their homes, their domestic occasions, and their esoteric and public religious gatherings. We learnt more from them about humanity than I have the skill to write of."

Radcliffe-Brown's influence on the British "school" of

anthropology derives from the skill with which he analyzed the social structures of primitive societies. Fortes's books, *The Dynamics of Clanship among the Tallensi*, and *The Web of Kinship among the Tallensi*, are magnificent studies of the structure of Tale society. Besides acknowledging his debt to Radcliffe-Brown in the Foreword to the first of these books, Fortes asserted that he considered "the first task of every field-worker to give an account of the social structure of the people he has studied." And in the following essay Fortes develops an essentially sociological analysis of Tale ancestor worship.

Besides field research among the Tallensi, Meyer Fortes worked in Nigeria in 1941–2, among the Ashanti of the Gold Coast in 1945–6, and in Bechuanaland in 1948. He received the Rivers Memorial Medal of the Royal Anthropological Institute in 1946, and was invited to deliver the Josiah Mason Lecture at the University of Birmingham in 1949. The following essay is based upon the Frazer Lecture that he delivered at the University of Glasgow in 1957. At present Meyer Fortes is William Wyse Professor of Social Anthropology in the University of Cambridge, and Fellow of King's College.

1

Oedipus and Job in West African Religion*

by

MEYER FORTES

¶ **FRAZER ON FATE**

It has been said that poets can be divided into two classes. There are those who write for other poets; and there are those who write for the common reader. Anthropologists can be similarly classified. There are the purists by conviction or by habit who write only for their professional peers, and there are the anthropologists of the forum and the market place who address themselves to the world at large. But there are also a few who seem equally at home in both worlds; and among these Sir James Frazer was and remains without rival. His influence on the progressive thought of his time is a by-word, and his writings are still held in respect bordering on awe outside professional anthropological circles. Why, then, has his influence among his professional successors declined in recent years? Chiefly, I think, because he was not only a great anthropologist and a man of letters, but also a moralist whose zeal in spreading enlightenment too often got the better of his scholarly judgment. That glittering prose hides too many rash conjectures. The hypotheses

* The following essay is reprinted by permission of the author and of Cambridge University Press. It was first published in book form: Meyer Fortes, OEDIPUS AND JOB IN WEST AFRICAN RELIGION, published by The Syndics of the Cambridge University Press, copyright Cambridge University Press, 1959.

paraded with so much learning turn out to be little more than descriptive labels for customs and institutions; and the historical and psychological speculations used to eke them out seem naïve today. The smug contempt for the exotic beliefs and customs paraded with such gusto, and contrasted disparagingly with the "civilized mind," repels us. Modern anthropology has largely grown away from Frazer; or rather it has outgrown him.

Yet, sooner or later, every serious anthropologist returns to the great Frazerian *corpus*. For beneath the encrustations of theory, speculation, and prejudice due to the climate of thought in which Frazer lived, there is a vision of mankind which still offers inspiration. It is a vision that takes in the whole of mankind. There lies its greatness. It shows in assiduous detail how varied and diverse are the customs and institutions of mankind. But its purpose is to bring home to us the unity behind the diversity. For Frazer this lay in supposed historical connections or common mental habits and dispositions. Fallacious though his theories now prove to be, in principle he was right. There are uniformities and common patterns in the customs and institutions of mankind; and if we want to understand them, we must take into account the common intellectual and emotional dispositions of mankind.

It would not have seemed strange to Frazer to place side by side Oedipus, Job, and the religious beliefs of a West African tribe of ancestor-worshippers, as I propose to do. But what he was interested in when he lumped together, as he habitually did, the customs of the Greeks and the Hebrews, other peoples of antiquity, and contemporary primitive and Oriental societies, was their most superficial descriptive features. To take an instance at random, Orestes the matricide, recovering sanity by biting off a finger, is quoted in the same breath as blood avengers among American Indians, Maori, and Africans who have to taste the blood of their victims in order to lay their ghosts.[1] That is what our informants tell us; but to see no more in these customs than diverse expressions of a fear of ghosts which acts as a curb on would-be murderers is, from today's standpoint, almost ludicrous. What is

[1] J. G. Frazer: *Psyche's Task* (1913), p. 56.

significant for us in the Orestes story is that he murdered a *kinswoman*, that this kinswoman was his *mother*, and that his expiation was to mutilate himself by *biting off a finger*. To go to such an extreme merely to taste his own blood would have been silly. The parallels that leap to mind, for an anthropologist today, are other apparently irrational mutilations of the body carried out in the context of an overt or suppressed conflict between successive generations. We think of the strange story of Moses' wife Zipporah circumcizing her son with a flint to save him from being killed by Yahweh,[2] and more particularly of the very widespread association of circumcision and other forms of mutilation with the initiation of youths and maidens into adulthood.

In short, we should now use the Orestes story not as one of a miscellany of examples to illustrate a particular kind of barbarous superstition, but as a model, or paradigm, from which we might be able to derive principles applicable in other cases.

In the same way Oedipus and Job both turn up in Frazer's *Folklore in the Old Testament*, but simply to illustrate widespread "superstitious" customs. Job is cited, curiously enough, in evidence for the statement that in the Old Testament it is the blood of a murdered man, not his ghost, which cries out for vengeance, the reference being to Job's "appealing against the injustice of his fate . . . 'O earth, cover not my blood, and let my cry have no resting place.'"[3] As for Oedipus, he appears as a parallel to the story of Moses in the ark of bullrushes. He is one of many examples of the hero who was "exposed at birth, and was only rescued from imminent death by what might seem to vulgar eyes an accident, but what really proved to be the finger of Fate interposed to preserve the helpless babe for the high destiny that awaited him. . . ."[4]

Fate, or Destiny, is the main theme of this essay. It is mentioned in many places in Frazer's writings, and invariably in the manner I have described. There is no

[2] Exod. iv, 25.
[3] J. G. Frazer: *Folklore in the Old Testament* (1918 ed.), Vol. I, p. 101.
[4] Ibid. Vol. II, pp. 438–46.

attempt to analyze the notion of Fate as a category of religious or philosophic thought. It is treated like any other customary belief—a belief in ghosts or in lucky and unlucky omens or in magical charms to fend off supernatural threats.

Supposing, however, that we consider the stories of Oedipus and Job from an analytical rather than a descriptive point of view.[5] What is notable then is that they epitomize, poignantly and dramatically, two religious and ethical conceptions that seem to be mutually opposed in some respects but complementary in others. These ideas are associated with different cosmological doctrines about the universe, and different conceptions of the nature of man and his relations with supernatural powers. I think that they represent, in a clear paradigmatic form, two fundamental principles of religious thought and custom. The Oedipal principle is best summed up in the notion of Fate or Destiny, the Jobian principle in that of Supernatural Justice.

Now I am not suggesting that the whole religious system of Greece of the fifth century B.C. can be reduced to what is represented in the story of Oedipus, or that the drama of Job contains the whole of Old Testament Hebrew religion. I am concerned only with the specific conceptions embodied in the two stories. That they are religious conceptions is taken for granted by all our authorities,[6] and what I want to show is that they also exist in West African religious systems.

¶ OEDIPUS AND JOB AS PARADIGMS

The myth of Oedipus is best known to us from the Theban plays of Sophocles; and what gives these plays their tragic intensity is not the horror they arouse of patricide and incest, but the "sense of the blindness and helplessness of mankind" [1] which, as Mr. Lucas notes, they convey. The catastrophe which overwhelms Oedipus

[5] Cf. Meyer Fortes: "Analysis and Description in Social Anthropology," *Advancement of Science*, Vol. xxxviii (1953).

[6] Cf. F. M. Cornford: *From Religion to Philosophy* (1912), pp. 12 ff.; D. W. Lucas: *The Greek Tragic Poets* (1950), pp. 133 ff.; J. Pedersen: *Israel: Its Life and Culture* (1926), 2 vols., pp. 358 ff.

[1] Lucas, op. cit. pp. 133 ff.

is due, Mr. Lucas adds, to causes that "lie hid deep in the nature of god and man," not to any faults of his. On the contrary, he is a man of virtuous and noble character choosing self-imposed exile rather than risk slaying his supposed father, a just and benevolent king, a faithful husband and devoted father. And he has one further quality which in the end proves his downfall: his resolute pursuit of the truth. When he discovers the truth about his birth and marriage, he can only bear to live by blinding himself and so blotting out the intolerable knowledge. For his sins are so infamous that not even death could atone for them.

But it is not just a matter of his having committed them unwittingly. It is as if his actions have been thrust upon him, or he driven into them, by some agency operating outside the bounds of human knowledge and unresponsive to human conduct. He is the victim of Destiny. The question of responsibility or guilt does not even seem relevant. Much later, when as an old man he is preparing for death, in the *Oedipus Coloneus*, the question does come up and he asserts his innocence. It was an appalling Fate and not his own choosing.

The part played by the concept of Fate, which is the usual translation of the Greek word *Moira*, in early Greek religion has been much discussed by classical scholars.[2] It was clearly a very complex notion, but our authorities seem to be agreed that its original meaning was "portion" or "lot." Furthermore, it seems to have had two aspects. One was the idea of Fate as an impersonal power representing the necessity and justice of the "disposition of Nature," as Professor Dodds puts it, and supreme over both gods and men. The other was its reference to the individual. Each person is conceived of as having a particular apportionment of good and evil for his lifetime which is decided at birth; and "this luck," to quote Professor Dodds again, "is not conceived as an extraneous accident—it is as much part of a man's natal endowment as beauty or talent."[3] This is the aspect most conspicuous in the Oedipus myth. But we see there also that an individ-

[2] E.g. Cornford, op. cit.; E. R. Dodds, *The Greeks and the Irrational* (1951); H. J. Rose, article, "Fate," Encyclopaedia Britannica. Fourteenth edition.

[3] Dodds, op. cit. p. 42.

ual's fate is in part determined by the fate of his parents and in turn affects that of his offspring. Professor Dodds relates this to the idea, very familiar to anthropologists from its occurrence in most primitive societies, that a son's life is the "prolongation of his father's life." By the laws of filiation and descent, a son who inherits his father's position in society *ipso facto* inherits both his material property and debts and his moral and ritual property and debts. Normally, however, filial succession is a deliberate and willing act. When Fate steps in, as with Oedipus, it occurs by blind and to some extent vainly resisted compulsion.

There is a similarity here to the notion of witchcraft.[4] Fate, like witchcraft, is an involuntary force and can, in the last resort, only be known in retrospect. This in itself generates efforts to discover it in advance and so to try to control it. Hence the appeal to oracles. But the oracles do not in fact enable men to master their fate. As with witchcraft, they merely help to reconcile men to its ineluctability. It is best of all, really, to accept this and not to seek arrogantly to probe destiny.

Job confronts us with a wholly different conception of man and of morality. There is no suggestion here of inscrutable influences ruling the course of an individual's life from the moment of his birth. The good and evil that accrue to a man during his lifetime are the rewards and punishments meted out by an omnipotent, personified God. But God does not act arbitrarily or capriciously. He is, as Pedersen points out,[5] bound by a covenant with his creature, man. It is almost a contractual relationship, in which God is bound to act justly and mercifully, and man is free to choose between righteousness and sin. There is a known code of righteous conduct, and a man who has consistently followed the way of righteousness is entitled to well-being, peace of mind, happiness, and even material prosperity as a gift from the Supreme Ruler of the universe. Hence Job rejects the arguments and consolations of his friends. He will not admit that his afflictions are due to his having sinned, however inadvertently. He even feels

[4] Cf. E. E. Evans-Pritchard: *Witchcraft, Oracles and Magic among the Azande* (1937).
[5] Pedersen, op. cit. pp. 358 ff.

entitled to demand of God "shew me wherefore thou contendest with me," [6] and spurns the advice of his comforters to admit his guilt and recover his happiness by asking God's pardon.

It should be emphasized that all the characters in the story believe that God is just, that the righteous man must therefore prosper, and that "the triumphing of the wicked is short." [7] The question is whether Job's confidence in his own righteousness is justified or whether his calamities are evidence of unadmitted sin. And there is a still deeper question. Even if Job is justified in denying that he is wicked, does righteousness, as understood in terms of human conduct, create claims on God? Is not God allpowerful so that he stands above all human norms of good and bad conduct and is not bound by a concept of justice founded on a rule of reciprocal obligation? For God is not only the creator of the universe but the very source of righteousness and justice. And this is the gist of God's speech in the magnificent thirty-eighth to fortieth chapters. Man is not God's equal, and however virtuous he may feel himself to be, he cannot measure himself against God to disannul God's judgment and condemn Him in order to justify himself.[8]

It is when he realizes the import of this speech that Job is saved. He does not admit guilt in the sense of responsibility for actions that are wicked by ordinary human standards. What he admits is having placed himself on a footing of equality with God, judging for himself what conduct is righteous and what wicked. This wrong relationship was his sin. He accepts, as he has not previously done, the omnipotence of God and his own dependence on Him. Job's God is a majestic and all-powerful fatherfigure, the source of his creatures' life, and in virtue of that vested with final authority over them; and reciprocally —as Job constantly pleads—with responsibility for their well-being and happiness. What Job has to learn is that God's authority is ultimate, inexplicable, not subject to coercion by obedience to rules of righteousness or bound by contracts. Job's sufferings are like severe measures of

[6] Job x, 2.
[7] Job xx, 5.
[8] Job xl, 8.

discipline that a father might use to correct a son who, while exemplary in his conduct, was getting too big for his boots and arrogating to himself a status equal to his father's; and Job's salvation might be compared to the son's realizing and accepting his filial dependence. This means accepting paternal authority without resentment and seeing it as always benevolent in intention, even when it is used punitively. This is the essence of filial piety, and Job had been on the brink of acting in defiance of it.

¶ THE NOTION OF FATE IN WEST AFRICA

The notion of Fate or Destiny as an innate, though not necessarily impersonal determinant of an individual's life-history, and its complementary, the notion of Justice as the actions of a personified and deified agency responding to the individual's moral conduct and to his moral relationships with supernatural powers, can and do occur in a single religious system. Both seem to be present in some form in the theistic Western and Oriental religions.[1] It is the more interesting and instructive to find that both occur in the nonscriptural religious systems of many West African peoples. Indeed, one of the characteristic marks of West African religions, as compared with other African religions (e.g., East and South African Bantu religions) in which ancestor-worship also plays a part, is the occurrence of the notion of Fate in them. What I wish to explore, with our paradigms to guide the inquiry, is how the two ideas are related in a West African religious system known to me at first hand.

But first let us take a few descriptive examples from other parts of West Africa. The Yoruba of Nigeria, Dr. Bascom tells us,[2] associate a person's "luck" with his "destiny." Luck is connected with the head and derives from one's "creator" or spirit guardian. One man may work hard yet remain poor. This is because his luck is bad. Another man may work little yet get rich because his luck is good. Bad luck affects not only its owner but also

[1] Cf. articles under "Fate," in Hastings's *Encyclopaedia of Religion and Ethics*, Vol. v.

[2] W. R. Bascom: "Social Status, Wealth and Individual Difference among the Yoruba," *American Anthropologist*, Vol. LIII, No. 4 (1951).

those with whom he associates. As to Destiny, it is best to quote Dr. Bascom's own words:

> A person's luck and his success in economic and other affairs is also a matter of destiny (*ayanmope, ayanmo*) or fate (*iwa*) which is also known as "to kneel and choose" (*akunleyan*). Before a child is born its soul is said to kneel before the deity (*Olo-dumare*) and choose (*yan*) its fate on earth. Those who humbly make reasonable requests for food, money or children receive what they ask during their life on earth. However those who make their requests as if they had the right to expect whatever they wanted, do not receive them. . . . A person whose destiny on earth is poverty may be able to acquire some money by working hard, but he will never have very much. Diviners of various kinds . . . are consulted to find out what is in store for the future and what can be done to avert evil or insure a favourable outcome . . . but while the diviners may be able to recommend sacrifices (*ebo*) which will influence events in the immediate future, they cannot alter the course of one's life or change his destiny.

Similar beliefs are held by the closely related people of Benin.[3] We learn that before he is born a person tells the Creator what he plans to do with his life and asks for the means to accomplish this. If he is unsuccessful he is said to be "fighting against the fate which he has determined for himself." Luck is associated with the head, so that a person is said to have "a good head" or a "bad head" according as he has been fortunate or not in his life, and he makes offerings to his head when he has a piece of good fortune.

These notions also form the core of the rich and complex cosmology and religious system of the Dahomeans, portrayed by Professor Herskovits.[4] Dahomean religion comprises three major categories of beliefs, mythology,

---

[3] Cf. R. E. Bradbury: *The Benin Kingdom* (Ethnographic Survey of Africa, Part xiii, 1957).

[4] M. J. Herskovits: *Dahomey* (1938), Vol. ii, especially Chap. xxx. See also B. Maupoil, *La Géomancie à l'ancienne Côte des Esclaves* (1943).

and associated cults: the worship of the ancestors, the worship of the great public deities, and the cult of personal gods and forces. These three categories are linked together by a "complex and highly specialized system of divination" which is constantly resorted to for fatidical guidance and ritual advice. This system of divination is under the aegis of the cult of Fa, "the destiny of the Universe as willed by the gods," as Professor Herskovits interprets it. But Fa is also a personal Destiny whose worship, as might be expected in a society with so highly developed a patrilineal descent organization, is restricted to men. What is significant is that a man does not acquire his full Destiny until he is mature. As a boy, his father, after consulting a diviner, endows him with his partial Destiny symbolized in some palm-kernels which form the nucleus of a small shrine, and in specific food, clothing, and other avoidances ascertained by the diviner. The incentive for a man to acquire his full Destiny is a series of misfortunes such as illness, the death of children, or the barrenness of a wife. Women have only a partial Fa, as they are deemed to share the destiny of their fathers or husbands, since they are dependent on them in the same way as children are.

"What is in store for a man," says Professor Herskovits,[5] "is foreordained." Yet there is a way out through the "divine trickster," Legba, the "personification of Accident." Legba is the messenger and spokesman of the gods, and if he is properly propitiated, he can divert predestined misfortunes. "In this world ruled by Destiny," Professor Herskovits explains, "man lives secure in the conviction that between the inexorable fate laid down for an individual and the execution of that fate lies the possibility of the way out. . . ." There is also a "way out" through the doctrine of the four souls. A man who reaches maturity achieves fulfillment of his life through his wives and children, his slaves and his entire household. His Destiny includes theirs, and this collective Destiny is watched over by his fourth soul. This is conceived as a kind of heavenly counterpart guarding an array of containers in which are stored good things like riches, health, and children, and bad things like poverty, illness, and death. The setting up

[5] Herskovits, op. cit. Vol. II, p. 222.

of a man's full Destiny as a cult object is a ceremony for persuading this soul to select the good things of life for the individual.

To cap it all, there is also the notion of Da, or luck, symbolized for the individual in the umbilicus and in cosmological terms by the snake and the rainbow. Da lies behind the vagaries of chance seen in particular incidents of good and ill luck. He pursues only men who have power and authority, such as heads of households or villages or kingdoms; and he manifests himself to them in the form of unexpected misfortunes which happen just when things are going particularly well. Hence he is regarded with apprehension. If he is neglected, he becomes resentful and dangerous. A man learns through dreams or through a diviner that his Da desires to be established. If he is wise, he establishes the Da in his house and worships it. This strengthens his luck and protects him against attacks from the Da of other men.

Brief as is this summary of Dahomean beliefs concerning Fate and Destiny, it can be seen that they bear comparison with those of the Greeks. The Dahomeans also have an elaborate Pantheon of sky and earth gods headed by a creator divinity which is both male and female, and a complex ancestral cult correlated with descent groups, local communities, and political units. The ancestors of a descent group are collectively enshrined and worshipped in a room specially set aside for this purpose. They are, as Professor Herskovits notes,[6] the focal point of the descent-group organization. Appeal is made to them through sacrifice and prayer to watch over the health and safety of any member of the group who is in hazard, and great ceremonial celebrations are held at set times, such as the harvest, to honor them. In very broad terms, therefore, their supernatural powers are called upon to safeguard the numbers and well-being of the descent group, whereas Destiny is involved in the play of chance in the individual's life-history.

The Yoruba, Bini, and Dahomeans are closely related in culture. All have a complex system of ancestor-worship and a cult of gods or deified beings, together with the notion of Destiny. I have dwelled on their beliefs because

[6] Herskovits, op. cit. Vol. I, Chap. XI.

they are characteristic of West Africa and the ethnographic data are so good. Similar patterns of cult and belief occur among other West African peoples, including some with no obvious linguistic or cultural links with the Yoruba. The Tallensi, whose social and religious institutions I have studied in the field, are typical of one such non-Yoruba cluster.[7] I turn to them with a particular aim in mind. Generalized ethnographic descriptions have one serious defect. They do not enable us to see how ritual or belief is actually used by men and women to regulate their lives. A Tale friend once remarked to me, as he was going home from the funeral of a clan brother: "Now that we have done the proper ritual our grief is soothed." Another pointed out to me that when you consult a diviner, you have the immediate relief of knowing what supernatural agency is causing your troubles and what ritual steps to take. It is only by considering it, in Malinowski's words,[8] as "a mode of action as well as a system of belief, a sociological phenomenon as well as a personal experience" that the living meaning of ritual and belief becomes apparent. For this we must see religious ideas and rites in the context of the situation, the context of personal history, and the context of social relationships: and these contexts can only be adequately supplied from one's own field observations.

¶ THE TALLENSI: KINSHIP AND ANCESTOR CULT

The religious institutions of the Tallensi cannot be understood without reference to their social organization. I have described this in detail elsewhere[1] and the barest summary must suffice here. We can begin with the domestic family living in its own homestead. This consists of a group of males, ideally a man and his adult sons and their sons, the wives of the adult men, and their unmarried daughters—in short, a typical patrilineal joint family. The men of this family form a minor branch of a more ex-

[7] The Mole-Dagbane peoples of the Voltaic region. Cf. Meyer Fortes, *The Dynamics of Clanship among the Tallensi* (1945); *The Web of Kinship among the Tallensi* (1949).

[8] B. Malinowski: "Magic, Science and Religion," *Science, Religion and Reality*, ed. J. Needham (1925).

[1] Fortes, op. cit. (1945, 1949).

tensive patrilineal lineage with common ancestry going back in some cases to ten or twelve generations. As the lineage is exogamous, the daughters marry out and the wives of its male members come from adjacent lineages. The lineage is a localized group with some political autonomy. But, as with the Dahomean descent group, its essential focus of unity and identity is the cult of the lineage ancestors. Just as there is a hierarchy of lineage segments of greater and greater inclusiveness, until finally the entire lineage is included, so there is a hierarchy of ancestors and ancestor shrines. Members of the smallest segment worship the founding ancestors of their segment, join with the members of the next more inclusive segment to worship their common founding ancestors, and so on till the most inclusive unit, the maximal lineage as a whole, is reached. The lineage ancestor cult is by definition a cult of the patrilineal male ancestors. But the ancestress of a lineage or segment is almost as important as the founding ancestor, and the spirits of maternal ancestors and ancestresses play as big a part in a person's life as his paternal ancestor spirits.

In this social system, jural and ritual authority is vested in the men who have the status of fathers. Until a man's father dies, he himself has no jural independence and cannot directly bring a sacrifice to a lineage ancestor. He is, as it were, merged in his father's status. Now paternal authority, however conscientiously and benevolently exercised, as it usually is among the Tallensi, inevitably gives rise to suppressed hostility and opposition in sons. This is quite explicitly recognized, and is dealt with by means of a number of ritual avoidances between a man and his first-born son. Indeed, so deep is the feeling of latent opposition between successive generations that ritual avoidances also hold between a woman and her first-born daughter.

Tale fathers are normally kind-hearted and tolerant, especially toward their young children, who are still in a stage of complete dependence on their parents. But when sons grow up and begin to farm for themselves and to look for wives, the wish for independence arises. Then the rights of the father—to command his son's labor and property, to take responsibility for him in law, to sacrifice on his behalf to ancestor spirits, to discipline his manners and morals—become irksome. The image emerges of the father as a taskmaster and minor despot. Tallensi say that a father's powers are absolute simply because he is his children's begetter. Whether he exercises his authority arbitrarily or benignly depends upon his own sense of duty, for there are no means open to children to constrain a father. A father who wishes to be respected, both by his own family and his kinsfolk and neighbors, should always make a just return to his son for his services and obedience.

A mother's rights are as absolute as a father's, but as women have no jural or economic or ritual authority, they take the form of moral claims upon, rather than jural power over, her children. A mother is thought of as a loving food-giver, ready to sacrifice herself for her children, their shield and comforter. This does not mean that mothers never discipline their children. On the contrary, it is they, not the fathers, who give children their earliest training in cleanliness, good manners, and elementary morality. But they use persuasion where fathers give commands, they are content to scold where fathers are sometimes provoked to punish.

Thus the patterns of customary sentiment toward the father and the mother differ. But one inescapable duty rests on children in relation to both parents. This is the duty of filial piety. It requires a child to honor and respect his parents, to put their wishes before his own, to support and cherish them in old age, quite irrespective of their treatment of him. The supreme act of filial piety owed by sons is the performance of the mortuary and funeral ceremonies for the parents. It is felt by the Tallensi as a compulsion of conscience, but there is a powerful religious sanction in the background. To fail in it is to incur the everlasting wrath of the ancestors. For the mortuary and funeral rites are the first steps in the transformation of parents into ancestor spirits, and the worship of the ancestors is in essence the ritualization of filial piety.

Tale social life is almost wholly organized by reference to relations of descent and of kinship. Precise genealogical knowledge is necessary in order to define a person's place in society and his rights, duties, capacities, and privileges. This is one reason why the cult of the ancestors is so elaborate among them. However, it is much more than a mnemonic for regulating their social relations. It is the religious counterpart of their social order, hallowing it, investing it with a value that transcends mundane interests and providing for them the categories of thought and belief by means of which they direct and interpret their lives and actions. This is quite explicit. Every important activity and every significant social relationship among them is expressed and sanctioned by the ancestor cult. And the pivot of this cult is the key relationship in Tale social structure—that is, the relationship of father and son. Only men may offer sacrifice to the ancestors, and a man cannot get ritual access to his forebears except through his father and mother. In his father's lifetime a man has no independent economic rights (for example, to land), or jural status (for example, in the matter of his marriage), except through his father; and it follows from this that he cannot officiate on his own account in religious rites. When his father dies and he succeeds to his father's place in society as an economically and jurally independent person, he also becomes ritually adult. He is now able to sacrifice and pray to his patrilineal ancestors through his father, who is among them. As maternal ancestors play an equally important part in Tale religion, the same rules apply with regard to the mother. In the most general terms, therefore, the ancestor cult is the transposition to the religious plane of the relationships of parents and children; and that is what I mean by describing it as the ritualization of filial piety.

Filial piety is in fact a kind of regulating mechanism in the relations of parents and children. Custom defines sons as their fathers' eventual supplanters but puts them in their fathers' absolute power. The hostility that this might generate is drained away in the ritual avoidances binding on an eldest son (who represents all his brothers). He may not eat with his father or wear his clothes or use his bow or enter his granary. He breaks these taboos in a solemn ritual during the final funeral ceremonies for his father. A father should exercise his authority benevolently. If he does not, his sons may be tempted to revolt and leave him. But filial piety binds them to accept paternal authority no matter how it is exercised, and they very rarely do revolt. If they do, usually on the grounds of economic necessity, they normally return to their father's home after his death, in submission to the mystical powers which he now has as an ancestral spirit.

Descent and kinship fix a person's place in society, and the rights, duties, and capacities consequential to it, in terms of his membership of such groups as the lineage and the family, and of his relations with other kin through his parents, spouses, children. But there is another pole of existence for him. There is the fact of his individuality. To be sure, in this homogeneous society every life-history is much the same, allowing for differences of sex and age. Yet every life-history is also unique. Some men achieve the supreme ends of life—health, longevity, and, above all, children to perpetuate their line of descent and care for them after death. Others do not. Each life is a particular fabric of good and ill, even though it is woven of fibers common to all. Meaning is given to this fact too in the ancestor cult.

The beliefs and practices of Tale ancestor-worship fit precisely into their social structure. We should note, first, that Tallensi are confronted with their ancestors in a very material way, for every homestead is full of shrines dedicated to the ancestor spirits. These shrines, built of dried mud and covered with a variety of relics and other ritual paraphernalia, differ markedly in appearance, for each type symbolizes a specific category, or configuration, of ancestor spirits. Tallensi explain that these shrines and objects are not inhabited by their ancestors, but represent them and form the altars where men can get into contact with them. In their prayers Tallensi always call on a particular group of ancestors, each by his or her name, to attend at their shrine to accept sacrifices.

Tallensi make contact with their ancestors by means of sacrifices, libations, and prayers, but they only take such ritual action after consulting a diviner. The diviner reveals which configuration of ancestors is involved in the situation at issue, and what sacrifices are demanded by them. Diviners are consulted by and on behalf of both individuals and groups at family crises like childbirth, sickness, or death, at public crises like drought, at seasonal and ceremonial turning points like sowing and harvest times, before hazardous undertakings like setting off for a hunt, and whenever the mood takes a responsible man. Thus the ancestor spirits are continuously involved in the affairs of the living; but they manifest their powers and interest characteristically in the unforeseeable occurrences which upset normal expectations and routines; and they do so in order to make some demand or elicit submission. These occurrences are sometimes deemed fortunate by their descendants, though more often they are experienced as unfortunate. Furthermore, ancestors manifest themselves in different ways for men and for women and with different effect at the successive stages of the individual's life.

¶ LIFE-CYCLE AND OEDIPAL DESTINY

If we consider any person's life-history, the essential starting point is the mere fact that he was born alive and survived to live. The Tallensi conceptualize this in their ancestor cult by the notion of the spirit guardian (sɛɣar). Soon after a child's birth, its father ascertains through a diviner which of his ancestors, associated with which configuration of ancestral powers, desires to take this child as its ward; and what the spirit guardian does is simply to watch over and try to preserve his ward's life itself.

The case of Dentiya illustrates this. One day he brought a sheep to be sacrificed to his spirit guardian. It appeared that in the past few years his first wife had died, his second wife had lost her baby, and now his third wife was pregnant. A diviner had revealed that all this was the doing of his spirit guardian. The spirit guardian declared that he had preserved Dentiya's life through many trials, but that Dentiya had neglected him. Therefore he had caused the death of his wife and child. Now that the third wife was pregnant, the spirit guardian demanded, first, reparation, and then the custody of the unborn child. The sheep was an offering of reparation, acquiescence, and conciliation given with prayers for the safe birth of the unborn babe, the welfare of its mother, and the health and prosperity of its father and his kin. In this case Dentiya was the ward of his patrilineal lineage ancestors grouped together in the configuration of the supreme lineage bɔɣar,[1] and the offering was made by the head of his lineage segment on

[1] Cf. Fortes: *Dynamics of Clanship*, pp. 52 ff.

the shrine dedicated to them. But all categories of ancestors take children as their wards. Furthermore, offerings are always made to a person's spirit guardian at decisive stages of the life-cycle. A man takes a fowl or a guinea fowl to be offered to his wife's spirit guardian by her father when she is advanced in pregnancy; and, most important of all, a person's spirit guardian must be informed as soon as he dies, for the life watched over is now ended.

But life—symbolized for the Tallensi in the breath (ŋovor)—is only the raw material for living. What one makes of it depends on other spiritual agencies. Let us take an extreme but common enough type of case. The six-year-old child of a close friend of mine suffered from a long, wasting illness. Medicines had been tried in vain and diviners had attributed the sickness to the anger of various ancestors who had been approached with promises of the prescribed offerings if the child should recover. But the child died. At the divination, which always forms part of the mortuary ceremony, it emerged that the cause of death was the child's mother's Prenatal Destiny (*Nuor-Yin*). A six-year-old's social identity is so merged in that of its parents, more particularly its mother's, that what happens to it is interpreted as deriving from *her* relationship with spiritual agencies. At about the same time a youth of about eighteen died of a similar wasting illness, and it was revealed that it was due to his own *Nuor-Yin*, he being mature enough to have an individual social identity. But when his twenty-five-year-old, newly married half-brother died of acute dysentery, divination ascribed it to the configuration of the lineage ancestors assembled at the supreme lineage shrine. And these differences in the attribution of the mystical causation of death, so obviously corresponding to the position of the individual in the social structure, are also reflected in the grief of the bereaved and in the range of kinsfolk and clansfolk concerned. When a small infant dies, the funeral rites are quickly over and only the closest kinsfolk and clansfolk of the parents attend; but when a lineage elder dies, the funeral rites are elaborate and protracted, and all the clans of the neighborhood, as well as a very wide range of kinsfolk and affines, take part.

However, the full significance of Prenatal Destiny is clearest from the way it affects women. In Tale eyes no one is so unfortunate or so unhappy as a woman who has no children. If, as happens only too often, a young wife loses her babies one after another by miscarriage or in early infancy, she becomes chronically miserable and dejected, and her husband, too, for that matter. It is then suspected, and diviners soon confirm, that the cause is her evil Prenatal Destiny. But while there's life there's hope, and, as elsewhere in West Africa, there is a customary way out of the dilemma. There is a ritual procedure for exorcizing Prenatal Destiny in cases of this sort. The rites are carried out by the woman's *father's* lineage, but at her married home, and the logic underlying the procedure is clearly expressed in the prayers. First a sacrifice is offered to her lineage ancestors. They are adjured to drive out the evil Prenatal Destiny. For was it not through their beneficence that she was born their child and was, moreover, born a woman? They must see to it that her womanhood is fulfilled. She was properly married, brideprice had been received for her, and her husband had a right to have children by her. What else is marriage for? A woman's offspring have close relationships of affection, duty, and privilege with her paternal kin and receive essential ritual services from them. Her paternal ancestors receive cattle of her bride-price in sacrifice. More than that, they receive ritual service from her offspring. Thus they benefit from her fertility both materially and spiritually, in ways that are directly parallel to and conditional upon the benefits her husband's kin receive from it. In justice to all, therefore, she must be enabled to bear children. After this follows a magical ceremony in which the woman is purged by washing, and the Prenatal Destiny is symbolically drawn off and cast away.

It is easy to see that a woman's Prenatal Destiny is linked with her filial status in her own lineage. For it is through being born a girl in her own lineage that she is endowed with fertility and it is through having been brought up to maturity by her parents that she is able to put her child-bearing powers at the disposal of her husband's lineage. When, more rarely, a man is the victim of Prenatal Destiny the symptom is usually failure, through some infirmity, to marry or to make a livelihood. Then his own lineage, assisted by members of his mother's lineage, perform the exorcism. He is their offspring and his native endowment derives from his birth and upbringing. If it has failed him, only his or their ancestors have the mystical power to save him.

What, then, is this Prenatal Destiny? Tallensi have a clear doctrine. The ultimate source of everything on earth is Heaven (*Naawun*). But there are no myths giving an account of the creation, or as they say, pouring out (*bah*) of the world, and no shrines for worship of Heaven. He or It is simply the Final Cause of everything that exists. Before it is born a child is "with Heaven," not in any literal sense, but in the symbolical sense of being in process of creation. At that time it declares its wishes to Heaven—hence the term *Nuor-Yin*, literally Spoken Destiny. It may declare that it does not wish to have parents or a spouse or children or farms or livestock. This means that it rejects ordinary human living though it cannot avoid being born. This is its evil Prenatal Destiny; and sometimes this is so powerful that its owner dies or else causes illness and even death to a parent, spouse, or child.

Very similar notions occur in other parts of West Africa, as we have already seen, but placing them in their context of situation and social organization throws significant light on them. For one thing, they explain and provide customary reassurance against the impact of diseases and failures that defy the knowledge and skill of the people. Thus it is very obvious to an observer that the ritual of exorcism brings relief and hope to the sufferers, as well as to their kin. But most serious disease is intractable by the magical and religious techniques which are the basis of all Tale cures. A further element comes in. The victims of Prenatal Destiny are a selected type. They are all out on a limb, or potentially so, in the social structure, being either too young to be implicated in responsible tasks and social relations or having apparently incurable physical or psychological defects that put them in danger of leaving no children and of thus eventually becoming socially forgotten. It seems that in these circumstances the notion of Prenatal Destiny serves as a legitimate alibi. It relieves the sufferer's kin, and therefore society at large, of responsibility and guilt for his troubles, and, indeed, exonerates him in his own eyes. For he is not aware that he is the victim of his Prenatal Destiny until this is revealed by a diviner.

¶ Good Destiny, Ancestor Spirits, and Parents

The notion of Prenatal Destiny among the Tallensi is, clearly, a simpler version of Oedipal Fate. There is, however, also another aspect of Destiny. In this, benevolence predominates; it does not commonly become effective till adolescence; and it pertains to men only. So every married man has his Good Destiny (Yin) shrine. While he is still young and dependent on his father, it stands in his mother's quarters. Later, when he has children, it is moved to his wife's quarters. And finally, when he succeeds to his father's place, it is moved outside to show that it owns and guards the whole family group. It is, in fact, a ritual record of a man's life-history. It begins with his emergence from infancy on to the threshold of adult jural status, and grows step by step as his involvement in responsible social relations expands through marriage, fatherhood, economic independence, family headship, and lineage eldership. Women are not independently endowed with Destiny in this sense because they have no jural or religious autonomy. As daughters and sisters in their parental family and lineage, they are under the authority and are the responsibility of their fathers. As wives and mothers in their conjugal families, they come under their husband's power. A woman's life-cycle is therefore interpreted as being governed first by her father's and subsequently by her husband's Destiny.

A man's Good Destiny springs ultimately from his unknown prenatal wishes and is sometimes spoken of as if it were the universal Heaven entering into the life and achievements of the individual. But it manifests itself through what we should call accidents and coincidences. This follows a completely stereotyped pattern; only the combination of elements in the pattern is unique for each individual. As Tallensi say, everybody gets ill sometimes, marries, has children, kills animals in the hunt, and so forth. Why, then, should illness strike a particular person at a particular time? Why should one man be fortunate in his marriages and have many children while his brother fails in these respects? One cannot foresee the course of one's life, for it is governed by forces beyond human knowledge and control; and these Tallensi conceptualize in terms of their ancestor cult. Thus each person's total life-history is unique, though the events it is made up of are similar to those of other people's lives; and its particular course depends on his Destiny. That is why an offering to a *Yin* shrine is often eaten only by the owner and his wife and children, his kin by birth not being allowed to share in it as in his other sacrifices.

Let us consider a few examples. As a youth of sixteen or so, Zaŋ went out herding his father's cattle one day. Coming to a pool, he saw a crocodile on the bank and promptly shot it. It was taken home and eaten by the elders. Zaŋ's father, as was his duty, went to consult a diviner about the incident. He revealed that it was a manifestation of Zaŋ's Destiny. It was his father's father and *his* mother who were manifesting themselves in the crocodile and the arrow which had killed it. They were Zaŋ's Destiny. He must set up a shrine and sacrifice to them, and they would watch over his well-being. So a small shrine was built of clay, the skull of the crocodile and the arrow which slew it being embedded in it as symbols of the ancestors who had chosen Zaŋ. At first Zaŋ's father always made offerings on his behalf. After his father's death, Zaŋ did this for himself.

This is a typical history of the beginnings of a man's Destiny shrine. Another, illustrating a different aspect of the notion, is Kunyaaŋba's. When he first began to farm like a grown man, at the age of about sixteen, a sickness of the feet laid him low. His father went to a diviner and it appeared that it was due to *his* father and father's father manifesting themselves as the boy's Destiny. The sickness had been a sign that they demanded to be accepted as his Destiny, his hoe being the material symbol of their interest and will. Furthermore, it was their wish that he should never eat any grain he himself cultivated. This is a very inconvenient personal taboo in the household economy of the Tallensi, and Kunyaaŋba at first jibbed at it. He was cured and went on farming. Then he became ill again, more seriously. This time divination revealed that his Destiny ancestors were angry at his defiance and now required him never to use a hoe, that is, to give up farming completely. This was a great blow, as there are no alternative equally rewarding occupations for an energetic and capable young man. But there was no choice, for to disobey would mean to risk illness or even death for himself, his wife, or his children. This taboo was one of the reasons why Kunyaaŋba went to work abroad. But he felt it as a serious privation. He spoke of it reluctantly, as if he felt ashamed, emphasizing that there was no redress.

Such personal taboos are often imposed by Destiny ancestors. They may forbid their wards from wearing cloth garments, from eating certain foods, from cutting their hair, from doing certain kinds of work, and so forth. These taboos are scrupulously observed, for the wages of disobedience are misfortune, sickness, and even the death of a wife or child. It is significant that Destiny ancestors rarely cause the death of their ward. This ultimate sanction is generally used against his dependants (as God did with Job) as a means of bringing the ward himself to heel. For Destiny is, ideally, beneficent, provided only that the ward accepts his Destiny ancestors, serves them, and obeys them. He shows this by faithfully keeping the taboos they impose, however arbitrary and inconvenient they may be from the rational point of view of normal Tale life.

Yet another aspect of Destiny appears in the case of Luoni. He slew a fully grown male crocodile at a distant river. It proved to be the vehicle of his Destiny ancestors. Ever since, he is woken up from time to time by a nightmare in which he sees himself pursued by the crocodile. He gets up, seizes a rattle, and runs in the night to the path leading to the river, then on to his mother's brother's home whence his Destiny ancestors originate, and this dispels the attack. His family takes no notice, for, as his son said: "It is his affair; we have nothing to do with it." A man's Destiny often asserts itself in this way when it was originally acquired through the killing of a big game animal. And it persists until the final establishment of the shrine. This takes place in the later years of life when his household, his children, and his survival are the tangible evidences of the beneficence of his Destiny. An elderly man frequently learns through diviners that his Destiny demands the sacrifice of a cow in gratitude for long-continued favors, and when this sacrifice is offered, it is a triumphant occasion.

A man's Destiny, then, consists of a unique configuration of ancestors who have of their own accord elected to exercise specific surveillance over his life-cycle, and to whom he is personally accountable. No one else, not even his brother, has the same configuration of Destiny ancestors.[1] They are always immediate forebears and most commonly paternal in character. They first manifest themselves through a critical experience or achievement at an appropriate stage of a man's life-cycle. It may be an illness; often it is through a productive achievement like slaying a game animal for the first time or excelling in farming. The material relics of these events form the shrine dedicated to the Destiny ancestors. In return for his submission and service, a man's Destiny is supposed to preserve his health, his life, and the well-being of his family, to bring him good fortune in his economic activities and social aspirations, and to confer on him, in due course, the immortality of ancestorhood by blessing him with sons and grandsons.

This is the supreme evidence of the goodwill of his ancestors, and the special power of Destiny in this matter is shown in two significant ways. First, though all categories of ancestors can and, as I have already mentioned, do elect to be the spirit guardians of a man's children, his Destiny ancestors predominate among them. Thus the most enduring fulfillment of a man's role in the social structure is identified with his Good Destiny.

Secondly, there is the appeal to Destiny in interpreting the ambivalence in the relationship of fathers and sons. Fathers want and need sons to perpetuate their social existence. But they become increasingly loth to yield their place to their sons as their bodily and social capacities wane and those of their sons wax with the passage of time. Sons accept their dependent status with affectionate respect and filial piety; but with every step toward jural autonomy, especially after they marry and have children, they chafe increasingly at their father's authority. Beneath the soli-

[1] Cf. Fortes: *The Web of Kinship*, pp. 229 ff.

darity due to common interests and mutual dependence lies the rivalry and opposition of successive generations. This is what generates the tensions symbolized and drained away in the taboos of the first-born. Tallensi explain it by means of the notion of Destiny. They say that a father's Destiny and his first-born son's Destiny are hostile to each other. During the son's infancy the father's Destiny is superior. As the son grows up, physically and socially, his Destiny grows stronger; indeed, it is because his Destiny is strong enough that the son succeeds in growing up. This is a threat to the father's Destiny. Father's Destiny and son's Destiny are enemies; each wishes to destroy the other so that its protégé may be master of the house and free to give it sacrifices and service. For this reason a married first-born son with children of his own is forbidden to use the same gateway as his father lest they meet face to face, Destiny against Destiny. This is reminiscent of the fatal effects an evil Pre-destiny may have on its victim's parents or children. The implication is that a person's Destiny (or, as the Greeks might have said, daemon), both in its malign form and in its benign form, asserts itself in opposition to that of his parents, or rather of his father, since his mother's is ruled by his father's.

Remembering that a son finally wins jural and ritual independence only on the death of his father, we must conclude that this is a victory for the son's Destiny. It is inevitable, yet Tallensi do not admit it. To do so would make the stabilizing effect of the first-born's taboos nugatory and destroy the very basis of the relationship between successive generations. Instead they emphasize the supreme filial duty of performing a parent's funeral rites. The effect of these is to transform the dead father (and, by the same principle, the mother) into an ancestor spirit and re-establish him in his family in his spiritual status. This transforms his mundane and material jural authority into mystical power—that is, power which is absolute, autocratic, and unpredictable because it transcends the human controls of moral and jural sanctions. It is as if fathers are exorbitantly compensated by society with spiritual powers for being deprived of material powers for the sake of the continuity of the society. It reconciles them with their sons who have ousted them and exonerates the latter of guilt, as can be discerned in the symbolism of the funeral ceremonies and in Tale beliefs about the ultimate causes of death, to which I will presently come.

What, then, is the service due to one's Good Destiny ancestors? In form it is just like the service due to any other ancestors in whatever configuration they are worshipped. First, they must be accepted [2] and enshrined. This takes place at their behest, conveyed through a diviner. It takes place according to the usual pattern, that is, as a result of misfortunes or coincidences which are interpreted as the manifestations of the ancestors. Being enshrined, the ancestors are restored in spirit form to the homes and hearths from which death cut them off in their physical form. They will continue to assert their power by causing troubles, but the means of placating them (and of thus allaying the anxieties and the disturbances of routine expectations due to their interventions) will be at hand. Secondly, they must receive regular offerings and libations. Tallensi interpret this as giving them food and drink, and thus expressing filial reverence and commemoration. And it is significant that this service is also normally given only in response to demands consequent on a warning misfortune or threat of misfortune. This applies even to sacrifices at fixed seasonal and ceremonial times, like the harvest. Every household head then sacrifices to all his ancestor shrines, but only in accordance with the demands received through a diviner. Thirdly, there is the observance of taboos which symbolize submission to the ancestors and compliance with the norms and customs instituted by them. In this aspect the fearful quality of the ancestors, particularly Destiny and Divining ancestors, becomes apparent. It is manifested directly in the case of Destiny ancestors in nightmares which can be allayed only by an act of quasi-ritual obedience, and indirectly in the anxious anticipation of supernatural afflictions for disobedience. Destiny ancestors are benevolent, not out of affection for their descendants, but out of self-interest and because they have the power. Their

---

[2] There is a special term (saɣ) in the ritual language of the Tallensi for accepting, or rather consenting to, the commands of ancestors, and it is noteworthy that the same word is used to describe the action of a parent, an elder, or an ancestor when he is thought to be responding benevolently to the conduct of a dependant.

solicitude is gained, not by demonstrations of love, but by proofs of loyalty.

What distinguishes the worship of Destiny from that of other ancestor configurations is the fact already mentioned, that it is a unique ritual relationship not shared, as are other ritual relationships, with kinsfolk and clansfolk. Tallensi have a shrewd understanding of individual differences in character and disposition; but this does not lead them to perceive individuality as a growth from within. Both to himself and to others the individual is what he sees himself to have achieved; and every significant achievement is credited to the goodwill of his Destiny. It supports him by bringing him luck, which the Tallensi, like the other West African peoples cited, associate with the head. It also aids him by warding off adversity. In Tale thought everything that happens has material causes and conditions, but they are effective only by grace of the mystical agencies which are the ultimate arbiters of nature and society. So they say that if a man wishes to prosper, he must have skill, industry, and thrift. But these are not enough; without the beneficence of Destiny they will be abortive; and even this is not enough, for behind Destiny is the collective power of all the ancestors, notably that of the omnipotent lineage ancestors.

In this special relationship of a man with his Destiny ancestors (as in his relationships with all his ancestors) morality in the sense of righteous conduct does not count. All that matters is service and obedience. A man who is wicked by Tale standards may flourish while his virtuous brother is a failure. But even assiduous service is not a guarantee of success. The ancestors are easily, and mostly inadvertently, offended, and this cannot be known until something goes wrong. That is why even fixed ceremonial occasions are potentially hazardous. It may then transpire that one group of ancestors has taken offense because they were overlooked in favor of some other group. Ancestors thus incensed may override a man's Destiny and bring disaster upon him. Divination after a death often reveals such a story. The result is that when a sacrifice is offered to any one configuration of ancestors, offerings must also be given, as advised by the diviner, to all the other ancestors in the officiant's custody. Thus if the main sacrifice is to be given to a man's Destiny shrine, he will first make the rounds of the other ancestor shrines in his possession. These will include his father's Destiny, his own divining shrine, the shrine dedicated to his mother if she is dead, and, if he is of sufficient seniority, the shrine of the lineage ancestors. Each receives a small sacrifice, perhaps only a libation of water, is told the circumstances of the occasion, and is besought to show goodwill. Tallensi account for this by referring to kinship. As a jural minor in your father's lifetime you need the consent, or at least the blessing, of your father and often of your lineage elders in order to undertake anything important for yourself. You must also tell your mother out of respect for her. The same pattern holds for transactions with your ancestors.

It is worth noting that this plurality of ancestral powers, thought of as competing unpredictably in their demands on their worshippers, actually works as a safeguard in everyday affairs. Since there is no single, sovereign god like Job's, one cannot feel entitled to rewards for following a code of conduct pleasing to him or deserving of punishment for knowingly transgressing it. One lives according to one's mundane lights, guided by the jural and moral sanctions of society, knowing that the ancestors dispense justice by their own standards and that one cannot please all of them at the same time.

Here there is an apparent inconsistency in Tale thought. For the ancestors are not considered to be wholly indifferent to moral values. On the contrary, they are the jealous guardians of the highest moral values, that is to say, the axiomatic values from which all ideal conduct is deemed to flow. The first is the rule that kinship is binding in an absolute sense. From this follows the second rule, that kinship implies amity in an absolute sense. The third rule is the fundamental one. It postulates that the essential relationship of parent and child, expressed in the parent's devoted care and the child's affectionate dependence, may never be violated and is, in that sense, sacred. It is indeed the source of the other rules. Tallensi believe that anyone who violates these rules is liable to the ultimate mystical penalty of death. For though every death has material causes, no death can occur except by the will of the ancestors.

We can see what the issue is. It is not a question of morality in the sense of righteous conduct. It is not a matter of, say, dealing honestly with one's neighbors, refraining from adultery, never committing a murder. Virtue in these matters does not earn the blessings of the ancestors, and a wrongdoer will escape their wrath unless his actions are also transgressions of the rule of kinship amity. It is a question of moral relationships, not of good deeds. What the ancestors demand and enforce on pain of death is conformity with the basic moral axioms in fulfilling the requirements of all social relationships; and these are the counterpart, in the domain of kinship, of the obligations posited between persons and their ancestors in the religious domain. This is understandable since the latter are derived from the former by extension and transposition to the religious domain.

The point I am concerned with here is well illustrated by the story of Pu-ɛŋ-yii. Tempted by the opportunity of gain, he deserted his own patrilineal kin to ally himself with a rival lineage. Then, at the height of his prosperity, he was involved in a truck accident. Luckily he escaped with a badly injured leg. On consulting a diviner, he learned that his mishap was brought about by his lineage ancestors. Deserting his paternal kin was a sin, for it meant that he could not join with them in true amity in sacrifices to his fathers and forefathers. This was tantamount to forsaking his ancestors, and in their anger they meant to kill him. However, said the diviner, his Destiny was propitious and had interceded to save his life. He must apologize to his lineage elders, offer up a sheep to his lineage ancestors to show his contrition and submission, and make a sacrifice of thanksgiving to his Destiny. He must also forthwith give up his association with the rival lineage. Pu-ɛŋ-yii was a sophisticated, much-traveled, and commercially minded man; but he immediately complied, believing that death would be the penalty of refusing.

¶ THE SUPREMACY OF THE LINEAGE ANCESTORS

In the religious system of the Tallensi the lineage ancestors have the last word. They are a person's or a group's fathers and forefathers by strict patrilineal descent from a founding ancestor and his wife to a deceased father. They are omnipotent, but not uniformly benevolent or malevolent. They are just;[1] and their justice is directed to enforcing the moral and religious norms and values on which the social order rests. They do this through the power over life and death in which they are supreme. Life, which surpasses all other forms of the good, and death, which is the end of everything, as the Tallensi phrase it, are dispensed by the ancestors by what can best be described as the right of primordial parenthood. Their powers are those of a father immeasurably magnified and sanctified—that is, removed from the controls of co-operation and reciprocity, conscience, and love as they work in the life of the family. They have this character in the specific configuration of the lineage ancestors with their special shrines. It will be remembered that a lineage ancestor can also become manifest in other configurations.

How, then, does their justice work? Take the case of a daughter of a lineage who is persecuted by an evil Prenatal Destiny. Whether or not she can be rid of it depends upon the will of her lineage ancestors. It is in their interests that there shall be children and children's children to keep the social order in being and to serve and commemorate them. And this may weigh more in the balance of ancestral justice than sins of omission or commission. Or take the case of a man who is fortunate in his Good Destiny and has a long and successful life. In the end his day, too, comes, as the Tallensi say, and he must die. The material cause, there for all to see, may be old age or disease; the exact moment and circumstances are the will of the ancestors. However virtuous, respected, and devout he may have been, his death is invariably interpreted as the consequence of a failure in his or his predecessors' piety toward his ancestors. It may be due to some long-forgotten sin, his own or his father's, which he and his kin had thought of as having been expiated but which now, in retrospect, proves to be still resented by the ancestors. Or it may be an apparently commonplace

[1] This is the attribute that distinguishes ancestors from other supernatural agencies in most religious systems which include the worship of ancestors. Cf. Monica Wilson, *Rituals of Kinship among the Nyakusa* (1956), for a striking analysis of this conception among an East African people.

ritual debt—and even the best of men have such debts at all times. Sometimes they are known to a man's sons and brothers, often they are not. For instance, every man of seniority has ritual obligations arising out of his status in his lineage and in society. Since, however, Tallensi think of an offering as a response to a demand from the ancestors, not as a spontaneous gift, they are very apt to put off these obligations. The demand may come with the usual sign of illness, chance mishap, or even a stroke of luck. But it may not be revealed until death overtakes a man or one of his dependants. Thus every mature man knows that he must someday complete the enshrinement of his Destiny ancestors. But he will procrastinate, thinking that it will be time enough when he gets older and there are children and grandchildren to prove the benevolence of his Destiny. This is a known obligation. If he dies before fulfilling it, it may be the mystical cause of his death. Diviners will disclose that his ingratitude had angered his Destiny ancestors, who had slain him with the consent of his lineage ancestors. Again, a man who succeeds to the custody of a lineage shrine may in good faith postpone the taking-over ceremony until he has enough grain for beer and livestock for the sacrifices. If he dies in the meanwhile, this delay may be revealed as the mystical cause. Then there is the "cow of the bride-price" which a man owes to his lineage ancestors when he has married off all his daughters, and putting off this sacrifice may end in his death or in that of one of his dependants. It may not even become known until he has long passed away.

In short, however conscientious a man may be in discharging his ritual obligations, there is always a loophole. For the will of the ancestors only becomes known after they strike, the range of ancestors who can manifest themselves in order to assert their rights is extraordinarily wide, and ritual debts to ancestors pass on from generation to generation. The system as a whole is impregnable, particularly since the criterion invoked is ritual service, not conduct that can be judged by men themselves. Whatever the ancestors do must therefore be, and is, accepted as just, and men have no choice but to submit. The parallel with Job is obvious. But unlike the Biblical hero, Tallensi do not attempt to dispute their ancestors' rights and authority, though they commonly plead with them for benevolence and sometimes protest their own deserts.

¶ Justice, Responsibility, and the Ancestral Cult

Tale religious beliefs and practices, like those of other peoples, serve a cathartic purpose. The grief, anger, and anxiety aroused by the afflictions of material loss or sickness or death are assuaged by them. But this is not the aspect of their religious system which concerns us here. What is of interest to us is the deeper catharsis, social as well as individual, made possible by the fusion in their religious system of Oedipal and Jobian notions.

I am thinking particularly of the question of fixing responsibility for the vicissitudes of life. Beliefs in witchcraft, magic, and sorcery have a relatively minor place in Tale thought, in contrast to many other African religions.[1] Tale cosmology is wholly dominated by the ancestor cult. Even the elaborate totemic institutions, the cult of the Earth[2] and the beliefs about the dangerous mystical qualities of evil trees, animals, and other natural phenomena, are subordinated to it. The result is that it is inconceivable for Tallensi to attribute serious misfortune to the sole agency of a witch, a medicine, or a mystically "bad" tree or animal. The final arbitrament rests with the ancestors. This means that ultimate responsibility is projected outside the living body politic, not on to neighbors or kinsfolk or natural phenomena, as happens in societies with extensive witchcraft and magical beliefs.[3] But this does not wipe out human responsibility entirely. What ancestor-worship provides is an institutionalized scheme of beliefs and practices by means of which men can accept

[1] Cf. Fortes: *The Web of Kinship*, pp. 32 ff. In this respect the Tallensi are very different from the other West African societies I have referred to.

[2] Cf. Fortes: *Dynamics of Clanship*, Chap. viii.

[3] As in the classical case of the Azande (cf. E. E. Evans-Pritchard, op. cit.). Cf. also Monica Wilson, op. cit., and an illuminating discussion of the same point by Professor P. Mayer in his paper *Witches*, Rhodes University, Grahamstown, 1957.

some kind of responsibility for what happens to them and yet feel free of blame for failure to control the vicissitudes of life. The moral responsibility for the manifestations of Destiny or the ancestors is always fixed on the person (or his jural superior) who is their object. When he accepts and later enshrines the ancestors who manifest themselves for him, or when he admits failure in service and makes reparation by sacrificing to them, he is accepting his own responsibility. But there is an implication of duress in this; and the very act of acquiescing in his own moral responsibility establishes the final, mystical responsibility of the ancestors.

The result is that the Tallensi can accept responsibility on a personal level for the good and ill in their lives without feeling morbidly guilty or having guilt fixed on them by jural and religious sanctions. Indeed, a striking feature of Tale response to misfortune is the absence of customary expressions of guilt, though grief, anger, anxiety, despair, and the comforting emotions of hope and relief are freely demonstrated.

Putting it in another way, we could say that when things go wrong, a person admits that he is in some sense answerable. But he is allowed, nay compelled, by custom to perceive his misfortunes as emanating in the last resort from his ancestors. Since they are invested with personality, they can be appeased by word and act, and this serves to restore both the sufferer's self-trust and his social esteem.

The mechanism of this is clear. By enshrining his ancestors and so taking them back into his home and his life a man gains direct access to them. By accepting the duty of preserving and caring for them he converts their potential hostility to potential friendship. It is not a contractual relationship, as some authorities say is the case with Job, but one of mutual interdependence and obligation, albeit an uneasy one, fraught with the constant possibility of mischance due to the incommensurable capacities and powers of the parties. It is, in fact, a reestablishment on a new plane of the filio-parental interdependence severed by death. For death is the culmination of the cleavage between successive generations that is basic to Tale social structure. In ancestor-worship it is transcended, and conceptually as well as emotionally reversed. The parents, metamorphosed into ancestors, are restored to a place in their children's life that reflects, in symbolic form, critical attributes of parenthood in real life. Real parents demand obedience, economic services, respect which goes so far, in special cases, as to turn into obligatory avoidance, as well as affectionate trust. Ancestors demand ritual services, sacrifices, reverence, and taboo avoidances. Real parents have economic power and jural authority over their children and possess knowledge and skill which seem immeasurably great to their children while they are young. Perpetuated in supernatural form, these attributes become mystical power and authority, ubiquity, and omnipotence. On the other hand, and this is equally important, real parents not only command and make demands on their children; they also care for them with affection and self-sacrifice. Ancestors, similarly, are benevolent if they are properly tended and served. The constraints of religion, experienced most acutely when ancestors act in a punitive manner, are the counterpart of the constraints of family life experienced whenever parents impose their will. In doing this they are bound to thwart their children and this is enough to arouse suspicions that they are angry, even if they seem to show no signs of this. At bottom, it is the same set of norms operating in the two spheres. Indeed, these spheres overlap, for, as we have seen, the powers and status of parents are backed by the sanctions of the ancestor cult.

Here it is worth repeating that the normal personal relationships of parents and children are warm and friendly. Fathers and sons trust and support one another at the same time that they carefully observe the restrictions proper to their relationship as members of successive generations. This too is reflected in the worship of the ancestors. The prayers offered at sacrifices are never abject. They explain the circumstances, perhaps express contrition, but end in phrases which, for all their persuasive and appeasing form, imply that the giver of the sacrifice expects a benevolent return. And this is the root of the attitude and belief that in the last resort whatever the ancestors decree is just.

¶ Fate in Relation to the Social Structure

We seem to have wandered far from the contrast between Oedipus and Job with which we began. Precisely in what sense are our paradigms applicable to the religious institutions of the Tallensi? Faced with this question, Frazer would have looked for connections in common human experiences and mental processes. As I remarked at the outset, I think he was right in principle but was misled by the premises which he took over from the science of his day. The descriptive parallels between Tale beliefs and our paradigms are patent, and Frazer would have given his attention to them rather than to the underlying meanings that primarily interest us.

Frazer derived ancestor-worship from a belief in the immortality of the soul, coupled with a fear of the dead, which he thought was virtually instinctive among mankind.[1] Such an explanation would be a ludicrous oversimplification for the Tallensi, or any other West-African people. The Tallensi have an ancestor cult not because they fear the dead—for they do not, in fact, do so—or because they believe in the immortality of the soul—for they have no such notion—but because their social structure demands it. To put it in other words, they have a complex and elaborate body of ritual beliefs and practices for perpetuating and regulating the significance of the dead in the lives of their descendants. They worship their ancestors because ancestry, and more particularly parenthood, is the critical and irreducible determinant of their whole social structure. Not fear, ignorance, or superstition but the moral bonds of the filio-parental relationship are the springs of Tale ancestor-worship. The significant parallels with Oedipus and Job lie in this.

We have seen that Tale jural and ritual concepts distinguish with precision a number of elements in the social and individual constitution of a person by reference to the different domains of social structure in which they are

---

[1] This is a typical Frazerian hypothesis. It is expounded at great and sesquipedalian length in *The Belief in Immortality* (1913); see especially Vol. I, pp. 23 ff., Vol. II, pp. 57 ff. It is also introduced in other contexts, e.g. *Totemism and Exogamy*, Vol. IV (1910), p. 32.

effective. We have noted that the mere fact of being born alive and remaining alive is the primary element. This receives a specific ritual imprimatur in the institution of the spirit guardian. The spirit guardian serves both to identify and to give value to the fact of individual life and to show how it depends on parental care. It is because one owes one's life to one's parents, Tallensi say, that one has irrevocable and absolute bonds with them.[2] First there are the affective and moral bonds which Tallensi derive from the relationship of upbringing. Parental discipline, authority, affection, and care create reciprocal dependence, obedience, and respectful love on the part of the children. Then there is the jural component of status in one's lineage and locus in the web of kinship, acquired by birth, through one's parents, and forming an element in the continuity of the social structure through time. The ritual imprimatur for this is the conception of the ancestors as sovereign and eternal, mirroring the total system of kinship and descent which is seen as an everlasting and fixed framework for the individual's social existence. Lastly there are the bonds created by the succession of generations. Sons must succeed fathers and daughters mothers in the passage of the generations. This is jurally expressed in the facts of inheritance and succession and ritually demonstrated in the worship of the spirits of the dead parents.

In this context the critical fact is that the individual has no choice. Submission to his ancestors is symbolic of his encapsulation in a social order which permits of no voluntary alteration of his status and social capacities. It is the common interest, the collective purposes that prevail.

We can see that an individual who was incurably impeded from fitting into the social structure would be an anomaly. Hence the great importance of giving specific ritual recognition to the individuality of each life-history. It acknowledges the need for the realities of life to be accommodated to the fixity of structural norms; and it is easy to see how notions of luck, chance, destiny and even, in a more sophisticated idiom, election, could be used to reconcile the determinism of jural and ritual status imposed by the social structure with the variability and un-

[2] Cf. what was said of Job, pp. 11–12 above.

predictability of the individual life-cycle. If we imagine a graph of a person's life among the Tallensi, one axis would stand for his movement into and through the social structure, the other for his personal development, the origin being the fact of his being born alive of particular parents.

This is where Oedipal concepts come into evidence. They recognize forces in social and personal development that cannot be changed or regulated by society. The Tale notion of Prenatal Destiny designates what, in more abstract language, could best be described as an innate disposition that can be realized either for good or for ill. The Tallensi themselves do not, of course, have the cultural resources for analyzing their religious symbolism in this form. Indeed, if they were able to do so the symbols would be denuded of their affective and expressive force. It is only the outside investigator, viewing the symbolism in relation to the other religious institutions of those who live by them, and in its context of social structure, who can perceive its abstract meaning.

What strikes us, then, is the criteria by which a person's evil Prenatal Destiny is diagnosed. Proof that it is working itself out in an evil way is the victim's irremediable but involuntary failure to fulfill the roles and achieve the performance regarded as normal for his status in the social structure. It would not be going too far to say that the Tallensi define a person as being afflicted by an evil Prenatal Destiny if he turns out to be incapable of being or remaining incorporated in the social structure. If, on the other hand, he gains and holds his due place in it, this is credited to his Good Destiny.

Why, then, is the victim of an evil Prenatal Destiny dissociated from the social structure? Tale doctrine and ritual usage imply that it is because he has, from the moment of birth, rejected society, preferring death to incorporation in the network of fundamental family and kinship relations and turning his back on the basic moral norms. This is not a conscious or deliberate rejection, since the sufferer is not aware of his predisposition until he learns of it through divination. From the point of view of society, as expressed in Tale doctrine, the fault lies in his inescapable, inborn wishes. But from the sufferer's point of view, as shown in his attitudes and conduct, his condition is forced upon him by society. He sees himself as implicitly disowned by his kin and his ancestors, since all the resources of social organization, therapeutic skill, ritual, and parental devotion have failed to open a way to social normality for him. He is justified in this because the sovereign authority over his life so obviously resides in society and because the notion of Prenatal Destiny is a last ditch defense. Those responsible for his well-being only fall back on it, with the sanction of a diviner's findings, when appeals to the ancestors to save him have come to nought. What is symbolized in the notion of evil Prenatal Destiny is, therefore, a failure in the relationship of belonging to society, which, for the Tallensi, means family, lineage, and kin. In developmental terms this means a failure in the primary relationships of parents and children, since it is through these relationships that the individual is fitted into society and the norms and the demands of society are implanted in him.

These structural considerations suggest a number of parallels in the story of Oedipus. His fate is evil; it enters into his life at the very beginning through his being rejected by his parents when they cast him away. He survives only because he is accepted by substitute parents, but he becomes an outcast again when his fate catches up with him. He is finally overwhelmed by his fate because he unknowingly violates the basic norms of the filial relationship. His tragedy can be described as that of a man blindly seeking to achieve his legitimate place in society, first as son, then as husband, father, and citizen against the unconscious opposition of an inborn urge to avenge himself by repudiating his parents, his spouse, and his children. When, in the end, he succumbs to this fate, he shows his revulsion against himself by mutilating his own eyes and so blotting out his relationship with his kin and his society. Nor is he ever accepted back into society. He dies in exile, almost like a ghost departing from this world rather than like an ordinary man.

We must remember, however, that the notion of Prenatal Destiny is not merely a label for a class of persons definable in structural terms. It is a religious concept, associated with ritual procedures for disposing, by symbolic displacement, of the emotional and moral tensions generated in the structural antinomies in which the fated individual finds himself. We have seen how it serves to exonerate both society and the sufferer by fixing ultimate responsibility on the ancestors and on a prenatal, that is, presocial, event. Thus the onus of the rejection is shifted on to the supernatural plane and the individual's feelings of helplessness and depression are made tolerable. In the case of Oedipus, too, the onus of guilt falls on fate. Even his father and mother are victims of this hereditary determinism. Where the Oedipus story diverges most strikingly from the simpler Tale pattern is in the place assigned to human will. Laius and Jocasta thought they could thwart Fate by casting away their child. They failed; and the Tallensi would understand this, for they do not believe that hostile supernatural forces can be averted by human prudence. Only ritual measures can, in their scheme of thought, defend them against supernatural threats.

The reason lies in the Tale concept of mystical causation mentioned earlier in this essay. Its effect is seen in the beliefs and practices related to the process by which the innate potentiality of Destiny is turned to beneficial ends. The evidence for its beneficence is demonstrated capacity to achieve the economic, jural, and social goals that are normal for a person's age, sex, and status. But continued beneficence is only ensured if particular (ideally paternal) ancestors accept the supernatural responsibility for his Destiny. We can readily see that this is the expression, in religious symbols and sanctions, of the ideal of the parents (particularly the father) as beings who accept their child in order to care for him throughout his life. Since Destiny ancestors are the agents of the collective ancestors, their role is also the symbolic equivalent of incorporating him into the political and jural domain of the social structure in his character as a person with a unique life-cycle. Consequently, when a man submits to his ancestors, he is accepting his dependence on his parents, particularly his father, and, a fortiori, his incorporation in society. This is an absolute—that is, supernaturally sanctioned—relationship, in which the duty to abide by the basic moral axioms of society is appropriated by each person as a supreme value. It is the very opposite condition to that of a supposed victim of evil Prenatal Destiny. In the abstract terms we have been using, we would say that harnessing the individual's inborn potentialities to the needs and values of society prevents them from becoming destructive and turns them into capacities for productive social development and normal life in society.

To put the argument in a slightly different way, if parents fail in their task of upbringing, the latent hostility of their children in their relations with them and sentiments toward them gets the upper hand—or at least it is deemed to do so—and eventually destroys the bonds between them. Evil Prenatal Destiny conceptualizes this experience. On the other hand, if parents succeed in this task, it shows that they have used the powers and authority vested in them by society with benevolence—in religious terms, with the blessings of the ancestors. Conversely, it also shows that their children have responded to parental discipline, care, and affection with growth to adulthood. This means that trustful acquiescence toward their parents has been more powerful than latent antagonism. The notion of the Good Destiny conceptualizes this experience and gives sanction and value to it as a lasting moral force in the individual's life. This is where Tale beliefs are quite unlike the story of Oedipus. For him there was no way of changing his evil fate into a beneficent destiny. But it is reminiscent of Job.

Figuratively speaking, therefore, we might say that an Oedipal predisposition is in this way transformed into a Jobian fulfillment. The drama of Job's life springs from the circumstance that he is chosen by his god in order to put his fidelity to test. It is comparable to the way Destiny ancestors choose their ward among the Tallensi and continually try his faith by making demands on him. This is one indication among many that Job is never disowned, avowedly or implicitly, by either his fellows or his god. The tribulations he endures are of a quite different order from the catastrophes brought on Oedipus by irrevocable fate. They can, as I suggested at the beginning, well be compared to a severe but just form of paternal correction, and that is why they are not tragic like those of Oedipus but simply pathetic though on a cosmic scale. They are, in fact, part of the total texture of a relationship with his fellows and his god in which he is cherished, despite appearances to the contrary, and which he never turns away from. Such a relationship is essential for God, the superior, to be in a position to chastize Job, and for Job, the inferior, to be in a position to defend himself by righteous conduct and argument. It is true that Job at first feels himself estranged from his fellows and persecuted unjustly by God. This is because he mistakes his status and believes himself entitled to recognition and reward in terms of his own standards of virtue and right. Tallensi would not fall into this error in relation to their ancestors.

Job's salvation comes when he recognizes his god's omnipotence as a phenomenon beyond human questioning. He perceives that submission to his god must be absolute, whether or not it corresponds to norms of righteous conduct among men. This is submission in the attitude of filial humility and faith toward all-powerful parents. In this relationship it is possible, and indeed inevitable, for the inferior to accept everything willed for him by his superior, whether it turns out to his advantage or not, as an act of justice. In Job's case it makes his tribulations appear as the means by which he was taught a true understanding of the nature of his dependence on God and of the services befitting to this relationship. It is appropriate that he is in the end restored not only to God's favor,[3] but to health, status, and rank. The Tallensi would understand this story very well by analogy with their ancestor cult; for Oedipus, such a road back to normality does not exist.

¶ RECAPITULATION

To recapitulate, the notion of evil Prenatal Destiny among the Tallensi serves to identify the fact of irremediable failure in the development of the individual to full social capacity. More than that, it gives symbolic expression to the implicit structural meaning of such failure as an indication of abortive filio-parental relationships. The possibility of these relationships going wrong is a threat to fundamental moral and affective ties and sentiments.

---

[3] We remember how, at the end of the drama, God declares: " . . . for him will I accept . . . " (Job, xlii, 8).

This is neutralized by ritual procedures based on the belief that evil Prenatal Destiny is in the last resort susceptible of control by the ancestors if they so will it. Thus the ill-fated are by implication those unfortunate people who are felt to be rejected by the parental institutions of society symbolized in the ancestor figures. The hostile component in the filio-parental relationship comes to the fore, and is given symbolic expression in the image of evil Prenatal Destiny which finally destroys its victim.

The notion of Good Destiny, on the other hand, symbolically identifies the fact of successful individual development along the road to full incorporation in society. It serves to make this fact comprehensible and to set a seal of religious value on it as implicitly significant of normal and successful filio-parental relationships. The symbolism utilized is the notion that Destiny operates in this way if it is absorbed and sanctioned by the ancestors. It thus accounts for the rewards that witness to successful development, and provides a basis for ritual procedures to neutralize the demoralizing effects, on fundamental moral and affective ties and sentiments, of the hazards that accompany each person's progress through life. The well-fated are by implication those fortunate enough to be accepted by the parental institutions symbolized in the cult of the ancestors and endowed with the ability to maintain relationships of mutual trust and support with them. This means that the hostile component in the filio-parental relationship is overcome in the attribution of a predominantly benevolent character to the ancestors. In this context the punitive aspect of the ancestor figures has a disciplinary, not a destructive, function. It is the instrument of their justice and a measure of their sovereignty paralleling, on the religious plane, the usages and forms of family government we have previously described. It helps to drain away individual feelings of anxiety and guilt by canalizing them into customary rituals of placation and expiation; and these are effective simply because the ancestors are believed not only to exact punishment for wrong conduct but also to behave justly and benevolently in the long run.

What can we learn from this limited inquiry? Frazer's own work is a warning against drawing facile generalizations from parallels between the customs and beliefs of widely different societies. However, my aim in this essay has not been to find parallels but to elicit basic common elements in the religious conceptions I have described. And one common element is patent. All the concepts and beliefs we have examined are religious extrapolations of the experiences generated in the relationships between parents and children in societies with a social organization based on kinship and descent. They are magnified and disguised extrapolations; and their effect is to endow the critical components of filio-parental relationships with an external reality and representation that belongs to the whole society and not to the realm of individual thought and fantasy. The religious conceptions of the Tallensi show us this process in a direct form. We can uncover the roots of these beliefs in the family system and observe how their branches spread through the entire social structure. We can see how they bind the internal domain of the family, where children are reared, to the external domain of political society, where they eventually run their life course; and we can see why parenthood, on the one hand, and the sovereignty of society, on the other, are invested with sacredness. Oedipus and Job dramatize the basic elements of this type of religious system. They, too, are reflections, partly exact, partly distorted, of family and kinship institutions. If they appeal more to our imagination and emotions than do the unsophisticated facts of Tale religion, this is because they deck out the bare bones of belief and concept in the rich panoply of the ethical thought and metaphysical doctrines of literate cultures. The core of fundamental beliefs and attitudes is the same.

Here, then, are the areas of common human experience to which our data must be referred. Ever since Freud's bold speculations in *Totem and Taboo* and Durkheim's great work on *The Elementary Forms of the Religious Life*, anthropologists have known that the springs of religion and ritual lie in kinship and social organization. What I have tried to do has been to relate particular religious conceptions to the significance, for the society, of the process of taking its individual members into itself. Considered merely as superstition, beliefs in Fate and the

Ancestors (or Job's God) seem to be antithetical. The first is amoral, the second is supremely moral. In fact, we have seen that in West African religions they are not opposed but rather supplement each other. For the Tallensi, at any rate, they can be described as supplementary conceptual moments in a religious apparatus for dealing with the commitments created for society collectively and for its members severally by the passage of the individual into and through society.[1] They reconcile the two main alternatives in the hazardous progress of the individual from the state of unchecked dependence, as an infant at the mother's breast, to that of constrained independence, as an adult and citizen. It is a law of nature that some people must fail in the whole or in parts of the task of becoming and remaining social persons. The predicament this gives rise to is interpreted, given moral value, and brought under control in the interests of society and of the individual, by means of the beliefs and rituals focused in the notion of Predestiny, or Oedipal Fate. Most people will succeed; but they can do so only by coming to terms with unforeseeable hazards and precarious rewards. To give meaning and absolute moral value to this experience, the Tallensi invoke personified supernatural figures cast in the mold of glorified parents who intervene justly in the life of the individual and of society. The image of the Good Destiny in which these ideas are focused is, in essentials, a simple version of Job's God.

In the ultimate sense, perhaps, the concept of Predestiny may be taken to designate tendencies that originate in organic sources and in the earliest experiences of infantile dependence. It is of profound interest that these tendencies appear to be intuitively recognized in many societies and are deemed to manifest themselves in unwitting resistance

[1] Cf. Jack Goody (ed.): *The Developmental Cycle in Domestic Groups*, Cambridge Papers in Social Anthropology, No. 1 (1958), for the analysis of other aspects of this problem. This essay is an expansion of the Frazer Lecture for 1956 delivered at the University of Glasgow on November 28, 1957, under the title "The Idea of Destiny in West African Religions." I am indebted to the Ford Foundation (Behavioral Sciences Division) for a grant for research assistance in preparing it for publication and to Dr. Christopher Scott and Dr. Lucy Mair for helpful criticism.

to the normal relationships of parenthood. Ancestor- or deity-worship, on the other hand, presupposes the triumph of parenthood. It recognizes the paramountcy of the moral norms emanating from society as a whole over the dangerous egotism of childhood.

A NOTE ABOUT THE AUTHOR

E. E. Evans-Pritchard

E. E. EVANS-PRITCHARD (1902–   ) received B.A. and
M.A. degrees in modern history from Exeter College,
Oxford, before studying anthropology at the London
School of Economics. At the present time he is Professor
of Social Anthropology in the University of Oxford, and
Fellow of All Souls College.

Evans-Pritchard has conducted field research in the
Anglo-Egyptian Sudan, the Belgian Congo, Abyssinia,
Kenya, and Upper Egypt, and his many publications report
a wealth of ethnological data with unrivaled clarity and
subtlety of organization. His first field work was in 1926–
7, among the Azande of the Anglo-Egyptian Sudan, whom
he studied again in 1928–9 and in 1930. And his book,
Witchcraft, Oracles and Magic among the Azande, is the
most comprehensive description in the anthropological
literature of the magical ideas and practices of an African
tribe.

The theoretical significance of Evans-Pritchard's books
lies not so much in the passages devoted to theory, which
are relatively few, as in the relevance of the ethnological
observations they contain to anthropological theories of
social organization, magic, religion, and world view. For
example, in his book on the Azande he writes: "I have
not . . . introduced current psychological and sociological
explanations of mystical notions and ritual behavior . . .
I have always asked myself 'How?' rather than 'Why?'
Azande do certain things and believe certain notions, and I
have tried to explain a fact by citing other facts from the
same culture and by noting interdependencies between
facts."

In his book, *Nuer Religion,* from which the following

selection is reprinted, Evans-Pritchard criticizes various theories of sacrifice and of the nature of religion, but not in order to advance general theories of his own. He remains close to the empiricist position he once advocated in a B.B.C. lecture. "To obtain objectivity in the study of primitive religions what is required is to build up general conclusions from particular ones. One must not ask 'What is religion?' but what are the main features of, let us say, the religion of one Melanesian people; then one must seek to compare the religion of that people with the religions of several other Melanesian peoples who are nearest to the first in their cultures and social institutions . . . the turning away of students from speculation to modest and detailed comparative research within restricted geographical provinces give hope that we may eventually reach by this means certain general and significant conclusions about the nature of the religions of primitive peoples as a whole." Within the rubric of this austere doctrine, Evans-Pritchard has made profound contributions to our knowledge of primitive peoples. He has received many honors, including the Rivers Memorial Medal of the Royal Anthropological Institute, and invitations to deliver the Frazer, Marett, Henry Myers, and Fawcett Lectures. He is a Fellow of the British Academy, and a former President of the Royal Anthropological Institute.

2

A Selection from
*Nuer Religion**

by

E. E. EVANS-PRITCHARD

The Nuer are a Nilotic people of between 200,000 and
300,000 souls living in savanna country near the Upper
Nile and its tributaries. They are a cattle people, the
ebb and flow of whose transhumant life follow the seasons.
They are divided into a number of tribes, the largest
political groups of their society, and these tribes are seg-
mented into sections and subsections corresponding structurally to the segments, or lineages, of the clans dominant
in each tribal territory.

Although Nuer religious ideas and practices were a
part of their way of life which greatly interested me, it
was that to which I was able to give least attention during
my short residence of a year in Nuerland. It was necessary
to learn their language and to study their manner of livelihood and their family, kinship, and political activities
before giving close attention to the more difficult problems of their religious thought. These tasks, all the heavier
in the arduous conditions in which they had to be carried
out, left me little time to pursue anything which could
be called a systematic inquiry into religious matters. What
I record I witnessed myself or is information given spontaneously during talks about other and more practical

* By permission of the author and of the Clarendon Press, the
following selection is reprinted from E. E. Evans-Pritchard, NUER
RELIGION, Oxford at the Clarendon Press, 1956.

affairs or in comment on some event or experience. Such observations may, however, be more valuable in a study of religious thought than those derived from purposive inquiry. This is especially so when a people lack, as the Nuer do, anything which offers easy scope for such an inquiry, for they have nothing which can properly be called dogma, liturgy, and sacraments (*in sensu stricto*), and they lack a developed religious cult and mythology. This is doubtless one of the reasons why for the most part those who have written about the Nuer have said so little about their religion.

A study of Nuer religion is a study of what they consider to be the nature of Spirit and of man's relation to it. I had previously spent many months among the Azande people of the Nile-Uelle divide. From my earliest days among them I was constantly hearing the word *mangu* (witchcraft), and it was soon clear that if I could gain a full understanding of the meaning of this word, I should have the key to Zande philosophy. When I started my study of the Nuer I had a similar experience. I constantly heard them speaking of *kwoth* (Spirit), and I realized that a full understanding of that word was the key to their—very different—philosophy. The attempt to reach it and, even more, to present my conclusions has occupied me for a long time and has proved to be a formidable task. The difficulties which had to be overcome will be very apparent in the pages which follow, but I mention some of them now.

One of the difficulties of presentation has been the different senses the word *kwoth* may have. I have tried to overcome it by speaking of "God" when the word has a sense near enough to our own conception of God to permit the usage; of "Spirit" where it refers, either in Nuer or more frequently, in my exposition, to spiritual nature rather than to any definite, precise, or stated form; and of "a spirit," "the spirit," and "spirits" where it specifically denotes some particular spiritual figure or figures other and lesser than God. The reasons for making these distinctions will become clearer as the book proceeds, and it will then also be perceived why it is impossible to adhere to them rigidly or to use them without any ambiguity.

A further difficulty relates not to Nuer words but to our

own. Although the considerable literature on primitive religions which appeared toward the end of the last century and the early years of the present century made us familiar with such terms as animism, fetishism, totemism, mana, tabu, and shamanism, their meanings are still obscure. The very fact that some of these terms are borrowed from native languages is an indication of the failure to build up an adequate and agreed-upon terminology in Comparative Religion, a subject which, moreover, has been since sadly neglected, especially in this country. In these circumstances sometimes even communication is difficult. If I speak of "spear" or "cow," everybody will have pretty much the same idea of what I speak of, but this is not so when I speak of "Spirit," "soul," "sin," and so forth.

This difficulty is not easily overcome, because it is not merely a matter of definitions but involves also personal judgment. It would be useless to deny this and rash to ignore it. It may be said that in describing and interpreting a primitive religion it should make no difference whether the writer is an agnostic or a Christian, Jew, Muslim, Hindu, or whatever he may be, but in fact it makes a great deal of difference, for even in a descriptive study judgment can in no way be avoided. Those who give assent to the religious beliefs of their own people feel and think, and therefore also write, differently about the beliefs of other peoples from those who do not give assent to them. This is not the place to discuss further this difficulty. I merely wish to recognize that it exists and that it introduces into writings about religion complications which are not present when writing about, for example, kinship or husbandry.

¶ SPIRIT AND THE SOCIAL ORDER

The Nuer word we translate "God" is *kwoth* (Spirit). Nuer also speak of him more definitely as *kwoth nhial* or *kwoth a nhial*, Spirit of the sky or Spirit who is in the sky. There are other and lesser spirits which they class as *kuth nhial* (spirits of the sky or of the above), and *kuth piny* (spirits of the earth or of the below).

The great variety of meanings attached to the word *kwoth* in different contexts and the manner in which

Nuer pass, even in the same ceremony, from one to another may bewilder us. Nuer are not confused, because the difficulties which perplex us do not arise on the level of experience but only when an attempt is made to analyze and systematize Nuer religious thought. Nuer themselves do not feel the need to do this. Indeed, I myself never experienced, when living with the Nuer and thinking in their words and categories, any difficulty commensurate with that which confronts me now when I have to translate and interpret them. I suppose I moved from representation to representation, and backward and forward between the general and particular, much as Nuer do and without feeling that there was any lack of co-ordination in my thoughts or that any special effort to understand was required. It is when one tries to relate Nuer religious conceptions to one another by abstract analysis that the difficulties arise.

When Nuer pray to God, though often looking to the sky as they do so, they usually address him simply as *kwoth* (Spirit), the "who is in the sky" being understood or expressed in gesture. On the other hand, the word may be used for some particular spirit—an air spirit, a totemic spirit, and so forth—without its being indicated by name, it being understood in the context that this particular spirit is referred to. Thus Nuer may say, for example, when speaking of the spirit of lion in reference to a certain lineage, *"e kwothdien"* ("it is their spirit"). They also speak of a *gwan kwoth* (possessor of a spirit), and of a *yang kwoth* (a spirit's cow), without specifying which spirit they have in mind. Those who are aware of the circumstances will know which particular spirit is being referred to. Those who are not aware of them will only know that the man possesses one or other spirit and that the cow belongs to one or other spirit, without knowing which one.

Since God is *kwoth* in the sense of all Spirit and the oneness of Spirit, the other spirits, while distinct with regard to one another, are all, being also *kwoth*, thought of as being of the same nature as God. Each of them, that is to say, is God regarded in a particular way; and it may help us if we think of the particular spirits as figures or representations of refractions of God in relation to particular activities, events, persons, and groups.

That the diverse spiritual figures of Nuer thought are to be regarded as social refractions of the idea of God will be understood better if some examples are given of the problem in action. The ceremony I am about to describe concerned a *nin diet* (a delayed homicide). When a man has been wounded and recovers but dies some months, or even years, later, his death may be attributed to the wound he received and compensation for homicide exacted. A blood feud is unlikely to break out in these circumstances, for the killing may generally be regarded as accidental, and, in any case, a long period of time has elapsed between the act and its consequence; and fewer, some twenty, head of cattle are demanded than for a straight killing, though the number seems to vary in different parts of Nuerland and is probably everywhere reached by negotiation between the parties, both of whom are anxious to reach a settlement as soon as possible. In the ceremony I witnessed, which took place in western Nuerland, the first and final rites of an ordinary homicide were combined, the slayer being cleansed of the blood and peace between the parties being made at the same time, and it took place after only some of the cattle had been paid.

It was held because a man of the Jikul clan had wounded a man of the Lual lineage with a fishing spear some years before, and he had just died. The fact that he had been wounded by a fishing spear was important because among the western Nuer less compensation is paid for a killing by fishing spear or club than for a killing by fighting spear, for it is less likely to have been premeditated. Apart from the slayer himself, there were no Jikul present at the ceremony, which on their side was conducted by their traditional allies the Ngwol lineage and in a Ngwol village. The absence of Jikul and the holding of the ceremony in a village of a third party made it easier for the Lual to be conciliatory.

After some drinking of beer, a sure sign that a settlement was certain, the people sat in the sun to watch proceedings. The heat was so intense that from time to time boys were told to place fresh cattle dung on the ground so that those delivering addresses could stand in it now and again to cool their feet. One of them interrupted his narration to ask God to send a shower of rain to cool him, and the downpour which closed the proceedings was regarded as an answer to his request. The ceremony began with the castration of the young bull to be sacrificed. A Ngwol man then drove a stake into the center of the kraal and tethered the ox to it, and many of the men present threw ashes over its back—a rite I discuss later. Then lengthy invocations, taking over three hours to deliver, were spoken by a Lual man, a Ngwol man, and a leopard-skin priest of the Keunyang lineage, the dominant lineage of the area in which all these lineages have their villages. I give only the gist of what they said because most of it little concerns the question we are considering.

Each speaker began his address by calling out his clan spear-name. He delivered his address walking up and down the kraal brandishing his spear. Most of what was said was addressed to the audience, who entered into lengthy arguments with the speakers about the matter in hand, besides carrying on conversation among themselves. But in the midst of their harangues the speakers frequently addressed *kwoth* by one or other title and explained to Spirit so addressed the circumstances which had brought the people together.

The Lual representative, who made the first speech, besides addressing *kwoth* (Spirit), and *kwoth a nhial* (Spirit who is in the sky), called on "*kwoth wicda, kwoth ngoapna*" ("spirit of our home or community [literally, cattle camp], spirit of our fig tree"), the fig tree being the totem of his lineage. He began with a long account of the history of the lineage of the man responsible for the death with interminable references to past disputes, threatening that if ever the Jikul or the Ngwol fought his people again the Lual would exterminate them, to all the events which led up to the quarrel in which the dead man had been wounded, and to cattle which had been paid or promised in compensation for the homicide and the further cattle which were being demanded. Among his observations he accused the Ngwol of having buried a living ox with some beads and a spear to kill the Lual, and this provoked a violent argument in which the Ngwol part of the audience retorted that the Lual had buried a dog alive in a byre to kill them (I do not know whether such practices ever really occur).

The Ngwol representative then delivered a rambling address. He often mentioned *kwoth* in it, though not, so far as I heard, with any particular specifications. His chief point was that the Jikul were paying compensation in cattle for the dead man and that if the Lual reopened the quarrel it would be to their disadvantage, the Jikul being fully able to look after themselves if it came to fighting again. He then, from the Jikul angle, repeated the whole history of the affair, a recapitulation which stirred up involved controversy with the Lual men present. In these invocations grievances, both real and imagined, are made public, not with the purpose of complicating the issue or inflaming passions, but because it is the rule of such gatherings that everything a man has in his heart against others must be revealed and no bitterness kept secret.

Finally, the leopard-skin priest, whose function is to cleanse a killer and to perform rites to terminate a blood feud, rose and addressed the assembly. In his invocation he frequently, in addition to speaking to *kwoth* and *kwoth a nhial*, called on "*kwoth riengda*," a phrase which literally means "spirit of our flesh" and which refers to the spiritual source of sacerdotal power. He told the slayer that as some of the cattle had already been paid and the remainder were about to be paid, he might go abroad without fear of vengeance. He told the kinsmen of the dead man that if they started a feud, their spears would miss their mark and that they would do well to take the cattle and settle the affair forever. He warned the kinsmen of the slayer not to try and hide their cattle, that is, send them secretly to the kraals of distant kinsmen and then say that they had not the wherewithal to meet their obligations. He, also, recapitulated the whole history of the quarrel, from the point of view of an impartial onlooker and mediator.

At the end of his address he speared the ox, and those present rushed in, as is the custom on this occasion, to obtain what they could of the carcass, hacking and slicing, waving their spears, and shouting. It was a scene of great confusion. When things had quieted down, the leopard-skin priest cut off some of the hair of the head of the man who had occasioned the death: "the blood which entered into his body is purged [*riem me ce wa pwonyde ba woc*], other hairs will grow [*bi miem ti okien dony*], the blood is finished" [*ce riem thuk*].

The ceremony I have described is typical in form of Nuer religious ceremonies. What I want here to draw attention to in it are the different titles mentioned in the invocations: *kwoth* (Spirit), without further designation, *kwoth a nhial* (Spirit who is in the sky), *kwoth wic* [*da*] (Spirit of the home), *kwoth ngoap* [*na*] (Spirit of the fig tree), and *kwoth rieng* [*da*] (Spirit of the flesh [the virtue of the leopard-skin priests]); and there may have been others which I did not hear. Besides these titles such expressions as *gwandong* (grandfather) and *kwoth gwara* (spirit of our fathers) were used. At other ceremonies at which people of different families and lineages from those concerned in this particular ceremony have been represented I have heard references in invocations to a variety of other spirits—totemic spirits, *colwic* spirits, and spirits of the air. How are we to interpret Nuer thought about the nature of Spirit as it is expressed in such ceremonies as the one I have described?

In this particular ceremony several groups were opposed to each other, and the leopard-skin priest was acting in his priestly capacity as mediator between them and to conclude a settlement by sacrifice. The persons who made the invocations therefore appealed to, or spoke about, God not only as God but also as God in his special relation to the groups they represented, and in the case of the leopard-skin priest to God in his special relation to the priestly function as well as to a particular priestly lineage. The circumstances may be compared to a war between European powers in which each prays for victory to the God of its fathers, Lord of its battle line. Those engaged in the struggle do not believe that two distinct deities are being appealed to. That this is the correct interpretation of the Nuer material is shown by a number of observations, one of the most significant being the fact that although the invocations were made to different titles, they were all made over the same victim, and this same victim was offered up by all the parties concerned. This appears to me to be proof that the sacrifice was made to one and the same being. Another significant observation is the fact that in situations in which no sectional interests are at stake but where men approach God simply as men and in the context of their common humanity, as, for example, when furious storms are raging, in times of severe drought and famine, or when a man is seriously ill, then God alone, or in certain circumstances one of his hypostases by which he is figured in relation to some particular natural phenomenon, is addressed, and he is not, as it were, divided by a variety of titles along the lines of the social structure. This may also be to a large extent the case even where different social groups are involved, so long as they are not antagonistic but have a common interest and intention. I give one such illustration.

A youth in a village where I was residing was badly wounded in the shoulder by a spear in a fight with a man of the next village. His antagonist had not intended to kill him, and the people of the two villages were on good terms, so his kinsmen at once sent the spear with which the wound had been inflicted to the injured youth's home with expressions of regret and wishes for a speedy recovery. The elders of the wounded lad's home bent the point of the spear and placed it point downward in a pot of cold water. This was done to lessen the pain of the wound, especially when it was washed, and to cool the inflammation. Next morning the wounder's village sent us a deputation, leading a goat for sacrifice. By this further indication of their regrets and of their willingness to pay compensation at once should the lad die, they anticipated a blood feud. It was hoped in any case that the danger of death would be obviated by the sacrifice of the goat. The wound would, as the Nuer put it, "be finished with the goat."

Before the animal was sacrificed, the visitors consecrated it by rubbing ashes on its back. It was then tied to a stake opposite the hut of the wounded youth's maternal grandmother, and an invocation was delivered over it by a man called Lel, a leopard-skin priest and also a prophet, who had been summoned from a distance to officiate, partly, I think, because his presence would give greater importance, and therefore perhaps efficacy, to the ceremony and partly because it would be a further insurance for a peaceful outcome to the incident. His address was largely taken up with reiterations that the youth would not die and with giving to God and the people a lengthy and detailed account of how the accident had occurred. He sacrificed the goat at the conclusion of his speech. Our home party then brought forward a wether and it was also consecrated with ashes. Afterward a man of the home poured a libation of water over its tethering peg as a prelude to delivering an oration. He told the story of the accident all over again and commented on it to God in this vein: "Ah God! We call on you about this wound. There is no enmity between us [the party of the injured youth and the party of the spearer]. This wound came of itself [they do not attribute it to the spearer because it was an accident and also because the youth will not die and so there will be no *thung*, debt of homicide]. Throw the badness away with this cow [they call a sheep or goat a "cow" in sacrificial contexts]. Let the wound heal. Ah God! it is only a headache [it is not a sickness of any importance—they speak of the most ghastly wounds in this way], let it be finished, let it go right on [heal without complications]. Let it be removed from the man's body. Let us be at peace." Another man of the home party also made an invocation in much the same language: "Friend [*maadh*], God who is in this village, as you are very great we tell you about this wound, for you are God of our home in very truth. We tell you about the fight of this lad. Let the wound heal. Let it be ransomed [with the sheep]"; and so forth. A representative of the visitors now said a few words to the same purpose and the sheep was then sacrificed. The meat of both sacrifices was eaten by the people of the home after the visiting deputation had departed; and also the carcass of a third animal, another wether, which the people of the home later sacrificed after three of them had made further invocations over it in much the same vein.

In this ceremony Spirit was addressed simply as *kwoth* and no designated refractions were mentioned, and when on such occasions Nuer speak to, or about, *kwoth* without differentiating specifications, they are, as I have explained, speaking to, or about, Spirit in the comprehensive conception of God the creator and the sustainer of life. This is often the case in their sacrifices, and it is the same when they pray for peace and deliverance from evil.

That emphasis is given to the refractions when a social group, acting as such and marking itself off from other groups, makes a sacrifice on behalf of itself or of one of its members in virtue of his membership of it, and that they are then to be regarded as diverse exclusive representations of God by which he is figured to the groups concerned in a special way as their patrons, is evident also from other considerations. It is clear that totemic spirits of lineages are Spirit conceived of in a tutelary relationship to the lineages. The *colwic* spirits are also Spirit in a tutelary relationship to the families and lineages to which they belonged in the flesh before they were metamorphosed into spirit. Also, the spirits of the air may have a tutelary relationship to families and lines of descent, and where their attachment is more to an individual prophet, he has public functions through which the spirit becomes patron of local and political communities. Totemic spirits may also, though in a rather different manner, have a secondary significance for political groups through the association of dominant lineages with tribal sections. Likewise, though to a lesser extent, nature sprites are Spirit in a tutelary relationship to families; and even fetishes, though of a rather different complexion, are Spirit in a tutelary relationship to individuals, and sometimes to local communities to which these individuals belong. The attachment of all these spiritual figures to social groups is indicated in various ways, most noticeably in ceremonial and in payment of cattle to them at marriages.

That these spiritual conceptions lack autonomy and are rightly regarded as social refractions of God is further shown by the fact that *kwoth*, without any distinguishing name, can become associated with any social group or office. Thus, as we have seen, Nuer speak of the *kwoth* of a leopard-skin priest, "the spirit of the flesh," and they speak also of *"kwoth muonde"* ("the spirit of his [the priest's] earth"). This is no particular *kwoth* but is Spirit seen in relation to priestly powers and functions. Likewise they speak of *kwoth cuekni* (the spirit of twins), to which sacrifices are made at the birth of twins and to which a cow of the bride wealth of the sisters of twins is dedicated.

Here again, this is not thought of by Nuer as some particular spirit which has an existence and name of its own but as God in a special relationship to twins, or rather to the event of a twin birth. Another example is the way in which they speak of the *kwoth* of an age set, the tutelary, nameless spirit which protects the members of the set and avenges wrongs done to men by their age mates. This cannot be a distinctive spirit in its own right, as it were, if only because the sets pass in turn into oblivion and are replaced by others. It is rather God thought of in relation to a particular set, just as he is also the separate, while still being the same, guardian spirit of the other sets. He is both the one and the many—one in his nature and many in his diverse social representations.

Moreover, though God is God of all men, he is not only conceived of, in the various totemic and other representations we have considered, as the special patron of descent, and sometimes of local, groups, but each family regards him, without specific differentiation of title, as having a particular relation to itself; and he may be spoken about in terms of a particular household, hamlet, or village community. One hears Nuer say in invocations, as in the one I have just recorded: "God who is in this village," or "God who is in this home." When a Nuer builds a byre, he holds a small ceremony before its central support is erected. Beer is prepared, and before the people drink it, the master of ceremonies or the owner of the byre pours a libation of it to God and the ghosts at the entrance to the byre and in the center of it, where the hearth and shrine will be, and asks God to give peace and prosperity to the home, its people, and its cattle. They think then of God looking after their home in a special way, of being particularly attached to it so that He then becomes, as it were, in a special sense the family's God, a household God. The shrine, a forked post, is the altar of God within the home, God of the hearth, as well as being associated with any of his particular representations—totemic, *colwic*, air spirits, etc.—in which he may stand in a tutelary relationship to the lineage or family of the owner of the homestead, and also with the ancestral ghosts. He is spoken of in this domestic representation as *kwoth rieka* (God of the post [shrine]). Further, every member of a Nuer lineage, whether or not it has totemic or other specifically designated spirits, will in invocations speak of *"kwoth gwara"* ("Spirit of our fathers") or in reference to the name of the ancestor of the lineage or clan, just as the Old Testament speaks of "the God of our fathers" or "the God of Abraham, Isaac, and Jacob." Similarly, one hears the leopard-skin priests address God as *"kwoth Geaka"* ("spirit of Gee"). Gee was the first leopard-skin priest from whom all the leopard-skin priests derive their powers, so that the expression refers to God figured as patron of priests; though it also has a wider, national, sense, for Gee was also the ancestor of the most important Nuer clans.

Apart from the use of names or titles as diacritical signs to indicate an inclusive or exclusive relationship to God, Nuer make the same distinction grammatically through their inclusive or exclusive pronominal suffixes. These particles are rather complicated when they are attached to family and kinship terms, as in reference to God as "father," and it is perhaps sufficient to say that they enable the speaker to indicate whether he speaks to Spirit as "Spirit of our fathers" in the sense of Spirit in relation to his lineage alone or in the sense of Spirit in relation to everyone. He can thus stress the unity of all present in relation to God or their separateness as social groups in a distinctive relationship to him as such.

The ambiguities which seem at first to be so puzzling a feature of Nuer religion are, at least to some extent, resolved by considering in this way their religious ideas in relation to their social order, for in all societies religious thought bears the impress of the social order. Given the segmentary political and lineage structure of the Nuer, it is understandable that the same complementary tendencies toward fission and fusion and the same relativity that we find in the structure are found also in the action of Spirit in the social life. Just as, for example, two lineages are distinct and opposed groups in relation to one another at one level of segmentation and are a single unit at a higher level of segmentation, so Spirit as conceived in relation to these segments must be divided at the lower level and undivided at the higher level. It is intelligible, therefore, that in its relation to the segmentary social order the conception of Spirit is broken up into diverse refractions, while in relation to nature and man in general the many become again the one.

In the light of what has been said above, it is not surprising that any number of new spirits may come into existence without disconcerting the Nuer, either being borrowed from neighboring peoples or derived from some unusual experience. We have good reason to believe that the spirits of the air, the fetishes, and, at any rate for the most part, the totemic spirits have been introduced, some of them very recently, into Nuerland, and probably the same is true of the nature sprites. I think it can be assumed—I do not see how it can have been otherwise—that there have always been different representations of *kwoth* among the Nuer, and if this is so, the old, or traditional, religion must have consisted, as far as the notion of Spirit is concerned, of the conceptions of God, of God figured to specific social groups by grammatical indications or by reference to their names, of *colwic* spirits, and of some totemic spirits.

The taking over of new spiritual conceptions from neighboring peoples may have been partly fortuitous, but I would suggest that it may also in part be accounted for by reference to recent Nuer history. During the last hundred years the Nuer have absorbed a great number of Dinka and have also been brought into closer contact, directly or indirectly, with other peoples of the Southern Sudan and also with Arabs and ourselves. This provided opportunities for borrowing foreign ideas. But it may be suggested that not only was the opportunity there, but also the need. Nuer statements lead us to suppose that certain social developments were taking place at the same time. They say that their clans and lineages were being broken up by expansion, and were incorporating into their stocks Dinka lines of descent, besides assimilating politically Dinka communities—hence the Dinka totems in Nuerland today; that prophets emerged who directed large-scale raids on the Dinka and defense against the "Turks" (the Arabs and the British)—hence the Dinka and other foreign spirits of the air; and that the peace and administration imposed on them by the government of the Anglo-Egyptian Sudan have given protection to those who wish to pursue private gain and vengeance—hence the introduction of fetishes and their spread. Ethnological evidences support what they say, and we can add that it is in accord with the logic of the Nuer conception of Spirit that it should be represented by figures corresponding to these new social phenomena. Dr. Lienhardt tells me that since I was last in Nuerland the number of spirits has increased and that they have spread widely and freely. This is what we would expect to follow further social disintegration.

God may thus be figured in numberless ways in reference to social groups and to persons, and in relation to effects which are significant for them; and in none of them has the figure any sharply defined individuality. This is fairly easy to understand when we are dealing with refractions which are referred to simply as *kwoth* of a group and without distinguishing name or title; but it may fairly be asked whether those spirits which are named can adequately be thought of as refractions and are not rather to be regarded as quite independent conceptions. We must distinguish here between class names and individual or personal names. The reason why Nuer divide the spirits into kinds, spirits of the above, spirits of the below, *colwic* spirits, *bieli*, and so forth, is that they regard them as different sorts of manifestation of Spirit and of varying degrees of importance. This is a matter I discuss later. It is rather the individual names with which we are immediately concerned.

The reason why some of the refractions have distinguishing names is, I think, mainly a matter of ownership. Spirit can be owned by persons. Now, no one in this sense owns God, but all the various spirits may be owned by persons; and it may be said that the most distinctive naming of them is where individual ownership is most marked, in the case of the spirits of the air and the fetish spirits, which have proper names and ox names. A prophet who is inspired by Spirit has in the logic of the situation to give it a name which distinguishes it as his particular spirit from the spirits of other prophets of his neighborhood who are his rivals for renown and influence; for the attachment here is to individuals who build up through it a personal following, and not, at least primarily, to social groups. When a spirit falls from above and enters into a man who becomes its prophet, it attains individuality by revealing through the prophet what it is called—its name; and when a person becomes possessed for the first time, the immediate endeavor of his neighbors is to get the spirit to reveal its name when he is in a dissociated state. The spirit gets its name, the *numen* gets its *nomen*, by being owned by the person it possesses and to whom, by possessing him, it brings power and prestige. Fetishes are also owned by individuals who compete, though in a different way from prophets, for prestige and power against one another, so they must have distinguishing names. Thus it is through the name that ownership is established. The individuality is, in a sense, that of the person and not that of the spirit, the spirit getting its name through him.

The conclusion we have reached is that the conception of *kwoth* has a structural dimension. At one end Spirit is thought of in relation to man and the world in general as omnipresent God. Then it is thought of in relation to a variety of social groups and activities and to categories of persons: to political movements connected with prophets, and in a special relation to warfare, as spirits of the air; to descent groups as *colwic* and totemic spirits; and to a variety of ritual specialists as totemic, totemistic, and similar spirits. At the other end it is conceived of more or less in relation to individuals in a private capacity as nature sprites and fetishes. God figured as common father and creator is patron of all men; figured in spirits of the air he is patron of political leaders; figured in *colwic* and totemic spirits, and also in unnamed refractions, he is patron of lineages and families; and figured in nature sprites and fetishes he is patron of individuals. I give only a general indication of the main lines of social demarcation between the various types of refractions, and I do not discuss exceptions and overlappings.

This impress of the social structure on Nuer religious thought is to be marked also in the natural and moral attributes of the different types of spiritual refractions. Mighty celestial phenomena, and great and terrible happenings, such as plagues and famines, and the moral order which concern all men are attributed to God, while processes and events which do not have so general a range of impact tend to be attributed to whichever particular refraction or type the situation and context evoke. Likewise the refractions tend to decrease in the degree of universality, stability, and morality attributed to them the smaller the social space to which they refer. I give a brief indication of this tendency, illustrated by a few examples.

God is everywhere; he is permanent and changeless in his relation to the constant elements in the natural and moral orders; he is one, and he is all-powerful, just, and compassionate. The spirits of the air are in particular persons and places, and even when their prophets are politically important persons, they have a limited spread of influence; they have fallen from the clouds in recent times and their renown depends on the personal prestige of their prophets and on political circumstances, both of which are unstable factors and may be ephemeral; they are multiple, though compared with lesser spirits they are few in number; and they are unpredictable, and even capricious and ill-intentioned. The *colwic* and totemic spirits are restricted to certain lineages and families; they became tutelary spirits of these groups at certain points of time and many are sooner or later forgotten; they are numerous; and compared to the spirits of the air they are unimportant. The nature sprites and fetishes are for the most part acknowledged only by the persons who own them and by their immediate kin. The fetishes certainly, and the nature sprites probably, are very recent introductions, and they enter into relationships with persons and families and are forgotten by their descendants. The sprites flit here and there, come into homes, and then return to the bush. The fetishes are bought and sold and pass from hand to hand. Their reputations wax and wane with those of their owners. They lose ground and are replaced by others. Both alike are potentially inexhaustible in number. Though some fetishes are feared, neither they nor the sprites are highly regarded, and the fetishes are in general disapproved of. On the other hand, the lower down the scale of Spirit we descend and the more it can be said to be owned, the more prominent do cult features appear. God is approached in simple prayer and sacrifice. The spirits of the air receive more elaborate ceremonial attentions, into which enter hymns, possession, and divination. Cult features are also prominent at the level of the *colwic* and totemic spirits. The most regular ritual attention appears to be given to the fetishes, which receive frequent offerings from their owners and in the most material form.

In relating the configuration of Nuer religious thought to the structural order of their society, I am, of course, relating abstractions to one another by a method of sociological analysis. It is not suggested that the Nuer see their religion in this sort of way. Nevertheless, the structural configuration we abstract by this process is of the same design as the symbolic configuration in which they think of their various *kuth*. The various spirits in their symbolic configuration occupy the same positions in relation to each other as they do in the structural configuration we perceive through sociological analysis.

In a typically Nuer way they represent the interrelationship of the spirits in a genealogical metaphor. God is the father of the greater spirits of the air, and the lesser of them are said to be children of his sons, of his lineage. The totemic spirits are often said to be children of his daughters—that is, they are not of his lineage, which is the Nuer way of placing them yet lower in the spiritual scale. The fetishes (and possibly also the nature sprites) come lowest of all in the representation of children of daughters of the air spirit *deng*. Another way of indicating this spiritual hierarchy is in terms of descent values in their political connotation. The spirits of the air are *diel*, true or aristocratic spirits, the totemic spirits are *jaang*, Dinka-like spirits, and the fetishes are *jur*, despised foreigners.

The interrelationship of the spirits is represented also in the symbolism of height or space, or more accurately in the relation of sky to earth. The spirits, as we have noted, are those of the above and those of the below. God is symbolized by the sky and the spirits of the air by the atmosphere, the clouds, and the breezes, the lesser ones being nearer to the earth than the greater ones. The totemic spirits as spirits are above and as creatures are below. The nature sprites may also be thought of as having a dual existence. The fetishes are the most earthly of the spirits, some of them speaking from beneath the ground. Implicit in this symbolic configuration is also an evaluation in terms of light and darkness, ranging from celestial brightness to subterranean darkness.

We see, and in their own way of looking at the matter Nuer see, degrees of immanence in this symbolic configuration. The cosmological representation of Spirit, and in particular the dichotomy between Heaven and earth, the spirits of the above and those of the below, is further indicated by the mode and manner of appearances, the forms in which Spirit is manifested to humans. At one end there is pure Spirit, transcendental being which is everywhere and in nothing particular, Spirit as it is in itself, God. God is seen only in the works of his creation, and he speaks only in the language of inner spiritual experience. The spirits of the air, on the other hand, and sometimes also the *colwic* spirits, appear to men in their prophets, through whom they are known and speak. Then Spirit is manifested in totemic species, which are mostly creatures, and at the farther end in things, the natural things associated with sprites and the magical substances which are the outward appearances of fetishes, which are Spirit in its lowest and most material form, Spirit which "eats" offerings and which is bought and sold. Nuer themselves draw these comparisons, and it is evident from their observations that they themselves perceive that they are dealing with Spirit at different levels of thought and experience, Spirit in itself, Spirit in persons, Spirit in beasts, and Spirit in things. Moreover, I think we may conclude further that they perceive these different levels of immanence also as levels in time. This is implied in the genealogical representation of Spirit, for father must come before children and children before grandchildren; and possibly also in its spatial representation in the falling of spirits from above in a succession of descents at points in time. But it is also explicit in Nuer statements of the order in which their various spirits appeared among them. God was always there; then at various points of time *colwic* spirits, spirits of the air, totemic spirits, nature sprites, and fetish spirits appeared on the scene, the fetish spirits being the most recent arrivals.

These refractions correspond, as we have noted, with different levels of social activity, but an interpretation in

terms of social structure merely shows us how the idea
of Spirit takes various forms corresponding to departments
of social life. It does not enable us to understand any better
the intrinsic nature of the idea itself. The varying degrees
of immanence in which the conception is expressed show
us that the different social levels at which Spirit is manifested are also different degrees of religious perception.
Spirit is sometimes perceived, intellectually and intuitively,
as one, transcendental, pure Spirit and at other times,
in relation to human affairs and interests, as one or
other of a great number of figures through which it is
made known, in varying degrees of materialization, concretely to human intelligence. Nor is it, even with strict
reference to a purely structural interpretation of the conception of Spirit in Nuer society, simply a matter of social
levels, for, as we have seen, God is also experienced un-
refracted at all levels, down to the individual; so that a
structural interpretation explains only certain characteristics of the refractions and not the idea of Spirit in itself.
I have only tried to show that, and how that idea is
broken up by the refracting surfaces of nature, of society,
of culture, and of historical experience.

¶ THE SACRIFICIAL ROLE OF CATTLE

I

Nuer are very largely dependent on the milk of their
herds, and in their harsh environment they probably could
not live without them, any more than the cattle could
live without the care and protection of their owners.
Their carcasses also furnish Nuer with meat, tools, ornaments, sleeping hides, and various other objects of domestic use; and their sun-dried dung provides fuel for the
great smoldering smudges that give protection from
mosquitoes to man and beast alike. Women are more interested in the cows, and this is natural, for they have
charge of milking and dairy work. Men's interest in the
cow is, apart from their value for breeding, rather for
their use in obtaining wives, and they are interested in
the oxen for the same reason, and also because they provide them with a means of display and, which is the
matter I am about to discuss, a means of sacrifice. But

for all Nuer—men, women, and children—cattle are their great treasure, a constant source of pride and joy, the occasion also of much foresight, anxiety, and quarreling; and they are their intimate companions from birth to death. It is not difficult to understand, therefore, that Nuer give their cattle devoted attention, and it is not surprising that they talk more of cattle than of anything else and have a vast vocabulary relating to them and their needs.

Though I restrict myself here to a consideration of the religious significance of their cattle for Nuer, we must not for a moment forget that this is bound up with their secular uses. Otherwise it will not be appreciated what it is that Nuer surrender in sacrifice, the most precious thing they possess. Nevertheless, if cattle were only used for food and obtaining wives, writers about the Nuer, and also about other Nilotic peoples, might have been content just to draw attention to the great interest these peoples have in them. But cattle figure so prominently in their lives in ways not directly concerned with their maintenance or their use for practical purposes that European observers have perceived that in the relationship between men and cattle there is something more than can be stated in simple terms of husbandry and exploitation. I mention only those whose observations refer specifically to the Nuer. Ernst Marno says that we may speak of their veneration (*Verehrung*) of cattle, that the largest and finest ox of a herd is regarded as a guardian genius (*schützende* Genius), and that they refer to this beast by the same name, "*nyeledit*," as they assign to the conception of a Supreme Being and to thunder. Likewise, Mr. H. C. Jackson tells us that the bull which a youth receives from his father at initiation "is a kind of guardian spirit of its owner who calls upon it in times of stress and difficulty," and in another place he speaks of this bull as the "tutelary spirit" of its owner. Captain H. H. Wilson says of the Nuer that, like the other Nilotic peoples of the White Nile, "what religion they possess is centred in the cow"; and Professor D. Westermann writes that "the attachment of a man to his cows and of a boy to the bull with which his father presents him may almost be called religious." There is, however, no evidence at all that cattle are venerated or in themselves are in any way regarded as guardian spirits, and in so far as it may be true to say that Nuer religion "is centred in the cow" or that their attachment to cattle "may almost be called religious," in so far, that is, that we may legitimately speak, as Marianne Schmidl did in her interesting paper on the subject, of *"die sakrale Stellung des Rindes,"* it is for a different reason.

Another writer about the Nilotic peoples and a very experienced anthropologist, my teacher Professor C. G. Seligman, said about Nilotic cattle that "it is difficult to describe their importance to their masters or the love and care the latter have for their beasts, but it is certainly no exaggeration to say that it amounts to what psychologists would term 'identification.'" What seems chiefly to have persuaded Professor Seligman to use this word is the Nilotic custom of taking personal names from their cattle in addition to the personal names they are given soon after birth. I have discussed elsewhere the general social significance of names and other modes of address among the Nuer, and here I speak only of their cattle names and principally of their ox names, these being of chief importance.

These names are often spoken of in writings about the Nuer as bull names, but ox names, in the use of the word "ox" to denote a castrated bull, is a more correct designation. Nuer speak always of such a name as *cot thak*, the name of an ox, and *thak* is a castrated animal in contrast to a *tut*, an entire animal. It is true that when a youth takes his name from a beast, it may be entire, but it will be castrated later. Nuer may not castrate a male calf till it is nearly two years old, but they do so before it is likely to gender with the cows. It is not for pedantry that I make the distinction: it has a logical, and perhaps psychological, appositeness to the equation of man and ox in sacrifice.

Ox names are essentially the names of men, males who have passed through the rite of initiation to manhood. Boys may take ox names in play, but only in imitation of their elders. Likewise, maidens may take ox names, from bull calves of the cows they milk, but they are mainly used only between girls themselves and in the nature of a game, copying their brothers; and the names are short-lived. Married women use cow names among themselves, but here again this is similitude, and it has none of the significance of the ox names of men. Perhaps also here again the distinction between the copy names of boys, girls, and women and those taken by men may be important because of its logical relation, which concerns our present discussion, to the fact that men, and not boys or women, are the sacrificial agents. The two sides of the standard equation are the human male and the bovine male, man and ox.

When a boy is initiated, his father gives him in sign of his manhood an ox or, as I have explained, a bull calf which will later be castrated; and this ox, which he describes as *"thak gareda,"* ("the ox of my cutting" [initiation]), becomes his *dil thak,* what I have spoken about as his favorite ox (Marno's *"Lieblingsstier"*), though the word *dil* has generally the sense of "pure," "true," "perfect," or "aristocratic." It is the ox of perfection. It is the young man's friend and companion. He plays with it and fondles it. He composes poems about it and sings them to it, and he gets a small boy to lead it around the camp in the morning or evening as he leaps behind it chanting poems. He walks among the cattle at night ringing a cattle bell and singing of his kin, his loves, and his cattle, and he praises this ox among all other oxen. He makes tassels to hang from one of its horns, and he loves to see it toss the tassel in the air with a sweep of the neck. He acquires an iron bell to hang around its neck, and no music, unless it be the ox's lowing, is sweeter to his ears than its tinkling in the pastures. He goes to the edge of the camp to meet it when it returns from grazing in the evening. He is never tired of describing its points, and as he does so, and also in dancing, he may hold up his arms in imitation of its horns. Should the ox die, he is downcast; and should he die, it must be sacrificed at his mortuary ceremony.

The youth now also enters through this ox into a new kind of relationship with God, the guardian spirits of his family and lineage, and the ghosts of his ancestors. When he has tethered it in the kraal for the night, he may pet it, removing ticks from its belly and scrotum and picking out adherent dung from its anus; and he may at the same time rub ashes on its back. Ordinarily I think he does this simply because the ox, which has suffered from para-sites throughout the day, gets relief from its back being rubbed, but I was told that he may occasionally, as he does so, speak a few words to God or to the ghosts. While it is not until a man marries and has children and an independent household that he sacrifices animals, dedicates them to spirits, and in other ways makes formal use of them for religious purposes, nevertheless, the ox a father gives his son at initiation provides him with a direct means of communication with the spiritual world. It is more than a possession, more even than part of his social personality—it is a point of meeting between soul and spirit and has therefore a sacramental character also.

From the colors, their distribution, the shape of the horns, and other peculiarities of the ox of his initiation, a youth takes, or is given by his companions, his *cot thak*, his ox name. It may be the same word as that by which the ox's markings are indicated, but generally it combines the name for the markings with a prefix descriptive of something connected with the ox. For example, a man whose favorite ox is black and white (*rial*) may call himself *Luthrial* or *Luerial*, *luth* being a large cattle bell and *lue* a long tassel attached to one of the horns. At first only his age mates may know his new name, but the older people soon get to know it, too, for they hear his mates greet him by it and they also hear him shout it out as he displays himself with the ox in the cattle camps which are formed soon after initiation. Also, young men of about the same age call out their ox names, with many embellishments, to one another at dances, often after a bout of dueling with clubs, and when in a dance two lines of youths stand opposite each other and shower ox names on one another preparatory to a spectacular jump into the air in unison.

The calling of a youth by a name the same as, or derived from, that by which his favorite ox is referred to is perhaps the most striking example of, and evidence for, what Professor Seligman speaks of as "identification." Indeed, in listening to Nuer poems, one is often in doubt whether it is the ox or the man that is being spoken about. The representations are never entirely distinct. Somewhat different, though related and also very striking, is the custom called *thak moc*, the calling out of the (name of the) ox. A man shouts out the name of his favorite ox— the ox's name, not his ox name, which may be an elaboration of the ox's name—when he hurls his spear at an enemy or at his quarry when hunting or fishing, for example: *"ma rial,"* ("black-and-white" [ox]), or *"thakda ma rial,"* ("my black-and-white ox"). In some of my earlier writings I have translated *moc* by "invocation" and "to invoke," following Driberg's translation of the Lango *gwongo*, but I avoid doing so in an account of Nuer religion partly because I have in it used these words to translate another word, *lam*, but also because nothing is in fact invoked, and it is precisely the use of the words in connection with oxen that has led to the erroneous conclusion that a favorite ox is a sort of "tutelary spirit." The ox is not called on, but called out. It is not an invocation, but a cry of excitement and triumph as the striker strikes his foe or prey. That the ox is not being called on for aid is conclusively shown by the fact that in the same circumstances a Nuer may shout out instead *"tet cueda"* followed by a kinship term, usually that referring to the mother's sister: *"tet cueda malene"* ("my right hand, my mother's sisters"). Nuer are not calling on their mothers' sisters for aid, but using an emotive ejaculation, in which the ideas of strength (the right hand) and good will (the mothers' sisters) are combined. When they cry out the names of their oxen, the ejaculation is a triumphant assertion of the self, for which the ox stands as a symbol. Also, a man may cry out the name of his ox on occasions when there is no question of success or failure: as he brandishes his spear as though to strike in dancing, when making spectacular leaps into the air (*rau*), and sometimes in making a sacrificial invocation. It is both self-expression and a drawing of attention to the self.

It should be borne in mind that a man normally retains his ox name and continues to be called by it and also to shout out the name of the ox from which it is derived long after the ox is no more in his possession. A man may part, though always with regret, with a favorite ox for marriage or sacrifice, or the ox may die. It is then replaced by another favorite, though when a man is older and has a herd of his own, he may not identify himself in quite the same way or to the same extent as when he was young with any one particular ox. If another ox takes the place of the first favorite, the ox of initiation, its owner may take, or be given, a new ox name derived from this second ox, the new name then either taking the place of the old or both being used; but most men keep for life the ox names they acquire at the time of their initiation. It is the name of this ox that a man shouts out in war, hunting, dancing and leaping, and in sacrificial invocations, and by which, in one form or another, he is addressed by his peers; though it has long ago departed. Fundamentally, therefore, it is not the ox of initiation itself with which there is "identification," but ox, the idea of oxen. The ox of initiation is the prototype of the ox-man relationship, and it is a kind of focal point at which the feelings a Nuer has toward cattle converge and run over into demonstration by word and gesture. When the ox is long ago dead, the relationship continues because ultimately it is not one between a man and a particular beast but a general relationship of a human being to cattle, an essential feature of which, I am about to suggest, is the sacramental equation of man and beast in sacrifice. Any ox will therefore serve the purpose, or, indeed, no ox at all— only the memory, or rather the idea, of an ox.

We may ask why the identification is with oxen and not with bulls. It might be expected that a man, who is himself a *tut* (bull), not only in the general sense of "male," but also in a common metaphor of speech derived expressly from cattle, would take his name from a bull rather than from an ox. The commonsense answer is that Nuer castrate all but a very few of their bulls, so that there would not be enough entire animals to go around, and this may be the right explanation. Even if it is not, or is not a sufficient explanation, we must here take it as given that the equation is between man and ox. We may, however, note further the fact, on which emphasis is later to be laid, that since an ox or a surrogate for an ox is almost always the sacrificial victim, the sacrificial equivalence is between men (the sacrificers) and oxen (the victims). If a beast is entire, it is castrated before sacrifice. It is perhaps also necessary to remark that Nuer evaluation of bulls and oxen is not ours. Our representation of an ox, in contrast to a bull, is a docile, inferior, and slightly contemptible beast destined for the slaughter house. In the Nuer representation a fat ox is a thing of grandeur and beauty. It is oxen which arouse their admiration. Bulls evoke utilitarian interest rather than emotional and aesthetic attention.

The facts I have related make it understandable that Professor Seligman should have spoken of "identification" of men with their favorite oxen. Had he had either a first-hand or a wider knowledge of the Nuer, he would no doubt have elaborated his theme, and especially by drawing on their ceremonies of initiation for illustrations.

A youth takes his cry and his personal name from the markings and other traits of the ox his father gives him at initiation. By the rites of initiation, boys are made men, and this means, among other things, a conspicuous change in their relation to the cattle. They now cease to look after the calves and sheep and goats and to perform the more menial services of kraal and byre. Instead they tend the adult cattle. The most marked change is that whereas before initiation they helped the women milk the cows, they now altogether cease to milk. But these external and evident changes are accompanied by a deeper, and hidden, transformation, men and oxen being brought into an intimacy of relationship on a different plane to that of mere proximity and association, however close, so that in some way an equation is brought about between man and ox. Such would seem to be the interpretation of certain very peculiar, though outstanding, features of the initiation rites. I have described these rites and discussed their social significance elsewhere, and in this place I shall only draw attention to those features which have special relevance to our immediate subject.

The rites direct our attention throughout to the relationship between men and cattle. It is the *wut ghok*, (man of the cattle) to which he stands in a special ritual relationship, who opens and closes the periods of initiation. During initiation the initiates may not have any contact with the cattle, which are a danger to them till their wounds are completely healed and they formally pass out of seclusion. The prohibition extends even to rubbing ashes of cattle dung over their bodies, a daily practice common

to all men and boys; and Dr. Mary Smith tells me that
Nuer say that it may harm the lads if the smoke of the
smudges reaches them; though the fact that they drink
milk suggests that the interdiction really concerns their relation to the oxen rather than to cattle in general, just as
the interdiction on women drinking milk during their
periods concerns their relation to cows and not to cattle
in general. In the terminal rite of initiation, when the
initiates are "loosened" (*lony rar*, the verb *lony* being
that used for loosening cattle from their tethering pegs),
they re-establish their contact with the cattle. They are
pelted (smeared) by their seniors with cattle dung (*buk
ke war*). Then they wash in a stream. On their return
to the homestead, they beat the cattle with wild rice,
and afterward rub themselves with ashes of cattle dung.
They spend the rest of the day leaping and chanting
behind the oxen given them by their fathers and possibly,
if they are lucky, by their paternal and maternal uncles also,
which are the first oxen they can call their own. The fact
that after initiation there is an interdiction on men milking also seems to point to an opposition between women
and cows on the one side and men and oxen on the other
side and further to emphasize the equation of man and ox.

One might perhaps feel that one was attributing to
the facts a symbolical significance which the evidence does
not sustain were it not that further, and very striking, observations push one to the interpretation put forward.
Thus, the name of the dances held at the initiation ceremonies is *ruath*, the word for a bull calf from the time
it is weaned—that is to say, a bull, normally destined to
be an ox, which has broken with its dam in the same
way as a youth at initiation cuts, as we would put it, the
apron strings which before have tied him to his mother,
especially in the matter of food, as some of the symbolism
of the rites indicates. Further, between the cutting of the
marks of manhood on a boy's forehead and his ceremonial
emergence from seclusion (or exclusion from the normal
life), he is known as *cot*, which appears to be the same
word as that used for a hornless cow or ox. It is remarkable also that Nuer compare to the initiation of youths
the cutting (*ngat*) of the horns of favorite oxen (they
are entire animals at the time) so that they will grow

against the cut at fancy angles, generally in a curve across
the muzzle (*ma gut*). They say that the operation, which
is performed before castration, is the *gar*, the cutting of
the marks of manhood, on the young bulls. If the operation has not already been carried out before a father
presents a young bull to his son at initiation, it is likely
to be one of the young man's first acts in the period
immediately following his own initiation. I have noted
earlier how soon after their initiation youths, if they can
procure the metal, fasten bracelets up their left arms so
tightly as to render them, for the time of their wearing,
incapable of use, and that they also render useless the
left horns of their favorite oxen by deforming them.

Human thought and expression are inevitably constructed out of man's experience of the world around him.
There is nothing that should surprise us in Nuer speaking
metaphorically of boys by the same word (*ruath*) as they
use for young bulls and for the male young of other animals, and, by contrast, of men by the same word (*tut*) as
they use for adult bulls and adult males of other animal
species. It is natural—it would be remarkable were it not
so—that Nuer use cattle metaphors in speech and gesture.
Nevertheless, the evidence, some of which I have presented,
suggests that there is more in it than that. Whether Professor Seligman's psychological use of the word "identification" is correct is a question that lies outside my own
competence and the scope of this book, but it cannot be
denied that there is a moral identification, a participation
imposed on the individual by his culture and inextricably
bound up with religious values. When henceforward I
speak of identification, it is to be understood in this sense.

II

We have noted that there is a personal side and a
collective side to Nuer religion and we may speak of
personal and collective types of sacrifice. We have noted
also that in the collective type the officiant represents the
whole clan, that the spear he holds in his hands is that
of the ancestor of the clan, and that he invokes God as
the God who created his ancestor and the God of his
fathers. We have further noted that the sacrificial victim,
although in fact it is an ox or a surrogate for an ox, is

not spoken of as *thak* (ox), but as *yang* (cow), a general term referring to any bovine beast, with a plural form *ghok* (cattle). This suggests that the victim embodies the general idea of the equivalence of cattle and men in the sacrificial act, and there is certainly what we may speak of as a collective identification of clans and lineages with their herds. This is expressed in the honorific titles of clans and lineages. We have been discussing hitherto the equation of man with ox. These titles introduce us to the idea of an enduring relationship between a social group and its ancestral herd.

On the day when, by the cutting of lines on his forehead, a boy becomes a man, there is much rejoicing of his kinsfolk, and especially of his father and paternal kin. In talking to Nuer about this day, they have impressed on me that what is uppermost in the minds of the older men, particularly at the initiation of an eldest son, is that the continuity of the family and lineage is now assured. Initiation is the threshold to marriage and the birth of sons who will remember their forebears; for as soon as the period of healing and seclusion is over, the initiates embark on a full sex life leading to courtship, marriage, and begetting. An initiate is part of a lineage and clan, and his initiation is seen in terms of its collective life. His new relationship with the cattle is then not only a personal one, important though that is, but the personal relationship is incorporated in a more general lineage one.

Nuer conceive of the ancestor of a clan, and likewise the ancestors of its component lineages, as having possessed a herd, the descendants of which have had, and continue to have, though distributed among different families, a constant relationship with the descendants of their original owners and are still thought of as one herd. This ancestral herd is a fiction, for the cattle are being constantly dispersed and replaced by others at marriages, but conceptually it is an enduring collectivity. There is ideally a constant attachment, the clan and its herd forming a joint community down the generations, so much so that a common, perhaps the commonest, explanation of a division in the clan is the fighting of bulls of the ancestors of the divided parts. The social cleavage is represented in tradition as a cleavage in the herd.

The unity of clans and lineages is symbolized in the names of the ancestral spears, which we have already discussed, and in honorific titles, chiefly derived from the names of cows. In both cases we are dealing with ideas and not actual things, with the idea of a clan spear handed down as an heirloom and with the idea of the present herds of the members of a clan being descended from the ancestral herd. Nuer say that *"mut kene paak jalke kel"* ("the spear and the honorific title go together"). If a man has a certain clan spear, he must have one or more honorific titles which go with it. Both have come down together from *tuok nath*, the beginnings of the Nuer. The *paak*, a word found with the same meaning in some of the other Nilotic languages, may be described as an honorific title used as a mode of salutation or address. It is commonly used on ceremonial occasions, as on formal visits, at dances, and at marriage and initiation ceremonies. Otherwise it is mostly a complimentary usage which expresses a formal relationship of reserve, as between a husband's mother and her son's wife, and then it is chiefly a woman's mode of address.

The title consists of *gat* (son [of]), or *nya* (daughter [of]), followed by a word which usually refers to a cow said to be that on whose milk the ancestor of the clan or lineage was nurtured in infancy, though it may refer to the place where the clan or lineage is said to have originated, or to some object connected with its ancestor, or to its totem. Nuer say that clans either *"ba paak ka kwi yangdien"* ("are saluted by reference to their cow") or *"ba paak ka kwi ciengdien"* ("are saluted by reference to their [original] village site"), but since the salutation generally refers to a cow, the expressions *"paak"* ("honorific salutation") and *"paakene yang"* ("honorific salutation of cow") are synonyms. The words are often exceedingly difficult to translate, or even to discover the meaning of, especially when they relate to cows, for here the Nuer language proliferates symbolism in luxuriant elaborations of fancy; and representations of ancestral cow, ancestral home, totem, and totemic spirit are sometimes fused in the titles, which are built out of a number of residues all of which derive from and express lineage values. I have listed and discussed some of these honorific titles elsewhere, and there is no need here for a detailed consideration of them. We have only to note the central place the idea of a cow has in them, the cow standing for the herd and hence also for the lineage of its masters.

It need not surprise us that it is a cow that is referred to and not an ox or bull. It would be inappropriate to refer to an ox since, as I understand the matter, the whole point of using a symbol from the herds is to express in a single representation the idea of the unity of a lineage and its cattle, the cattle which sustain the lineage by their milk (the cow suckles the ancestor) and by constant calving provide them with bridewealth for marriages whereby sons are born and the lineage continued, and with a means of maintaining communication with Spirit and ghosts. Male animals do not answer the requirements of the symbolism. The great majority of the bulls are castrated, and, if not later disposed of in marriage, those which survive murrains are sacrificed; and the animals which are left entire are not thought of as being, like the male members of a human lineage, a line of descent. In tracing back the lineage of a beast, which Nuer can sometimes do to several generations, they do so by the points of the dams and not the points of the sires: an ox of certain markings was born of a cow of certain markings and it of a cow of other markings. Descent in the herd is, so to speak, traced matrilineally; and it is the cows which are seen as the stable element, which calve cow-calves, which calve cow-calves in their turn, and so provide the constant and continuous nexus between herd and lineage. Consequently, if at marriage most of a herd is dispersed and only a core is retained, it is some cows which are kept so that the herd may be built up anew through them. Therefore, it is to the cows of the ancestors, and not to their bulls, that the honorific titles of clans and lineages refer.

The lineage-herd equation can thus be considered as a collective expression of the man-ox equation. The one does not derive from the other, but they are parts of a single complex representation, which finds its most logical expression in the rites of sacrifice. The name of the ox of the speaker may be shouted out in sacrificial invocations because its name stands for his own, but when the sacrifice is on behalf of a whole clan, the exordial words are the spear name of the clan, which goes together with the cow title of the clan, representing the relation of the clan to its ancestral herd. The two symbols, ox name and spear name, represent two aspects of the sacrificial relationship between men and cattle, the personal and the collective. The one or other aspect is emphasized according to the nature of the sacrifice.

III

The facts we have examined, taken severally or together, point to the conclusion that there is the idea of equivalence between men and cattle, and the only plane on which there is anything that can be called equivalence is that on which men and cattle are things of the same order, so that one can be substituted for the other, namely in sacrifice, or, in other words, in relation to God. We have seen that in those sacrifices which have the most significance for the study of Nuer religion, the personal ones, the lives of oxen are substituted for the lives of men. This is not only evident in what Nuer say, but is indicated also in the rites themselves, and especially in the rite of consecration. In discussing this rite, I speak for the present only of personal sacrifice.

When ashes are rubbed on the back of an animal in giving it to a spirit, I speak of the act as one of dedication. When they are rubbed on its back in sacrifice, I speak of it as consecration. It is useful to make this distinction for several reasons. Animals are not dedicated to God except on rare occasions when sacrifice is to take place shortly afterward, but they are consecrated to him in sacrifice. Cows are the animals usually dedicated to spirits, whereas it is oxen which are sacrificed. Though even a cow dedicated to a spirit may ultimately be sacrificed and at least one of its male calves is destined for sacrifice, sacrifice does not follow dedication, if at all, for months or even years after the dedication. What is devoted by dedication to a spirit is the animal and its milk, but when ashes are rubbed on the back of a beast at sacrifice, what is devoted is its life. That there is a difference of meaning between the two acts is shown by the fact that an animal which has been dedicated to a spirit by ashes being rubbed on its back has ashes again rubbed on it when it is sacrificed to that spirit. It is—if we care to use these terms—dedicated to the spirit in the first act and consecrated for sacrifice to it in the second. The difference is that the rubbing of ashes in dedicating an animal to a spirit is the sign and the manner of its passing out of man's possession (though in fact he does not part with it) into a spirit's possession, whereas the rubbing of ashes in consecrating an animal for sacrifice is a substitution of life of man for life of beast and hence also an identification of man with beast, sacrificer with victim.

It will be remembered that in sacrifice the animal is consecrated with ashes, has an invocation spoken over it, and is speared. I have already discussed the *lam*, or invocation. What concerns us now is the *buk*, the consecration. This word, which in other Nilotic languages has the sense of "to smear" and sometimes of "to sacrifice," means in Nuer "to rub" or "to smear" and generally "to rub with ashes." In a sacrificial context it describes the placing, and usually lightly rubbing, of ashes on the victim's back. It is clear that it is a rite of consecration, the animal's life being thereby devoted to God; but also in the personal and piacular sacrifices it is, as we have seen, sanctified for sacrifice in substitution for the life of a man. It would seem, therefore, that the laying of the right hand on the animal's back identifies the man who lays it, or the person on whose behalf he is acting, with the beast, the right hand standing, as we have earlier noted, for the whole person. If this is so, then it is himself, or the person for whom he is proxy, that the officiant offers up; or, to put it in another way, in the act of consecration the representations of man and ox, of sacrificer and victim, are fused.

This interpretation is supported by the fact that when ashes are ritually rubbed on persons, the meaning which fits the action best is unity, solidarity, or identification, the expression of the idea of "I am with you," as when, for example, before initiation a boy's father, maternal uncle, and family's master of ceremonies rub (*buk*) his forehead with ashes, uttering an invocation, or when a man returns from a long journey and his father rubs ashes on his forehead. It is confirmed by two other observations. As we have noted, there is no laying of hands on cattle sacrificed at mortuary ceremonies, nor is there, Dr. Smith tells me, in sacrifices at *colwic* ceremonies. They are given to God, but the person on whose behalf they are sacrificed is dead. Also, cattle slain for reasons other than for sacrifice may have an invocation said over them, but there is no laying on of hands.

I discuss this question again later in relation to the whole rite of sacrifice and the various theoretical interpretations of it which students have put forward. We may here note further, however, that the fact that it is ash which is placed on the back of the victim and not something else and that this ash must be that of cattle dung (*pou*) and not wood ash (*ngeth*) may be significant, for the ash is taken from the *gol*, the household smudge which symbolizes for Nuer the home in various senses. *Gol* means primarily the home in a domestic sense. It is identified with the father of a family, *gol* so-and-so being the "home" of that man and hence his "family" also. But it can also be used for the lineage, "the family" in that wider sense. The ash comes from the *gol* which represents the family or the lineage, and the officiant who places it on the animal's back represents, according to the type of sacrifice, either the members of the family or the members of the lineage.

IV

It may be asked how the fact that in piacular sacrifice an ox is substituted for a man affects the general relationship of men to cattle. The answer is that all cattle are reserved for sacrifice. It is not just that in a particular ceremony a particular ox stands for a particular man. The equivalence is a general one between men and cattle. Some caution is necessary here. Nuer are very fond of meat, and whether an animal is killed in sacrifice or dies a natural death, its flesh is eaten. All cattle, sheep, and goats, except those sacrificed in holocausts, eventually go into the pot. Also, it is very noticeable that on ceremonial occasions which are not also occasions of calamity most people show more interest in the festal than in other aspects of the ceremonies. People show their desire for meat without reserve, and it is the festal character of sacrifices which gives them much of their significance in the life of the Nuer. This is perhaps most noticeable at weddings, when, moreover, those who get the flesh are not those who sacrifice the animal; and also on those occasions when men scramble for meat. Further, Nuer themselves recognize that some men are too eager to sacrifice an ox, sheep, or goat on the slightest excuse, a craving for meat rather than a pressing need for spiritual aid being the incentive for sacrifice. It is undoubtedly true that it is sometimes craving for meat which reminds a man that sacrifice to some spirit is long overdue, religious obligations providing a ready excuse for a feast. However, the fact that Nuer accuse men of making unnecessary sacrifices to have feasts of meat in itself shows that animals should not be slaughtered except in sacrifice; and there is indeed a very strong feeling, amounting to a moral injunction, that domestic animals—sheep and goats as well as cattle—must not be slaughtered except in sacrifice, and, save in very special circumstances, they are never slaughtered for food, a fact noted by Ernst Marno nearly a century ago. This injunction explains why Nuer are not expected to, and do not, provide meat for guests, and also why I was unable to buy beasts from them for food for my own household.

The very special circumstances in which cattle are killed for food are times of severe famine and in what are called *nak*, or in some parts of Nuerland *kanar* or *cuel* (camps). Within my own short experience, in 1931, a year of great hunger, the Lou Nuer killed many oxen for food, and during a famine in western Nuerland in 1935 a great number of beasts were slaughtered to keep the people alive. Dr. Howell says that in the Zeraf valley in 1943, likewise a year of famine, animals were being killed for food. The Lou Nuer even have a reputation, of which they are ashamed, for killing oxen when hungry, for not waiting, that is, till faced with starvation. How often this situation used to occur is not, and cannot, be known. If it is not altogether a modern phenomenon, we may suppose that it was much less likely to have arisen before rinderpest depleted the herds and imposed peace prevented their rehabilitation through raiding, the milk supply thus being lessened. *Nak* camps are presumably so called because they are formed for the express purpose of killing (*nak*) oxen. They are formed in some years only, in the rains or at the commencement of the dry season, by youths, each of whom takes an ox to the camp, where one by one they are slaughtered and the young men gorge themselves on their flesh. Now that cattle have become scarcer, two youths may share a single animal, though it is still thought that there ought to be an ox to a man. There is some doubt about the precise significance of this custom. When I published an account of the Nuer age-set system, I considered that it did not form an integral part of the rites of initiation but was only incidentally connected with them. I may have been wrong in this conclusion, and my own later researches revealed features which incline me to accept Dr. Howell's contention that they are connected with the age-set system. Certainly there is more in the *nak* than merely killing oxen for feasting. That it has a ritual significance is clear from the fact that the youths who take part in it are segregated. Girls are not allowed to enter, or at any rate to sleep in, the camps. Abstinence is imposed at a time when the company of girls and their favors are a Nuer's chief interest. Nor may the young men attend dances, which therefore do not take place at this time. Also, they may have no contact of any kind with the herds other than with the oxen with which they are segregated. It is to be noted further that the borrowing from kin and neighbors of oxen for slaughter by youths whose families are unable to provide them with suitable animals is no ordinary loan but is of a peculiar and ritual character. The owner of a beast who is asked for it by a youth may not refuse the request, and not only for social reasons but also, says Dr. Howell, because "he would run the risk of spiritual contamination resulting in sickness or even death among the members of his family." Nor may he demand repayment for some years. These facts considered in the light of the great reluctance, to say the least of it, of Nuer to kill an ox other than for sacrifice suggest strongly that a slaughter on this scale has some religious significance. I asked Dr. Lienhardt and Dr. Smith to inquire about this matter. The former informs me that an old man makes an invocation over one of the oxen, which stands for all of them, and the latter that the older men who have contributed the beasts make invocations over them, though they do not consecrate them with ashes. It would seem, therefore, that if their slaughter is not a proper sacrifice, it has to some extent a sacrificial character. It is significant also that not only is the killing obligatory, but also that each youth ought to provide an ox for slaughter, an ox for a man, for we seem to have here again the equivalence of a man with an ox, which is the basis of piacular sacrifice; and it can easily be seen that the death of an ox at the termination of the rites of initiation would be a sacramental act appropriate to the whole setting of initiation.

Except on those rare occasions when dire necessity or custom compels them to do so, Nuer do not kill cattle except in sacrifice; and it is regarded as a fault to kill them *"bang lora"* ("just for nothing"), the Nuer way of saying that they ought not to be killed for meat. This is clearly shown, apart from the facts I have already instanced, by the statement that an ox slain simply from desire for meat may *cien* (take ghostly vengeance on) its slayer, for it has *cuong* (right) in the matter. Maybe Nuer do not take this very seriously, but that they say it at all is an indication of how they regard the matter, for, as we have seen, they fear ghostly vengeance and hold that it operates only because God is permissive, seeing that an injustice has been done. The man had no right to take the life of the ox, and by doing so, he committed a fault. In sacrificial invocations Nuer explain to God why the life of the ox is being taken, and they may also address the ox and tell it why it is being killed—not that they think it understands. They are justifying themselves in taking its life.

Consequently, I was not surprised to learn from Dr. Mary Smith, whom I asked to inquire into the question, that when cattle are killed in time of famine, Nuer, though they do not consecrate the beasts, may make an invocation over them asking God that "the meat may be soft in their stomachs and not bring them sickness." This does not constitute sacrifice, there being no sacrificial intention, but it shows that there is a feeling of guilt about killing animals for food even when hunger compels it, and we can say that all cattle, and also sheep and goats, are reserved, or set apart, for sacrifice and their lives should not be taken, except in the special circumstances I have mentioned, for any other purpose. In that sense we may speak of cattle as being "sacred." If we do so, however, we must note that they are not sacrificed because they are regarded as sacred intrinsically, or for reasons extraneous to the sacrificial situation, but, on the contrary, they are regarded as sacred only because they are reserved for sacrifice and in the sense defined by that purpose. I have discussed beasts of the herd only and not those of the flock because, as we have noted earlier, in sacrifices they are "cattle," surrogates for oxen. It is pre-eminently their role to play the victim's part in sacrifice, and they are consequently also reserved for sacrifice, but the sacrificial equivalence is always between *ran* and *yang* (man and "cow"), never between man and sheep or goat, for even when it is a sheep or goat which is being killed, the ideal equivalence is preserved in speech.

In order that the sacrificial killing of beasts of the flocks and herds may be seen in a wider setting both of the taking of lives of creatures and of the eating of flesh, it should be realized that, except for fish, Nuer seldom kill wild creatures, but rely almost entirely on the flesh of their domesticated animals for meat. For religious reasons they are averse to killing birds, except occasionally the ostrich, to which the same symbolism does not attach, for its feathers; and also reptiles, except the turtle and the crocodile (perhaps occasionally the monitor lizard). But even where there is no objection to killing animals, as in the case of mammals, Nuer seldom go out of their way to kill them. They do not go out to hunt lions, leopards, and hyenas unless they molest the flocks and herds, and usually they only pursue those graminivorous animals which come to drink near their camps and seem to offer themselves for slaughter. It is not that it is thought to be wrong to kill them, but that except in time of famine, Nuer are little interested in hunting. They speak of it as a Shilluk and Dinka practice beneath the serious attention of a Nuer who can boast of a herd—as a pursuit, that is, of foreigners or of men without cattle. Even those who deliberately set out to hunt elephants and giraffe do so less to obtain meat than to acquire ivory and hair which can be exchanged for cattle, sheep, and goats. This lack of interest in hunting may be due to the fact that their flocks and herds supply them, through sacrifice, with meat and to the nature of their country which renders hunting difficult, but whatever the reason, they are not interested, so that any killing of animals outside sacrifice is rare; and we may here say again, as has been said before in a rather different context, that the Nuer mind is turned inward toward his own society of men and cattle. He is not unobservant of nature, but he sees it with a contemplative and not with a predatory eye that seeks to destroy and exploit. He sees wild creatures as something in their own right, and his disposition is to live and let live. His folk stories reflect this attitude and the feeling that killing, like death, is something which has come about almost by accident and is not in the original nature of things.

A large part of Nuer folklore consists of stories about animals. There are stories about ogres; a cycle of adventure stories about how cunning fox tricked hyena; many just-so stories which tell why hyenas limp, why plovers have thin legs, why guinea fowl crouch, why millepedes are blind, why cows have no upper incisors, and so forth; and stories of yet other sorts. God sometimes figures in these stories as a judge in a way which appeals to the Nuer sense of humor as well as to our own. For example, fish, finding that they were visible to man in the water and hence easily speared, appealed to God, who let them be invisible. God sometimes figures in them because the animals are made to act like men after the manner of fables. They are given human speech and feelings, live in villages and camps, and have kinship relations on the pattern of human relations; and as men stand in a certain relationship to God in real life, so the animals are placed in a similar relationship in the make-believe of the stories. Miss Huffman says of these stories that the Nuer "implicitly believe" in them. This was not my impression. It appeared to me that they realize that their folktales are just tales which are true only in the sense that they are, as we say, true to life, a dramatization of real situations and an accurate characterization of human and animal, and indeed also of spiritual, qualities. It does not, therefore, worry them that their folk stories may not accord with, and may contradict, both evidences of the senses and those of tradition and myth, and also each other.

These stories reflect an attitude of mind about man's relation to other creatures, and I mention them in this place, without, however, laying great stress on their significance, because they tell of an original age of innocence in which all cre..tures lived in amity in a common camp. Various stories, though separate tales and not related as parts of a coherent structure or dramatic plan, nevertheless taken together, give us a picture of man at that time, or rather in that state, for the setting of myth and folklore lies outside time. He is entirely simple. He does not suffer from hunger, because what later became his stomach lives a life of its own in the bush where it feeds on small insects. He does not have to labor to live because, according to another story, which contradicts the last one, a single grain of millet soaked in water makes a sufficient meal. In this Nuer Eden there is no desire and mating, for the male and female organs are also not yet part of man and woman, but live apart from them and separate from each other. As other, and once again contradictory, stories have it, man does not know how to beget or woman to bear. Man has no knowledge of fire and he does not know the spear. Then all changed. The new order is sometimes presented as arising from a quarrel in the camp started, it would seem, by fox persuading mongoose to throw a club into elephant's face. The animals separated and each went its own way and began to live as they now live and to kill each other. Stomach entered into man, and he is now always hungry. Elephant taught him how to pound millet, so that he now satisfies his hunger only by ceaseless labor. The sexual organs attached themselves to man and woman, so that they are now constantly desirous of each other. Mouse taught man how to beget and woman how to bear. Dog brought fire to man. And we are told that while fox was plotting to sow dissension among the beasts, he gave man the spear and taught him how to use it. It was then that man began to kill, and his first killing seems to have been that of the mother of cow and buffalo, or rather the mother of cattle, for at that time cows and buffaloes were the same. This led to a feud between men and cattle, buffaloes avenging their mother by attacking men in the bush and cows by causing men to quarrel and slay one another.

It may perhaps sharpen our focus on sacrifice to know not only that Nuer seldom kill wild animals, but also that

they can imagine a state in which man did not kill, that
there might have been a beginning to killing as to coitus,
to pounding grain, and to other things men do now.
Viewed in relation to the dialectic of the stories, the killing
of cattle is then seen not to be, as it were, derived from a
state of nature in which men kill animals for food, as just
one sort of killing among others, but as a product of a
new dispensation in which cattle are allotted a sacrificial
role and are set apart for this purpose. Other animals may,
as a matter more or less of chance, and now and again,
be killed, but it is the role and destiny of cattle to be
slaughtered in sacrifice. Sacrificial slaughter thus stands at
the very center of the idea of killing, and sacrificial flesh
at the very center of the idea of feasting.

We may conclude, therefore, that the observations we
have made earlier concerning the relationship of a man
with his favorite ox, the ritual of initiation, etc., must be
viewed in the light of the identification of men with
cattle in sacrifices. A Nuer does not look upon his cattle
as a stockbreeder or dairy farmer does, for in his case his
relationship to his beasts is complicated, apart from their
use in marriage, by their reservation for sacrifice. And it is
not just that he must not kill cattle except in sacrifice,
because if he were to slaughter them for meat, he would
lower his resources for food, marriage, and religious purposes. It is not merely a negative injunction. It is not
"thou must not kill," but "thou must sacrifice." It is not
that they must only kill for sacrifice, but that they must
sacrifice to kill.

We must not be led astray by this conclusion to suppose
that in the everyday life of the Nuer they think of and
treat their animals in a "religious" manner. They do not
even treat those dedicated to spirits in any special way.
Ordinarily Nuer think of their beasts from the practical
point of view of herdsmen who are largely dependent on
them for food and are dependent on them entirely for
marriage. But if it would be a mistake to leave out of
consideration the practical uses of cattle, it would be no
less a mistake were we to ignore the religious significance
they have for Nuer. This is easier to do for two reasons.
Firstly, because Nuer are themselves reticent in speaking
of their cattle in this connection. They tend to be reserved

in discussing religious matters, and it may even be said that a certain secrecy adheres to them; and those whom a European tends to know best, the younger men, have less awareness of the sacramental role of cattle than the older people. Secondly, because we have no direct experience of our own which associates animals with anything similar in our culture. We are, therefore, inclined to reason that cattle have ritual significance because they have great practical value. If this were really so, the cow, and not the ox, would be the object of identification, but apart from that consideration, an attempt to interpret the religious importance of cattle on this one-way track of reasoning changes the whole character of the relationship between men and cattle. It makes the animals themselves to be in some way the object of religious attention, and nothing could be farther from the truth.

The religious significance of cattle is of a very different kind. Cattle are necessary to Nuer not only for food and marriage but also for salvation, for the sanctification of their social undertakings, and for overcoming evil in its twofold character of sickness and sin. As Professor Westermann's text has it, "she [the cow] was ordered [by God] for the deliverance of souls." This soteriological function pertains to cattle as much as their economic, bridewealth, and other functions. It is not just that in Nuer sacrifices something that for other reasons is valuable obtains through its consecration and sacramental death a religious significance, which would consequently be secondary and momentarily derived from the immediate sacrificial act. The sacrificial role is always dormant in cattle, which in sacrifice are being used for an ordained purpose for which they are set apart. This is why the rubbing of ashes on an ox's back while uttering some short prayer or invocation is a rite which can at any time be performed. The animal, even when not dedicated to a spirit, is already destined for sacrifice. The sacrificial situation is present, as it were, in the act, though no actual sacrifice is made.

When, therefore, we seek to estimate what their cattle are to Nuer and how they see them, we have to recognize that they are the means by which men can enter into communication with God, that they are, as Father Crazzolara puts it, "the link between the perceptible and the transcendental." In fulfilling this role, his cattle shield a man and his family from disaster, and he conceives of them also collectively as a herd which, from the beginning of time, has helped his fathers in distress, performing in each generation the same sacrificial service. In the time of the ancestor of his clan the "cow" gave her life for his salvation and so it is today. Whence springs the identification of man with ox, of lineage with herd, and of men with cattle.

¶ SOME REFLECTIONS ON NUER RELIGION

The theories of writers about primitive religion have not been sustained by research. During the last century what was presented as theory was generally the supposition that some particular form of religion was the most primitive and that from it developed other forms, the development being sometimes presented as a succession of inevitable and well-defined stages. The form of religion presented by a writer as the most primitive was that which he considered to be the most simple, crude, and irrational; to exhibit most conspicuously "crass materialism," "primeval stupidity," "naïve eudaemonism," "crude anthropomorphism," or "daemonic dread." Many such origins have been propounded: magic, fetishism, manism, animism, pre-animism, mana, totemism, monotheism, etc. All this was for the most part pure conjecture. The determination of the *primordium*, in the absence of historical evidences, was, as Schleiter, among others, has shown, quite arbitrary.

Nuer religion, like any other, has, of course, a history, but we can only trace it in so far as it survives in the memories of the Nuer themselves, for reports by travelers, which start barely a century ago, are on this matter slight and unreliable. Ethnological research can supply us only with indirect evidences; archaeological research, were it to be undertaken, probably with none at all. However, Nuer statements, supported by ethnological evidences, enable us to say with a fair degree of probability what have been the main lines of development during the last hundred years. Now, if we take the Nuer as we find them today and as we have good reason to think them to have been in the recent past, an account of their religion at least shows the inadequacy of most of these so-called evolutionary theories and exposes the conceit of the assumptions on which they were based. The Nuer are undoubtedly a primitive people by the usual standards of reckoning, but their religious thought is remarkably sensitive, refined, and intelligent. It is also highly complex.

Explanations of primitive religions were often couched at the same time both in terms of historical origins and of psychological origins, which made for great confusion, especially as the logical and chronological senses of "primitive" and "origin" were also seldom kept distinct. The psychological explanations were very varied, changing with changes in psychological theory. Intellectualist interpretations were succeeded by emotionalist interpretations and they by psychoanalytical interpretations. Religion was discussed and explained in terms of association of ideas, of personification of natural phenomena, of awe, of thrill, of fear, anxiety, and frustration, of projection, and so forth. Most of these theories have long ago been discredited as naïve introspective guesses.

Certainly one cannot speak of any specifically religious emotion for the Nuer. One can only judge by overt behavior on occasions of religious activity, and, as I have noted, on such occasions Nuer may be afraid, anxious, joyful, indifferent, or in other states, according to the situation and the degree to which they are involved in it. Miss Ray Huffman says that their religion is one of fear, and I feel I ought to say, and I do so with her permission, that this is the one point with which Dr. Mary Smith finds serious fault in my account of it. She, like Miss Huffman, holds that it is a religion of fear, even of terror. For me this is an oversimplification and a misunderstanding. It is true that Nuer, like everyone else, fear death, bereavement, sickness, and other troubles, and that it is precisely in such situations that they so often pray and sacrifice. It can be admitted also that, in that these troubles are manifestations of Spirit, they fear Spirit and wish to be rid of it. But we cannot say that on that account their religion is simply one of fear, which is, moreover, a very complex state of mind, and one not easy to define or assess. On the contrary, it is because Nuer are afraid of these misfortunes that one might speak of their religion as one of hope and comfort. But I think what fits the facts best is to say that it is a religion of both fear and trust, which may be opposites but are not contraries, or that the Nuer attitude toward Spirit might be described as ambiguous, and perhaps as ambivalent. The question is much complicated by the different ways Nuer represent Spirit to themselves and their different attitudes to it at different levels of representation. We have further to recognize that the sense of guilt which is often so evident in misfortunes is not just fear but a complex psychological state, and also that it varies in intensity from one situation to another. Nuer thought in these matters is involved, for a serious danger may not be just an adventitious intrusion of Spirit into human affairs. It often has a moral significance. It is then not so much regarded as a natural crisis which can be overcome by spiritual aid as a moral crisis brought about by human action, and of which the outcome, it is thought, may depend on so delicate and indiscernible a factor as intention. Faced with so complex and variable a problem, to speak of Nuer religion simply as one of fear or awe, or as a projection or as cathartic, and so forth, must be a distortion, and one that does not greatly help us to understand it. All emotions enter into it; they blend; and there is nothing constant that we can say is characteristic of the religious life, which is rather to be defined in terms of disposition than of emotion.

Sociological theories of religion have frowned on evolutionary and psychological explanations alike. They have rather sought to understand primitive religions, or certain aspects of them, as products of social life. Fustel de Coulanges, Robertson Smith, Durkheim, Mauss, Hertz, and others have shown successfully that many features of these religions can be understood only by sociological analysis, by relating them to the social structure. This is true of Nuer religion. I do not think, for example, that the configuration of Spirit, the faults which are regarded as sins, and the roles of master of ceremonies, priest, and prophet in sacrifice can be fully understood without a knowledge of the social order. But Durkheim and his colleagues and pupils were not content to say that religion, being part of the social life, is strongly influenced by the social structure. They claimed that the religious conceptions of primitive peoples are nothing more than a symbolic representation of the social order. It is his society that primitive man worships in the symbol of a god. It is to his society that he prays and makes sacrifice. This postulate of sociologistic metaphysic seems to me to be an assertion for which evidence is totally lacking. It was Durkheim, and not the savage, who made society into a god.

All these theories about primitive religions, evolutionary, psychological, and sociological, suffered from a common weakness. The facts on which they were based were both inadequate and unreliable. Indeed, such wide generalizations could only have been put forward at a time when systematic studies of the religions of primitive peoples were lacking, and by persons with no direct, however slight, experience of them. That they were in reality *a priori* assumptions posited on the facts rather than scientific conclusions derived from them became increasingly apparent as new knowledge of these religions came to light and their variety and complexity were better appreciated. It is indeed surprising that these writers, whose speculations were for the most part attempts to explain religion as a general phenomenon, should have turned their attention exclusively to the religions of present-day primitive peoples or to the earliest forms of the higher religions—to those religions, that is, about which information was the most lacking and the most uncertain—rather than to the contemporaneous world religions with their vast literatures and known histories, to Christianity, Islam, Hinduism, Buddhism, and others. Had they done so, however, and, even more, had they conducted research into what these religions mean to ordinary people rather than into how philosophers, theologians, lawyers, mystics, and others have presented them, they would have seen how inadequate their theories were. Also, the religions of primitive peoples could not then have been treated, as they so often were, as something so unlike the religions of civilization that they appeared to require a special kind of interpretation and a special vocabulary.

INDIA

INDIA showing the approximate locations of the
societies described by Milton Singer, McKim Marriott, and David G. Mandelbaum in the following
pages.

A NOTE ABOUT THE AUTHOR

Milton Singer

MILTON SINGER (1912–   ) has not passed through the usual passage rites of the professional anthropologist. He studied social psychology as an undergraduate at the University of Texas. And in 1936, drawn to the University of Chicago by his interest in George Herbert Mead's theories of self, language, and mind, he undertook graduate study in philosophy. This was the period when Charles Morris was developing his general theory of signs, when Rudolf Carnap, fresh from Europe, was crystallizing his ideas on testability and meaning, logical syntax, and semantics, and when Bertrand Russell went to Chicago to reopen his career in technical philosophy. In this heady atmosphere Singer turned his main energies to the philosophy of science and symbolic logic. He wrote his doctoral dissertation under Rudolf Carnap on "Formal Method in Mathematical Logic," and received his Ph.D. in 1940.

From 1942 to 1953 Milton Singer was active in the College of the University of Chicago. He was a member of that remarkable group of scholars, including David Riesman, Robert Redfield, Daniel Bell, Herman Finer, and many others, who designed and taught a three-year social-science program in the College at Chicago. It was during this period that Singer developed a serious interest in professional anthropology, particularly in the study of personality and culture. With Gerhart Piers, a psycho-analyst, he wrote *Shame and Guilt: A Psychoanalytic and a Cultural Study*, published in 1953.

In 1951, when the Ford Foundation made the first of a series of grants to Robert Redfield for the development of intercultural studies, he asked Singer to serve as associate director of the project. A series of volumes on China, India, and Islam grew out of this project, and were published as *Comparative Studies of Cultures and Civilizations*, under the general editorship of Redfield and Singer. The essay reprinted in the following pages is taken from one of these volumes, *Traditional India: Structure and Change*.

Milton Singer's work in Madras was not a "field study" in the usual anthropological style of an intensive study of a small community. He went to India in 1954–5 to explore the problem of how to select appropriate units for field research on the interaction of great and little traditions within a civilization. In his work in Madras he hit upon the idea, developed in the following essay, of "cultural performances" as units for observation and comparison. He plans to return to India for more intensive field research, collecting the kind of data reported in a preliminary manner in his study of Madras.

Milton Singer is Paul Klapper Professor of the Social Sciences in the Department of Anthropology, and in the College of the University of Chicago.

3

The Great Tradition
of Hinduism in
the City of Madras[*]

by

MILTON SINGER

The movement of modern nationalism in India, as in most
other countries, has always shown a strong interest in the
recovery or reinterpretation of India's traditional culture.
With the achievement of national independence, this
interest has received an official definition. Language, national history, archaeological monuments, folk arts and
crafts, classical music, dance, and drama have become
symbols of a modern Indian identity alongside the national
emblem, Five Year Plans, parliamentary institutions, and
atomic installations.

The definition is selective and creative. A traditional
culture, notably that of India, is far too varied and rich a
growth to be adequately displayed in Republic Day celebrations. And not all cultural traditions will be thought
suitable for display; some are perhaps thought best left to
grow or wither in provincial obscurity. Those cultural
traditions that become symbols of national identity

[*] *The following selection is reprinted by permission of the author,
and of the editor of the* JOURNAL OF AMERICAN FOLKLORE. *It first
appeared in the* JOURNAL OF AMERICAN FOLKLORE, *Vol. 71, No. 281,
1958, and in* TRADITIONAL INDIA: STRUCTURE AND CHANGE, *Milton Singer,
editor, Publications of the American Folklore Society, Bibliographical
Series, Vol. x, 1959.*

undergo, by virtue of their new role, a sea change; they take on a life of their own, quite different from their life as regional and local traditions. They have become the chosen representatives of a national tradition.

Theoretically, any element of traditional culture is a potential candidate for selection, but in fact only a small number are so chosen at any given time. In this selective and creative process, cultural traditions take on a fluidity and self-consciousness that reflects constantly changing moods and aspirations, and changing conceptions of national identity. They reflect, too, the fact that a civilization is a process of becoming, as well, a state of being, as Nirmal Kumar Bose has remarked apropos the modern history of Bengal. Now, this is not the way we ordinarily think of traditions; they are, ordinarily, the things that we take for granted, the unquestioned assumptions and the handed-down ways of our ancestors. But it has become a commonplace of modern history that even the most traditional societies are no longer sure of what it is they can take for granted. Confronted by swift currents of internal and external change, they have been compelled to restate themselves to themselves in order to discover what they have been and what it is they are to become. Their cultural traditions have become problematic hypotheses in an inquiry into the design for a meaningful and worthwhile life.

The professional student of culture and civilization may contribute something to this inquiry through an objective study of the variety and changes in cultural traditions, freed from the immediate necessity of choosing among them a single meaningful pattern of existence. In an article entitled "The Cultural Role of Cities" [1] Robert Redfield and I suggested that Great Traditions get fashioned out of local folk cultures, or Little Traditions, through a process of continuous development by professional literati centered in orthogenetic towns and cities. And we also said there that in metropolitan centers, ancient and modern, another process—heterogenetic transformation—operates to destroy or supersede the great cultural

[1] Robert Redfield and Milton B. Singer: "The Cultural Role of Cities," *Economic Development and Cultural Change*, Vol. III, No. 1 (1954), pp. 53–73; reprinted in *Man in India*, 36 (July-Sept. 1956), pp. 161–94.

traditions of an indigenous civilization. This transformation is carried on with the help of a new social type of professional intellectuals—the intelligentsia—who stand astride the boundaries of the cultural encounter, mediating the alien cultural influences to the natives and interpreting the indigenous culture to the foreigners.

We also suggested in that article, however, that the two processes—that of primary urbanization leading to the growth of a Great Tradition in orthogenetic centers, and that of secondary urbanization leading to a heterogenetic transformation of that tradition—are not always discontinuous. There seem to be civilizations, or at least particular historical phases of some civilizations when they undergo imperial and colonial expansion, in which we can almost see how one process is succeeded by the other and how a new social type, the intelligentsia, takes over from the old, the literati. Indic civilization appeared to us to be particularly well characterized by such lines of continuity, and the communities of western Guatemala with their well-established institutions of trade and travel may even represent a simpler pre-urban phase of the process.

The details of the subsequent fate of a Great Tradition as it undergoes secondary urbanization have, we must confess, remained shadowy because there are few intensive case studies to give a detailed picture. In the general literature on cultural and civilizational history, this kind of change is usually presented as a sharp one and a change for the worse, representing a decadence, fossilization, or secularization of the great cultural traditions. Because I suspected that this common view of the matter is, in part, influenced by a particular kind of cultural analysis— the textual study of the outstanding products of art and learning, abstracted from social and cultural context and the matrix of little and popular cultural traditions—I undertook in a preliminary way a functional and contextual study of what happens to a Great Tradition and its literati in a metropolitan urban center in South India.[2]

---

[2] A preliminary report of this study was published by the author under the title "The Cultural Pattern of Indian Civilization" in the *Far Eastern Quarterly*, Vol. xv, No. 1 (Nov. 1955) pp. 23–36.

The six months' period my wife and I spent in India during the autumn and winter of 1954–5 (and only about two and a half months in Madras city) was not sufficient for an intensive field study. It was a

Because Madras is a heterogenetic and was a colonial city, it is a good place to investigate the effects of urbanization on cultural traditions.

The urban characteristics that usually go with large metropolitan centers are found in Madras city, the capital of Madras State—a large population, rapid growth, predominance of males over females, a high proportion of immigrants, high literacy rates, a highly specialized non-agricultural occupational structure, an abundance of social and cultural facilities and organizations, and a heterogeneity of linguistic, religious, and ethnic and social groups. These characteristics do not always have the same high absolute values in Madras that they have in other metropolitan centers of the world, but the degree of urbanization is high if compared with the city's hinterland in Madras State or with India's present degree of urbanization. The city's hinterland is about eighty per cent agricultural villages and small towns. It includes a predominantly Telugu-speaking North as well as a predominantly Tamil-speaking South.

Located on the coastal plains of the Bay of Bengal in Southeast India, Madras is India's third largest city with a population at the 1951 census of 1,416,056. This is exceeded only by Bombay, with a population of over 2,800,-

sufficient period, however, to establish the relevance of a method of analyzing cultural traditions for a study of urbanization and culture change, and also for exploring some of the problems involved in applying the method. In this sense the study was a "methodological field study" and not a descriptive sociological or ethnological study. If, in the summary of a part of this study which follows, there are many more positive statements than seem to be warranted by the evidence presented, this is not because I regard these statements as proved. On another occasion I shall publish what detailed evidence I do have. In the meantime, the apodictic formulations will serve as a greater stimulus to discussion and further research than statements properly qualified with a "perhaps" or "maybe."

I am grateful to Robert Redfield and the Program on Comparative Cultures and Civilizations, directed by him at the University of Chicago, financed by the Ford Foundation, for making my trip to India possible; to V. Raghavan, of Madras University, for generously putting at my disposal his profound knowledge of Indian culture; and to David Mandelbaum for an opportunity to do further research at the Institute of East Asiatic Studies at the University of California. To the three of them and to M. N. Srinivas, McKim Marriott, and Hans van Buitenen I am also indebted for helpful comments on an earlier draft of this paper. Free time for travel and research was granted by the University of Chicago.

000, and by Calcutta, whose population is over 2,500,000. The year 1921 marks an important change in Madras's population growth. For at least thirty years before that date the rate of growth is fairly steady; after that there are a series of spurts probably induced by immigration to escape famine, or to take advantage of opportunities in employment or of the city's medical and educational services and cultural amenities. The population figures in round numbers for these periods are: 1891, 450,000; 1901, 500,000; 1911, 518,000; 1921, 526,000; 1931, 645,000; 1941, 776,000; 1951, 1,416,000.

Before 1891 the population figures are less reliable and the earliest accurate figure is probably that of the 1871 census, which gives 399,552 as the population of the city.

The steady and slow growth of Madras until very recent years has permitted the survival of many parts of the villages and small towns which have become incorporated into its limits as it has expanded. As late as 1908 the Imperial Gazetteer describes Madras as "a collection of villages." And even today many of the pre-urban characteristics are visible: large tracts of unused land with palms growing on them, paddy fields and irrigation tanks, buffalo and washermen in the city's rivers and lagoons, fishermen's thatched huts and catamarans on the beach. The accelerated growth of the last twenty years is, however, quickly filling up the vacant land and sending an increasing number of daily commuters farther and farther out of the city on the electric trains.

In its origin Madras city resembles many other pre-European towns in India and some medieval European towns: it began in 1640 as a settlement of traders around a fort and several villages. But because the fort was one of the trading factories of the English East India Company, the settlement soon developed a character and career distinctive of the British colonial city in Asia. These cities, like Madras, Surat, Bombay, Calcutta, at first *entrepôts* for European trade with Asia, later became bases for the spread of European political and military control over the entire country. The history of these cities is the story of the encounter of differing civilizations and of their mutual transformations.

As early as 1688 the East India Company's directors in

London were so impressed with the prosperity and growth of Madras that they decided to call it a city rather than a town. In 1752 it became the seat of Madras Presidency, and from 1774 it was subject, through the Bengal government, to the control of the British Parliament.

The city's importance as an administrative center has continued to the present, with a concentration of state and union government offices. It is, however, also a foremost commercial, transportation, and cultural center. With ninety-eight per cent of its population depending on nonagricultural employments—production other than cultivation (twenty-five per cent), commerce (twenty-two per cent), transport (nine per cent), government and professional services (forty-two per cent)—and only two per cent on agriculture, Madras is a highly urbanized metropolitan center.

Localization of the Great Tradition in Sacred Geography and in Social Structure

Where in a metropolitan center shall we find the Great Tradition of Hinduism? It is natural for a Westerner to assume that a large modern city is not a very likely place to look for it, but in India this assumption does not hold. It is true that the full-blown "classic" version of the tradition as it might be constructed from selected texts is not evident in the city today. In fact, there is not a single unequivocal version of the Great Tradition in Madras, but several overlapping and competing versions with varying degrees of admixture of regional and local traditions. This is not surprising in a study which begins with a functional analysis in a limited region. Only as the accumulation of studies in different regions and in different historical periods permits an extension of comparisons will we be able to say with some confidence what is common and pervasive and what is local and episodic in Indian civilization as a whole.

There are three general methods for localizing a great tradition within a limited area: through a study of its sacred geography, of its professional representatives and their social organization, and of its cultural performances (including religious rites and ceremonies). Since in this paper I shall be dealing chiefly with the third method, let me comment briefly on the first two.

Although modern Madras is not a major temple city or pilgrimage center, its relation to the sacred geography of Hinduism is not insignificant. For the modern city grew up around historic temple villages like Mylapore and Triplicane, whose large Śiva and Viṣṇu temples, respectively, continue to be actively patronized today. And even as the city developed under the East India Company, the local merchants and landlords continued to build new temples and to patronize Sanskrit scholars, traditional poets, musicians, and dancers. It would be interesting to trace the continuity of the historical cultural associations of the city with the neighboring religious and cultural centers like Kanchipuram (the present residence of the head of the Śaṅkara *maṭh*), Sriperumbudur, and Tirupati, and with the many other temples and *maṭhs* in South India, as well as with the modern temples and religious seats which have located in the city, e.g., the Ramakṛṣṇa Mission, the Divine Life Society, a Śiva-Viṣṇu temple, and a Sai Baba temple in honor of a Hindu-Muslim saint, among others.

Contemporary Madrasis not only visit the major and minor temples (of which there are hundreds) within the city but also make frequent pilgrimages to other shrine centers in South India and in North India. This practice has been helped by modern improvements in transportation. Automobiles and buses, planes, and trains now take large numbers of pilgrims on organized tours of the major temple and shrine centers. These pilgrimages now tend to merge with patriotic sight-seeing, which has become popular even with the secular-minded.

The 1951 census tells us that 81.62 per cent of Madrasis declared themselves as Hindus, 9.91 per cent as Muslims, and 7.2 per cent as Christians. But we cannot assume without further evidence that every Hindu is a representative of the Great Tradition, even an active participant in it, or that there is a single system of Hinduism.

Hindus in Madras city are subdivided into a number of sectlike groups. The most important of these are the Smārta Brahmans, followers of Śaṅkara (?788–820),

believers in monistic or Advaita *vedānta* who are supposed
to conform to Smṛti traditions; the Śrivaiṣṇava Brahmans
and non-Brahmans, followers of Rāmānuja (1017–1137),
and believers in a qualified monism; the Madhvas, predominantly Brahman followers of a dualistic Vaiṣṇavite
system developed by Mahhva, a Canarese theologian of
the thirteenth century; and the predominantly non-Brahman Śaivasiddhantins, followers of a dualistic and mono-
theistic system of Tamil Śaivism. Each of these groups has
its distinctive theology and philosophy, canonical scriptures, ritual practices, shrines, and centers of religious
teaching and leadership known as *maṭhs* in different parts
of the South. They do not generally intermarry.

In addition to these major Hindu groups, there are also
in Madras city small numbers of Sikhs, Jains, Buddhists,
and Zoroastrians. Of these only the Jains exceed 1,000,
numbering about 6,000 in 1951. The 1951 census returned
1,267 self-declared atheists for Madras city and very few
members of the Ārya Samāj, the Brāhmo Samāj, and the
Rationalists. The increase in atheism in Madras city and
state (the 1921 census listed four for the state as a whole)
is generally attributed to the active antireligious propaganda
of two non-Brahman organizations, the Dravidian Federation and the Dravidian Progressive Federation.

The second method which I used to identify the Great
Tradition in Madras city was essentially an application of
Robert Redfield's suggestion that a great tradition is
cultivated and transmitted by a class of learned specialists,
the literati, who have a definite social structure and organization.[3] This idea is very apt for India, where for
thousands of years a special learned and priestly class, the
Brahmans, have had almost a monopoly as officiants,
teachers, and scholars of Hinduism. And in Madras city
I was able to locate many different kinds of these Brahman
literati: temple priests, domestic priests, gurus, *paṇḍits*
specializing in sacred law, in logic, in poetics, in Vedic
exegesis; astrologers, ayurvedic doctors, and others. But I
also found that not all Brahmans are literati; they are also
lawyers and high-court judges, businessmen, physicians,
movie producers, authors and journalists, professors and

[3] Robert Redfield: "The Social Organization of Tradition," *Far Eastern Quarterly*, Vol. xv (1955), pp. 13–21; *Peasant Society and Culture* (Chicago; 1956).

architects, cooks and chauffeurs. Many of those in the higher professions have been trained abroad and have been agents of Westernization and modernization in India. Some of the literati, on the other hand, are non-Brahmans.

These findings raise the question of whether the Brahman literati in Madras are changing their social role, giving up their traditional role as cultivators of the Great Tradition (and agents of Sanskritization, as M. N. Srinivas would say)[4] to become intelligentsia, i.e., agents of Westernization and modernization. To some extent I believe this is occurring, but it is difficult to give a clear-cut answer to this question because there have always been important social and status differences between priestly Brahmans (*vaidikas*) and worldly Brahmans (*laukikas*), because some Brahmans are traditionalizing and Westernizing at the same time, and because new forms of Sanskritization have been developing under urban conditions. A detailed study of how the worldly Brahmans have been recruited into modern professions, of their family histories, of the statistics of changes in traditional occupations, of how they relate themselves to Hinduism, and of the ancient parallels and precedents is necessary before definite answers can be given.

These sociological studies are just beginning to be made in different parts of India, and I shall not report them at this time. There is some evidence, however, from Madras, which suggests that the Brahmans are relating themselves in new and constructive ways to the charges affecting Indian traditions and are not schizophrenically split down the middle into traditional Indian and modern Western halves. This evidence is indirect and comes chiefly from observation of cultural changes. I should like to present some of it because it is intrinsically interesting and also because it illustrates a third method of approach to the problem of urbanization and culture change.

Localization of the Great Tradition in Cultural Structure: Comparative Analysis of Cultural Performances

This third method emerged naturally in the application of the second method. Whenever Madrasi Brahmans

[4] M. N. Srinivas: "A Note on Sanskritization and Westernization," *Far Eastern Quarterly*, Vol. xv, No. 4 (Aug. 1956).

(and non-Brahmans, too, for that matter) wished to exhibit to me some feature of Hinduism, they always referred to, or invited me to see, a particular rite or ceremony in the life cycle, in a temple festival, or in the general sphere of religious and cultural performances. Reflecting on this in the course of my interviews and observations, I found that the more abstract generalizations about Hinduism (my own as well as those I heard) could generally be checked, directly or indirectly, against these observable performances. The idea then occurred to me that these performances could be regarded as the most concrete observable units of Indian culture, the analysis of which might lead to more abstract structures within a comprehensive cultural system. Looking at performances from this point of view, it soon became evident that the rites and ceremonies performed as ritual obligations, usually by domestic or temple priests, had many elements in common with the more secular cultural performances in the theater, concert hall, radio programs, and films, and that these linkages revealed not only the outlines of a cultural structure but many indications of trend and process of change in that structure.

Through an analysis and comparison of these cultural performances and their constituents, e.g., the media and themes, the place and occasion of performance, the performers, the audience, it is possible to construct the structure and organization of particular kinds of performances. Then by tracing the linkages among these structures and organizations it is possible to arrive at the more comprehensive and abstract constructs of cultural structure, cultural value system, and a great tradition. To the extent that exact dates or relative temporal orderings are available for the different performances or their constituents, it is also possible to analyze continuities, trends, and processes of change in these structures and organizations. Given such data about the persistences and transformations of cultural traditions, it is then possible to relate these persistences and changes to urbanization and other relevant causal conditions.

This method is an operational one: it begins with concrete units which can be directly observed, the cultural performances, and proceeds, through analysis and abstraction, to constructions which are not directly observable at all or only indirectly so. It thus makes up two methodological deficiencies in holistic concepts of culture—directly observable units of observation and a "ladder of abstraction " that leads from these units to the holistic constructs. In studies of the relations of urbanization to culture change it is more usual to begin at the societal end—with particular social groupings, their structure, organization, interrelationships; the impingement on them of economic, demographic, geographical, and other changes. This, too, is a legitimate procedure and is required in a complete analysis of the problem to complement the procedure which begins with culture traditions.

I shall now present some examples of the method of comparative analysis of cultural performances. The generalizations to be considered concern the changes in religious orientation adopted by Madrasi Brahmans under the influence of the urban environment. These changes are verbalized by some of the Brahmans as involving a change in preference among the ancient paths to religious salvation within Hinduism.

The Widening Path of Devotion in Urban Culture: An Easier Path to Salvation: Bhakti

The path of ritual observance (*karma-mārga* or *karma-yoga*) and the path of devotion (*bhakti-mārga* or *bhakti-yoga*) are two of the three standard paths within Hinduism that lead to eternal bliss and salvation. The third path is that of knowledge (*jñāna-mārga* or *jñāna-yoga*). The three paths have been interpreted as providing a variety of roads open to an individual depending on his degree of spiritual evolution and type of personality:

. . . to those intent on work, there is Karma-yoga, the path of fulfilling the ordained duties and performing such meritorious acts as have been perscribed by scriptures. To those who are of an emotional nature, whose heart is not satisfied with impersonal acts or principles of ethical conduct and in whom there is an inner cry for hugging a supreme personality to whom it could pour forth its love and homage, there is the path of devotion, Bhakti-yoga. And to those of the highest class who can revel only in the Abstract, there is the path of knowledge, Jnāna-yoga, and the goal of realising the one impersonal Absolute Brahman, which is of the essence of Being, Light, and Bliss, *Sat, Chit,* and *Ananda.* Truly cultivated, these are not mutually conflicting, but different paths to the one ultimate goal.[5]

What is particularly significant about these paths in Madras city today is that orthodox Brahmans traditionally committed to the paths of ritual observance and of knowledge are turning to the path of devotion, that they seem to be doing this as a result of moving to the city, and, finally, that the paths themselves are acquiring some new content and form in an urban setting.

There is a very general consensus among the Brahmans of Madras city that they have neglected the paths of knowledge (*jñāna-mārga*) and the path of ritual observance (*karma-mārga*). It is the path of devotion (*bhakti-mārga*) which is now most popular and considered to be a last defense against atheism. As one public speaker put it: "We modern men and women who have learnt, or are being taught, that we need not follow the *Śāstras* but can follow our own inclinations, are sure to derive very great spiritual profit and mental comfort by studying the hymns of the popular saints." This is a constant refrain in the speeches of cultural leaders, who never tire of extolling devotional puranic recitations, plays, films, music and dance concerts as an accessible path to salvation open to "modern" man. Even Svāmī Śaṅkarācārya, the spiritual leader of *advaitins* in Madras State, who does not regard *bhakti* as a very deep or lasting form of Hinduism, has sponsored conferences of Tamil hymn singing for "inculcating the spirit of *bhakti* among the people at a time when atheists were doing their best to poison the minds of youngsters through propaganda."

This turning to devotional religion is, in part, a response to antireligious movements and trends, and, in part, represents a distinctive development of religious and popular culture in an urban environment. To some extent, this development is a continuation of revival of traditional

[5] V. Raghavan: "Some Leading Ideas of Indian Thought," *The Vedanta Kesari* (Madras; February 1955).

devotional movements in which Brahmans have always played a leading part, but it has also entered into modern cultural and mass media and serves new needs.

Bhakti movements are very old in India and have been traced all the way back to Vedas.[6] Most generally, however, they have been associated with the post-Vedic and post-Buddhist sectarian movements: Vaiṣṇaivite primarily in North India, Śaivite and Vaiṣṇaivite in South India. In Tamil tradition there are sixty-three Śaivite singing poet saints (called *Nāyanārs*) whose canon of hymns (*devāram*) was collected in the tenth century A.D., and twelve Vaiṣṇaivite singing poet saints (called *Ālvārs*), whose canon of hymns (*divyaprabandham*) was collected in the eleventh century. These hymns, together with the *Bhāgavata Purāṇa*, particularly the story of Kṛṣṇa's life, are part of the scriptures of Tamil Śaivism and Vaiṣṇavism, and have been placed on a par with the Vedic and Āgamic scriptures.

Traditionally the doctrine of *bhakti* taught that religious merit and even salvation could be acquired by those deficient in sastric learning, ritual observance, and ascetic penances if they would but love the Lord and sing His name and praises in the presence of other devotees (called *bhāgavatas*). This doctrine gave the movement a mildly anticaste and anti-intellectual tone. The following verses illustrate this mood of many of the Tamil hymns:

Though they give me the jewels from Indra's abode,
　　Though they grant me dominion o'er earth, yea o'er heaven,
If they be not the friends of our lord Mahādev,
　　What care I for wealth by such ruined hands giv'n?

But if they love Śiva, who hides in His hair
　　The river Gaṅga, then whoe'er they be,
Foul lepers, or outcastes, yea slayers of kine,
　　To them is my homage, gods are they to me.

Why bathe in Gaṅga's stream, or Kāviri?
　　Why go to Comorin in Koṅgu's land?
Why seek the waters of the sounding sea?

[6] V. Raghavan: "The Vedas and Bhakti," *The Vedanta Kesari* (Madras; December 1955).

Release is theirs, and theirs alone, who call
In every place upon the Lord of all.

Why chant the Vedas, hear the Śāstras' lore?
    Why daily teach the books of righteousness?
Why the Vedāṅgas six say o'er and o'er?
    Release is theirs, and theirs alone, whose heart
    From thinking of its Lord shall ne'er depart.

Why roam the jungle, wander cities through?
    Why plague life with unstinting penance hard?
Why eat no flesh, and gaze into the blue?
    Release is theirs, and theirs alone, who cry
    Unceasing to the Lord of wisdom high.

Why fast and starve, why suffer pains austere?
    Why climb the mountains, doing penance harsh?
Why go to bathe in waters far and near?
    Release is theirs, and theirs alone, who call
    At every time upon the Lord of all.[7]

These sentiments of an easier path to salvation have naturally been popular among non-Brahmans and lower castes. They have given devotional groups the distinctive emotional tone of a brotherhood of mystical devotees of Kṛṣṇa or of Śiva. Among some devotional groups in contemporary Madras this emotional tone persists, but the brotherhood is now conceived in terms of modern democratic and equalitarian ideology. And Brahmans from orthodox families have become active participants and leaders of the devotional movement. The devotional movement in Madras city has become ecumenical, an expression of democratic aspirations within Hinduism. It links village and town, traditional and modern, the folk and classical, the sacred and secular spheres of culture. It brings together, at least within the religious and cultural sphere, different castes and sects, different linguistic and religious communities. Historically, devotional movements have had similar tendencies but have usually resulted in the formation of exclusive sects. The contemporary movement does not so much inspire sectarian and denominational forma-

[7] Tirunavukkarasu Swami (more commonly referred to as Apparswami), in F. Kingsbury and G. E. Phillips: *Hymns of the Tamil Saivite Saints* (Calcutta and London; 1921).

tions as a diffuse emotion of brotherhood which softens the rough edges of group differences.

Urban Pastoral: Bhajans

The kind of cultural performance which is closest in form and spirit to the older *bhakti* movements is a form of group hymn singing called *bhajans*. These are very informally organized as part of temple processions around the streets of the city, or in private homes and halls. Older men distinguished for their devotion and knowledge of the songs (and known as *bhāgavatars*) act as *bhajan* leaders, but many *bhajan* groups meet without special leaders. Some of the leading singers, of whom there are about 100 in Madras city, come from families who have been devotees for four or five generations. Every Saturday night it is usual for these groups to hold a *bhajan* at home with friends. These usually last three or four hours from seven to ten thirty at night and consist chiefly in chanting of the Lord's name and singing of devotional songs. A larger all-night *bhajan* is held about once a month. For these it is usual to have a leader who knows the technique, and also some musicians. The more elaborate of these long *bhajans* include, not only chanting of the Lord's name, but a greater variety of songs and acting out by the devotees of the story of Kṛṣṇa and his beloved milkmaids or *gopīs*, as well as of the wedding of Rādhā and Kṛṣṇa.

A full *bhajan* program, several of which I attended, includes a complete *pūjā* to Kṛṣṇa, who is invoked with songs, in lithographs on the walls, and in a lamp placed on the floor in the center of a circle of devotees. All of the "attentions" (*upacāras*) offered to a temple image by a priest are offered to the lamp by the singing devotees. The offerings are chiefly in the songs, although some articles like fans, garlands, and sandal paste are also used.

One leading devotee, a well-educated *bhāgavatar* who very kindly gave me running comments on the *bhajan* in which he was participating, explained that these "attentions" represent "services of all kinds." My devotee friend declared: "We let the Lord enjoy all kinds of happiness, comforts, conveniences and so forth. We offer all these to Him as servants or Devotees who always think in this way, 'What shall I do to the Lord next? What service shall I offer? Shall I hold an umbrella for Him? Shall I fan Him? Shall I do this thing for Him? Shall I do that thing for Him?' and so forth. We do all imaginable kinds of service to Him."

As they sit singing in a circle around the lamp, the devotees imagine themselves to be milkmaids or *gopīs* playing with Kṛṣṇa. "The philosophy here," the *bhāgavatar* explained, "is that all men and women in the world are spiritually women, and the Lord alone is male, because the woman's love for her lord or husband is the only greatest possible love, and we can acquire such great love only by imagining ourselves as women—as the *gopīs*—and love the Lord, calling after him."

The marriage of Rādhā and Kṛṣṇa in a complete *bhajan* is a replica of an orthodox Hindu marriage. The form of it, according to the *bhāgavatar*, was supposed to have originated in Sītā's marriage to Rām. In *bhajans* the Vedic part is usually left out, but all the rest is included, with the pictures of Rādhā and Kṛṣṇa, and the devotees, playing the roles of bride and bridegroom. A marriage string (*tali*) is put on Rādhā's neck in the picture; the devotees' feet and those on the pictures are painted with sandal paste or turmeric powder; the pictures are taken in procession, flowers are thrown, *pān supārī* is offered, a miniature swing is used, etc. Some of the Rādhā-Kṛṣṇa love songs for this part of the *bhajan* are taken from Jayadeva's *Gīta-Govinda* and sung in Sanskrit.

The songs and dances of the *bhajan* follow a definite sequence which is known to experienced devotees and can also be learned from printed books. The songs come from various traditional sources—the *Bhāgavata Purāṇa*, and from the regional devotional songs. Some are in Sanskrit, others in Tamil, Telugu, Hindi, Marathi. There are many songs in praise of the ten incarnations of Viṣṇu and also some in praise of Śiva, "to show that we do not dislike Śiva though we have been praising Kṛṣṇa all along."

The dances include the *Ras Krīḍā*, a Kṛṣṇa dance, and the *Kummi* and *Kolaṭṭam*, both folk dances, the former usually performed by women at work. These dances were called "sports" by my *bhāgavatar* informant, a translation of *līlā*. They represent the *gopīs*' expression of joy at being with Kṛṣṇa. "There may be several other sports as well—

all imagined to be resorted to by the *gopīs* as they are now most happy, having got back Kṛṣṇa and enjoying His company once again. Happy people will sport in a variety of ways."

In the eyes of the devotees the climax of the *bhajan* comes when they embrace one another and roll on the floor to take the dust of each other's feet. A young devotee, a college instructor and the *bhāgavatar's* son, explained that this part of the *bhajan* expresses "the spirit of equality without respect to young or old, caste or creed. Each devotee shows that he considers the others as his equals and is willing to worship them as the Lord." One of the verses which they sing at this point says: "Let us purify ourselves with the dust that has fallen from the feet of the devotees. Let us praise the two glorious feet of our guru. Let us enjoy the bliss by mutual embraces and attain ecstasy."

Local interest in *bhajans* has greatly increased in the last twenty years. Non-Brahmans as well as Brahmans hold *bhajans*, although Brahmans predominated at the ones I attended. There are *bhajans* of the "sitting type" where only Tamil songs—usually from the *Devāram*—are sung and where Brahmans do not give the lead. Non-Brahman Vaiṣṇaiva *bhajan* halls and *bhajan* parties are also common.

The group of about fifteen to twenty devotees I have seen at two *bhajans* are mostly Brahmans and have been doing these *bhajans* together for about six or seven years. They are all personal friends and have generally developed their friendship from meeting at the *bhajans*. "That is why the *bhajans* are so good; they make us friends. We accept all, we accept even foreigners."

Women who attend the *bhajans* may also join the singing, although they usually sit silently on the side. In the last ten years there have been efforts to organize all-female *bhajans* where women do the singing and the men are silent. In fact, there are now probably as many of these *bhajans* of women as there are *bhajans* of men.

Bhakti in the Storytelling Media

A less dramatic kind of devotional performance consists of readings and recitations from the epics and *purāṇas*. India is a storytelling civilization. Stories from the *Rāmā-*

yaṇa, the *Mahābhārata,* and the *Bhāgavata Purāṇa* are a staple upon which the Indian imagination feeds in all parts of the country. While I was in Madras I saw hundreds of people daily sitting in public halls avidly listening to the recitation of these familiar stories. The reciters were usually professionals (called *paurāṇikas*); some were Brahmans, some non-Brahmans, some were Śaivite, some Vaiṣṇavite, and there were women as well as men among them. One woman I heard usually had an audience chiefly of women, while the male reciters drew mixed audiences but with the men sitting on one side of the hall and the women and children on the other. The style of recitation varied from the austere, erudite manner of the *paṇḍit* who would not depart from the Sanskrit texts he knew well, to the folksy, humorous, and anecdotal manner of the reciter, who traded on his histrionic and comic talents rather than on his learning. An individual recitation lasts about two or three hours, although it is customary to arrange a sequence lasting seven or fifteen days.

Not all the reciters were professionals. In the home, parents and grandparents will tell the stories to the children. And if the householder is orthodox, he will also read, or have read, a canto from the *Rāmāyaṇa* (or *Mahābhārata,* or a *purāṇa*) every day as part of his morning prayers. Because the section on the discovery of Sītā (*sundara kanda*) has greater merit, it will be read at the rate of seven cantos a day. This ritual type of reading is usually done in the Sanskrit text, and is carried on over a period of about a year and a half until the entire epic is completed. Then a new cycle of reading is begun either in the same text or in another one like the *Mahābhārata.*

Recitation of stories from the epics and *purāṇas,* whether done by amateurs or professionals, in ritual Sanskrit, or in the vernacular, is only one of the media through which these themes are presented. The same stories may also be sung in ballads, danced, dramatized, painted in pictures, carved on temple towers, and written in books. Each medium has its own special development and combines in many ways with several of the others. This variety of storytelling media is reflected in the numerous Sanskrit words for "story"—*kathā, harikathā, kālakshepa, pravacana.*

Historically all of these media have been used to communicate and transmit the traditional religious culture. Professional specialists in these media are known from remote times, performing in the temples of village and town and in palace courts on the occasion of religious festivals, weddings, and royal celebrations. These media came to have a special "popular" function because the masses of the people were not ritually excluded from them as they were from Vedic ceremonies and recitations. For the orthodox, this distinction persists today, the Vedic culture being reserved to the Brahmans and "twice-born," the epic and puranic literature being the vehicle of dissemination for the "masses." Yet many changes have occurred and are occurring to blur and shift the distinction. Non-Brahmans, Śūdras, and untouchables are being given direct access, not only to temples, but to Vedic rites, artificially revived, and to discourses on the Upaniṣads. Brahmans participate, not only as performers, patrons, and organizers of the popular cultural media, but have become an eager audience for them. The development of the newer mass media of print, radio, and movies has not eliminated the older cultural media and these traditional themes, but has transformed and incorporated them. The increasing concentration of population in urban centers has also brought with it changes in cultural media, specialists, and places and occasions of performance. How far all these changes have produced a mass, secular culture different in values and in organization from the traditional religious culture is a question which I shall now consider.

Cultural Effects of Mass Media: Bhakti in the Films

Mass media like the movies, the radio, the daily newspaper, and the printed book tend to reinforce the trend toward greater popularization. Whether privately or governmentally controlled, they cannot afford to cater to a limited caste, sect, or linguistic group, but must seek to maximize the audiences for continuous performances of their media. Popular entertainment is for them a more important value than religious merit and salvation. The technology and organization of the mass media make these shifts possible and introduce, as well, new characteristics in the cultural transmission which are quite different from the traditional cultural media.

Most important of these characteristics is that the mass medium produces an impersonal record—on paper, wax, wire, tape, or film—which exists separately from both performer and audience and can be mechanically reproduced. This makes it possible to send the program to mass audiences quickly and in practically any location.

There is a further difference in quality as well as in quantity. The mass media develop their own times, places, and occasions of performance on a principle of continuous daily "showings." This cuts them off from the ceremonial calendar geared to the important events of the life cycle and of the agricultural cycle which were the major occasions for the cultural media. On these new occasions and cultural stages it becomes possible to by-pass the distinctions of caste, sect, language, and sponsorship that were important in the traditional performances. Another difference is that the cultural media were equally at home in village and in town, and traveling performers used to spread a living cultural network over the countryside. The mass media, on the other hand, are centered in the large city, and require elaborate mechanical equipment and personnel to operate. Although their programs are sent to towns and villages, it is the impersonal record and not the performers who travel. They remain in the urban centers.

These distinctions tend to place the mass media in a relation to the traditional culture, its social structure, and its religious values, which is very different from the relation of the cultural media to those traditional elements. A constant repetition of themes in the mass media is no longer regarded, at least by the producers, as "eternally new," but is merely a source of dependable income or an obstacle to novelty. The cultural tradition which in India is thought of as being transmitted from what has been revealed to the seers (*śruti*) and through that which is remembered (*smṛti*), by *paṇḍits* and storytellers, undergoes a transformation when it is transmitted impersonally over the mass media without the benefit of seers, gurus, or reciters.

But even these changes introduced by the mass media

have not yet resulted in a secularization of religious culture. Print, radio, and film are used to disseminate puranic stories and devotional music, and *bhakti*-inspired audiences have their own ways of personalizing the impersonal mass media. In Tirupati, in some of the bigger temples of the Tamil country, and in Annamalai University, the loudspeaker and gramophone record are used to broadcast devotional music, hymns and prayers. Recently, the availability of tape recorders at about Rs. 1,000/ has led to a number of people keeping recordings of such devotional recitals at home and listening to them regularly. The hymns recited at the Tirupati shrine in the small hours of the morning to wake up the Lord have been tape-recorded and kept by some devotees.

The example of the "mythological" and "devotional" films is instructive. During our stay in Madras, a non-Brahman and practically illiterate chauffeur kept urging us to see the film *Avvayyār*, which was then very popular and which he characterized only in an enthusiastic murmur as "*bhakti, bahkti.*" We did eventually get to see this film and also to interview its producers. The story is about the female saint and poet, Avvayyār, of the Tamil country who goes about performing miracles with her devotional songs. Usually each song is connected with an incident teaching a moral lesson, and as it is sung, the incident is dramatized on the screen. A giant image of Gaṇeśa was kept in the theater lobby.

This technique of narrative song sequence in the *Avvayyār* film has also been used in other devotional and historical films, as well as in radio dramas and in epiclike narratives about Ghandi and the Congress Party struggle for independence. It is an adaptation of a village ballad form called "bow song" (*viḷḷu pāṭṭu*) to urban mass media. One person responsible for these adaptations was the producer and director of the *Avvayyār* film. He is a folk poet by avocation and is known as "the Bobby Burns of Tamil," and has a nickname which means "soaked in the soil." He has composed over 1,000 folksongs in village meter on harvest festivals, weddings, war, and modern themes. The village background of folk plays, folksongs, ballads, and puranic recitations to which he was exposed as a child have provided him, he believes, with great literary wealth. His was the only Brahman family in the village, and their relation to the non-Brahmans was very good. He came to Madras in 1935 at the age of twenty-five, but mentally he still lives, he says, in the village. He goes back at least once each year. And in town he tries to live as in the village with some thirty-five to forty relatives under one roof—including four different generations.

The *Avvayyār* picture is expected by its producers to run five years and make a large profit for the company. Its great success has encouraged Indian film producers to turn once more to "devotionals" and "mythologicals" as dependable sources of investment. One film producer stated that about eighty per cent of the stories in Indian movies are now traditional, reflecting the desire of the movie companies to play for safety by relying on the familiar. Many of these traditional stories are drawn from the epics and *purāṇas* or from stories about the lives of regional saints like Avvayyār or Caitanya.

This trend, which represents a return to the mythological themes of the early Indian films, is considered regressive by some of the modern producers. They do not feel that this traditional subject matter is as "educational" as "social" or "landscape" films. The educational value of the "mythological," according to one producer, is restricted to "what has already happened." This comment sounds paradoxical to a Westerner, but probably reflects the Indian's realistic acceptance of his mythology. This same producer also worries a good deal about whether a medium like the films is not too powerful in a country like India, "where people are so ready to believe." He seemed particularly impressed by the case of an actor who played the role of a saint in one devotional film and was for several years afterward followed around and worshipped by large crowds as if he were really a saint.

On the other hand, this producer is convinced that the filmmaker must think of the Indian "man in the street," the rickshaw puller in the city, and the villager as his audience, and suit the film to their taste and understanding. Film music and dancing cannot be classical or even authentically Indian. Film music is a mixture of Spanish, Hawaiian, and Indian, and the dancing is a mixture of streamlined classical Indian dances and European styles like the waltz.

Not all Indian films have traditional or devotional themes. As in the United States, comedy and variety films are also very popular. There is an Indian "Costello" who is in such great demand at the studios in Calcutta, Bombay, and Madras that he spends much of his time flying from one studio to another. This emphasis, too, needs no special justification in the filmmakers' minds: "The cinema is often all the rickshaw puller or the villager has. It has to combine everything in an evening's entertainment—dancing, comedy, fighting, romance, and lots of songs." The villagers see the films in the nearest towns or in the village at the mobile theaters sent out by the film companies or the government. The government films are documentaries, shorts, and information films, and must also be shown in urban theaters.

Comedy, variety, social, and educational films belong to an international urban culture and are not especially associated with the devotional outlook, as the mythological, devotional, and historical films are. Yet even these purer "international" films retain many distinctive Indian features—traditional song and dance forms, the combining of many different media in one program, the long and rambling sequences, the use of regional languages. The mass media have brought in new urban forms of devotional and nondevotional storytelling, but they are also still linked in themes and techniques to the folk and traditional storytelling media.

A very similar continuum can be traced in popular urban drama. The village folk play (*terukkuttu*) has migrated with the low-caste communities and thrives on city lots as vigorously as it once did around village temples. As in the village, these are all-night performances, given about four times a year during festivals and important occasions. The actors are all amateurs, young men of the community who are rehearsed for several months by an older man who happens to know the plays. The most popular of these are based on incidents from the *Mahābhārata* and *Rāmāyaṇa* and from Tamil epics and legends all familiar to the audience. Comic interludes and farce, usually having no relation to the play, help to sustain interest through the night. There are also presentations of garlands and gifts to the leading actors on first appearance because they are the important people who organize the plays and raise the money for city license fees. This little ceremony and the colorful costumes of the leads give a touch of glamor to the kerosene-lighted, roped-off lot on which Arjuna and Draupadī, Rāma and Sītā, Kōvalan and Kaṇṇakī act and sing their roles.

While the folk play persists unchanged in the city, there has also developed within the last fifty years a form of popular devotional drama that corresponds to the devotional films and the urbanized forms of puranic recitation. Specializing as these other media do in mythological, devotional, and historical themes, the devotional play incorporates with its bright costumes, professional lighting, and stage effects some elements of the court theater and of the modern stage. To a Western observer, the action in these devotional plays seems predominantly of a tableau form, with occasional songs and dances and numerous sound and trick stage effects. This serves to highlight the mythological incidents and personages and to present each in as luminous a manner as might be desired from a chromolithograph.

These devotional plays are probably the most popular dramatic performances in Madras, with all classes of the population paying to see them at a commercial theater. They have been developed by a professional actor and producer, "Nawab" Raja-Manickam, who has a reputation for *bhakti*. Before the curtain goes up on one of his plays, puffs of smoke roll out under it and from the sides indicating that he is performing a *pūjā* to Gaṇeś. He has produced plays based on Rāmdās and the life of Christ, as well as on South Indian deities like Murugan, to teach the message of devotion and national unity. The first scene in the Murugan play, *Kumāra Vijayam*, opens with a singing tableau representing Indian unity. Various figures, all young boys, appear with papier-mâché heads of Gandhi, Nehru, and other Indian leaders, as well as regional types, against a backdrop showing a temple, a mosque, and a Christian church.

This devotional drama is a more colorful and urbanized

form of the folk play. It is performed by professionals on a commercial stage for mixed audiences and uses modern stage techniques. Its themes remain devotional and its tableaus are more akin to the painted scenes on temple towers than to the modern theater.

Within the last fifty years, however, there has been rapidly developing in the city a modern theater which cuts across caste and sect and has some resemblances to Western theater. Sponsored at first by amateur dramatic societies, particularly of male college students, this move-ment is now in the hands of professional companies, per-forming in permanent theater halls. As in the cinema, which is the chief medium now for popular drama, the aim is to reach a wide audience, so Tamil is the major language. Types of plays are categorized, again as in the film, into devotionals, mythologicals, and historicals on the one hand, and socials and comedies on the other. The first group is regarded as representing the indigenous Indian theater, and the latter as being largely Western influenced. The Sanskrit drama is virtually neglected by the professionals, although a recent Sanskrit revival may bring it back into popular esteem.

The social play replaces the traditional puranic stories and the traditional media of presentation with modern problems and prose dialogues. It corresponds to the novel, the short story, and modern poetry, and tends in the main to be cultivated by a similar group of people, those with modern education and in the middle and upper classes. The urban theater prefers to use Tamil and the other Indian vernaculars or even English. It is also more secular than the traditional drama in being less determined by caste and sect. Performances are in public halls open to all who can pay the price of admission. The times and occasions of performance are not geared to temple fes-tivals or other religious occasions; they are brief and are set in accordance with the commercial and cultural exi-gencies as perceived by the owners of the theater halls, the performers, and their organizers and sponsors. In these respects, dramatic media resemble the cinema and the radio and tend to develop their own "festival" calendar.

The involvement of drama in the political arena is reminiscent of the storytelling media. Both the state government and the national government have shown active interest in dramatic activities. In addition to the officially sponsored academies and drama festivals, there has also been use of dramatic media to tell villagers the story of independence, of the Five Year Plan, and of specific projects for village improvement. Both the traditional and modern dramatic forms have been employed for this purpose. And not only the government has made this political use of drama. Private voluntary groups, opposition political parties and movements have also made similar use of this medium. An attempt by some followers of the Dravidian Progressive Federation to enact a dramatic parody of the *Rāmāyana* has recently led in Madras State to riots and to highly restrictive legislation regulating dramatic performances.

The Classicists

Pervading almost all cultural media and mass media and appealing to all classes of the population, the path of devotion has become a main highway. It is nothing exceptional that Brahmans, too, should find themselves on it as performers, patrons, and audience. Those belonging to Bhāgavata sects of course find this situation congenial to their traditions, despite the novel elements that have appeared in it. Many Smārtas, too, have been drawn into it, although their tradition has stressed the paths of knowledge and ritual more than that of devotion.

Not everyone, however, has taken this path of *bhakti*. Beside it and overlapping it, another path, far smaller, is clearly discernible. This is the path of classical art cultivated by a very distinctive class of patrons, critics and connoisseurs, among whom Brahmans predominate.

The classicists are not regular or frequent participants in *bhajans*, which they regard as too emotional and uncontrolled a form of religious expression, suitable perhaps for less cultivated people. If they go to puranic recitations, they prefer the austere *Paurāṇika* who knows the Sanskrit texts well and adheres faithfully to them, to the reciter who caters to popular tastes and humor. They may not themselves always have sufficient Sanskrit to follow, but they nevertheless insist on purity of standards.

The musical form of puranic recitation known as

harikathā they consider as an art form superior both to *bhajans* and to traditional recitation without music. In the field of the drama, they fail to see how the modern social play has improved on the classical play and they prefer the devotional and folk play to the "social." Highest in their esteem are the classical South Indian dance, the *bhārata nāṭyam,* and the classical South Indian or Carnatic music, vocal and instrumental, which they regard as the very peak of aesthetic achievement.

For the classical critics there is, in other words, a definite hierarchy of cultural media and performances. This hierarchy does not only depend on the general character of the media, but on the degree of sophistication, knowledge of the art tradition, and cultivation of taste with which they are rendered. As one ascends the hierarchy, the values of popular entertainment as well as of *bhakti* become less and less, and the values of "pure art" become more important. The "pure art" at the top is to some extent an "art for art's sake," but it is not completely secularized. It represents a fourth and distinctive path to release and the absolute, and a kind of sublimation of the paths of ritual observance and of knowledge.

Story and Song: Harikathā

The distinctive technique of reciting, called *harikathā kālakṣepam,* uses songs in several languages—Sanskrit, Tamil, Telugu, Kannada, Marathi, and Hindi—dramatic exposition in Tamil, and musical accompaniment, and is considered an art form since it demands a knowledge of music, languages, and dramatic technique. This form of *harikathā* was developed in the Tanjore Court about 100 years ago through adaptation of a Maharashtrian form. The Senior Madras performer in this technique is Saraswati Bai, a lady Brahman noted for her knowledge of music, both North Indian as well as South Indian, a gifted voice, excellent pronunciation of a wide range of Indian languages, and for erudition and good taste in the selection of song and story material. Her style of *harikathā* is regarded as unique because it combines the best styles of her predecessors.

Krishna Bhagavatar of Tanjore is credited with the creation of the distinctive Tamil *harikathā* from the

Maharashtrian model. Saraswati Bai, who claims descent from him through her guru or teacher, believes that this form began in the South in the nineteenth century. She considers herself as equally a storyteller, a singer, and a religious teacher. "All three must be present in equal proportion: no one is primary." She does not restrict her moral teaching to one special lesson or sect but teaches about Hinduism. She performs before both Vaiṣṇavite and Śaivite sects. She herself comes from a Madhva Brahman family. Her repertoire includes stories about Śiva, Viṣṇu, Subrahmanya, and many other gods. These are usually taken from the *Rāmāyaṇa*, *Mahābhārata*, minor *purāṇas*, and the hagiology of the saints. When I asked whether she repeated the same story many times, she said that she did but insisted that there is no such thing as "repetition." People love to hear the same story over and over and will call for it in advance. A popular favorite is the story of Nandanar, the Tamil Śaivite Harijan saint, which she thinks she has told at least 10,000 times.

The occasions on which she performs include festivals and festivities, usually of special castes; marriages; temple festivals; before institutes and *sabhās* associations and before Maharajas. She has performed before the Maharajas of Mysore, Travancore, Cochin, and others. "Three generations have heard me: I have been doing it for forty-eight years." Marriages are the most frequent occasions, festivities next, temple festivals next, performances for *sabhās* and Maharajas least. Temple festivals are now slightly less frequent occasions probably, she thinks, because of the spread of atheism. To some extent, too, musical associations and concerts are taking the place of temple festivals.

She is willing "to tell any kind of story everywhere, provided it is about God. But the essence must be devotion [*bhakti*] and I would not sacrifice this anywhere." *Harikathā* she thinks is the most appropriate medium for the expression of *bhakti*. In a public speech she said: "Music is not only a medium of entertainment in this world but also the means of realizing the Godhead."

She has given *harikathā* performances all over India, as well as abroad, in Calcutta, Bombay, Banaras, Rangoon, and Ceylon. Before foreign audiences who do not understand her Tamil narration, she always selects songs in the language of the region, and with these and her "mono-acting" she can hold them. The audiences are, of course, already familiar with the stories and have shown great enthusiasm wherever she went.

She has also traveled to the villages. "I have not spared a single village and not a single village has spared me." Whenever she traveled by cart, crowds of villagers would come out to greet her and would follow her from one village to another. The arrangements for village performances are usually made by a landlord who invites her for a marriage or a temple festival. The landlord gives a fee for her, her musicians, and her guru; the villagers will also give her shawls and other presents. The musicians include a drummer who has been with her for nearly forty years, a harmonium player who has been with her for nearly as long, and a supporting singer who also plays cymbals. The harmonium is used instead of the *tambura* for a drone because the *tambura* is big and difficult to transport. The traveling party also includes her cook and servants.

The trips used to last two or three months, but now she goes only for a week or ten days. A manager makes the arrangements for the distant trips; for the near ones she makes them herself. Local arrangements are usually made by the inviter, who pays all the expenses of the party, and, in addition, pays her a fee. When she was in Bombay, she received a fee of about 2,000 rupees. For performances close to Madras she usually receives about 600 rupees. No written contracts are drawn, but "it is all written in letters, so it is like a legal contract."

Village audiences and town audiences are not too different, she said, but she has found village audiences more appreciative of both her stories and music. This is not because, as I suggested, they are more religious, but because "they just respond better." Thousands of villagers will come to hear her from neighboring villages. Southerners show more interest in art and music than Northerners, and when they settle outside of South India, they always organize music and art activities. In Rangoon, Burma, where there are many "overseas Tamils," 10,000 people came to hear her at one performance.

The most difficult thing in *harikathā*, she thinks, is to take the many different parts in a single story. She has been highly praised just on this score. One admirer has written: "I have seen her, in her Kalakshepams, put great actors in the histrionic field to shame, by her masterly impersonation of the characters of a Rāvaṇa, a Hanumān or a Garuḍa, a giant or a cooing bird, a Bhakta or a scoffer, a lover or a libertine, a god or a goddess, a saint or a sinner, a man or woman, King or peasant, with equal ease and yet remain in her decorous Sari—'rich but not gaudy'—the sweet, simple, generous and loving Lady Bhāgavathar she has been and is today." [8]

These varied roles require knowledge, too, of the appropriate dialects, of some Urdu for the story of Ramdas, and of Tamil slang for that of Nandanar. As one scholar has written, *harikathā* is a kind of concentrated drama, a "monodrama," in which one gifted actor enters swiftly a whole series of characters, moods, and manners.

The day before my interview, one of the local newspapers carried an announcement that the Union of India government was going to use *harikathā* to publicize the Five Year Plan. In reply to a question about this program, Saraswati Bai said she hoped that the government would set up a national academy for *harikathā*, as it has set up an academy for letters and the dance; otherwise the art would be lost. I asked her whether *harikathā* could be used to get people to dig pits and clean wells, whether devotional songs were not inappropriate for this purpose. This question aroused much laughter from her and the members of her family who were present. But then she said, seriously: "No, the devotional songs would not be appropriate. But I would be willing to compose new songs if I were asked. This is a matter of patriotism and I would be willing to sing about pits and wells, too."

Several *harikathās* about Gandhi's life have been written and performed. One of these was recorded by another lady *bhāgavatar* who comes from a Brahman Vaiṣṇava family in Mysore. In her version the story of Gandhi's life is told after the fashion of the lives of the saints. In fact, Gandhi

---

[8] *Commemoration Volume*, in honor of Srimati C. Saraswati Bai (Madras; 1939). See also Y. B. Damle: "A Note on Harikatha," *Bulletin of the Deccan College*, Vol. XVII (Poona).

is treated as an incarnation (*avatāra*) of God who has come to deliver India from foreign domination. Gandhi's death is also effectively told as the death of a martyr. Gandhi Bhagavatar (Rajaram), a Tamil Smārta Brahman and a Tamil poet, was a pioneer in this line.

To tell Gandhi's story the reciter uses all the songs and Sanskrit verses that are used in the traditional *harikathā*. She begins with the famous song of the Gujarāti saint Narasimha Mehta, which starts with the words "*Vaisnava janato*," and declares that "he is a true devotee of Lord Visnu who knows the suffering of others." This was Gandhi's favorite song. The reciter emphasizes the great faith which Gandhi had in devotion (*bhakti*) and in the recital of Rāma's name. Gandhi's doctrine of help and uplift for the poor and his belief in equality are also stressed.[9]

Classical South Indian Dance and Music

In *harikathā*, *bhakti* is still an important element, although considerations of artistic and dramatic technique and learning also loom large. In the classical South Indian dance called *bhārata nātyam*, and in classical South Indian or "Carnatic" music, aesthetic standards and the rules of art predominate. In fact, it is primarily these two media that are most frequently associated with the ideas of classical art. They are almost never referred to without the prefix "classical." Their more active revival is dated from two political events, the Madras meeting of the Indian National Congress in 1927, and the All-India Khadi and Swadeshi Exhibition organized by the Tamil Nadu Provincial Congress Committee in Madras in 1935.

On the occasion of these meetings local cultural leaders organized an All-India Music Conference in 1927 and a Music Festival in 1935. Before this, voluntary organizations called *sabhās* arranged periodic public performances of music and *harikathā*. Apart from the publicity given at these times to dancing and music, one of the most important results of the early meeting was the organization of the Music Academy of Madras. Funds remaining after the expenses of the All-India Music Conference of 1927 were met were donated by the Reception Committee of

[9] I am indebted to V. Raghavan for information about this Gandhi Kathā.

the Congress for establishing a Music Academy. This institution soon became an important center for the promotion of Indian dance and music. It has sponsored regular performances of leading artists, holds annual conferences at which both scholars and artists come together to exchange knowledge, encourages new talent, sponsors music and dance schools, and tries to set high standards of public taste. The *Journal of the Music Academy* has become an all-India forum for learned discussions of the technicalities of Indian music and dance, and enjoys an international circulation as well. The success of the Music Academy stimulated the organization of other voluntary associations, and now there are about twenty "cultural *sabhās*" in Madras carrying on similar programs. During the Christmas season, which also usually falls in the Hindu holy month of Mārgaśīrṣa, these different cultural associations vie with one another to bring the best artists to Madras and to put on the most interesting programs. The most elaborately planned among these programs is that of the Music Academy and usually consists of expert demonstrations and discussions in the morning, popular auditions and programs in the afternoons, and classical concerts in the evenings. Two of the halls most frequently used for these programs are the Museum Theater in Egmore and the *Rāsika Rañjanī Sabhā* of Mylapore (Association Which Pleases Connoisseurs).

These cultural associations, or their leaders, also organize special local programs for visiting dignitaries, foreign cultural delegations, and for the national drama, music, and dance festivals which are now held in New Delhi on Republic Day. These programs are not always the same, although there is usually a common core of classical South Indian dance and music in them. In 1955, on the occasion of the Congress meetings at Avadi near Madras, free cultural programs for the delegates and visitors included in addition to classical music and dance several varieties of folk dances, a puppet show, a dummy-horse dance, a folk play, a devotional drama, a social drama, and devotional singing or *bhajans*.

The Music Academy and the other local cultural associations, while tolerant of "folk" and "popular" culture, regard the promotion of classical music and dance as their own primary responsibility. It has been the influence of these associations that has secured a hearing for the "classics" on the radio, to a lesser extent in the films, and has prompted the organization of state and national academies of music, dance, drama, and letters. They are the institutional representatives of the classic revival, and although Brahmans have played an active part in their formation, they are not restricted with respect to caste or sect.

The Revival of Classical Dancing: Bhārata Nātyam

The "revival," strictly speaking, was not only a revival, but brought in major innovations. This is particularly true of the dance. Before it was revived it was known as the *nautch* or *sadir nautch* and was performed by hereditary families of dancing girls. These were called *devadāsīs* (servants of God) because they were usually "dedicated" or given to particular temples where they sang and danced at the temple processions. Their "dedication" involved a "marriage" to one of the deities in the temple so they could not become widows. If they had children, these would take the mother's father's name and could inherit his property as well as the mother's. The dancing girls were trained to sing and dance by professional teachers known as *nattuvanārs*. These were men who came from hereditary families of teachers and musicians and were also attached to the temples. Some of them were the male members of the *devadāsī* community, while others came from a different community. The dancing girls, their teachers, and musicians performed not only on the occasion of temple festivals and ceremonies but also for private parties, particularly at weddings, and at palace parties. Special troupes of dancing girls and musicians were sometimes permanently attached to the courts.

Because of the association of some of the dancing girls with prostitution, an "anti-*nautch*" campaign was waged at the turn of the century by British and Indian reformers to stop temple dancing and "dedication" of girls to temples. In 1905 the Executive Committee of the Prince and Princess of Wales' Reception Fund unanimously decided that there should be no performance by *nautch* girls at the entertainment to be given to Their Royal

Highnesses at Madras. In 1947 Madras State forbade the "dedication" and temple dancing.

After the revival, the name of the dance came to be called *bhārata nāṭyam;*[1] daughters of respectable families, including Brahmans, now take it up; it is taught in high schools, and in diluted form has become one of the most popular items in cultural programs in the films, on the stage, and at private gatherings. Although in the recent past it was developed in South India, especially around Tanjore, it is now popular all over India and has also been performed abroad by Uday Shankar, Ram Gopal, Shanta Rao, and other dancers.

The major agents of the change are, as usually happens, transitional figures. Three kinds of transitional figures have played an important part in transforming the *sadir nautch* into *bhārata nāṭyam*—dance critics, the traditional dancing teachers, and some dancing girls.

One influential critic highly respected by friends of the art and by professionals was K. V. R. His perspective was gained from a wide academic background, since he was a keen student of ancient Indian art, sculpture, and painting and of all aspects of traditional culture. He was a technically well-informed critic of classical dance and music and a sharp-tongued enemy of mass culture and everything he considered counterfeit.

K. V. R. wrote one of the first technical appreciations of *bhārata nāṭyam* in a series of articles published in 1935 in the magazine *Triveni, Journal of Indian Renaissance.* This journal, founded in Madras in 1928, became a major organ of the cultural revival in the South, in form and format like the old *Dial*. The articles are highly detailed analyses of the dance movements of the *nautch*, still so called at this time, and of its affiliations with the Brahman dance drama, the Tamil folk play, and Bhārata's *Nāṭya*

---

[1] *Bhārata nāṭyam* means dance based on the technique originally laid down by the sage Bhārata, author of the oldest surviving text on the art, the *Nāṭya Śāstra.* This name was introduced and came to be regularly used for the first time by V. Raghavan, who played a significant part, on the learned and academic side, in the renaissance of the art. Before this the dance was called the art of *bhāratam* as well as *sadir* and *nautch*. *Bhāratam* or *bhārata Śāstram* is still in use and it was also independently known as *nāṭyam*.

Śāstra. The article is illustrated with photographs of many of the movements posed by R. and his wife.

Since 1942 K. V. R. has lived in Coimbatore, where he does a flourishing business making and selling a very popular hair tonic. The formula for this scalp treatment he discovered himself about 1929 when his wife began to lose her hair after the birth of their first child. They were living in Madras at the time, where he ran a small druggist shop. The success of the tonic made the problem of living much easier and enabled him to devote more of his time to the study of classical Indian dance and music. He has also studied Western music because he regards himself as a "citizen of the world whose antennae spread all over the world." He knows Mozart, Beethoven, Wagner, and Handel, and is especially fond of Debussy, in whose music he finds Javanese influence.

K. V. R. comes from a Smārta Brahman family learned in music and Sanskrit. Four of his uncles were musicians and some of his cousins were paṇḍits. He himself studied music and Sanskritic tradition. He first became seriously interested in the classical dance when he was in college in Madras from 1915 to 1919. The stimulus was his reading of Coomeraswamy, Otto Rothfeld, and Havell. But even as a boy he had been attracted by the aesthetic charm of the dance and used to watch the *devadāsīs* and their dancing teachers at marriages and temples as often as he could, both in the city and when he went to the villages during vacations. At that time there were at least 500 professional dancing teachers in Madras and many *devadāsīs.* This was before the anti-*nautch* movement came to a head and before public concerts were popular. He thinks that the first public-dance concert was held in Madras in 1933 and that Chokkalingam Pillai was the teacher.

His reading of the secondary works on the dance stimulated him to go to some of the original sources like Bhārata's *Nāṭya Śāstra* and to the temple-dance sculptures at Chidambaram and Tanjore to reconstruct the original forms of the classical art. The dance poses on the temple sculptures, while valuable, have to be reconstructed with caution, since they represent only a single "frozen section" within a moving sequence. However, he believes that through a careful study of these literary and temple sources and of the "authentic living traditions of the art," in Java and Bali as well as in India, it is possible to recover the true classical dance.

When he was married in 1925, he encouraged his wife to learn dancing from a professional temple dancer in Mylapore and from a Brahman dancing teacher who taught her the art of interpretation (*abhinaya*). He often corrected his wife's poses as well as those of professional dancers who came to him for advice. He has also encouraged his daughters to take up dancing and singing.

K. V. R. believes that Brahmans have always played an important role in transmitting the classical dance. Because of their knowledge of Sanskrit and rhetoric, they were especially qualified to teach *abhinaya*. This tradition has almost died out, although remnants of it can still be found in the dance dramas (*bhāgavata melā nāṭaka*) performed by male Brahmans in a few Tamil and Telugu villages. At some point the Brahmans taught the art to the guilds of non-Brahman teachers or *nattuvanars* who have jealously guarded it since.

The *devadāsīs*, too, have played an important part in keeping the dance traditions alive, R. believes. The dancing girls themselves rarely married, but were kept as concubines by well-to-do patrons. The children were raised by the mother and her relatives without any stigma. The male members of the community were usually dancing teachers and musicians and married within the community. Whatever faults moral reformers may have found with their social life, R. thinks their mode of life did not prevent these professional dancers from achieving very high standards of proficiency, taste, and judgment in the art and general culture as well.

K. V. R.'s sympathies have always been with the Congress movement although he did not belong to the party. He ran classes for Harijans when Gandhi was in jail and has always been a nationalist at heart. When he was a child, he used to have his hands caned for singing the *Vande Mātaram*. His elder brother was very active in the movement and went to jail and later became a leading journalist. He does not, however, believe that Congress has been very sympathetic to cultural pursuits. Its claims to extend the Swaraj to Indian culture he cannot take seriously. The founding of the Music Academy in 1927, on the occasion of the Congress Party meeting in Madras that year, he regards as merely a coincidence, and the Madras 1935 Music Festival sponsored by the Tamilnad Congress Committee, in which he himself participated, was of the same character. "The political movement just makes a show of patronage but has really very little influence and never picks the right people. The politicians are like flies on the wheel of culture."

His attitude to present trends is highly critical. Dance performances have been commercialized, "the mob calls the tune"; the art has lost refinement, and the artists are interested only in revenue. The emphasis on translating all songs into Tamil so that everyone can understand them has not increased the number of people who can understand the music. And "acoustical cranks" who are themselves quite unmusical have become music critics.

But he is not without hope for the future: "We will die before these things die." With a long-range view and a "better class of people," the classical arts can be kept alive. The proper approach would be first to understand what you have, then to clear up misconceptions and only after this to undertake to develop new forms within the frame of the old. He thinks even temple dancing could be restored if political conditions were favorable, since people at large are not bothered by "morality."

In Indian villages today little survives of the classic forms. They have more of the folk arts, which, he supposes, may be "the soul of the classics, like a child lisping," but these do not become important until they have been influenced by classical forms.

The renaissance of Indian culture which started with great hopes in the twenties and thirties he thinks has, in its contemporary sequel, proved a failure. The "cinema people" have taken it over and now "the monkey has got it." Indian culture has become more and more attenuated in every generation and "like a child with an enlarged liver lives on in an enfeebled way." The development of modern dance and music schools have "merely increased the scope for fraud."

The reason it was possible for a classic culture to flourish in the past was that performances were regularly held in temples and palaces, that the patrons were themselves musicians and connoisseurs, that the audiences were highly critical, and that the artists were responsive to this atmosphere. Now the audiences are very uncritical and the "artists play down, not up to the audience." In the past, too, the artists considered it a privilege to perform before the deity, and there was no stress on personality and the ego; the compositions were impersonal and anonymous. The cultivation of the art through family tradition was also a factor.

Himself a student of Tamil before he studied Sanskrit, K. V. R. believes the present effort to Tamilize the arts by "the left-wingers" is culturally suicidal. Although *bhārata nāṭyam* developed in Tamil country, its life source has been its connection with Sanskrit. Without this connection it will dry up or have a lopsided development.

K. V. R. regards the classical dance as an expression of a spiritual reality. In his presidential address in 1956 before the Indian Institute of Fine Arts in Madras he refers to some of the religious elements in the dance, especially to its connections with temple worship. He speaks of the first item on a *bhārata nāṭyam* program, the *Alarippu*, as "a divine adoration." "While the main root connects Naṭya with the Vedas, others connect it with the Agamas which govern and regulate temple worship and tantric rituals."

Secularizing trends in the dance he regards as unfortunate. "By secularizing it, we have converted it into an affair of the drawing room; and imported the spirit of the market place into the tabernacle . . . all our arts were auxiliary to our religion; a restoration of faith in that religion might help to restore the arts."

The image of the classical dance constructed by the dance critics needs to be supplemented by the reports of the surviving traditional teachers and dancers. One of these dancing teachers is now conducting a *bhārata nāṭyam* dancing school in Madras. We had an opportunity to visit his school and to interview him twice and also to learn from him something of the traditional ways of teaching and dancing as practiced in the villages.

The city dance class was held in a small school hall

during the hours when school was not in session, about two hours early in the morning and another two hours in the late afternoon. We visited it one afternoon and watched teacher and students communicate perfectly without the use of language. The teacher sat cross-legged at one end of the room. He vigorously tapped the time with a small round stick and chanted it in nonsense syllables. With his free left hand, he would describe the positions that the hands or feet should assume in the different steps. Occasionally he would put down the stick and use both hands to describe these positions. These movements of his hands were intermittent and highly abbreviated, like the sketchiest line drawings. But the pupils followed them intently and were guided by them and by the beats of the stick through the complex intricacies of *bhārata nāṭyam*.

There were eight students in the class, a young girl from Orissa, an older Parsī girl from Bombay on a government scholarship, an American woman from New York, and five little girls from eight to ten, most of whom came from Brahman families in the city. They were all learning *bhārata nāṭyam*. Only the small girls knew the teacher's language, Tamil; the others communicated with him through the medium of the dance's gestures and rhythms.

The class and teacher were sponsored by the Indian Institute of Fine Arts, a cultural association devoted to the promotion of classical Indian dance and music. "We teach only the purest classical type of dancing," said the wife of the Institute's secretary, who had received us at the class. She and another official of the Institute were proud that Chokkalingam Pillai, the dancing teacher, attracted students from all over India and from abroad. The Institute had given diplomas, representing usually the completion of three years' training, to at least twenty dancers. Some of these graduates have become professional dancers, but many are interested in the art only for its own sake, and the families of the younger students are not interested in having their daughters become professional dancers, but in learning a social accomplishment.

Chokkalingam Pillai himself is a traditional dancing teacher, a *nattuvanar*, who once taught *devadāsīs*. He is the son-in-law of Meenakshisundarum Pillai of Pandanallur village, a famous *nattuvanar* who, before he died, attracted some of India's best dancers to come to study with him in his village. There are three different families of dancing teachers in Pandanallur village: Chokkalingam's family, Meenakshisundarum's family, and a third family. These families are all interrelated and directly descended from a famous "Tanjore quartet" of *nattuvanars.* They have been historically attached to the two temples in the village, one Śiva temple and one Viṣṇu, to some temples in surrounding villages, and to the Big Temple in Tanjore, about fifty miles away. Chokkalingam Pillai believes that the families of dancing teachers in the village can trace their affiliation to the Tanjore temple back to the Cola kings who founded it in A.D. 900.

Chokkalingam was very insistent that the community of dancing teachers were in no way related to the community of dancing girls (*devadāsīs*) whom they taught, contrary to the opinion that the women of the *ṇattuvanar* community were sometimes dancing girls and that the men of the *davadāsī* community were dancing teachers and musicians. The two communities do not intermarry or interdine. No dancing girl would be allowed to sit in front of a *nattuvanar;* she only came to the house to learn.

Meenakshisundaram Pillai, who taught the art to Chokkalingam, came from a distinguished family of musicians and dancing teachers. His mother was the daughter of Ponniah, one of the famous Tanjore quartet. Meenakshisundaram first studied in the village and was then sent to Tanjore city for further study. He learned Tamil, Telugu, and Sanskrit well enough to compose songs in all of these languages. When he returned to the village, he taught music, dancing, and singing. He died in 1954 at the age of eighty-six in his village. One son and several sons-in-law carry on his tradition.

Chokkalingam's early memories are of young girls from *devadāsī* families and boys from the whole community coming to learn dancing and music from his father-in-law. The children would begin their training from their fifth year. Some came to live with his father-in-law; others returned home daily. The routine of the house was very strict and severe. It began at five a.m. with music lessons for all. The first meal of the day, cold rice and curry, would be served by seven thirty. From eight thirty to twelve the girls practiced dance steps under his father-in-law's supervision, and the boys sat on the side, following with sticks of their own. Mistakes, whether made by the girls or by the boys, were punished by slaps or rappings with the stick. Shaming insults with the help of the other children were also used.

Between one and four o'clock in the afternoon, after the noon meal, the children went to a modern school to learn languages. In the training, Tamil was the medium of instruction, but Telugu songs were also learned. On their return, there was dance practice again from four to six, music lessons from six to eight thirty, lessons in *abhinaya* (interpreting songs through dance gestures) from eight thirty to ten, another rice and curry meal at ten thirty, and to bed at eleven. They did not find this routine exhausting, Chokkalingam Pillai said, because "the food was right."

Serious lessons would begin when a child was about ten, and continue until about the thirteenth year. This meant that a total period of training would usually last from seven to eight years. The completion of the training was marked by the giving of a first performance—*Aragentram*—by the pupil. This was usually given in a temple and only for the girls; there was no special ceremony for the boys, who always assisted their teacher and never performed independently of him.

At the *Aragentram* ceremony, the teacher usually received presents from the mother of the pupil as well as from others. Thereafter, if the pupil performed in public and received any compensation, she would give half to the teacher, who assisted at such performances by keeping time with small cymbals.

This system continued until seven or eight years ago, when temple dancing girls were abolished by law. Chokkalingam and his father-in-law were brought to Madras by Rukmini Devi, who, although herself a Brahman, learned to dance, and organized a dancing school at *Kalakeshetra*. He does not think, however, that the old methods of instruction can be followed now or that the same type of dancer can be produced. The pupils do not have so much time to give to training, and the traditions are not in their families.

Chokkalingam's family was attached to a temple in a village several miles from their home village of Pandanallur. To this village some members of the family went every day to participate in the *pūjās* held at the temple. Dancing by the dancing girls was involved in these *pūjās* in the form of *mudrās* (hand gestures) to the nine deities of the nine directions. In these *pūjās* the *nattuvanar* kept the time with cymbals and drums, and the *pūjāri*, or temple priest, gave the orders. Sometimes there was singing and pipes.

But the biggest performances came at the *Brahmotsavam*, or the chief annual temple festival, which comes in April and lasts for ten days. The festival begins with a hoisting of the temple flag and a propitiation of the nine gods of the directions. Once the flag is hoisted, no villager can leave the village until it is lowered at the end of the festival. During the festival the *devadāsīs* would dance for about an hour and a half each day accompanying the processions of the gods and dancing at the street corners. The *nattuvanars* assisted at these dances and also helped with the morning and evening *pūjās* each day.

The ninety-minute festival dance program was quite similar, Chokkalingam Pillai said, to the present *bhārata nāṭyam* programs, both in arrangement and in types of songs used. The songs were mostly devotional about Kṛṣṇa and the Gopis and other gods. In a dance program one of his pupils performed in 1954 in Madras, we found only one song out of ten which could not have been used at the temple festival. This was a song which praised a human being, the only type that was prohibited at the temple.

The song is given below in English translation, and immediately after, another song addressed to Śiva which was included on the same program and which would have been allowed in temple dances. The dancer does not sing these songs but acts them out with a standardized gesture language (*abhinaya*) as they are sung in Tamil or Telugu by specialized singers.

Oh my friend! I am deeply in love with Him
Take Him quickly and secretly

He Ramalinga endowed with all good qualities and a
    generous mind.
I feel the cool moonlight very hot.
Manmatha [God of Love] is tormenting me with his arrows
Do take him here at once.

This song was written by Ponniah Pillai, one of the
famous *nattuvanars* of Tanjore, and a relative of Chokkalingam's. The second song was written by Marimuttu
Pillai, a devotional singer.

Will He not come down the street
Oh! if only He could favor me with a fleeting glance
That Lord Nataraja, who burnt Manmatha and Tripura
Oh! if only He would tarry in front of my door and have
    a word with me
That I may conquer the God of Love whose arrows are
    tormenting me?
Time does not move
I have none to carry my message of love.
I am blameless:
He whose dancing feet are worshipped by Lord Brahma
    and Vishnu, the three thousand holy Brahmans of
    Chidambaram and all the celestials
Will he not come down the street and favour me with a
    fleeting glance?

Even to this prohibition there is an exception. At the
Tanjore temple, e.g., on the eighth day of the festival, a
dance drama called *Kuravanji* is performed by the dancing
girls in honor of King Serfoji. There was no *Kuravanji* at
his village, but they are also performed at other temples
in honor of the elephant-headed deity, Ganes.

For their participation in these festivals and the performance of their other temple duties, the *nattuvanar*
family usually received two or three rupees a month and
a portion of the cooked-rice offerings from the temple.
The *devadāsīs* received less than this. They could also
augment their income by taking pupils and by performing
at marriages, private parties for a "big man," and other
festivities. The structure of the dance programs was the
same on all of these occasions although the songs were
usually "lighter." Thinking that "lighter" meant secular,
I asked about these "lighter" songs. No, they too were de-

votional. Even Maharajas at their parties insisted on hearing the songs in honor of their deities. Some of the temple songs were in honor of local temple deities and could not be used outside, but in general all the songs were similar.

In the old days the village audiences knew as much as town audiences. They knew who the best dancers and teachers were and would go for miles to other villages to see them and to appreciate the science of the art. Now the audiences in the city *sabhās* and in the villages do not know very much about the art, but the audiences in the towns are beginning to learn.

The *devadāsīs* and their dancing teachers were not attached to temples exclusively. Royal courts also made claims on their time. There is a record of a troupe of Tanjore dancing girls, dancing teachers, and musicians which was in the service of the Maharaja Sayajirao III of Baroda until Baroda was merged with Bombay.[2] Two of the dancing girls, who were retired with pensions in 1941, came from *devadāsīs* families attached to the Kamakshi Temple at Tanjore, and two of the dancing teachers were grandsons of the same Tanjore dancing teacher whose granddaughter married Chokkalingam's father-in-law. The entire group had come to Baroda from Tanjore as the wedding dowry of the Tanjore princess who married the Maharaja in 1879.

At the Baroda palace the troupe was subject to the supervision of a State Department of Artists which fixed the regulations and recorded them in print. The two dancing girls were paid together 433 rupees per month, and their musicians a total of 272 rupees per month. A dearness allowance was later added. The dancers had to provide their own costumes.

Leaves and discipline were governed by strict rules. The women were given a regular monthly leave of four consecutive days and three months leave with pay when in pregnancy. All the artists had to register every Saturday at the State Department in a special book. If Saturday was a holiday, they had to go the following working day.

The dance team had to perform for the Maharaja every Wednesday and Saturday after dinner. Dance per-

[2] Moban Khobar: "Bharata Natya in Baroda," *Indian Institute of Fine Arts, Proceedings* (1954). The author is head of the Department of Dance, Maharaja Sayajira, University of Baroda.

formances also had to be given in Durbar for ceremonies
and for distinguished visitors. No performances were required when the Maharaja was away. The Superintendent
had to give the dance team at least two hours notice before
a performance. Gifts in cash and presents from the audience had to be surrendered to the Superintendent, who
divided some of it among the artists and put the rest into
the State treasury.

The dance repertoire included the standard *bhārata
nāṭyam* program (it was called the *Tanjori Nautch* at this
time) and some "light" dances at the end. The five
"light" dances, which were performed by the two dancing
girls as a team, were called the Radha Kṛṣṇa Dance, the Kite
Dance, the Scorpion Dance, the Drunkard's Dance, and
the Snake Charmer's Dance. Although these included
some of the *bhārata nāṭyam* movements and gestures,
they were, in general, more free and frivolous than the
regular *nautch* and very popular with the Court audience.
As was the custom, the ruler's name was included in some
of the dance songs. A Tanjore song in honor of Shivaji,
coming in the Varnam part of the program, was slightly
changed to honor the Maharaja of Baroda.

When the original dancing girl, Gowri, retired fifty-
two years after she was brought to the Baroda court at the
age of ten, the Maharaja had a metal statue made of her
in one of her dance poses at a cost of 50,000 rupees. This
is still in the Lakshmivilas palace in Baroda.

In 1949, when Baroda merged with Bombay, the State
Department of Artists was abolished. A dance department
was, however, organized in the M.S. University of Baroda
with the son of one of the Tanjore dancing girls as a
dancing teacher. *Bhārata nāṭyam* and *kathak* dancing are
taught and both the B.A. and M.A. degrees are awarded.

The National Academy of Song, Dance, and Drama
(Sangeet Natak Acadami) selected for the first time, in
1955, outstanding Indian artists in music, dance, and drama
for "Akadami awards." The award for the outstanding
bhārata nāṭyam dancer was presented by the President,
Rajendra Prasad, to Balasaraswati of Madras. Balasaraswati's great-great grandmother was a famous *vina* player
and her mother is a famous singer. Yet she is a transitional
figure belonging neither wholly to the family tradition of

devadāsīs nor to the modern trends which she is helping to bring in. She is the only one of four daughters who took up dancing, and that against her family's wishes. Because of the anti-*nautch* movement she did not have too many opportunities for seeing the old-style dancing during her childhood. And she was not "dedicated" to a temple. She was trained by a *devadāsī* who was once attached to the Mylapore Temple and by a *nattuvanar* from Tanjore. Her own dancing, usually to be seen at public concerts, is distinguished for its expressive *abhinaya*. Because of her artistic proficiency and because she is now considered a representative of the authentic classical tradition, the Music Academy of Madras sponsors her dancing school, where, with the help of her teacher's son, she teaches *bhārata nāṭyam* to the young girls coming from different classes and families of Madras.

Carnatic Music

The classic revival in music has had a smoother, if less spectacular, course than in dance. Music has not been so closely associated with the controversial dancing girls. Although many famous musicians have come from the *devadāsī* community, this is an art which Brahmans and other castes have also cultivated for a long time. Technical development in music has a long continuous history in the South, and has reached greater specialization and refinement than the dance. Technical virtuosity with instruments like the *vīṇā* (a kind of lute), the *flute,* the *mṛdaṅgam* (South Indian drum) and the *nāgasvara* (or long pipe) has been so highly developed that it is not at all uncommon to hear musical concerts devoted exclusively to performances on these instruments. Vocal music is similarly highly developed, and the large number of "modes" (*rāgas*) gives the individual singer, who is as often a female as a male, great opportunity for virtuosity. While some of these instruments still have a ritual use, particularly the long pipe and the drum, which are played at weddings and other functions to frighten away evil spirits, their purely musical development began very early. The ancient Tamil epic of the second century A.D., *The Lay of the Anklet,* mentions four kinds of *vīṇā*, five kinds of flute, thirty-one kinds of percussion instruments, and lays down the technical qualifications for a singer, male and female, a drummer, a flutist, and *vīṇā* player. There are other discussions on music, and the system is based as it is today on melody and rhythm and a basic scale of seven notes.[3]

Many features of this southern musical system are also described in the Sanskrit treatises, in the *Nāṭya Śāstra* of Bhārata, where it is directly derived from Vedic chanting, and in later treatises like the *Saṅgīta Ratnākāra* of Śārṇgadeva in the thirteenth century. From the sixteenth century, when the Carnatic composer saint Purandara Dās flourished, southern, "Carnatic Music," developed in distinction from northern, or "Hindustani music." The present classical form of the Carnatic system is usually attributed to three Tanjore composers, all Brahmans, of the early nineteenth century: Tyāgarāja, a Telugu living near Tanjore, Mathusvāmī Dīkṣitar, and Śyāma Śāstri, both Tamils. They are often referred to as occupying the same position in the recent history of classical southern music as is occupied in the nineteenth century by the "Tanjore quartet" of dancing teachers. After them, musical development is seen in decline because of an overemphasis on rhythm, a failure to co-ordinate theory and practice, loss of princely and patrician patronage, and weakening of the gurukal system of training. The revival aims at restoring the Carnatic classical tradition to its historic path.

The distinction between "classical" and "folk" music is frequently invoked by music critics who regard it as equivalent to the ancient Sanskrit contrast between *mārga* and *deśī* respectively. In a recent paper on "Popular Music and Classical Music" [4] V. Raghavan of Madras University undertakes a systematic definition of the folk-classical distinction as it applies to music, and also traces some of the historical interaction of the two types. He includes in "popular music" folk music as well as popularized classical and "light" music. The main difference between "popular" and "classical" he finds in the rendering: "when the rendering is sophisticated, it is art or classical music; when it is plain and simple, it is the popular or folk variety." Sophis-

---

[3] The *Śilapparikāram*, translated with notes by V. R. Ramachandra Dikshitar (Oxford; 1939), pp. 57–62.

[4] Presented at the Symposium held by the Bharatiya Kala Kendra, Delhi (February 5–7, 1956).

tication depends on rules and principles into which an art is codified and systematized. Just as "to evolve a principle and to conduct oneself in conformity to it is the mark of culture," so it is in art where the standard of judgment is based on "artistic criteria" that have evolved. This is what connoisseurs care for and enjoy, whereas the layman likes other things. "That is art-music in which artistic considerations alone prevail; the moment one sings down to the populace, one relaxes the high austerity of his art."

Folk or popular music, then, Raghavan finds, is not bound by strict rules and principles and is characterized by features likely to appeal to popular tastes: simple rendering; accentuated and obvious rhythm; group singing; stereotyped, monotonous form; emphasis on words; basis in a festival, a season or an event; emotional and dramatic tone.

These elements are present in art music but must be "duly proportioned" and made subservient to "expression." Melody (*rāga*), rhythm (*tāla*), and idea and feeling (*bhāva*) must be "evenly integrated" into a "fine synthesis."

Even the classical pieces of the great musicians who have been mostly saints and teachers are often overloaded with thought and words, and "when they are rendered as vehicles of teaching or as a means of devotional transport, they depart from the concert and take the turn towards *harikathā* and *bhajan.*"

Art music should evoke its *rasa* (mood) by the actual music and not by importing extraneous elements. "To evoke Rasa with the words alone is to surrender music to poetry; to evoke it through overloading one's rendering with pure feeling is to surrender it to drama; to evoke it by pure music is really pure music, and the Rasa which this pure music evokes leaves far behind that realm in which the mundane sentiments of Śṛiṅgāra (love), Vīra (heroism), etc. have their meaning; it is that ineffable bliss in which one gets absorbed as in Samādhi (Yogic concentration). Thus does *Nāda* (sound) become the nearest portal to the *Brahman* (world spirit)."

Raghavan's summarizing characterization of "art music" is that it is music in which "the canons and requirements of art, the rules of balance, harmony, proportion, propriety, concentration on pure artistic resources to the exclusion of adventitious circumstances are to hold sway or absolute sway." To dilute these strict standards and to make concessions in any direction to please a lay audience is to make the music popular, "or if it is purposely done for subserving another art or other purpose it is applied music."

In this same paper Raghavan describes how "folk" and "classical" have interacted on each other. This is a further development of the view which he has stated more comprehensively elsewhere that the historic formation of the major Indian cultural tradition has involved a two-way give-and-take interaction with local and regional traditions. "Almost always, the major cultural tradition spreads out and consolidates itself over new regions by absorbing, incorporating within itself and adjusting to its own scheme such of the local elements as are valuable and attractive. So do all major traditions become national cultures, of significance to every region and group of people." [5]

This give-and-take cultural process is particularly clear in music and dance, although it may also be traced in language, social organization, and in other departments of human activity. Many of the musical "scales" (rāgas) have regional and tribal names and probably represent sophistications of tribal melodies. The association of the Rāja-mātaṅgī rāga with the vīṇā as the goddess of music may be connected, he suggests, with a tribe called Mātaṅgas who were once numerous and artistically endowed but later were degraded socially as Cāṇḍālas and untouchables. Numerous musical technical terms, names of instruments, of varieties of voice, are still in the local language of western India and reflect the movements of the cultural tradition across India. Deśī terminology not only occurs in the classical music, but the treatises stipulate that a musician is not entitled to the foremost status of Gandharva unless he is proficient in both the mārga and the deśī styles.

In the classical dance, too, there are deśī strands. The treatises on music and dance include descriptions of local and folk dances. Jayasenāpati's Nṛttarattnāvalī devotes its last three chapters to the varieties of folk dances. Someśvara, the author of another treatise, "was captivated by the

[5] V. Raghavan: "Variety and Integration in the Pattern of Indian Culture," Far Eastern Quarterly, Vol. xv, No. 4 (Aug. 1956).

dance of the hunters, the *Goṇḍalīs*, and systematized it in a set scheme and described it in his work from which it passed into the regular repertoire of dancers elsewhere also."

Raghavan finds these folk influences beneficial; they contribute "a frequent invigoration and enrichment of the main tradition by local forms which are fitted into the basic technique and higher ideology of the classical tradition. The *deśī* supplied the material, the *mārga* refined it and assigned it to a place and wove it into the larger and richer scheme. The popular and the classical were the two currents, so as to say, of the energy of our culture. Our art and culture thus soared forth like the image of Pārvatī and Śiva in one, the Ardhanārīśvara, a synthesis of the two into an inseparable unity."

Summary and Implications for a Theory of Culture Change: Little and Great Traditions in Village and City

A cultural tradition needs to be conceived both culturally as a cultural structure and societally as a social organization. Looked at as a structure of culture content, it is made up of sequences of cultural performances combining various cultural media, verbal and nonverbal, performed at cultural centers by professional and semiprofessional performers. These performances, media, centers, and performers have each of them a complex and differentiated structure of their own. It is possible to place each of these structures along a two-dimensional line of variation between two poles—an uncultivated Little Tradition of folk culture at one end, and a cultivated and learned Great Tradition at the other. The line, however, is a continuum, and there seems to be constant interaction between the extremes, whether one looks at performances, texts and media, cultural centers, or cultural performers. In India the Great Tradition is still closely tied to a sacred culture, so that the performances are frequently religious rites and ceremonies, the centers are temples and shrines, performers are priests and spiritual teachers, and the media are linked to a canon of sacred scripture and myth. Little and Great Traditions are not neatly differentiated along a village-urban axis. Both kinds of tradition are found in villages and in the city in different forms. Folk and ritual kinds of performances survive in fragments in the city, but they are very old forms and are common in villages and towns. The popular devotional and the classical forms are essentially urban developments of the last hundred years, although they have more ancient precedents. The modern urban forms are the most recent of all, and are essentially urban in origin. These different kinds of performances are but points on a single continuum when we compare their media, performers, language, place and occasion of performance, and themes. In such folk forms as the folk play, folksongs, folk dances, and ballads, the performers are generally non-Brahman men in the case of the plays and ballads, women in the case of dances and songs. There is some hereditary cultivation of skill within certain families, particularly in ballad making, but in general the performers are amateurs who "pick it up" or are trained by some teacher. The language of the folk forms is usually a regional dialect of Tamil or Telugu and is rarely written or printed. Non-Brahman village temples have been the place for the performance of the folk plays on the occasion of seasonal festivals, while the songs, dances, and ballads may be performed at almost any place and time. The audiences at these performances are generally members of the non-Brahman community. Puranic themes are mixed with themes from local legend and history and from the commonplaces of daily life. These folk performances are close to the little traditional pole of cultural performances, but not completely cut off from great traditional influences.

At the opposite pole, but still found in villages as well as in towns, are the ritual kinds of performances, the life-cycle rites and ceremonies, temple festivals, chanting and recitation of scriptures, and until about 1947, temple dances and religious dance dramas. These belong to the sacred sphere of the culture and are closely associated with Brahman priests and *paṇḍits* as performers, teachers, and patrons. The performers are men, except for the community of temple dancers, and belong to families who have cultivated the special media for many generations. The verbal texts used are generally Vedic and classical Sanskrit and have been transmitted through an oral tradition, although books are used as aids to memory. In some Vaiṣnavite and Saivite rites, Tamil hymns and scriptures have been incorporated into the ceremonies. The themes are mainly Vedic and puranic. Some ritual performances differ in one other respect from other kinds of cultural performance: the daily rites performed by householder or temple priest do not require an audience; they are addressed only to a deity.

The popular devotional and classical types of cultural performances which have developed in an urban environment differ from the village forms in a number of important respects. The duration of the performance is much shorter in the city; a puranic recitation usually lasted from six months to a year in the village; in the city it has been condensed into seven- or fifteen-day sequences. The devotional films and plays, as well as the *harikathā* performance, do not exceed three or four hours, whereas a village folk play or temple festival play went on through the night, and at the major festivals for ten days. The performers at these urban performances are nonhereditary professionals who have usually been trained in modern schools. They come from all communities, Brahman and non-Brahman, and include women as well as men. Since the place of performance is a public hall or theater and the occasion is the performance itself, there are no caste or sectarian restrictions on the audience. The language of the popular devotional performances is predominantly the urban colloquial vernacular of the region, with some verbal texts in Sanskrit and other Indian languages, used by the more erudite performers in *harikathā*, in classical concerts, and of course in Sanskrit plays. Stories from the epics and *purāṇas* and from the lives of the regional saints continue to provide thematic material for the urban forms, but these are increasingly mixed with secular and political themes.

The greatest transcendence of local folk and ritual forms is reached in the strictly modern urban forms—the social play, the social film, the short story, and the novel. In these the language is predominantly a regional vernacular or English, and the themes are the social, economic, and political problems of the day. The language and the distinctive cultural content of some of these problems—intermarriage of castes, the plight of the villager, a foreign-trained graduate's qualms about an arranged marriage

—add a distinctive flavor to this younger branch of a world-wide urban culture.

Two Rhythms in Culture Change

The differentiation of folk, ritual, popular devotional, classical, and modern urban cultural performances in relation to urbanization suggests the operation of more general processes of culture change operating in different spheres of culture. The differentiation between classical (*mārga*) and folk (*deśī*) in art styles is paralleled, as Raghavan has pointed out, in the field of language by the differentiation between *Samskṛta* (perfected, refined, civilized) and *prākṛta* (unrefined, vernacular), and in the field of social customs by the distinction between customs sanctioned either by *śruti* (revealed scripture) and *smṛti* (remembered scripture), or customs sanctioned by local usages (*deśācāras*) and family usage (*kuladharmas*).[6]

Each sphere of culture seems to be subject to opposing directions of change, one type of change tending to push a given cultural sphere in the direction of greater refinement and strict codification, the other in the direction of maximum popularity and practicality. At any given time, the outcome within a given cultural sphere is something of a compromise between the two extremes, a range of intergrading cultural forms. The prevalence of the refining tendencies sustained in several departments of culture over a long period will result in a level of aesthetic and intellectual achievement deservedly called a Great Tradition.

The question now arises as to whether the operation of these opposing rhythms of change within differing spheres of culture is merely formal and structural or whether there is some direct and organic relationship among changes in the different spheres. And is there, in particular, a distinctive pattern of change which a great tradition undergoes in a metropolitan environment? Perhaps a process of secularization?

Culturally, the effect of urbanization, so far as the Madras case is concerned, has been to shift attention and activity away from ritual observances and sacred learning

[6] Raghavan: "Popular and Classical Music," *Journal of the Music Academy*, Vol. XXVIII.

and to the fields of popular culture and the arts. This shift carries with it a shift in values from those predominantly connected with religious merit to those of mass entertainment and aesthetics. There are also associated changes from cultural media to mass media and from sacred centers and occasions of performance to cultural centers and secular occasions. Movie actors and concert artists compete with priests and *paṇḍits* as performers. "First nights" succeed "first fruits."

It would be inaccurate, however, to apply the Western concepts of secular urban mass culture and of "art for art's sake" in interpreting these changes. There are, indeed, secularizing tendencies, but they have not yet cut off urban culture from the traditional matrix of sacred culture. There is no sharp dividing line between religion and culture, and the traditional cultural media not only continue to survive in the city but have also been incorporated in novel ways into an emerging popular and classical culture. Much of the urban popular culture is seen as an extension of the path of devotion (*bhakti-mārga*), more easily accessible to modern man than the paths of strict ritual observance (*karma-mārga*) or the path of sacred knowledge (*jñāna-mārga*). The classical arts, as well, are viewed as offering a special path and discipline for those able to cultivate it that is akin to yogic concentration.

Nor are these religious interpretations of popular and classical culture limited to the verbalizations of religious leaders. They are interpretations which are borne out by the many continuities in themes, media, audience reaction which link the urban culture to the traditional sacred culture. The films and other mass media, e.g., although disposed by technical and economic organization to cater to a mass market without respect to caste, creed, or language, have nevertheless found it profitable to draw on the old mythological and devotional themes and to adapt freely the media of folk and classical culture. The newer political themes introduced with the struggle for independence, and now with economic development, are also effectively communicated when joined to the traditional themes and media. The effect of the mass media, in other words, has not so much secularized the sacred traditional culture as it has democratized it.

In the revival of classical South Indian dancing and music, the strands connecting these arts with the sacred culture are evident. The revival, to be sure, has its creative aspects, particularly in having introduced new classes of people as teachers, performers, audience. It also tends to make the concert stage and the social recital, rather than the wedding of the temple procession, the normative cultural forum for the performance of these arts. It is still the hereditary teachers and performers, however, or those directly trained under them, who are in greatest demand and have the highest prestige. And a program of authentic classical dancing or music is still pretty much what it was when part of a ritual calendar. The *pūjās* of invocation, the devotional songs, the hand gestures (or *mudrās*), many of the dance movements, and the musical instruments used for village festivals fifty to 100 years ago are now used by modern artists in city concerts. In judging these performances, the critics and connoisseurs will apply standards of technical virtuosity and aesthetic refinement, but they take for granted the puranic themes and also judge whether the performance is a "worthy offering to the deity."

Many of these very same media, or elements of them, enter into the performances of more popular culture—puranic recitations, devotional plays, *bhajans*—since the difference between popular and classical culture rests, not on a sharp difference in kind of media or theme, but depends rather on the degree of sophistication, technical refinement, and balance between aesthetic, devotional, and entertainment values which characterize the performance.

The continuum implied here of media and themes extends right into the sphere of ritual observance. The *pūjās* and *mudrās* of the temple and domestic priests are clearly similar to the *pūjās* performed in *bhajans*, devotional plays and films, and in classical dancing. And it is not too far-fetched to suggest that the modern classicists' doctrine of pure music with its insistence on preserving fixed rules of art and its de-emphasis of the meaning of the words may be analogous to the ritual necessities of Vedic chanting. In the Sāma Veda chanting, e.g., there is a highly developed technique of vocal and instrumental music with specialized singers and instrumentalists. The singing was part of mystic sacrifices and highly esoteric. The Sāman singers are still reluctant to disclose their special techniques. The verses of the *Rig-veda* furnish the libretto for this singing, but there are also many syllables without particular meaning (*stobhas*) which are used as aids in the singing. The mystic efficacy of the singing depends on the correct enunciation of the sounds, and it thus became all-important to repeat the sounds each time without any change.[7]

Classicism in art may be a sublimation, if not an actual derivation, of ritual singing and dancing. And popular mass culture, to which it is opposed, is itself an extension of the devotional reaction to ritualism. The dialectic of the two rhythms of culture change continues on a new plane with some new, some old, media and themes.

The new plane on which this dialectic of cultural rhythms is operating is an urban one. Although several of the older ritual and village folk forms survive in the urban environment of Madras, the distinctive cultural developments in the city have been the revival and modernization of classical forms and the creation of popular devotional forms in each of the major media—literature, puranic recitation, drama, music, and dance.

These classical and devotional forms are not without ancient precedents, but their immediate and contemporary sources are urbanized ritual forms and urbanized folk forms. Urbanization has adapted the traditional forms to create modern versions of class and mass culture. It is also beginning to produce a form of urban culture that derives neither from the sacred culture or from the local folk culture. This is either an importation from another urbanized culture—as in the novel, the social play, the symphony—or represents a creative synthesis of indigenous and foreign sources.

A Profile of Urbanized Literati

To this point the discussion has been primarily cultural, basing itself on a comparative analysis of cultural performances. Can such a method throw any light on the sociological question raised at the outset: are the Brahman literati turning into intelligentsia in the urban environ-

[7] Raghavan: "An Outline Literary History of Indian Music," *Journal of the Music Academy*, Vol. xxiii (Madras; 1952), pp. 64–74. For a musical analysis of the Sāma Veda in relation to classical Indian music, see Strangways: *The Music of Hindustan*.

ment? The results of the cultural analysis suggest one natural inference, that urbanization differentiates the literati into social types corresponding to the cultural types of performances. There would then be ritualists who follow the path of ritual observances (e.g., domestic and temple priests, and strictly orthodox householders); sages who follow the path of sacred knowledge (e.g., *paṇḍits*, yogis, swamis); popularizers who follow the path of popular devotionalism (e.g., the puranic reciters, *bhajan* leaders, dramatists); and classicists who follow the disciplines of the classical arts. All of these are literati in the sense that they seek through their activities to continue the Great Tradition. But the last two types, the popularizers and the classicists, represent new urban types who seek to restore, revive, or adapt elements of traditional culture under modern urban conditions. The ritualists and the sages are old literati types who are found in a metropolitan center but do not feel at home in it.

On this scheme of classification only the modernists, who seek to introduce modern and western cultural forms even where they conflict with the traditional culture, would be classed as intelligentsia. These are the novelists, short-story writers, playwrights of modern plays, producers of films, artists and composers in Western music, scientists.

The folk performer (bard, reciter actor) is a proto-*literatus* who cultivates the cultural forms of the Little Tradition. In India, however, where little, great, and urban traditions interact so freely, he also performs some of the functions of the literati and of the intelligentsia, bringing the local traditions into the culture of the city and taking the city's cultural products back to the countryside.

This typology of intellectual types suggested by a typology of cultural performances deserves to be checked against direct sociological studies of the groups concerned. Such studies, I think, will find a good deal of overlap among the different types because there is a continuity of social types, as there is of cultural forms. The modernist film producer who attends *bhajans* regularly is not an unusual person, and the new literati are also responsible for introducing some novel forms within the frame of traditionalizing change.

Rather than scan the cultural data for additional indications of social typology, I should prefer, in these closing pages, to sketch a composite profile of the urbanized Brahman literati in Madras city.

Madras city would not appear to be a very good place to study the Great Tradition of Indian culture. It is a large metropolitan center and a major cultural, political, and commercial center of South India. Nevertheless, it presents an unusually good situation in which to trace the heterogenetic transformation of a great tradition that results from secondary urbanization, because the leading professional representatives of that tradition, the Brahmans, and the non-Brahman merchant patrons, have been closely associated with the city from its very beginnings in 1640. They have come to the city from adjoining villages and towns to help build up its educational, cultural, administrative, and economic services and themselves to take advantage of these services. For these tasks they were particularly well qualified by their relatively high literacy, linguistic abilities, and long association with learning and literary activities. As they exercised these abilities within an expanding urban center and passed through the modern educational system into modern professions, they came to perform in increasing numbers the role of intelligentsia, or agents of culture change, and less and less that of traditional literati. That is to say, they found in their new preoccupations less time for the cultivation of Sanskrit learning and the performance of the scripturally prescribed ritual observances, the two activities for which as Brahmans they have had an ancient and professional responsibility. They have not, however, completely abandoned these activities, and to some extent they have developed compensatory activities which have kept them from becoming completely de-Sanskritized and cut off from traditional culture.

They continue, e.g., to make pilgrimages to Banaras and the Ganges as well as to many of the shrine centers in South India, albeit with modern means of transportation and new motives of patriotic and cultural sight-seeing added to the old religious ones. They employ family priests (*purohitas*) to help them conduct domestic rites, and those who can afford it are very lavish on the occasion of a sacred thread or wedding ceremony in observance and expenditure. They go to the temple for the big festivals several times a year and visit their *jagadguru* and their *maṭh* at least once a year. Legislative restrictions against these sacred institutions are actively resisted, and organizations to finance ritual activities and to promote Vedic learning have been formed by them. While they deplore the passing of the old *gurukula* system of education and the decline in the number of sastric *paṇḍits*, they are interested in keeping Sanskrit learning alive and support moves to incorporate more of it into high schools, colleges, and universities. Their ritual status as Brahmans may have been somewhat lowered through increasing violations of some of the pollution taboos, and a generally more careless attitude toward them, but the taboos against intercaste marriages are still very strong, and pollution from death or birth in the family and from many other sources is still carefully expiated.

Above all, these urban Brahmans have taken an increasing interest in popular religious culture, traditionally designed for the lower castes, women and children. They form *bhajan* groups, listen to recitations of the hymns of Tamil saints, organize and attend puranic recitations, devotional plays, and movies, and discourses in English or Tamil on the Upaniṣads delivered by non-Brahmans, contrary to sastric sanction. These cultural performances are increasingly held at public halls and theaters rather than in temples or at domestic ceremonies and are open to all without respect to caste or sect. They are considered an extension of the devotional form of religion of the older *bhakti* cults and sects to a democratic mass culture. Brahmans not only make up part of the audience, but are also some of the leading performers, producers, directors, and writers for these programs.

A relatively small group among the more educated and sophisticated Brahmans (and non-Brahmans, too) have kept aloof from these mass religious cultural activities. To their taste, these activities are too emotional, unrefined, and unauthentic. They are classicists, and insist on greater fidelity to the ancient Sanskrit texts in readings and recitations, and on the predominance of purely artistic values (as articulated in the ancient *śāstras* and exemplified in temple sculpture and cultivated by hereditary performers) over the values of popular entertainment or even religious devotion. This group is responsible, both as leading critics and as an audience of connoisseurs, for the revival of classical South Indian dancing and music. The revival, as some of the more percipient classicists have observed, is not entirely backward-looking. It contains creative innovations linking it to the modern urban scene and to its popular culture. These include a change in the methods of instruction from the apprentice system to the modern school, a change from hereditary families of teachers and of performers to nonhereditary teachers and pupils drawn from all quarters, including the most respectable families, and the substitution of the social accomplishment or a commercial career for a ritually defined role. Some of the classicists deplore these innovations and call for a total restoration of the traditional pattern—temple dancing, the apprentice method of teaching, a practically hereditary professionalization of performers and teachers. Others are content to seek a wider hearing for classical culture in the mass media and to raise the levels of popular taste. Most of them look upon their classicism not as a secular doctrine of "art for art's sake" but as offering a distinctive path of release and religious salvation, akin to yogic concentration, to the sophisticated and cultivated individual.

There is a kind of built-in flexibility within the orthodox Vedānta position which permits an easy incorporation of a wide variety of changes. The *paṇḍits* who are called upon to decide difficult cases say they follow a fixed hierarchy of authorities and standards in their deliberations and decisions. At the top of the hierarchy are the revealed scriptures (the *śruti*, including the Vedas and Upaniṣads). Next come the remembered scriptures (the *smṛti*), including the treatises on religious law, the epics and *purāṇas*, and the auxiliary sciences. In case of a conflict among scriptures, the opinion of a wise man should be consulted. Local customs and usages, and individual conscience, finally, may be followed if the scriptures are not available.

This hierarchy gives the wise man—the *paṇḍit*, the guru, the head of the *maṭh*—a comfortable scope for interpretation and reconciliation of scriptural sanctions. He quite freely invokes considerations of logic, experience, the convenience or inconvenience of a particular circumstance, and local usages in coming to his decision. In this process the wise men and particularly the learned literati are an institutionalized agency for changing tradition, so long as they regard the change as primarily preservative of the tradition's essentials.

The long-run result of this process has been consolidative and selective. Some elements of language, learning, and the arts, as well as of ritual custom, drop out (e.g., Vedic sacrifice); new ones are added (e.g., temples and monastic organizations). Aspects of heterodox sectarian movements and of tribal and regional custom are assimilated to orthodoxy. Fragments of little traditions have been absorbed into the Great Tradition, and the culture of the villages and tribes has, in the long run, also been responsive to the authoritative teachings of literati. And just as a large and famous temple will contain numerous shrines to stones, snakes, trees, and the planets, as well as to the pantheon of major deities, so a learned and sophisticated Brahman will make offerings to these shrines and follow many local and family usages, as well as adhere to a very abstract *advaita* philosophy. As one of them said, describing just this kind of situation: "I suppose I am a museum."

Some limits are recognized, however, to what can be assimilated by the orthodox tradition. The anti-Brahman, anti-Sanskrit, anti-Hindu movement now popular with some Tamil groups is certainly looked upon as an attack against the essentials of Hinduism. And the weakening of the caste system, particularly as a ritual structure, is viewed in the same light by the more orthodox. Svāmī Śaṅkarā-cārya, the most authoritative spokesman for Madrasi Smārtas, thinks that what is distinctive and essential in the nature of Hinduism is the caste system considered as a set of hereditary family disciplines. If these decline, he thinks Hinduism will not be very different from other religions, many of which have similar systems of ethics, theology, and philosophy, but lack the hereditary sociological foundation for them. The Brahman community, he believes, has become lax, for one reason and another, in the observance of these disciplines of diet, marriage, social intercourse, ritual observance, and sacred learning. He is inclined himself to appeal to devout non-Brahmans to preserve the essentials of Hinduism in these difficult times, since the Śāstras make less severe demands on them and they are able to conform.

Even in the face of this uncertain future, the Svāmī and his Brahman followers remain detached and resilient. Their long-run cosmic perspective gives them a hopeful serenity in the face of disturbing changes. Discussing the recent restrictive legislation against temples and *maṭhs*, one of these Brahmans said cheerfully: "Well, many of these temples and maths are only seven hundred or eight hundred years old. They have been destroyed before and revived. New values must be admitted. Life will grow, if old values are not destroyed. Life is one huge, infinite ocean in movement."

McKim Marriott

McKim Marriott (1924–   ) began the study of cultural anthropology and linguistics at Harvard College under the tutorial guidance of Clyde Kluckhohn. During World War II he joined the United States Signal Corps, and in 1945 he was stationed in New Delhi. Fascinated by India, Marriott decided to devote himself to the study of Indian civilization.

Taking up graduate training in anthropology in 1946, Marriott attended the University of Chicago, where his leading teachers were W. Lloyd Warner, Fred Eggan, and Robert Redfield. He also prepared for field research in India by studying Sanskrit, Hindi, Indian history, and philosophy. In 1950–2 he returned to India for his first intensive field work. His research was designed to examine the way in which the political and social changes consequent upon India's emergence as a self-governing nation influenced the life of a single village. The essay reprinted in the following pages is based upon that research. In this essay Marriott describes the local culture of the village of Kishan Garhi as evolving within the broad context of India's history. In other publications he has examined immediate practical problems of agricultural technology, health, and political organization. A major additional aspect of his work in Kishan Garhi has been a fresh approach to the nature of the Hindu caste system, and at present he is preparing a book on kinship and caste in this community.

Not far from Kishan Garhi is Etawah, the cradle of India's vast projects for rural agricultural development. *Pilot Project, India,* edited by Marriott and Richard L.

Park, tells the story in the words of Albert Mayer and other pioneers of that development.

In 1956–7 McKim Marriott undertook a second and quite new sort of anthropological field research. He settled in the city of Wai, a center of learning and place of pilgrimage in the Marathi-speaking region of southern India. In close touch with Robert Redfield and Milton Singer, he there planned a wholistic study of a natural segment of Indian civilization in its full complexity. He is now developing much further the ideas opened up in the following essay, looking upon the civilization of India as a network of communication channels.

McKim Marriott is now Associate Professor in the Department of Anthropology and in the College of the University of Chicago.

❦ ❦ 4 ❦ ❦

Little Communities

in an Indigenous

Civilization[*][1]

by

McKIM MARRIOTT

If we would describe the small world of a village within the universe of Indian civilization, we must at some time consider two related questions of method: (1) can such a village be satisfactorily comprehended and conceived as a whole in itself, and (2) can understanding of one such village contribute to understanding of the greater culture and society in which the village is imbedded (Redfield and Singer 1954a)? In this paper I undertake to answer both

[*] Permission to reprint the following essay in abridged form has been granted by Milton Singer and the Department of Anthropology of the University of Chicago. Reprinted from VILLAGE INDIA: STUDIES IN THE LITTLE COMMUNITY, edited by McKim Marriott, by permission of The University of Chicago Press. Copyright 1955 by Robert Redfield. All rights reserved. Published 1955. Third Impression 1958.

[1] This paper is based on field work in Aligarh District, U.P., from December 1950 to April 1952, and in the village here called Kishan Garhi from March 1951 to April 1952. Field work was supported through an Area Research Training Fellowship granted by the Social Science Research Council. Writing was made possible by the Indian Village Studies Project, Institute of East Asiatic Studies, University of California, Berkeley.

For their useful comments on this paper I am grateful to Dr. Alan R. Beals, Dr. E. Kathleen Gough, Professor Oscar Lewis, Professor David G. Mandelbaum, Mr. Jack M. Planalp, Professor Robert Redfield, and Mrs. Gitel P. Steed.

questions of method by describing some ways in which the village of Kishan Garhi (*Kiṣan Gaṛhī*) in Uttar Pradesh is articulated with the Indian universe: first, through certain aspects of its social structure; and, second, through parts of its religious culture.

¶ SOCIAL STRUCTURE

Kishan Garhi is an old Hindu village in an old cradle of Hindu civilization. Its ancient mound rises above the western plains of Uttar Pradesh in Aligarh District, between the Ganges and Jumna rivers, 100 miles southeast of Delhi. Landlords of *Jāṭ* caste live in the crumbling mud fortress which tops the village mound, while the houses of farmers and specialists of twenty-three other castes huddle on the slopes below. Brahmans are the most numerous in the population of 857 persons. As tenants, farmers of Brahman caste in 1952 possessed about one half of the village lands. Kishan Garhi is off the beaten track and far enough from newer urban influences for its people to feel conservative about much of their old culture.

Kishan Garhi as Not an Isolated Whole

First I consider how Kishan Garhi is *not* a world in itself by examining the outlines of its economy, its patterns of kinship and marriage, the social organization of its religion, and its political structure. In each of these aspects Kishan Garhi's society is cut deeply by internal divisions, and in each it also reaches out to form part of a wider system of relationships.

In Kishan Garhi there are internal divisions of economic interest among groups of landlords, tenants, share croppers, laborers, artisans, domestic servants, and shopkeepers. There are many external economic relationships, too. About one third of the village crops, measuring them by their cash value, are sold every year outside the village. Approximately three quarters of the 300-odd animals now in Kishan Garhi were brought there from outside, just as were many other essentials, such as clothing. One third of the credit which finances agriculture in the village was obtained from outside sources. The Brahman priests,

Barbers, Potters, Carpenters, Watermen, and Sweepers who live in Kishan Garhi go out to serve hereditary patrons in some fifteen other villages and derive about one half of their income from those outside patrons. Traders who live in Kishan Garhi regularly range over many miles of the countryside on their trading trips. Wage workers who maintain homes in Kishan Garhi during the present generation have gone out to work in at least twenty-five other places, including ten cities. During one period of three months I counted forty-four different specialists coming into Kishan Garhi from outside to provide goods and services; probably there were many more whom I did not count.

Internal divisions are apparent within Kishan Garhi's society also in matters of marriage and kinship. At least twenty-four caste groups are represented locally; each caste is perfectly exclusive in marriage. There are forty-six local lineage groups in Kishan Garhi, each wholly separate from every other in descent. There is no marriage inside the village within or among any of these groups. Daughters of the village move out and wives of the village move in at marriage, moving to and from more than 300 other villages. Fifty-seven marriages currently connect Kishan Garhi with sixteen towns and cities. Half of the marriage ties of groups in Kishan Garhi connect them with places more than fourteen miles away, while 5 per cent connect them with places more than forty miles distant.

Social relationships concerned with religion in Kishan Garhi are fragmented to an extreme point. There is no temple of the whole village, no one cremation ground, no sacred tank or well. Instead, dozens of different trees and stones and tiny shrines are made objects of worship separately by members of the many caste and lineage groups. Four different priests divide the eligible families among them for domestic services; no priest serves families of the eight low and lowest castes. Most festivals are observed separately by each family, when particular family tradition does not forbid observance. Different families and sometimes even different individuals of the same family give their allegiance to many different religious preceptors and shrines outside the village. In the course of a few weeks of conversations, I found that I had recorded the names of more than fifty distant places to which villagers of Kishan Garhi had gone on pilgrimage.

Politically, also, Kishan Garhi is noncommunal and disunified in some obvious ways. Within the village there are factions whose members fight on the average a new court case each month. Usually there are three cases in progress at any one time, and many people become involved. Persons of other villages are frequently interested and involved in local disputes. And the organs of government—the bureaucracies of the police, the revenue system, etc.—are intimately intrusive within the village of Kishan Garhi.

These structural facts make Kishan Garhi seem very much less than an isolated whole in the primitive sense. Viewed as a society, as an economy, as a church, or as a polity, this little community has no close coherence or well-bounded physical locus. The very things which I must identify as parts of the little community reach beyond the physical village, while many parts of other communities and of the great community reach inside the village. This little community of Kishan Garhi cannot be very satisfactorily conceived of as an isolated structure or system.

Kishan Garhi as Isolable

But still I am compelled to go on to say that the village of Kishan Garhi is like a living thing, has a definable structure, is conceptually a vivid entity, is a system—even if it is one of many subsystems within the larger socio-politico-religio-economic system in which it exists. Especially am I so compelled if I look at the concerns and emphases that the people of the village express, and if I try to evaluate the structural aspects of their lives as they evaluate them.

Economically, for instance, the village constitutes a vital nucleus of activity through its lands. Nine out of ten persons, despite their nominal caste specializations, depend in part directly upon the land for a living. Ninety-five per cent of the land on which they depend is contained within the village area.

Socially, the village of Kishan Garhi is a nexus of much informal activity among nonkinsmen and noncastemen.

People come together casually, and sometimes convivially, because they are neighbors in their fields or houses, or because they use the same wells and adjacent threshing places. People of Kishan Garhi visit separately outside the village with their own respective relatives by marriage whenever they are called to a feast of birth, marriage, or death. But people of Kishan Garhi attend four times as many ceremonies and feasts inside the village, often with nonkinsmen, as they attend outside the village with relatives. Domestic ceremonies in all families above those of the lowest castes require that representatives of many other local caste groups and lineage groups participate.

Marriage ties outside the village are strong and compelling. But the quality of social relations that obtain among relatives by marriage is rarely one of much friendliness, or even reciprocity. Marital relationships are formally one-sided and unbalanced: the boy's side is the high and demanding side, while the girl's side is the low and giving side. At the wedding ceremony the groom proceeds to the bride's distant village in a procession of military style with as many guns and horses as he can muster. The groom's men demand and receive formal hospitality as their due by formal contract. When they ultimately carry off the bride to their own village, she weeps, clutches her brothers, and screams that she is dead.

To illustrate the quality of relations between marital relatives after the wedding, an anecdote which I heard told for entertainment at one wedding will serve. Villagers thought that this story was terribly funny, and it did touch on some sensitive points in their extralocal social organization.

A man comes to a village one evening and asks to be directed to the house from which a girl has been married out to a boy of Rampur village, a place twelve miles away. He is directed to that house, and there he demands the hookah to smoke. The girl's father, who of course cannot visit his daughter in her village of marriage, says to himself: "This must be someone from my daughter's father-in-law's house." He gives his hookah to the stranger and asks solicitously: "How is Ram Lal, my son-in-law?"

But the stranger just smokes and says: "Bring food!" He washes and sits on a cot. The girl's mother prepares a fine meal, and the girl's father brings it to the stranger on a brass tray. After the stranger has eaten, they ask him again: "Now tell us about our relatives. How are Ram Lal and his brothers?"

But the stranger just says: "I'll sleep now," and he goes to sleep. In the morning, as the stranger is ready to leave, the girl's father presses him hard, begging for news. "Say! How is everyone there in Rampur in your house?"

"My house in Rampur?" asks the stranger as he leaves. "How should I know? I'm from another village!"

This story makes two points about the supralocal organization of marriage. (1) A stranger may pass himself off as a relative by marriage. Relations between marital relatives are generally formal and distant, are sometimes even hostile, and may remain so throughout life. (2) To persons of the outside world a villager's primary identification must be with his own village. Hence the absurd twist of the story depends on the fact that the stranger had not been properly identified as a man of Rampur village before he was granted hospitality.

The first inquiry which is customarily made of anyone who is away from his home is: "What is your village, sir?"—not "What is your caste, clan, name, etc.?" A person's village must be known before anything else about him can become significant, before any other claim can be validated. Village identifications are not mere subjective matters; they are essential to the inclusive fictional kinship system by which everyone is placed in society.

Each village in the countryside around Kishan Garhi is regarded as a fictional agnatic group. People use agnatic terms for each other systematically, taking note of fictional generational standing throughout the village, ignoring all actual differences of caste and lineage. All villagers in Kishan Garhi tend accordingly to observe the same rules of intervillage hypergamy. They tend to classify the affinal villages of fellow villagers consistently as high or low, thus recognizing the fiction of common local descent which binds the residents of each of those other affinal villages, as well. In the countryside around Kishan Garhi, village is as important a fact for identifying a person as is clan in aboriginal Australia. A man must be identified with his own natal village before his place can be established in the intervillage web of marriages. The wide range of exogamy, which seems to deny the local community and to diffuse social relations over a wide area beyond the village, serves in fact also to define what the village is and who its members are, and to give each village a distinctive position in rural society.

Politically, too, there is in some senses an isolable whole community in Kishan Garhi in spite of internal conflict and in spite of the weakness of formal local government. Factional groupings not only divide people but also unite people who would otherwise act together but rarely. In a sample of thirty-six groups of persons engaged in litigation, half the groups cut across caste lines and joined diverse persons together by allying them in common hostilities. The fact of intense factional struggle raises another question: If there were no compelling awareness of the village as a distinguishable world, then why would people fight inside one village so intensely as they do through litigation and through ceremonies? Indeed, there is a local stage on which relative dominance and relative prestige must be fought out in the village. Few fights within castes but outside the village can compare in intensity with these many local fights.

Ways of Conceptualizing the Situation

Thus far I have admitted that a North Indian village society such as Kishan Garhi's is much less than an isolated whole. It has no neatly definable boundaries that are coextensive with its physical self. The social system of the village reaches beyond its central locus far into the outside world, while the outside world in turn reaches into the most central core of village society. In attempting to characterize Kishan Garhi as an isolable whole, I have had to call it a "stage," a "nexus of activity," a focal point of reference for individual prestige and identification. Although Kishan Garhi is a conservative and a relatively traditional village, I cannot say that it is a self-contained, complete little community comparable with primitive little communities. Nor, on the other hand, can I doubt that it is a community, and a very clearly isolable community for its residents. So how am I to conceive it within its larger universe? [2]

The folk-urban continuum offers one constructive way of conceiving intermediate states of society. Betty Starr (1954), building on the concepts of that continuum, invites me to view Kishan Garhi as a step in a series of "levels of communal relations" like those which intervene between little communities and great cities of Western type in modern Mexico. Structurally, Starr's levels of communal relations comprise a hierarchy of inclosing greater communities, each community having its discrete nucleus. At the level of each successively wider community, social relations tend to become less frequent, less personal, and more affected by the principle of superordination and subordination.

But the concept of levels of communal relations contrasts with much that is most characteristic of Kishan Garhi. A series of inclosing, nucleated greater communities is not evident; instead, social relations of each different kind spread out in widely different patterns. Thus Kishan Garhi's most frequently exercised ties—its ties with its principal market—place it within the sphere of one small town five miles to the east, while its administrative ties join it with a center of government seven miles to the west. Its hundreds of marital ties recognize no inclosing boundary, but are dispersed over tens of thousands of square miles of the countryside. The village's dozens of ties with places of pilgrimage are limited only by the boundaries of the whole nation, one of the most popular pilgrimages requiring a round trip of 600 miles. The spatial patterns of Kishan Garhi's livestock trade may be taken as another illustration of the complexity of that village's situation: cows are bred and obtained mainly in the village or from low affinal relatives in the south, following the web of marriage; bulls and bullocks are obtained largely by purchase at markets or from traveling traders, often from the far north and west. Inside the village, neighborhoods are indistinct and lack discrete nuclei; families are inclosed

[2] Some of these alternative ways of conceptualizing peasant communities were suggested to me by a reading of the manuscript of *The Little Community* (Redfield 1955).

within lineage groups, and lineage groups are inclosed within caste groups, but because of the small size of each of these groupings, social relations are almost inevitably more frequent outside than inside them. Finally, social relations within the village of Kishan Garhi are already maximally affected by the principle of superordination-subordination; further movement toward the urban pole cannot increase but can only decrease the effects of that principle.

The concept of levels of communal relations traces the passage of the folk community toward a type of civilization which is its opposite—the type of civilization which is familiar to us in the urbanism of the modern West. To distinguish it from an older, indigenous kind of civilization, Redfield designates this newer type of civilization as "secondary" (1953: 41–42 and Chap. III). Urban communities and urban culture in such secondary civilizations are necessarily different from the society and culture of the indigenous folk. Secondary civilizations are heterogenetic in origin and in manner of growth; in content they continue to include much that is foreign and to recognize it as such. Urban ways in secondary civilizations are often seen as foreign to folk ways, and are also often regarded as superior to folk ways in authority. The same urban ways, since they oppose folk ways, may simultaneously be regarded by the folk as morally corrupt.

Differing from the concept of secondary civilization and emphasizing continuity rather than discontinuity is the type of "primary civilization" illustrated with Indic urban materials by Redfield and Singer (1954b). This concept of a primary civilizational type and process is one of the most inviting of available models for conceptualizing Kishan Garhi's relations with its universe. A primary or "indigenous" civilization is one which grows out of its own folk culture by an orthogenetic process—by a straight line of indigenous development. The "great tradition" which is characteristically developed by such a primary civilization is a carrying forward of cultural materials, norms, and values that were already contained in local little traditions. If the great tradition absorbs foreign materials, it subjects them to syncretism. An indigenous great tradition remains in constant communication with its own little traditions through a sacred literature, a class of literati, a sacred geography, and the rites and ceremonies associated with each of these. One effect of the development of an indigenous great tradition is to universalize the cultural consciousness of persons within it as they become aware of a greater sphere of common culture.

Given such a primary continuity of culture and society, little communities would almost seem to cease to exist as isolated, distinctive wholes. Redfield and Singer have described the development of an urban community in a primary civilization as "one of a series of concentrations and nucleations within a common field" (1954b: 71). The same description would appear also to suit the little communities of a primary civilization. It seems to fit the facts of Kishan Garhi most aptly.

The remainder of this paper is an attempt to extend the concept of an indigenous or primary civilization by examining its implications for one little community. I have outlined above the general situation of the village of Kishan Garhi in its larger context. I turn now to a more detailed examination of village data on two aspects of social structure which particularly relate the village to the outside—governmental land administration and the organization of caste—and then to an examination of data on village religion.

Little Communities and the State

"In government and administration," write Redfield and Singer in describing the indigenous type, "the orthogenesis of urban civilization is represented by chiefs, rulers and laws that express and are closely controlled by the norms of the local culture . . ." (1954b: 63). Such orthogenesis was evident in the administration of many villages around Kishan Garhi in 1951–2. The revenue-collecting headmen (*nambardārs*), appointees of the state government, are descendants of the same *Jāṭ* chieftains who seized control of the region some 300 years ago. They are the heads of the leading families of their localized lineages, the principal proprietors of the village lands, and, by the same token, quasi-officials of the state. Ancestors of the present *Jāṭ* headmen, being in *de facto* control of hundreds of villages, had secured rights of revenue collection under provincial officials of Shah Jehan and Aurangzeb (Nevill 1909: 92–3). Before the *Jāṭs*, chieftains of a *Rājpūt* clan had held the same villages and lived in the same mud fortresses in much the same manner, according to local tradition.

Such an orthogenetic relationship, by which government grows upward, as it were, from village to state, is evident in North India generally (Baden-Powell 1892: II). Studies of other single villages convey detailed views of the indigenous administrative forms. In Senapur village in Jaunpur District, U.P., a division of the village lands and administration first into halves, then of each half into thirds, reflects a genealogical division within the local ruling *Rājpūt* family (Opler and Singh 1948: 468–9). In village Rani Khera in Delhi State, the two *pannās*, subdivided into four *ṭolās*, are both segments of the lineage group of the *Jāṭ* proprietors and basic units of state land administration (Lewis 1954: 424). Land administration representing three or more levels of kinship segmentation is not uncommon elsewhere: thus one village next to Kishan Garhi was held in 1952 by local proprietors under the superior proprietorship of a *Rāja* who is the living heir of the senior lineage of their own *Jāṭ* clan. The clan corporation of these proprietors had grown to be in effect a part of the state government. All these villages of northern India have in common a kind of administrative connection with the state by which parts of local kinship organization and parts of state government mutually interpenetrate one another to the point of becoming indistinguishable.

Little Communities and Caste

If integration and continuity between little communities and civilization are evident in the structural relations of village and state in India, they are evident even more plainly in the organization of caste. The existence of an extensive system of castes, present in all villages and cutting across many villages, perhaps provides the ultimate in proofs of the ancient inseparability of the little communities of India from the greater community which they collectively constitute. Three aspects of caste organization in particular demonstrate the mutual influence of little and great communities: (1) its complex ethnic composition; (2) its partial correlation with and determination by differential allocation of wealth and power; and (3) its maintenance by elaborate ritual usages.

1. Villagers in Kishan Garhi today refer to the twenty-four caste groups of the village by the terms *zāt* (birth, race) and *kaum* (tribe, people)—in other words, as representatives of different ethnic groups. Each caste group in each village is one of many dozens or hundreds or thousands of local caste groups which make up the whole membership of any endogamous caste. As villagers see the situation today, the village is a local association of representatives of many ethnic groups, some being early settlers, some later immigrants, and others conquerors. One conventional metaphor for the "whole" of any large village in the region of Kishan Garhi is "all the seven peoples" (castes). While some of the groups which are now ethnically separate may have originated by fission within formerly united populations, many are likely once to have existed in something like actual spatial separation. Taking the middle-run perspective of India's civilizational career, we know that the development of local and regional caste systems could have occurred only by such local accommodations among once separate peoples as a large-scale political order can make possible. There is some evidence that such has been the history of certain present castes and of the caste system (e.g., Majumdar and Pusalker 1951: 356, 386–7). The present highly differentiated and extensive caste system may be regarded thus in part as a living monument to a primary adjustment among tribal peoples emerging into a civilization of greater organized range and scope.

2. A second kind of interaction of greater and lesser communities is evident in the differential allocation of wealth and power to the ethnic groups which are presently higher and lower castes. In the region around Kishan Garhi today, as in the village itself, the two highest castes —Brahmans and *Jāṭs*, by local opinion—are the two castes whose members possess the greatest amount of landed wealth. In part, such correlations of wealth with the caste order may represent a recognition in the general caste order of indigenous *de facto* stratification. From remote Coorg we have the relevant example of a people, the

Coorgs, who follow a number of habits that are repugnant to Brahmanical custom: they drink liquor, eat domestic pork, and permit the remarriage of their widows. They could by these tokens be counted as a very low caste, possibly untouchable. But since they also control the lands of an entire district, they are more conveniently admitted to the caste hierarchy as "*Ugras*" or "*Kṣatriyas*" (Srinivas 1952: 33–4). The Coorgs' high position may be considered as an instance of orthogenetic addition to the general system of castes, an addition which has passed directly from the little communities of a region into the great categories of the wider civilization. More complicated sequences of interaction, many of them originating immediately in the orthogenetic state, may be found to have brought about the correlations of caste rank and power now existing in many other little communities. The Brahmans of the Tanjore village of Kumbapettai, for example, appear to owe their wealth, their secular power, and much of their effective ritual authority to a royal land grant (Gough 1952: 531). Whatever the hieratic, feudal, bureaucratic, or indigenous origins of unequal wealth and power as between higher and lower castes, some formality and fixity of lands and offices through the devices of a greater state seems everywhere to underlie the order of caste ranking.

3. A third kind of link between the caste hierarchies of little communities and the great tradition of the greater community can be described only speculatively: this is the body of ritual usages by which the ranking of castes is managed in each place. The castes of Kishan Garhi place each other in positions of relative rank according to an elaborate order of ritual usages, especially usages concerned with the giving and receiving of food, water, and services on ceremonial occasions in each household. It is difficult to imagine how such elaborate ritual usages capable of ranking so large a number of different castes could have come into being without something like deliberate contrivance, without some context in centers more sophisticated than those of the village households. Even within such a village as Kishan Garhi, a stratification of these ritual usages is already evident, for the number of services and the rules of handling food and water are

more elaborate in the highly literate landlord's household than in the tenants' and are more elaborate in the higher castes than in the lower.

Beyond the village and far back beyond the present we can have glimpses of the processes of filtering down between great and little communities which may have given rise to present village usages, but glimpses only. In later vedic times there were two classes of sacrifices: simpler ones which could be conducted by householders themselves, or with the assistance of kinsmen, and more elaborate ones which could be conducted only by kings with the help of professional ritual specialists. Royal sacrifices grew more elaborate in time, their ritualists more specialized (Renou and Filliozat 1947: 348–9; Majumdar and Pusalker 1951: 386–7). By comparison with their Aryan forefathers, villages in Kishan Garhi probably now practice more elaborate household sacrifices, too, and employ a larger number of specialists.

Hocart points out that many of the kinds of ritual relationships which exist among Indian village castes today may be regarded as results of a "degradation of the royal style" (1950: 155). If the king has a royal chaplain or a royal barber in his retinue, then no peasant home can afford to be without one. Even a poor householder in Kishan Garhi today retains six or seven servants of different castes mainly to serve him in ceremonial ways demonstrative of his own caste rank. Householders and their servants formally address each other by courtly titles. Thus the Brahman priest is called "Great King" (*Mahārāj*) or "Learned Man" (*Panditjī*), the Potter is called "Ruler of the People" (*Prajāpat*), the Barber "Lord Barber" (*Nāū Thākur*), the Carpenter "Master Craftsman" (*Mistrī*), the Sweeper "Headman" (*Mehtar*) or "Sergeant" (*Jamādār*), etc. About half of the twenty-four castes of Kishan Garhi also identify themselves with one or another of the three higher *varna*, thus symbolizing their claims to certain ritual statuses in relation to the sacrifice or the sacrificer of Sanskrit literary form. "Thus the apparent degradation of the royal style becomes a step in social evolution" (Hocart 1950: 155).

If communication with the great tradition of the greater community has had much to do with the development of a ritual hierarchy of castes in the village, then the village has also provided a social unit whose small scale of relationships among its members is essential to the flourishing of such a ritual hierarchy. The village and the royal court have this small scale in common. Villagers are able to maintain their many ritual ranks precisely because they are able to recognize each other individually as a Brahman, a Barber, a Potter, or a Sweeper. A villager of one place cannot move to a village far from his own or to any town without loss of caste recognition and without confusion as to caste ranks, for both individuals and intercaste usages of rank vary from place to place. Whether a *Jāṭ* Farmer may accept a hookah handed him by a certain Barber may depend on whether the local Brahmans accept food handled by that Barber. The intricacies of the Hindu system of caste ranking cannot be imagined as existing in any but small packages.

Summary

Viewed from the perspective of Kishan Garhi, the villages which are the little communities of India today may be conceived as relative structural nexuses, as subsystems within greater systems, and as foci of individual identification within a greater field. They cannot be conceived as things in themselves in their organization of marriage and kinship, residence patterns, modes of conflict, or caste organization. Nor are they ever likely to have been conceivable as isolates since Indian civilization began. The traditional social structure of the greater community of India similarly cannot be understood as apart from its continuing existence in relation to hundreds of thousands of little communities. Both little communities and greater communities are mutually necessary conditions of each other's existence in their present forms. One must consider both in order thoroughly to understand either.

¶ FESTIVALS AND DEITIES

To add another dimension to the answers given above from social structural materials alone, I turn at this point to examine some cultural contents of the religion of the people of Kishan Garhi. If I would describe the religion

of these people as it exists within the universe of Indian
religion in general, I must consider as a matter of method
(1) the extent to which the religion of the little community can be conceived as a whole apart from the religious
great tradition of Indian civilization and (2) the extent
to which the religious great tradition of Indian civilization
is understandable through study of the religion of one little
community. Fortunately, I can take as my guides in
answering these questions both the concept of a primary or
indigenous civilizational process (Redfield and Singer
1954*b*) and that set of hypotheses concerning the spread
and effects of Sanskritization which has been drawn up by
Srinivas (1952, Chap. VII).

Festivals as Products of Great and Little Traditions

Table 1 gives immediate proof of the existence of the
great tradition of Hinduism within Kishan Garhi, if that
tradition is understood to be the literate religious tradition,
embodied in or derived from Sanskrit works which have a
universal spread in all parts of India. At least fifteen of
the nineteen village festivals are sanctioned by one or
more universal Sanskrit texts. The festivals of Tenth and
of Lights, for example, are sanctioned as celebrations of
climactic events in the *Rāmāyana* epic, while most of the
other festivals are connected with stories in one or several
Purānas.

Nearly half the festivals in Table 1 not only have connections with great-traditional text but are themselves observed very widely, if not universally, in India. Eight of
these festivals of Kishan Garhi may be listed as probably
universal, at least in name. The eight are *Durgā* Ninth,
Eleventh, Charm Tying, Nine *Durgās*, Tenth, Lights,
Śiva Night, and *Holī*. Possibly parallels of two or three
others among the festivals of Table 1, such as *Krsna*'s
Birthday Eighth, *Kanāgat*, and Awakening of the Gods,
might also be found in the annual cycles of villages in
most regions of India.

The remaining half of the festivals observed in Kishan
Garhi have more limited regional or local distributions.
Regional festivals include Cow-Nourisher Worship, Pitcher
Fourth, Old Clerk's Worship, and probably others. The
Fair of the Well Godling and Leftover Food Worship

TABLE 1

Principal Annual Festivals in Kishan Garhi

Month	Fortnight and Day	Local Name	Translation [or Implication]
Cait (Mar.–Apr.)	1:11	1. Ekādaśi	"Eleventh"
	2:1–9	2. Patthvārī Pūjā or Durgā Naumī	"Stony One Worship" or "Durgā Ninth"
Baisākh (Apr.–May)	Varies	3. Bāsor Pūjā or Devī-Devatā kī Pūjā	"Leftover Food Worship" or "Goddess-Godling Worship"
	Varies	4. Kue kā Devatā kā Melā	"Fair of the Well Godling"
	2:1–15	5. Pitar kī Pūjā	"Ancestor Worship"
Sāvan (July–Aug.)	2:3	6. Tīj	"Third"
	2:15	7. Salūno and Rākhī Bandhan	"Beautiful" [?] and "Charm Tying"
Bhādon (Aug.–Sept.)	1:8	8. Kṛṣṇa Janam Aṣṭamī	"Kṛṣṇa's Birthday Eighth"
Kuār (Sept.–Oct.)	1:1–15	9. Kanāgat	[Ancestor Remembrance]
	2:1–9	10. Naurthā or Nau Durgā	"Ninenights" or "Nine Durgās"
	2:10	11. Daśahrā	"Tenth"
Kātik (Oct.–Nov.)	1:3	12. Karvā Cauth	"Pitcher Fourth"
	1:15	13. Divālī	"Lights"
	2:1–2	14. Gobardhan Pūjā	"Cow-Nourisher Worship"
	2:11	15. Devuthān	"Awakening of the Gods"
Pūs (Dec.–Jan.)	Varies	16. Būṛho Bābū kī Pūjā	"Old Clerk's Worship"
Māgh (Jan.–Feb.)	1:1–2	17. Sakaṭ	. . . .
Phāgun (Feb.–Mar.)	1:13–14	18. Śiv Rātrī	"Śiva Night"
	2:13–15	19. Holī	[Saturnalia]

must probably be counted as local festivals, although they are not without resemblances to festivals elsewhere in the region. Only for the last four festivals mentioned have I been unable to find any trace of great-traditional sanction, however.

The great tradition of Hinduism is not merely present as a part of most festivals of Kishan Garhi, but it has achieved, through the festivals, an integrated position in village life. Great festivals of Sanskritic rationale and no-menclature provide, along with domestic ceremonies, the principal occasions on which most villagers may engage in concerted symbolic activities. Most of the festivals in Table 1 are observed by most of the castes, lineage groups, and families of Kishan Garhi, and many festival observances cut significantly across the routine barriers of social structure.

From such a simple listing of the names and distributions of principal festivals in Kishan Garhi one might presume that there is not much in the festivals of this little community which conceptually could be set apart from the predominant Sanskritic great tradition. One might well expect to find the great tradition predominant in a village which, like Kishan Garhi, lies in the heartland of Aryan settlement. One might with reason imagine even that Kishan Garhi once knew a purely Aryan religion, and that the process of Sanskritization first began to operate there between Aryan and non-Aryan religious traditions (Hutton 1946: 192–201). In any event, the religion of Kishan Garhi must have been subjected to constant Sanskritization over a period of about 3,000 years. If time and geographic location have important effects upon the degree of Sanskritization—on the spread of the great tradition—then one might expect to find that the religion of Kishan Garhi is notably closer to the religion of the great tradition than is, for example, the religion of the Coorgs in remote mountains of southern India.

But the presumption that the festivals of Kishan Garhi are approximately identical with those of the great tradition needs to be qualified in at least four ways. These four qualifications bring us to confront the little tradition of Kishan Garhi.

First, there are four festivals which have no evident

Sanskritic rationales: Leftover Food Worship, Fair of the Well Godling, Pitcher Fourth, and Old Clerk's Worship.

Second, those festivals of Kishan Garhi which do have Sanskritic rationales represent only a small selection out of the total annual cycle of festivals which finds sanction in the great tradition. Of the thirteen major Hindu festivals recently listed by a group of Hindu scholars (Morgan 1953: 423), only seven are observed in Kishan Garhi. Of the thirty-five presumably all-Indian Hindu festivals listed by Swami Sivananda (1947: 1–57), only nine occur in Kishan Garhi. Of the 270 festivals of the Hindu religious year in the list compiled by Underhill (1921: 136–59), only eleven are observed in Kishan Garhi, and then on somewhat variant dates. Even lists of festivals drawn up especially for the state of Uttar Pradesh or its districts rarely include as many as half of the festivals which are observed in Kishan Garhi and listed in Table 1; conversely, all the festivals observed in Kishan Garhi are rarely equal to more than a small fraction of even regional compendia (e.g., Growse 1880: 246–9).

Third, between the festivals of Kishan Garhi and those sanctioned by the great tradition, connections are often loosened, confused, or mistaken because of a multiplicity of competing meanings for each special day within the great tradition itself. Each festival of Kishan Garhi is likely to have at least two or three Sanskritic stories available to explain it. To explain *Holī*, for instance, a villager in Kishan Garhi may choose between or combine the puranic story of *Prahlād* and *Holikā* and that of *Kṛṣṇa* and *Rādhā* or the *Gopīs*. Particularly auspicious dates of the calendar tend to accumulate layer upon layer of mythical events—birthdays of deities, victories of gods over demons, etc.

When I went with villagers of Kishan Garhi to witness the Car Festival (*Ratha Yātrā*) in a town nearby, I found that different villagers held very diverse explanations of the festival. When they saw the focal idol being towed through the streets on a great car, with swordplay, hymn singing, and roll of drums, some said it represented the Goddess (*Devī*), others that it represented *Ṭhakurjī* riding triumphant after a victory, others that it represented the divine epic couple *Sītā-Rām*, and still others that it represented *Kṛṣṇa* celebrating his birthday. Accustomed to an interminable variety of overlapping Sanskritic mythology, villagers have ceased to be much concerned with distinguishing the "right" great-traditional explanation of a festival from such Sanskritic-sounding and possibly newly invented ones as may be convenient.

Fourth, behind their Sanskritic names and multiple great-traditional rationales, the festivals of Kishan Garhi contain much ritual which has no evident connection with the great tradition. The festival of Lights, for example, as it is celebrated in Kishan Garhi, contains many elements which are not connected either with a celebration of *Rām*'s triumphal return from *Laṇkā* or with a celebration of *Lakṣmī*'s wedding. To be sure, villagers do set out oil lamps in the evening and say that they do so in order to celebrate either or both of these great-traditional events; many do also worship *Hanumānjī* by name the next morning to celebrate his part in *Rām*'s triumph.

But on these same dates of the festival of Lights villagers also perform the following other rituals. (*a*) Small incendiary sacrifices are made by each householder in the name of each of his personal gods and godlings and ancestors, as well as in the name of *Hanumānjī*. (*b*) A crude figure of a goddess called "*Saurtī*" is drawn in each household, usually on the wall, and is variously worshipped, then implored to grant prosperity and preservation to the family and its animals. A few villagers identify *Saurtī* with *Lakṣmī*, but most do not, because, as several men said, "*Lakṣmī* is a goddess only of rich people." (*c*) Another female deity called "Lampblack" (*Siyāho*), represented by a mound of dung with a straw stuck on top, is worshipped with songs by some women of the higher castes at 4:00 a.m. Actual lampblack is manufactured while the songs are being sung, and this lampblack is applied to the eyes of children during the ensuing year to protect them from evil eye. Most people in Kishan Garhi do not know about the worship of *Siyāho*; I could find no one who was willing to connect *Siyāho* with any other deity or story (but cf. Rose 1919, I: 915). (*d*) An old winnowing fan is beaten through the rooms of each house, also at about 4:00 a.m., the owner crying as he beats: "Get out, Poverty!" (*e*) Some of these old winnowing fans are immediately burned by small boys, and some are burned along with the straw image of an old man. This image is called Flag Grandfather (*Jhaṇḍī Bābā*), possibly to commemorate a garrulous man of that name who actually resided in Kishan Garhi a generation ago. Here, then, contained within what seems from its name to be a major festival, sanctioned in the great tradition of Hinduism, are many elements having precedents only in lesser traditions without literary form.

Like the festival of Lights, the contents of most other festivals in Kishan Garhi also show a combination of some great-traditional elements with many other distinctive, non-Sanskritic elements. Although we cannot conceive of all the contents of religious festivals in Kishan Garhi as existing apart from a great tradition which is both within and beyond the village, we can nevertheless distinguish a substantial body of festival contents which are partly unique to the region and to the village and which partake, therefore, of lesser traditions. A part of village religion thus remains conceptually separable, both for the people who live in Kishan Garhi and for the outside analyst.

If we consider this same combination of great- and little-traditional rites as representing the extent of "the spread of Sanskritic rites, and the increasing Sanskritization of non-Sanskritic rites" (Srinivas 1952: 208), then we must conclude that spread and Sanskritization in Kishan Garhi have scarcely begun, despite their having continued there for some 3,000 years. While elements of the great tradition have become parts of local festivals, they do not appear to have entered village festival custom "at the expense of" (p. 208) much that is or was the little tradition. Instead, we see evidence of accretion and of transmutation in form without apparent replacement and without rationalization of the accumulated and transformed elements.

Whatever the processes that lie behind the present combination of great and little traditions in the religion of Kishan Garhi, villagers now regard both traditions as old and indigenous. When I asked for explanations of the diversity of the seemingly unconnected rituals which were being observed at the festival of Lights, villagers replied that the dark-moon day of the month of *Kātik* is a very auspicious day for many gods and for themselves, hence that all these rituals naturally fall together.

Since the great tradition derives its authority from faith in its native belongingness, hardly anyone thinks of replacing elements of the little tradition with elements of the great. Bright lithographed pictures of *Lakṣmī* and *Hanumānjī* in Sanskritic regalia are available in the shops at Kishan Garhi's market town, and have long been used by villagers as household decorations. But only one young man of lower caste, a critic of his father and of the social order, put one of these printed pictures on his wall for worship at the festival of Lights in place of the little-traditional *Saurtī*, rudely drawn with rice flour or ghee.

1. *Universalization.*—For understanding why Sanskritization has gone so short a way in so long a time in the festivals of Kishan Garhi, and for understanding why Sanskritic rites are often added onto non-Sanskritic rites without replacing them, the concept of a primary or indigenous process of civilization again offers useful guidance. By definition, an indigenous civilization is one whose great tradition originates by a "universalization," or a carrying forward of materials which are already present in the little traditions which it encompasses (cf. Redfield and Singer 1954*b*: 68).[3] Such an indigenous great tradition has authority in so far as it constitutes a more articulate and refined restatement or systematization of what is already there (pp. 6–7). Without subsequent secondary transformation of its contents and without heterogenetic criticism of the little tradition, the indigenous great tradition lacks authority to supplant the hoary prototypes that are the sources of its own sacredness.

I am not able, from having visited Kishan Garhi in 1951–2, to report that I have witnessed the whole process of universalization upward from festivals of a little tradition into sacred events of the great tradition of Hinduism. "Time to simmer is an essential part of this concept . . ." just as it is of the concept of filtering down—"time to

[3] Redfield and Singer in the paper cited use the term "universalization" only in the phrase "universalization of cultural consciousness." From this point onward, I use the term in the broader sense indicated here to designate the carrying forward and upward, not only of cultural awareness, but also of cultural contents.

integrate . . . to rework" (Foster 1953: 164). Such a festival as the festival of Lights nevertheless suggests and allows me to speculate upon the course which such processes might have taken in middle-run perspective. The Sanskritic goddess *Lakṣmī*, for example, appears to be a credible literary apotheosis of such local figures as the unlettered *Saurtī* and the inchoate *Siyāho*; she is the antithesis of poverty and old things, and is an object appropriate for worship on a day already held sacred in the little tradition for renewing one's reverence to the multitudes of gods and spirits. And what better day than this auspicious dark of the moon could have been chosen by the puranic poet for staging the marriage of *Lakṣmī*, or by the epic poet for staging the curtain scene of *Rām's* adventures (cf. Crooke 1896b, II: 295–6)?

Materials suggestive of such ancient processes of upward universalization are ready at hand in many other festivals of Kishan Garhi. The festival of Charm Tying can supply one further example here. This all-Indian festival coincides and blends in Kishan Garhi with the festival known regionally as *Salūno* (Beautiful [?]), a festival which marks the end of that annual fortnight during which most young wives return for a visit with their parents and siblings. On *Salūno* day, many husbands arrive at their wives' villages, ready to carry them off again to their villages of marriage. But, before going off with their husbands, the wives as well as their unmarried village sisters express their concern for and devotion to their brothers by placing young shoots of barley, the locally sacred grain, on the heads and ears of their brothers. Since brothers should accept nothing from their sisters as a free gift, they reciprocate with small coins. Brothers and brothers-in-law then join in sports contests.

On the same day, along with the ceremonies of *Salūno*, and according to the literary precedent of *Bhaviṣyottara Purāṇa*, among other Sanskrit works, the ceremonies of Charm Tying (*Rākhī Bandhan* or *Rakṣa Bandhan*) are also held. The Brahman domestic priests of Kishan Garhi go to each patron and tie upon his wrist a charm in the form of a polychrome thread, bearing tassel "plums." Each priest utters a vernacular blessing and is rewarded by his patron with cash, for it is thought impious to accept anything as a free gift from a priest. Parallels between the familial festival of *Salūno* and the specialized Brahmanical festival of Charm Tying—between the role of the sister and the role of the priest—are obvious. The likelihood that Charm Tying has its roots in some such little-traditional festival as *Salūno* tempts speculation. The ceremonies of both now exist side by side, as if they were two ends of a process of primary transformation.

A further, secondary transformation of the festival of Charm Tying is also beginning to be evident in Kishan Garhi, for the thread charms of the priests are now factory-made in more attractive form and are hawked in the village by a local caste group of *Jogīs*. A few sisters in Kishan Garhi have taken to tying these heterogenetic charms of priestly type onto their brothers' wrists. The new string charms are also more convenient for mailing in letters to distant, city-dwelling brothers whom sisters cannot visit on the auspicious day. Beals reports,[4] furthermore, that brothers in the electrified village of Namhalli near Bangalore tuned in to All India Radio in order to receive a time signal at the astrologically exact moment, and then tied such charms to their own wrists, with an accompaniment of broadcast Sanskrit *mantras*.

2. *Parochialization.*—If the indigenous origins and connections of the great tradition limit its authority to uproot any little tradition, the essentially unlearned and non-literate nature of the little tradition also obstructs the direct transmission or spread of elements downward from great to little. Downward spread, like universalization, is likely to be characterized by transformations.[5]

The festival of Cow-Nourisher Worship as it is celebrated in Kishan Garhi exemplifies some of the kinds of limits upon, and changes that take place during, the course of a downward transmission of cultural contents from great to little traditions. Villagers today know at least two stories to explain this festival, both of them evidently derived from Book X of the *Bhāgavata Purāṇa*, a Sanskrit work of the tenth century A.D. (Renou and Filliozat 1947: 418). The contents of this Sanskrit book, which

---

[4] In a personal communication, April 1954.

[5] My attention was first called to this process by Professor Morris E. Opler.

comprise a biography of *Kṛṣṇa*, have been popularized among villagers by a succession of vernacular renderings, among which one of the latest is the nineteenth-century Hindi version entitled *Prem Sāgara* (Lallū Lāl 1897: 1–2). The story from this great-traditional book which is most generally taken to explain the Cow-Nourisher Worship concerns *Kṛṣṇa*'s adventures with his cowherd companions at a hill named *Gobardhan* (Cow Nourisher), which is actually located about forty miles distant from Kishan Garhi. In this story, *Kṛṣṇa* directs the cowherds of Braj to worship the hill that is near at hand rather than such great but distant gods as *Indra*. The cowherds comply with *Kṛṣṇa*'s directions. In anger over the resulting defection of his worshippers, *Indra* sends violent rainstorms to destroy the cowherds and their kine. *Kṛṣṇa*, however, lifts up the hill to provide them shelter, and all are saved (Lallū Lāl 1897: 65–72). At the actual hill of Gobardhan, in Mathura District, an annual ceremony of circumambulation and worship is still enacted (cf. Growse 1880: 280).

By the time that this great-traditional story has reached ritual enactment in a festival of Kishan Garhi, it has taken on a cruder form and accumulated a number of homely details which have no evident justification in the Sanskritic myth. Villagers, indeed, seem to have taken the story's parochial moral to heart. "Cow Nourisher" (*Go+vardhana*) has become by a village etymology "Cow-dung Wealth" (*Gobar+dhan*) (cf. Grierson 1880; Temple 1883: 38).[6] The sacred hill of the *Purāṇa* has become in each household yard a literal pile of cow dung, shaped into a rough homunculus with four embracing walls appended to its neck, and decorated on top with "trees" of straw and cotton. Within these walls are crowded rude loaves representing all the cows, bullocks, and buffaloes that the family owns or would like to own. To secure any possible benefit to the family's milk and fodder supply, feeding troughs, milking vessels, churns, etc., are also represented in fecal model. The family cowboy is there, too, modeled in dung—the real family cowboy gets a rupee on this day—and so is a model tank to which the cowboy can take the animals for water. The women and children

[6] Thanks are due to Professor Murray B. Emeneau and to Dr. Norvin Hein for pointing out this etymological shift.

of each family finish this dung construction by day; in the evening all the agnates of each family worship it jointly by placing a lamp on its navel, winding a thread around its trees, and shouting in solemn procession: "Long live Grandfather Cowdung Wealth!" Members of the Weaver caste of Kishan Garhi add their bit, too, for on the next morning they must be paid to sing a Cowdung Wealth awakening song before the dung images can be broken up for use as daily fuel. But a portion of the cow dung remaining from the celebration must be set aside: this portion is reshaped and scored into the form of an enormous cracker; the cracker is dried and preserved as sacred until it can be contributed to the great annual all-village bonfire at the *Holī* festival six months later.

To refer to the kind of transformation of cultural contents which is apparent in the festival of Cow-Nourisher Worship—the downward devolution of great-traditional elements and their integration with little-traditional elements—a term is needed. For this movement, which is the reverse of "universalization," I suggest the term "parochialization." Parochialization is a process of localization, of limitation upon the scope of intelligibility, of deprivation of literary form, of reduction to less systematic and less reflective dimensions. The process of parochialization constitutes the characteristic creative work of little communities within India's indigenous civilization.

The festival of Nine *Durgās* in Kishan Garhi presents another specimen of parochialization. This festival has innumerable precedents in Sanskrit literature of the great tradition. The nine days on which it takes place are sanctioned in myth for the worship of *Durgā, Kālī, Pārvatī, Śakti,* and all other names and aspects of the great Goddess (*Devī*) and the spouses of *Śiva*. During this festival in Kishan Garhi, bas-relief idols representing a feminine deity called *"Naurthā"* are constructed of mud in some variety in about every tenth household of the village. Each morning and evening during the nine days, small groups of women and girls worship *Naurthā* by bathing, by singing songs before their respective idols, and by making mudballs or figurines, which are piled below each idol in a little mud hut. On the ninth day of the festival, each worshipping group carries its accumulated mudballs or figurines and deposits them on top of the mound of another deity, called the Stony One (*Patthvāri*), which is located at the west end of the village's residential area.

In dozens of houses and from dozens of worshippers I inquired who or what *Naurthā* represents. Eventually, from those few persons who were willing to hazard an identification, I received a variety of somewhat contradictory answers including "*Durgā*," "*Śiva Śaṅkar*," and "*Sītā*." But most worshippers told me firmly that *Naurthā* is herself one of the "Nine *Durgās*," is another one of the many aspects of the Big Goddess (*Baṛī Devī*). No one whom I asked in the village was able to tell me what seems obvious from comparison with the Sanskritic name of the festival—that the word "*Naurthā*," considered in the region around Kishan Garhi to be the name of an indigenous goddess, is nothing more than an old dialectic variant of *nava rātra*, which means "nine nights."

The festival of Nine *Durgās* in Kishan Garhi thus exemplifies the continual fertility and creativity of little communities within Indian civilization: by sheer linguistic confusion and loss of meaning in the contact between great and little traditions, a new minor goddess has been created. But no sooner has the parochial goddess *Naurthā* been born into the villages of Aligarh than she is reabsorbed by peasant conception as a new manifestation of the great Goddess principle.

3. *Residual categories.*—The processes of upward universalization and downward parochialization, if we could in every instance trace their courses, might serve to conceptualize some of the characteristic relations between little and great traditions and might account for the present distributions of many religious elements between great and little communities in India. In practice, however, since universalization and parochialization have both proceeded for a very long time, we are ordinarily unable to trace the course of either process with certainty, or to decide whether a given present configuration of religious contents is the result of one, and not also the result of the other, of these two processes. Thus in the festival of Lights and in the festival of Charm Tying, which have been described above, certain apparent homologues between little and great traditions suggest that a process of univer-

salization has occurred. But some of the same pairs of apparent homologues may equally well be imagined to have originated as precipitates of the process of parochialization. *Lakṣmī* may be a universalized *Saurtī*, or *Saurtī* may be a parochialized *Lakṣmī*; the priestly charms of the Charm Tying festival may be universalizations of sisterly barley shoots, or the barley shoots may be parochializations of the priestly charms. Thus also in the festivals of Cow-Nourisher Worship and Nine *Durgās* we have no guarantee that the movement of cultural contents has been wholly parochial in direction. The Sanskrit tale of *Kṛṣṇa's* adventure with the cowherds' hill may have arisen out of still more ancient peasant rituals of animal prosperity in which dung had played a part. As for parochialization in the festival of Nine *Durgās*, the worship of goddesses, even by techniques like those in use today, is attested to be far older in India than the verbal manufacture of the goddess *Naurthā* could possibly be (Wheeler 1953: 68, 83): the great Goddess, who seems to be *Naurthā's* mother, may herself be a village goddess grown great by devouring her little sisters.

In dealing with so ancient a phenomenon as the festival of Nine *Durgās* in Kishan Garhi, if we choose between universalization and parochialization as *the* explanation for similarities and differences between great and little traditions, then we are stopping arbitrarily in mid-cycle what must in fact be a circular flow. Circular flow is familiar to European folklorists (e.g., Foster 1953: 169 and 172, n. 12). Describing the culture of Switzerland, Weiss writes that the little tradition "can well be considered as a catch-basin, as an ocean in which the springs, brooks and rivers of the creative cultural processes of the millennia collect and to some extent remain. However, this ocean is no stagnant swamp in spite of the continuity dictated by tradition. Instead, the entering flows are transformed and mingled upon their entrance. And as the water of the ocean rises afresh to the clouds, so also does the folk culture return once more to its own sources. As in the eternal cyclical course of the waters, so in the giving and receiving of cultural contents a continual exchange takes place between the two levels of culture" (1946: 42).[7] Further re-

[7] I am indebted to Mr. Per Gräslund of Stockholm for directing me to this parallel analysis by Weiss.

search—literary, ethnographic, distributional, and historical—may diminish our present ignorance and assist in answering some of these questions as to opposite processes and possible cycles of exchange between great and little traditions in the festivals of village India.[8]

Apart from our ignorance of past processes, however, residual categories seem likely to remain necessary for conceiving the distribution of cultural contents within either the great or the little tradition. These residual categories of cultural contents represent neither the results of upward movement nor the results of downward movement, but rather the stability of contents, created and retained within either tradition. Created within the great tradition and by necessity remaining there in their details are the hundreds of Sanskrit works of literary invention and of philosophic subtlety which have been woven about the legendary histories of Śiva and Viṣṇu, of Rāma and Kṛṣṇa. Such works can rarely be translated for peasant understanding without some loss of their distinctive refinement. Unintelligible but more Sanskritic and therefore more authoritative versions of literary works are often retained in village use along with their vernacular renderings (cf. Hein 1950).

The little tradition also has its residuum of festival contents which appear neither to have arisen out of nor to have descended into it. Parts of the festival of Lights as it is celebrated in Kishan Garhi have already brought us to confront the little tradition as a residuum of religious elements which are separable from the great tradition. Almost all the contents of the festival of Pitcher Fourth appear to belong to the residual category of the little tradition, *sui generis*.

[8] Professor W. Norman Brown (1919) finds himself at a similar threshold of ignorance in his efforts to discover the extent of borrowing into oral Indic folklore from literary sources. After reaching an estimate that at least half of all known oral Indic folktales are derived from Sanskrit or Persian literature, Brown cautions the reader that his estimate of the borrowed proportion grows constantly larger as his own knowledge of the written literature grows (p. 11). The same caution may be applied to the problem of estimating the little- and great-traditional proportions in the deities and festivals of Kishan Garhi. This caution may be applied not only to the problem of estimating the borrowed portion of the little tradition, however, but also to the problem of estimating the borrowed portion of the great tradition. The more one knows of either tradition, the more one becomes able to find evidence suggestive of communication and borrowing from it to the other.

The little-traditional festival of Pitcher Fourth is in essence a celebration of wifely devotion for the sake of the welfare and long life of the husband. Wives of all castes but the *Jāṭ* caste fast by abstaining from bread during the day. While they are fasting, each wife completes a mural picture showing two "moons" and depicting the events of the Pitcher Fourth story. The story is told before each picture by one of several elderly ladies, mostly Brahmans, who make a specialty of storytelling. Wives gather in small groups to hear the story, and then all sing any devotional song which they may know. Their fast continues until the real moon rises in the evening. Then each wife goes to where she can see the moon, sketches a sacred crossroads at her feet, and pours water onto the crossroads out of a spouted earthenware pitcher as an offering to the moon. She next worships the moons of her mural picture by pressing food against their "mouths"—a few wives also make mud figurines of a goddess at this point—and then breaks her fast after serving food to the men of the family. The moon is here often spoken of as having masculine gender rather than as the "Moon Mother" of usual speech.

From one storyteller I heard the story of Pitcher Fourth in the following version. There were seven married brothers living together. They had a younger sister, who was also married. Once, on Pitcher Fourth day, the younger sister kept fast at her brothers' house along with the wives of the seven. The youngest brother, feeling pity for his sister in her hunger, climbed a tree and showed a lamp behind a sieve, saying: "Sister! The moon is already up!" The sister offered water, then broke her fast. Her husband at once died. But she sat by her husband's cot for a whole year, not allowing ants or worms to come near, and not allowing his corpse to decay. The next year, when the festival of Pitcher Fourth come again, she once more kept fast. Her brothers' wives said: "You can't keep fast with us, because you are a widow." But the younger sister said: "I'll keep fast anyway!" When the moon rose, all the seven wives went to offer water. The sister took hold of her youngest brother and said: "Give me back my husband! Revive him!" Then she split open her finger and let the blood flow into the mouth of her dead husband. He came back to life, chanting the names of God.

In a second version of the Pitcher Fourth story, the sister avoids being deceived at all. In a third version, the brothers are five rather than seven. In several other versions, one of the wives, strangely called "maid servant" (*dūtī* or *mantharā*), is herself said to be involved in the plot to deceive her husband's sister; she is represented in some of the mural pictures as undergoing punishment by hanging from her heels.

Even this essentially little-traditional story of Pitcher Fourth is not without minor echoes of Sanskrit literature, however. The story's theme of wifely devotion bears an over-all resemblance to the theme of the *Sāvitrī* legend— a legend which occurs both in *Mahābhārata* (*Vana Parva*, 293–9) and in *Matsyapurāṇa* (208–14). The detail of the intriguing wife or servant seems clearly to have been borrowed from the episode of the intriguing Queen Kaikeyi and her servant in the *Rāmāyaṇa*. And the variant which begins with five brothers cannot but hint at the *Pāṇḍava* brothers of the *Mahābhārata*.

The Pitcher Fourth ritual of worshipping the moon seems furthermore to derive by direct descent, as it were, from an even older upanishadic cosmology in which the moon was the transitory abode of dead spirits awaiting re-birth, and the heavenly form of the life-giving *soma*. The wife's pouring of water from a spouted pitcher held before the moon with the aim of preserving or reviving the husband suggests a magical enactment of the prayer that moon-dwelling spirits descend through rain, then through the husband's semen to enter the wife's womb for re-birth (cf. *Chāndogya Upaniṣad* 5. 10. 3–7; *Bṛhadāraṇyaka Upaniṣad* 6. 2. 16).[9] But, in speculating on the possible Sanskritic cosmology which underlies the mute ritual of Pitcher Fourth, I am going beyond what is conscious or relevant to villagers today.

Whatever their ultimate origins, most of the ritual contents of the festival of Pitcher Fourth appear now to refer not to any greater tradition but rather to the residual little tradition. The story of the younger sister and her devotion to her husband, which provides the manifest rationale of the festival, is unmistakably built up out of the objects

---

[9] I owe the second part of this interpretation of the ritual of Pitcher Fourth to a suggestion made to me by Dr. Norvin Hein.

and life of the village. As far as I have been able to determine, and as far as villagers in Kishan Garhi were aware, neither the story nor the ritual of Pitcher Fourth has resulted from the devolution of any Sanskritic myth. As for universalization, the *Purāṇa* of the younger sister's fast has yet to be written. In this festival, which seems to be distributed at least as far as Hardoi (Crooke 1896a, I: 172) and Mainpuri districts (Wiser 1936: 89) on the southeast and Muzaffarnagar District on the north,[1] we seem to have isolated an original, if not pristine, contribution of the regional little tradition in its creative aspect.

¶ DEITIES, GREATER AND LESSER

An examination of the deities of Kishan Garhi may serve to review the questions and answers which have been suggested above through analysis of more complicated materials concerning festivals. The deities lend themselves to finer discriminations, even to some rough statistical statements, and to further understanding of social processes which are involved in the relations of great and little traditions.

These deities may be examined through a collection of information concerning ninety gods, goddesses, and godlings made between March and October 1951 in Kishan Garhi. About half of these ninety deities were mentioned to me spontaneously in various contexts over a period of five months; the other half of these deities came to my notice for the first time during the festival of Lights, when I consulted forty-six persons throughout the village as to the deities which they were themselves worshipping on that sacred day. The list of ninety does not exhaust information about deities in Kishan Garhi; it does seem, however, to represent an approximation to the total list of deities whose cults are actively practiced in the village today.

To what extent can the religion of the little community be conceived as a whole apart from the religious great tradition of Hinduism? For the deities, as for the festivals,

[1] For evidence from Muzaffarnagar, thanks are due to the personal recollections of Urmila (Mrs. Satya P.) Agarwal, originally of that city.

the answer must be "to a very limited extent only." About thirty of the total list of ninety deities, or one third of the whole list, are recognizably gods of the great pantheon. Among these gods of the great tradition are *Viṣṇu, Lakṣmī, Hanumān, Rām, Kṛṣṇa, Śiva* or *Mahādev,* etc.

These gods of the great tradition not only are in the villager's range of knowledge but are found within the common core of objects worshipped by castes of all ranks (cf. Srinivas's "vertical spread" [1952: 218]). Fifteen deities may be specified within the common core of objects worshipped by members of at least three out of the four major blocs of castes in Kishan Garhi (Brahmans, high castes, low castes, lowest castes). Of these fifteen core deities whose cults are actively practiced, seven or eight deities may be identified as gods of the great tradition. Just as in the festivals, great-traditional elements thus play a part of central importance among the gods of this little community of Kisham Garhi.

But there is yet another substantial portion of the list of ninety deities—about sixty deities, or two thirds of the total list—which does not seem to require us to take much notice of the great tradition of Hinduism. In this portion of the list we meet once more a part of village religion which approaches separability.

The less-than-great-traditional portion of the list of deities may be subdivided into shorter lists, descending from more widely known, regional deities with vernacular literatures, temples, and professional devotees down to purely local ghosts and spirits. People of Kishan Garhi worship at least twelve deities which have elaborate cults and which are known over areas of from several districts to several states. Such regional gods include the "Saint Apparent" (*Zāhir Pīr*), the "Goddess of Nagarkot" (*Nagarkoṭvālī Devī*), the "One of Agra" (*Āgrevālā*), the "One of the Well" (*Kuāṇvālā*), "Auspicious" (*Kalyāṇī*), the "Old Gentleman" (*Miyāṇ Sāhab*), *et altera.* Among these regional gods, as also among local gods, are included several of Muslim name or origin, notably the Saint Apparent (cf. Temple 1884–1900, II: 121, III: 264; Rose 1919, I: 172–92), the One of Agra, and "Saint Adam" (*Ādham Pīr*). Sectarian or other differences of origin are of slight concern in a civilization used to adopting and syncretizing any material that meets the criteria of interest and local availability.

The remainder of the list from Kishan Garhi, about one half of the whole collection, consists of deities whose names are foreign even to any vernacular literary tradition, and whose cults have but little professional elaboration. Among these minor deities are "They of the Garden" (*Bāgvāle*), "They of the Twelfth Day" (*Doādśīvāle*), a goddess named "*Lańgubir*," "She of the Tray" (*Thālvālī*), etc. Here are found some forty-five names in all. In this list are the names of many mother goddesses: "Mother of Jalesar" (*Jalesarvālī Mātā*), "Mother of Gurgaon," "New Spaghetti Mother" (*Nayī Semarīvālī Mātā*), etc. Although some of these nonliterate deities are known to the little traditions of other districts—four of the forty-five are found in Wiser's list for a village seventy miles away in Mainpuri (1933: 262–3), while one occurs in Griffiths's list from Rewa 300 miles away (1946: 133–4)—all lack felt connection with any thing or place far away from the villages where they are worshipped, and may therefore be counted as local deities. Only a handful of these deities have sufficient spread or fame to have made their ways into even so large a compendium of Uttar Pradesh village religion as Crooke's (1896*b*). A few of these local deities appear to be known only to the people of Kishan Garhi village, and then not to all of them. Partly because of the wide range of country from which wives of the village are drawn, there is nevertheless great diversity in adherence to such local and regional deities from family to family and from individual to individual. The village list from Kishan Garhi appears to contain a sampling of the local theological diversity of a large area.

In the common core of objects of worship—that is, among the fifteen deities which are worshipped by members of most blocs of castes in Kishan Garhi—these little-traditional deities play a large part. While Sanskritic deities make up seven members of the common core, or nearly half of the total, regional deities account for four members and local deities for another four members. This little-traditional core component is subjectively important to villagers in Kishan Garhi, for next to the worship of

their own respective ancestral spirits of the last two generations, villagers are most attached, I would estimate, to the
worship of four local godlings of no refinement whatsoever:
Cāmar̥, *Alop*, "Earthy" (*Bhūmiyā*), and the "Stony One"
(*Patthvārī*). In these little-traditional deities, as in festivals, in caste rituals, and in kinship organization, we
again come upon an area in which the little community feels
itself to be and can be conceived as a partly distinctive and
partly isolable nexus within greater communities. Here
again we come upon the paradox of isolability within non-
isolability, for the theological great and little traditions,
like the great and little communities which bear them, are
continuous with each other.

1. *Stratification of deities and their slowness of spread.*
—The distribution of deities through the caste hierarchy
of Kishan Garhi helps to explain why great-traditional religious elements are unable to achieve exclusive dominance
in the little community, despite the many continuities between great and little traditions.

Adherence to deities of the great and little traditions is
distributed through the hierarchy of castes in Kishan Garhi
in the relative proportions which have been stated hy-
pothetically by Srinivas (1952: 218). Sanskritic deities of
the great tradition play a larger part in the devotions of
members of the Brahman caste and generally in the bloc
of the high castes of Kishan Garhi than they do in the
devotions of the lower castes. Forty-five per cent of the
deities worshipped by Brahmans are Sanskritic; 35 per cent
of the deities worshipped by members of ten high castes
below the Brahmans are Sanskritic; but only 15 and 19 per
cent, respectively, of the deities worshipped by members of
the low and lowest castes are Sanskritic deities.

That so small a proportion as 45 per cent of the deities
worshipped even by Brahmans are Sanskritic may occasion
some surprise, considering that Kishan Garhi stands in an
ancient area of Brahman settlement and characterization
(cf. O'Malley 1935: 129). The lands between the Ganges
and the Jumna appear to have been a region of Aryan settlement in the time of the *Brāhmaṇas* (Majumdar and
Pusalker 1951: 251–2); they appear as the *Brahmarṣideśa*,
as the *Madhyadeśa*, and again as the domain of the ancient
Pañcālas. Brahmans still hold a quarter of the lands of the

district as hereditary cultivators and still form more than
10 per cent of its population. In each village of the countryside around Kishan Garhi a Brahman lineage group
controls the hereditary office of priesthood of the village
site (*kheṛāpatī*). The *Sanādh* Brahmans of Kishan Garhi
are thus people of the soil rather than people of the book.
They are vernacular Brahmans: excepting the four individuals who are professional priests, the Brahmans of Kishan
Garhi address their deities with familiar prayers in the
local dialect of Braj Bhasha, not with vedic *mantras*. In
spite of the ancient habitation of Brahmans in this original
area of orthodoxy—perhaps, considering the conservatism
of local custom which is inherent in an indigenous civilization, one should say *because* of their ancient habitation in
this area—more than half of their deities in Kishan Garhi
are non-Sanskritic and still un-Sanskritized.

The relatively slight Sanskritization of the Brahmans in
this area contains a clue to the general slowness of Sanskritization and to the relatively small proportion of great-
traditional contents in the religion of the rest of the castes
in Kishan Garhi. Brahmans are, by their position in the
caste hierarchy and by their association with priesthood,
the best potential local agents of the great tradition. Since
their religious forms are in large part little-traditional, what
filters down from the Brahmans to lower castes in Kishan
Garhi must also be in large part little-traditional. Thus the
festival of Pitcher Fourth, whose lack of Sanskritic reference is described above, is explicitly identified in Kishan
Garhi as a festival of Brahman wives, who may not re-
marry if they are widowed; this festival is said to have been
taken up in recent generations by the lower castes of
Kisham Garhi. So, too, the priesthood of the village site,
which descends in the most influential Brahman lineage of
Kishan Garhi, is the priesthood of the non-Sanskritic
mother-godling called by the untranslatable name of
"*Cāmaṛ*"; when persons of lower caste would propitiate
this powerful mother-godling of the Brahmans, they must
take their offerings, not to any temple of the great tradition, but to *Cāmaṛ's* rude mound of stones and mud.

No doubt there has been through the millennia some
spread of Sanskritic deities from higher to lower castes in
Kishan Garhi, as posited by Srinivas for Hindus in general

(1953: 218, 226). But those few persons and groups of Kishan Garhi who have demonstrably in recent times taken on more Sanskritic, great-traditional forms of religion seem in every instance to have obtained them, not from the local higher castes, but from itinerant teachers of exotic cults, from urban-centered associations of recent growth, from new state schools, or from the market place. A newly standardized great tradition is thus externally available to the people of Kishan Garhi as a transformed, now heterogenetic criticism of the indigenous religious order of the village (cf. Hutton 1946: 204–5).

2. *Civilizational processes: parochialization and universalization.*—We may learn more of the processes of growth in Hindu civilization from the careers of these deities of Kishan Garhi if we conceive of civilizational growth not only as a process of Sanskritization which proceeds from high caste to low caste, or from place to place, or as a process of the distribution of literate elements to nonliterate people, but more broadly as all those processes by which many little traditions come to be related to a more universal great tradition. The processes of universalization and parochialization move along a vertical axis of Sanskritization and de-Sanskritization, but their range of play extends somewhat below its nether pole.

Parochialization—the downward movement and transformation of contents between great and little traditions—is evident among deities as it is among festivals in Kishan Garhi. In the festival of Nine *Durgās* described above, the local female godling *Naurthā* thus seems to have descended into the little tradition through linguistic change and loss of the meaning of a Sanskritic *tadbhava.*

The career of the Sanskritic divine sage, "Master of the Sperm" (*Śukrācārya*) (Renou and Filliozat 1947: 491), in Kishan Garhi further exemplifies the process of parochial devolution. "Master of the Sperm" is said by some Brahmans of Kishan Garhi to be the same as the planet Venus, the star which governs marriage and acts as a special patron of Brahmans. Possibly in pursuance of some one of these beliefs, ancestors of the leading lineage of Brahmans in Kishan Garhi at some time now forgotten seem to have erected a stone for the worship of "Master of the Sperm" beside a tree in a disused cremation ground. Every new

bride brought into that Brahman lineage is still taken out
with her groom a few days after her first arrival in order to
worship at that stone. But only two or three old men of
the lineage now recall the former Sanskritic significance
of the stone. As far as women of that lineage are concerned, as far as anyone else in the village knows, including
the Barber woman who must serve at every ceremony of
worshipping the stone, that stone in the old cremation
ground is no Sanskritic planetary deity, but simply the
abode of the ancestral spirits of the Brahman lineage whose
members placed it there. Such instances of downward
movement and eventual severance from the great tradition
may be compared with the downward growth and eventual
fall of a stalactite.

The beginnings of universalization, like the precipitates
of parochialization, are apparent far below the level of
Sanskritization among the deities of Kishan Garhi. Universalization among these deities appears to begin especially
through the deification of spirits of ancestors or of famous
other local residents of the village who are now deceased.
Thus the "Lord" (*Thākur*), the "Lady" (*Thākurānī*), and
"They of the Garden" in Kishan Garhi, who are the spirits
of powerful landlords of two or more generations ago, have
become public ghosts; for the most part, they operate
within the area of Kishan Garhi itself, but occasionally
they seize people of other villages who pass through. So
I was told by one professional exorcist of Kishan Garhi.

Building upward from the littlest tradition toward a
slightly greater tradition is the spirit of one late villager
named Happy Eyes (*Nain Sukha*). In life, Happy Eyes was
a famous curer of scabies, of the seven-year itch. Since his
death, he has gained a public shrine, which consists of
two dung-plastered bricks, located at the base of a tree in
front of a Sweeper's house. Happy Eyes's shrine is now
worshipped along with the local shrines of many mother-
godlings of skin diseases by all women of the village on the
day of Leftover Food Worship, or Goddess-Godling Worship. The Sweeper, who receives all offerings to Happy
Eyes's monument, is naturally interested in promoting
Happy Eyes's cult, since he thereby gains leftover food with
which to feed his pigs. Happy Eyes is still called a [male]
"godling" (*devatā*), but change of sex or the status of con-

sort seems to be destined for him sooner or later, considering his many feminine companions.

Further along toward a more universal deification is the deity who is worshipped in Kisham Garhi under the name of "Auspicious" (*Kalyāṇī*). Auspicious is the deification of a famous Hindu ascetic who actually resided long ago in the next district of Etah (Crooke 1896b, I: 220). Auspicious is now worshipped not merely at a pair of bricks by the people of one village, as is Happy Eyes, but at a temple shrine in Etah which is attended annually by thousands of persons coming from several districts.

Still more widely known and more broadly intelligible among the deities worshipped in Kishan Garhi is the "Old Gentleman" (*Miyān Sāhab*), a deity of pneumonia, fertility, etc. The cult of the Old Gentleman has grown up around the combined spirits of two Muslim personages who lived at different times in two different districts of western Uttar Pradesh, according to Crooke's sources (1896a, II: 274, III: 180–1; 1896b, I: 217). Unlike the cult of Auspicious, who has little if any popular sacred literature in Kishan Garhi, the cult of the Old Gentleman has developed several long vernacular songs. Members of the local caste group of Weavers in Kishan Garhi sing the songs of the Old Gentleman with enthusiasm, especially when they are paid to do so for therapeutic purposes. The Old Gentleman has substantial templelike shrines at both of his abodes in Jalesar and in Amroha. From so elaborate an indigenous cult as that of the Old Gentleman to the cult of an authenticated Sanskritic deity is but a short distance. The cult of the Old Gentleman, like the growth of a stalagmite, has nearly reached the ceiling.

The role of the material interests of Brahman priests in spreading the cults of Sanskritic deities has often been noted elsewhere. In Kishan Garhi the Weavers' interest in the cult of the Old Gentleman, like the Sweepers' interest in the cult of Happy Eyes, reminds us that the cults of local godlings may also be spread upward through the self-interested action of many other castes. One local caste group of Kishan Garhi, the Ascetics (*Jogīs*), combines the proselytizing of both a Sanskritic and a non-Sanskritic cult. These Ascetics derive a large part of their income from singing two devotional songs, one describing the wed-

ding of *Śiva*, the other describing the miraculous history
of the Saint Apparent (*Zāhir Pīr*), a merely regional deity.

In the careers of the little-traditional deities worshipped
in Kishan Garhi one can also trace the elaboration, the
refinement, and the systematization of the cults as such
toward more universal cultic forms. One can also trace in
them spatially the beginnings of a sacred geography which
is continuous with the sacred geography of India's great
tradition (Redfield and Singer 1954*b*: 19–20). The rudi-
ments of Hinduism's sacred geography are perhaps evident
in the Fair of the Well Godling in Kishan Garhi. This
fair and its godling, villagers say, were deliberately instituted by a landlord of Kishan Garhi some thirty years ago
in order to produce for himself a source of tolls and rents
from concessionaires. He installed the godling in the form
of a flat stone beside a well in his own garden, and announced that a fair would be held. The godling's fair has
prospered, and so have the owners of the garden. But the
landlord who founded the fair is now gone. People of
Kishan Garhi at the present day hold mixed views as to
the name and possible affiliations of this godling of the
fair. Some villagers say that since he is the "Well Godling"
(*Kue kā Devatā*), he may therefore be the same as the
famous "One of the Well" (*Kuānvālā*) whose abode is in
a village of nearby Mainpuri District (Crooke 1896*a*, II:
364). Other villagers say that he is the "One of Agra"
(*Āgrevālā*), identifying him with another Muslim deity
said to be installed in or at a well in the city of Agra, fifty
miles away (cf. Crooke 1896*a*, III: 81, 367). People of
Kishan Garhi also hold mixed views as to whether their
Well Godling is the apotheosis of a Brahman, a Muslim, a
Sweeper, or several of these. Whatever their particular
views, most villagers feel sure that the local Well Godling
is the "branch office" of one or another greater deity.
And, whatever their views, Brahmans, Weavers, Muslim
Beggars, Sweepers, and Goatherds pitch into the festival as
functionaries, while crowds from the nearby villages pour
in to obtain the benefits thought to derive from adoring
this parochial deity.

Of somewhat greater age and of greater areal sway than
Kishan Garhi's own Well Godling is the "Garden Godling" (*Bāg kā Devatā*) of one village neighboring on

Kishan Garhi. Sweepers of the neighborhood, who also serve as midwives for all castes, have played an important part in spreading the Garden Godling's reputation as a protector of babies. Each year at the time of the Garden Godling's festival they collect sugar and oil for his worship —and for their own use—from each of their clients in Kishan Garhi.

At still greater distances, many another local godling, goddess, mother, and cremation ground spirit (*masānī*) competes to draw worshippers from Kishan Garhi. Some of these local deities never rise to any greater refinement, but others take on more articulate and lettered forms of expression through competition. Without necessarily developing a homogeneous community of worship in any continuous region or even among the families of one village, the upward growth of such localized cults serves to connect the members of each little community with an overlapping congeries of greater communities of worship.

3. *Sanskritic identifications: effects on solidarity.*—Between the beginnings of upward universalization among parochial deities and the downward parochialization of universal deities there remains a gap in the kinds of evidence which one village can furnish in a short time. A few months or even a few years is too short a time in which to observe the actual composition of a new literary *purāṇa* or of a new subsidiary episode in the *Mahābhārata* out of materials developed in the cult of a deity risen from some little tradition. And perhaps the modern anthropological observer is arriving on the scene a little too close to the end of the puranic age to expect to observe its phenomena in full flower.

Less conclusive than the full literary Sanskritization of a little-traditional deity, but very much alive in Kishan Garhi, is the technique of identification. By the technique of identification each local or regional apotheosis is equated with some more universal deity of the great tradition, the lesser often being interpreted as an additional form or incarnation of the greater. Identification is perhaps the premier technique of the more inclusive process which Srinivas has called "Sanskritization" (1952, Chap. VII).

By identifying their local or regional deities with more widespread Sanskritic ones, Srinivas suggests, the Hindus of a region such as Coorg or the Hindus of all India come to have the same objects of worship, and therefore to have the sense of constituting a single regional or national community, respectively (p. 208).

The suggestion that solidarity arises out of Sanskritic identifications needs to be qualified for Kishan Garhi. Deities of the little tradition in Kishan Garhi are identified with deities of the great tradition in varying ways; the result is not necessarily an increased sense of community or an enlargement of cultural consciousness.

In the festival of Nine *Durgās*, for example, the mud idol is capable of the most diverse Sanskritic identifications. As noticed above, *Naurthā* is thought by many villagers to represent *Durgā*, *Kālī*, *et al.* or the goddess principle in general. But she is thought by others to represent *Śiva* and, by still others, to represent *Sītā*. While nearly all women and children in Kishan Garhi can agree that they have a common object of worship in the *Naurthā* of the little tradition, by no means all worshippers of *Naurthā* can agree on what object of the great tradition they simultaneously hold in common reverence.

The identifications of three other important little-traditional deities of Kishan Garhi demonstrate similar difficulties which would arise if villagers were to attempt to communicate with each other by triangulation through the great tradition. These three deities are the feminine godlings Stony One, Earthy, and *Cāmar̥*. Sanskritic identifications are easily enough made for each of these feminine godlings separately; indeed, these lady godlings of the village are on the whole the most upwardly mobile of all little-traditional deities. The Stony One, for example, has for at least a generation and probably much longer been identified with a famous manifestation of the great goddess *Pārvatī* or *Satī Devī* at Nagarkot in Kangra District, Punjab. The Goddess is said to manifest herself at Nagarkot in the form of a sulphorous mountain which still glows at night with the fires in which she was herself extinguished. Members of nearly every Hindu family in Kishan Garhi worship the Stony One and identify her explicitly with the Goddess of Nagarkot. Thus when pilgrims are ready to depart each year from the village to go to Nagarkot, public worship is held at the mound of the Stony One. And while the pilgrims are away, members of their families continue to make offerings of fire and water at the Stony One (cf. Channing 1882: 35).

But this identification of the Stony One with the Goddess of Nagarkot and thence with the goddess complex of the great tradition does not go unchallenged. In the neighboring district of Agra, for example, *Patthvārī* is said by a different Sanskritic etymology to be the "Goddess of the Roadways" (Crooke 1896a, II: 426). Srinivas cites an instance of a similar conflict in the identification of cobras with the Sanskritic deity *Subrahmaṇya* in Coorg and Mysore, and with *Nāgās* elsewhere in India (1952: 218). Such competing and inconsistent Sanskritic identifications are not unusual but quite the rule in and around Kishan Garhi.

While Sanskritic identifications of the Stony One vary from place to place, in Kishan Garhi itself Stony One competes with *Cāmar*, the mother-goddess of the village site, for identification with the Goddess of Nagarkot. Some years ago, *Cāmar's* powers were apparently believed to be very great. Refugees are said to have settled in Kishan Garhi during the Mutiny of 1857 because of the supernatural protection which she offered. *Cāmar's* credentials as local representative of the Goddess of Nagarkot were at that time also made firm. One pilgrim to Nagarkot brought back some fragments of stone sculpture from the greater goddess's temple and placed those fragments atop *Cāmar's* mound for all to see. In more recent times, however, identification with the great goddess seems to have shifted largely to the Stony One.

Like the Stony One, *Cāmar's* own identifications within the lesser traditions are not without uncertainty and conflict. By general opinion in Kishan Garhi, she is certainly a goddess: many persons refer to her as "*Cāmar* Mother" (cf. Crooke 1896a, II: 225). But in other parts of Aligarh District and in Agra District, a local deity of the same name is said to be masculine in gender (Crooke 1896a, I: 46; III: 81).

Earthy (*Bhūmiyā*), a third mother-goddess of Kishan Garhi's little tradition, is beset by similar Sanskritic complexities. If we join villagers of Kishan Garhi in identifying Earthy with the greater Mother (*Mātā*) and Goddess complex of Hinduism, then we will be confused in Delhi District to find Earthy identified with the masculine Sanskritic deity called Field Protector (*Kṣetrapālā*) (Crooke 1896*b*, I: 105). We will be further confused in another district to find that a local godling of the village site is called alternatively *Bhūmiya* or *Bhairoṇ*, and is therefore identified with a manifestation of the great god *Śiva* (Crooke 1896*b*, I: 107–8). We will be still further confused in Patna District, Bihar, for Crooke reports that Earthy is there identified as a manifestation of *Viṣṇu* (p. 107). Earthy's diverse identifications indicate that villagers of Aligarh, Delhi, and Patna might more accurately sense their actual community of worship by sticking with that identical nomenclature provided by the common ground of their respective little traditions rather than by resorting to indirect, triangular communication through the discrepant *Mātā*, *Kṣetrapāla*, *Śiva*, and *Viṣṇu* of greater traditions.

The careers of these four female deities of Kishan Garhi demonstrate the facility with which identifications may bridge the gap between great and little traditions in India's indigenous civilization. They also demonstrate the confusions which resort to the medium of the great tradition can put in the way of communication between two adjacent and only slightly variant little traditions. Sanskritization may obscure as well as clarify the nearness of two little traditions: the Delhi villager who identifies his Earthy with *Kṣetrapāla* will be closer by Sanskritic idiom to the Coorg villager who worships his *Kētrappa* as *Kṣetrapāla* one thousand miles away (Srinivas 1952: 223) than he will be to the villager of Kishan Garhi 100 miles away who also worships Earthy, but in another Sanskritic guise. Although Sanskritic identifications do not necessarily bring adjacent little communities closer to each other, they do bring the great community closer to all little communities. To each little tradition, Sanskritic identifications lend the sense of derivative participation in the great tradition which is authoritative, not only because it is indigenous, but also because it is refined, learned, and ecumenical. Sanskritization thus heightens and dignifies the sphere of communication for each little community; it does not necessarily widen that sphere.

If reference to the Sanskritic great tradition of Hinduism sometimes confounds or prevents communication within and among adjacent little traditions, it also, of course, provides a saving doctrine for some persons at a higher level. In place of disordered polytheism and endless polymorphism, the philosophic villager in Kishan Garhi is free to put pantheism—the conception that all deities everywhere, no matter how parochial or non-Sanskritic, are but manifestations of a single divine Oversoul (*Paramātma*). If all deities are one, then accurate communication about particular objects of worship becomes a matter of irrelevant details.

¶ SUMMARY AND CONCLUSION

Seen through its festivals and deities, the religion of the village of Kishan Garhi may be conceived as resulting from continuous processes of communication between a little, local tradition and greater traditions which have their places partly inside and partly outside the village. Only residual fragments of the religion of such a little community can be conceived as distinctive or separable.

Since both great and little traditions exist within the religion of little communities and there communicate, study of the religion of a little community can contribute to understanding of processes of universalization and parochialization which are generally operative in Indian civilization. Preliminary study of the contents of religion in Kishan Garhi indicates, for example, that great and little traditions may remain in equilibrium within the little community, neither tending to exclude the other: elements of the great tradition undergo parochial transformation as they spread, while the great tradition itself, where it originates as a universalization of indigenous materials, lacks authority to replace elements of the little tradition. Communication between indigenous greater and lesser traditions may proceed vertically without necessarily effecting any contiguous lateral enlargement of the community of common culture. A focus upon the small half-world of the village and a perspective upon the universe of Indian civilization thus remain mutually indispensable for whole understanding, whether of Hinduism or of the traditional forms of India's social structure.

REFERENCES CITED

BADEN-POWELL, B. H.

1892   *The Land Systems of British India.* 3 vols. Oxford: Clarendon.

1900   "The Villages of Goa in the Early Sixteenth Century." *Journal of the Royal Asiatic Society*, pp. 261–91. London.

1908   *The Origin and Growth of Village Communities in India.* London: Swan Sonnenschien.

BAILEY, F. G.

1953   "An Oriya Hill Village." *Economic Weekly*, Vol. 5, pp. 326–8. Bombay.

BEALS, ALAN ROBIN

1953   "Change in the Leadership of a Mysore Village." *Economic Weekly*, Vol. 5, pp. 487–92. Bombay.

1954   "The Government and the Indian Village." *Economic Development and Cultural Change*, Vol. 2, pp. 397–407. Chicago.

BROWN, W. NORMAN

1919   "The Pañcatantra in Modern Indian Folklore." *Journal of the American Oriental Society*, Vol. 39, pp. 1–54. Baltimore.

CARSTAIRS, G. MORRIS

1952   "A Village in Rajasthan—a Study in Rapid Social Change." *Economic Weekly*, Vol. 4, pp. 75–7. Bombay.

CHANNING, F. C.

1882   *Land Revenue Settlement of the Gurgaon District.* Lahore: Central Jail Press.

CROOKE, WILLIAM

1896a   *The Tribes and Castes of the North-Western Provinces and Oudh.* 4 vols. Calcutta: Superintendent of Government Printing.

1896b   *The Popular Religion and Folk-Lore of Northern India.* 2 vols. Westminster: Archibald Constable.

FOSTER, GEORGE M.

1953   "What Is Folk Culture?" *American Anthropologist*, Vol. 55, pp. 159–73. Menasha, Wisconsin.

GHOSHAL, U. N.

1929   *Contributions to the History of the Hindu Revenue System.* Calcutta: University of Calcutta.

GOUGH, E. KATHLEEN

1952   "The Social Structure of a Tanjore Village." *Economic Weekly*, Vol. 4, pp. 531–6. Bombay.

GRIERSON, GEORGE A.
   1880   "Proper Names." *Indian Antiquary*, Vol. 9, p. 141.
          Bombay.
GRIFFITHS, W. C.
   1946   *The Kol Tribe of Central India*. Calcutta: Royal Asiatic
          Society of Bengal.
GROWSE, F. S.
   1880   *Mathurā: A District Memoir*. Second ed. Allahabad:
          North-Western Provinces and Oudh Government
          Press.
HANSSEN, BÖRJE
   1953   "Fields of Social Activity and Their Dynamics." *Trans-
          actions of the Westermarck Society*, pp. 99–133. Copen-
          hagen.
HEIN, NORVIN
   1950   "The Ram Lila, a Pageant of the People." *The Illus-
          trated Weekly of India*, Vol. 71, No. 43, pp. 18–19.
          Bombay.
HOCART, A. M.
   1950   *Caste: A Comparative Study*. London: Methuen.
HUTCHINSON, J. R.
   1856   *Allygurh Statistics; Being a Report on the General
          Administration of That District from A.D. 1803 to
          the Present Time*. Roorkee: Thomason College Press.
HUTTON, J. H.
   1946   "Hinduism in Its Relation to Primitive Religions in
          India," in *Caste in India* by J. H. HUTTON, pp. 195–
          232. Cambridge at the University Press.
LALLŪ LĀL
   1897   *The Prema-Sāgara, or Ocean of Love*. . . . Translated
          by Frederic Pincott. Westminster: Archibald Constable.
LEWIS, OSCAR
   1954   "Group Dynamics in a North-Indian Village: A Study
          in Factions." *Economic Weekly*, Vol. 6, pp. 423–5,
          445–51, 477–82, 501–6. Bombay.
MAJUMDAR, R. C. and A. D. PUSALKER, eds.
   1951   *The Vedic Age. The History and Culture of the Indian
          People*, Vol. 1. London: George Allen & Unwin.
MANDELBAUM, DAVID G.
   1952   "Technology, Credit and Culture in an Indian Village."
          Economic Weekly, Vol. 4, pp. 827–8. Bombay.
MARRIOTT, McKIM
   1952   "Social Structure and Change in a U.P. Village."
          Economic Weekly, Vol. 4, pp. 869–74. Bombay.
   1955   "Western Medicine in a Village of Northern India,"
          in *Health, Culture and Community: A Book of Cases*,
          ed. Benjamin D. Paul. New York: Russell Sage Founda-
          tion. (Forthcoming.)

MILLER, ERIC J.
  1952 "Village Structure in North Kerala." *Economic Weekly*,
        Vol. 4, pp. 159–64. Bombay.
MISRA, B. R.
  1942 *Land Revenue Policy in the United Provinces under
        British Rule*. Benares: Nand Kishore.
MORELAND, W. H.
  1937 "The Revenue System of the Mughal Empire," in *The
        Mughal Period*, ed. Sir Richard Burn. The Cambridge
        History of India, Vol. 4. Cambridge at the University
        Press.
MORGAN, KENNETH W.
  1953 *The Religion of the Hindus*. New York: Ronald
        Press.
NEVILL, H. R.
  1909 *Aligarh: A Gazetteer*. District Gazetteers of the United
        Provinces of Agra and Oudh, Vol. 6. Allahabad: Gov-
        ernment Press.
NEWELL, WILLIAM H.
  1952 "A Himalayan Village." *Economic Weekly*, Vol. 4,
        pp. 208–10. Bombay.
O'MALLEY, L. S. S.
  1935 *Popular Hinduism*. Cambridge at the University Press.
OPLER, MORRIS E. and RUDRA DATT SINGH
  1948 "The Division of Labor in an Indian Village," in *A
        Reader in General Anthropology*, ed. C. S. Coon, pp.
        464–96. New York: Henry Holt & Co., Inc.
PETER, P. C.
  1952 "Theocratic Landlordism." *Journal of the University of
        Bombay*, Vol. 20, No. 4, pp. 44–9. Bombay.
REDFIELD, ROBERT
  1953 *The Primitive World and Its Transformations*. Ithaca:
        Cornell University Press.
  1955 *The Little Community*. Chicago: University of Chicago
        Press.
REDFIELD, ROBERT and MILTON SINGER
  1954*a* Comparison of Cultures: The Indian Village. Chicago,
          Department of Anthropology, University of Chicago.
          (Hectographed.)
  1954*b* "The Cultural Role of Cities." *Economic Development
          and Cultural Change*, Vol. 3, pp. 53–73. Chicago.
RENOU, LOUIS and JEAN FILLIOZAT
  1947 *L'Inde classique, manuel des études indiennes*, Vol. 1.
        Paris: Payot.
ROSE, H. A.
  1919 *A Glossary of the Tribes and Castes of the Punjab and
        North-West Frontier Province*. 3 vols. Lahore, Super-
        intendent of Government Printing.

SMITH, MARIAN W.
1953 "Social Structure in the Punjab." *Economic Weekly*, Vol. 5, pp. 1291–8. Bombay.

SRINIVAS, M. N.
1951 "The Social Structure of a Mysore Village." *Economic Weekly*, Vol. 3, pp. 1051–6. Bombay.
1952 *Religion and Society among the Coorgs of South India.* Oxford: Clarendon Press.
1954 "Village Studies." *Economic Weekly*, Vol. 6, pp. 605–9. Bombay.

STARR, BETTY W.
1954 "Levels of Communal Relations." *American Journal of Sociology*, Vol. 60, pp. 125–35. Chicago.

STEWARD, JULIAN H.
1951 "Levels of Sociocultural Integration: An Operational Concept." *Southwestern Journal of Anthropology*, Vol. 7, pp. 374–90. Albuquerque.

STEWARD, JULIAN H. and ROBERT A. MANNERS
1953 "The Cultural Study of Contemporary Societies: Puerto Rico." *American Journal of Sociology*, Vol. 54, pp. 123–30. Chicago.

SWAMI SIVANANDA
1947 *Hindu Fasts and Festivals and Their Philosophy.* Rikhikesh, U.P.: Sivananda Publication League.

TEMPLE, RICHARD C.
1883 *A Dissertation on the Proper Names of Panjābīs. . . .* Bombay: Education Society's Press.
1884– *The Legends of the Panjāb.* 3 vols. Bombay: Educa-
1900 tion Society's Press.

THOMASON, JAMES
1838 "Report on the Settlement of the Ceded Portion of the District of Azimgurh . . ." *Journal of the Asiatic Society of Bengal*, n.s., Vol. 8, pp. 77–136. Calcutta.
1858 *Directions for Revenue Officers in the North-Western Provinces of the Bengal Presidency. . . .* New ed. Calcutta: Baptist Mission Press.

UNDERHILL, M. M.
1921 *The Hindu Religious Year.* Calcutta: Association Press.

WARNER, W. L.
1949 *Democracy in Jonesville.* New York: Harper & Brothers.
1953 *American Life: Dream and Reality.* Chicago: University of Chicago Press.

WEISS, RICHARD
1946 *Volkskunde der Schweiz.* Zurich: Eugen Rentch Verlag.

WHEELER, Sir MORTIMER
1953 *The Indus Civilization.* The Cambridge History of India, Supplementary Volume. Cambridge at the University Press.

WISER, WILLIAM H.

  1933   "Social Institutions of a Hindu Village in Northern India." Unpublished Ph.D. dissertation, Cornell University, Ithaca.

  1936   *The Hindu Jajmani System.* Lucknow: Lucknow Publishing House.

❦❦ ❦❦

A Note about the Author

David G. Mandelbaum

DAVID G. MANDELBAUM (1911–   ) was an undergraduate at Northwestern University when he took a course in
anthropology with Melville Herskovits. Encouraged by
Herskovits, he undertook graduate study at Yale University
just as Edward Sapir was organizing a new Department of
Anthropology.

Mandelbaum conducted field research in 1937–8 among
the Kotas, an aboriginal tribe in the Nilgiri Hills of South
India. The essay here reprinted is based upon that research.
Together with the preceding essays by Milton Singer and
McKim Marriott, it forms a sequence on urban, peasant
village, and tribal levels of religion in India. Although
Mandelbaum describes a religious innovation among the
Kotas by paying particular attention to the personalities of
the innovators, the change itself is another example of the
relationship between the great traditions of Hinduism and
the little traditions of local communities discussed by
Singer and Marriott. In a Postscript written especially for
this edition of his essay, Mandelbaum reports a more recent visit to the Kotas.

As a Guggenheim Fellow in 1949–50, Mandelbaum
conducted field research in India, and in 1958 he traveled
in the country under UNESCO auspices. He is presently
working on problems of social organization in India, with
the intention of improving our theoretical understanding
of civilization.

At Yale University Mandelbaum's main teachers were
Edward Sapir, Leslie Spier, and Clark Wissler. He did
his first field research in 1933 with a Laboratory of An-
thropolgy linguistic group among the San Carlos Apache.
In the summers of 1934 and 1935 he did further research

in Canada in Plains Cree communities. This work provided the materials for his Ph.D. dissertation, and for a monograph published by the American Museum of Natural History.

David Mandelbaum has been on the faculty of the University of California, Berkeley, since 1946. He was Visiting Fulbright Professor at the University of Cambridge in 1953, and in 1957–8, a Fellow of the Center for Advanced Study in the Behavorial Sciences. He has been a member of the Executive Board of the American Anthropological Association, and is now serving his second term as a member of the United States National Commission for UNESCO.

Social Trends
and Personal Pressures[*][1]

by

DAVID G. MANDELBAUM

In March of 1924 an epidemic of relapsing fever—a louse-borne disease—struck the Kotas of the Nilgiri Hills in South India. Of all the tribe, the village Kolme·l was hardest hit. Within a month almost one fourth of its 300 inhabitants were dead; before the epidemic burned itself out in September, well over half the villagers had fallen

* The following essay is reprinted by permission of David G. Mandelbaum. It was first published in LANGUAGE, CULTURE, AND PERSONALITY: ESSAYS IN MEMORY OF EDWARD SAPIR, edited by Leslie Spier, A. Irving Hallowell, and Stanley S. Newman; Sapir Memorial Publication Fund, Menasha, Wisconsin, 1941.

1 The Kota field work was financed by the National Research Council and by the Institute of Human Relations, Yale University. It was carried on while Dr. M. B. Emeneau was conducting researches on the Kota language. I am deeply indebted to him for aid and advice in the field. An interpreter was used with all informants save one, Sulli.

This essay first appeared in a volume of essays honoring Edward Sapir. Professor Sapir was much interested in the interplay between culture and personality. He felt that there was an invidious dissociation between the ethnologist's studies of cultural forms and the psychologist's or psychiatrist's studies of individual behavior. In his teaching and writing, he led the way to a field of dynamic ethnology wherein the two approaches to the study of man could be brought together. The problems in that field have to do largely with the meanings for the individual of the patterns which culture recognizes. If he may not be called the father of this realm of research, he is certainly one godfather who stood sponsor for it and steadfastly worked to make its name respectable and its importance recognized. This essay illustrates some of the principles propounded by Sapir with case examples from a field study which he fostered.

victims to the disease. During the following years, a new set of gods was adopted by the villagers, shrines built to them, and new ceremonies conducted by special officiants consecrated to their worship.

In 1937–8, when the writer was with the tribe, the new religious complex was firmly installed in Kolme·l. Those of the villagers who worship the new gods also fulfill their duties to the ancient deities of the tribe. Some, however, stubbornly refuse to admit the innovation and continue to follow only the older religious forms. The shift of religious allegiance is an event of significance in the historical career of the tribe and is a matter of concern to the individuals involved. Since this bit of culture change is of recent occurrence, the chief participants could be used as informants. It is the purpose of this paper to trace the genesis and development of the new religious idea complex in terms of the pressures, both personal and societal, which affected its growth.

To set the scene for a discussion of the event, we may briefly outline the salient features of Kota culture. The two great mountain ranges which run parallel to the east and west coasts of the Indian peninsula meet in the south to form the Nilgiri plateau. This high, isolated tract, often capped by mist, is much cooler than the plains which surround it. Rolling grasslands cover the plateau, with scattered groves and thickets in the sheltered valleys and hillsides. The flora and the fauna of the Nilgiris are different from those of the neighboring lowlands, and the aboriginal inhabitants, too, are culturally distinct from the peoples who live below.

Four tribes live on the plateau: Todas, Kotas, Kurumbas, and Badagas. The Badagas are agriculturalists, whose staple of diet was and is millet. The Todas are purely a pastoral people whose whole interest—economic, social, religious—revolves about their herds of buffalo. The Kurumbas live on the fringes of the plateau where the jungle creeps up the hillsides. They depend partly on hunting and food gathering, but mostly on the yield of their tribal trade, sorcery. The Kotas are artisans and musicians who live in seven villages which are scattered among the Toda and Badaga settlements.

The long cultural isolation of the Nilgiri tribes may be

attributed to the steepness of their hills and to the climate of their highland terrain. They formed a cultural enclave which was unperturbed by the great goings and comings that went on below, not fifty miles away. But when the English came to India, all this was changed. The English sought some refuge from the summer heat of the plains, and about 100 years ago discovered the Nilgiris. Before long a road was hacked through to the plateau, and every summer the provincial government was moved up to the hills. With the Europeans came their servants and an influx of merchants. The cultural solitude of the tribes was broken; they were exposed to the simultaneous impact of two differing cultures, Indian and English.

Although the old patterns of intertribal relations have been weakened, they still are maintained. The tightly integrated Toda culture has been little affected by alien influence; the Kurumbas in their jungles are remote from it; many conservative Badagas still carry on the old relations with the Kotas. At the present time the Kotas still practice their traditional trades, and the Kota village functions much as it did a century ago.

In each Kota village there are three exogamous patrilineal sibs, making a total of twenty-one father sibs for the tribe. There is some cultural differentiation among the villages, but all adhere to a general pattern of religious observance. Three deities are worshipped: Ayno·r, Amno·r, and Kunayno·r—Father God, Mother God, and Younger Brother God. Three temples are to be found in every Kota village, one for each deity.

A seasonal cycle of ceremonies is devoted to the worship of the gods. Every village has its own set of religious officiants for the enactment of the ceremonies. The priest leads the people in prayer, makes the offerings, and conducts the sequence of ritual observance. In some villages there is but one priest; in others there are two, one to care for the male gods, the other for the female deity. The priest's life is dedicated to the service of the gods and is surrounded with interdictions and taboos. The priest must keep apart from all other men, and may not mingle with them too freely.

At specified times during the course of every major ritual, the priest stands aside and the focus of attention rests on another religious officiant, the diviner. Every village has three diviners, one for each god. It is through them that the deities make their voices heard and their desires known to men. When the appropriate time arrives for the presence of the divinity to manifest itself, the priest addresses a special prayer to the god. A spasm of shivering works through the diviner, then another, and his head begins to shake from side to side. The head movements continue with increasing velocity until it seems as though no human vertebrae could stand the strain. The diviner may fall to his knees and beat his palms against the earth with furious tattoo, but the deity does not speak through him until his hair is loosened. The long Kota locks are tied up with a cord which has ritual significance, and this cord must be dislodged by the force of the head motion. When the diviner's hair does fly free about his oscillating head, a strangled sob bursts forth from him—the first articulation of the god speaking through its chosen medium. With jerky, strangulated utterance, the diviner's voice serves as the mouthpiece of the deity. The voice tells the tribesmen wherein they have transgressed, and what they must do if the gods are no longer to frown. Questions are asked of the god—why has the south field not yielded a crop? why is my wife barren? why is my child ill?—and the queries are answered. The messages imparted, the god withdraws. The diviner's gesticulations come to an abrupt end and he sinks limply to the ground.

The life of the diviner, too, is hedged about with ritual restraints. But these are not as numerous or as exacting as those which govern the conduct of the priest. A widower may not hold either office. Priest and diviner alike must relinquish his office upon the death of his spouse.

When either office is vacant, the post is filled by divine appointment. During the course of the God Ceremony, the most important on the calendar, all eligible men stand before the temple, and a group prayer is addressed to the god who is to choose one of them. If it is a priest who is to be chosen, the diviner becomes possessed and pulls one of the worshippers forward to bow before the entrance to the temple. Later, a consecration ceremony is held to dedicate the nominee to the service of the god. The new priest occupies a special house, is given cattle by the community, and should he be unmarried, may have any woman, be she maid or wife—though not widow—for his own.

When a diviner is to be chosen, the men similarly assemble before the temple. The priest, who never becomes possessed himself, fervently prays for the appointment of a new diviner. One of the assembly begins to shake in the stereotyped manner of diviners, comes forward, touches the front pillar of the temple, and forthwith becomes the new Voice. Sometimes it happens that more than one man will quake and shiver on this occasion. The one who comes forward and touches the pillar first is the choice of the god.

The questions asked of the diviners in their trance have usually to do with misfortunes, personal and communal. And misfortunes usually are the work of Kurumbas. A Kurumba may have been offended by too small a fee and has laid a spell on a child in revenge. Or a fellow villager, in envy of his neighbor's fine crop and bonny son, has hired a Kurumba to send a blight to both. The only remedy is to secure the services of another Kurumba to practice more powerful sorcery and exorcise the evil.

But exorcism was of little avail in 1924. People were dying so rapidly that the Kurumbas themselves were afraid to come near the village. As the epidemic blazed on, the cremation ceremonies for the dead were not forgotten or stinted. In a few months the scanty village stores of food and fuel were exhausted. Cold and hunger were added to the general misery. Sulli, the schoolmaster, the only Kota who understands English and who has had some education among the Hindus, counseled the villagers to abandon their customary funeral rituals and bury the bodies with little ado. But the villagers had no desire to abandon this morsel of certitude, this familiar traditional form, in the moment of greatest stress. As is often true for other men, so too for the Kotas. At the time of greatest uncertainty they clung most desperately to the known, and had least desire to venture out into unknown procedures. Though they knew that the traditional ceremonies for so many dead would sorely deplete their reserves, still they felt that when all seemed uncertain, when life itself was perilously balanced, they must fulfill this ceremony unchanged.

Toward the end of the year the epidemic finally burned itself out. The daily round of Kota life was re-established; men tried to carry on with their former ways. A month or so after the "dry funeral" in December, the Kotas celebrate the God Ceremony. This is the great event of the ceremonial year. Solemn rituals entail weeks of preparation, extend through days. All that pertains to the gods is renewed or refurbished. If a sacred office is open, a recruit is divinely chosen to join with the old priests and diviners in the performance of the service. But at the God Ceremony in January 1925 there were no old priests or diviners. To a man, the former officiants had died of the fever. The men eligible for the offices stood before the temples as always. The assembled villagers prayed with deep fervor for the appointment of successors as always. But as had not happened before in the memory of the people, no man was supernaturally propelled to the temple pillar to be diviner; none was seized as priest.

Soon after, another strange occurrence took place. Kusvain became possessed. Kusvain had once been a diviner, but had had to give up the office when his wife had died. As an unfrocked diviner, he could not officially be chosen as the vehicle of a deity. Stranger still, the voice that came through him in his possession announced that it was that of Raŋgayṇo·r. This deity was a Hindu god, worshipped at a temple in the hamlet of Karaimadai, near the foot of the plateau. Moreover, the voice of this new deity announced that priests and diviners could not be chosen for the old triad until shrines were built for Raŋgayṇo·r and two other deities who were to form a new Trinity.

Now, Kusvain is a person of little prestige. Shiftless, irresponsible, he commands small respect. It is understandable, then, why the villagers would have none of his revelations and did not heed the injunctions which issued from him. But when a year passed, and the God Ceremony was held once again, and still no priests or diviners were chosen, then the villagers were more disposed to take note and obey. Sulli, especially, advocated the acceptance of the new revelation and urged the others to heed the new gods.

So, when Kusvain became possessed again and the god

Raŋgayṇo·r spoke through him, the people worshipfully saluted and replied that they would take heed. Shaking with the spirit of the deity, Kusvain led the congregation to a pasture near the village, and the voice commanded: "Here shall you build me a temple." Some men, Ka·kn among them, had little enthusiasm for the venture and tried to counter with some objections. But in the end the shrines were built, small structures of brick with one side open and roofs of corrugated iron. Kusvain's spirit told of the proper procedure for the service of the new gods. For them coconuts and plantains must be offered on brass platters before a lamp lit within the shrine. The ritual of the old gods included none of these elements. Coconuts and plantains were unobtainable before roads and the railroad were built; temple lamps and ceremonial platters were used in Hindu temples on the plains.

Not long after Kusvain had led the villagers to the site of the shrines, two other men became possessed. One had never been a diviner before. His voice proclaimed him to be the vehicle of Beṭdamn, a female deity, whose worship is known to the plainsmen. The other had once before been a diviner, but, like Kusvain, had been relieved of the position by the death of his wife. He became diviner for Ra·mayṇo·r, the Kota version of the Hindu deity Rama. Kusvain chose a priest for these gods.

Kusvain had prophesied that sacred retainers for the old gods would be chosen after shrines for the new were built, and so it came to pass. When the villages had made their obeisance to the new Trinity, the God Ceremony was resumed. The men of Kolme·l stood before the temples; the spirit of the old gods came upon three men, and they were the diviners. They seized two men who became the priests.

In the years that followed, the ritual for the service of the new gods became established. In general pattern the worship of the new gods closely parallels the worship of the old. The priest of the ke·rva·y gods—so-called from the pasture, ke·rva·y, in which the shrines were built— must pray before the shrines at dawn and again at dusk, just as do the other priests for the ancient gods. Kusvain and his fellow diviners of the new dispensation become possessed and speak with the voice of their particular deity.

It is noteworthy that the voice of the new gods never advises the abandonment of the worship of the old gods. And the diviners of the orthodox convention never revile the upstart supernaturals.

During the celebration of the ancient ceremonies, the adherents of the new gods go through the traditional ritual and then come to the ke·rva·y shrines to make additional offerings and intone more prayers. But the form of the prayers is exactly the same as those repeated before the old temples save that the names of the new gods are substituted for those of the old.

Only one ceremony is celebrated exclusively for the newer divinities. After the traditional God Ceremony is completed, another God Ceremony is staged for the new gods. It is somewhat less elaborate than the first, extends over a much shorter time, but maintains essentially the same ritual procedure. In like manner the whole corpus of taboo and duty toward the new gods is less rigorous than that for the old, but the general pattern of worship is the same for the two.

The names of the new gods have been taken from the Hindu pantheon, and lowland traits have been introduced into the new ritual, but apart from these particulars the ke·rva·y complex closely resembles the older religion. For barriers of language and social status separate the Kota villager from any intimate contact with followers of the Hindu deities; hence he cannot obtain fresh ideas concerning the nature of the gods or new concepts about the proper behavior of religionists. A casual Kota observer, peeping into a Hindu temple, can see the use of plantains and coconuts, lamps and platters, incense and camphor, and can easily obtain these things in the bazaar. But he is shut off from any glimpse of the attitudes which surround the use of these material traits. Here, as in much of the history of culture change, we find that material traits and formalized modes of action are more amenable to diffusion than are the less readily apparent complexes of behavior. The villagers of Kolme·l, no less than other peoples, have integrated the borrowed bits of material culture and formal procedure into a pre-existing larger pattern which remains, in bold outline, but little altered.

At this juncture we can make certain preliminary statements to answer the question—how have the Kota come by this new element of their culture? The evidence of diffusion is clear and simple. Men of the tribe occasionally ride the railroad down to the plains, and sometimes visit the temple at Karaimode. There they have learned of a deity called Rangen, as well as of Rama and Beṭdamn. Hindu temples have also been established on the plateau, and a Kota can hardly escape observing certain gross features of Hindu ritual. These have been borrowed by the tribesmen and adapted to their tribal usage. Since Kota deities have names ending in the suffix -ayṇ (father), or -ayṇo·r (father god), the Hindu names Rama and Rangen become Ra·mayṇo·r and Raṇgayṇo·r. Since the old pattern calls for a Trinity, the divine couple of the Karaimadai temple are accompanied by another Hindu deity. Other aspects of the new pattern also demonstrate the process of diffusion and integration.

This piece of historic reconstruction clears the way for an approach to further questions. Why were these new elements introduced precisely at this time? What factors eased the change; what conditions hampered it? What meaning did the new cult have for different individuals within the village? Why has it been embraced by some and rejected by others? The answers to these questions can best be couched in terms of the personalities involved. To establish the fact of diffusion it was possible and advisable to speak of culture complexes and of the diffusion and integration of culture traits. But if we are to make sense of the succeeding problems, reference must be made to the human *dramatis personæ*, the living characters who took part in the event.

The locus of this culture change lies in the fact that Tom and Dick of Kolme·l village began to do certain things they had not done before. Harry did not join them in this new behavior and did his utmost to prevent them from going on with it. If we are to understand why Tom and Dick were impelled toward a certain mode of action while Harry recoiled from it, we must have a look at the personal make-up of Tom, Dick, and Harry. True, it will never be possible to plumb the depths of each personality involved in a social situation, but a good deal of light can be thrown on the dynamics of social interaction by a consideration of key personalities. Three men have played major roles in the action at Kolme·l.

Kusvain appears to be the prime mover in all that went on. A brief account of the occurrence, such as that above, must give Kusvain the center of the stage. He is the vehicle of the new divinities; their words through him institute the new worship and direct the form of the ritual; he speaks (with the voice of the Gods, to be sure), and the people listen and obey. But a closer study of Kusvain's personal history and of his relations within the society must relegate him to a part of considerably less importance.

Kusvain has never been a person of any consequence in the regard of his fellow tribesmen. Men may acquire prestige via several avenues. Able craftsmanship, accumulation of wealth, adeptness in catching buffalo, skillful argumentation in council—all enhance the status of a man and enable him to influence the behavior of others, to be a leader. Kusvain often has to beg for his food, is not a craftsman at all, has never gained particular acclaim in the buffalo chase, and does not open his mouth in council. Several informants characterized him as a shiftless ne'er-do-well.

The one way in which he is able to distinguish himself, to win personal victories, is by being a diviner. The diviner, by his very office, commands the accouterments of prestige and respect. He stands before the assembled congregation during ceremonies; he is accorded a special place when he visits another house; he is respectfully attended by the priest during ceremonies. But despite these symbols of respect, a diviner's prestige status in the group depends on how he measures up to the requirements for prestige which apply to all men. Moreover, the utterances of a diviner in possession may be disregarded if he is known to be a fool in the daily round of life, or obeyed to the letter if he is a man of standing. The formal dogma of the religion has it that anything revealed by the diviner during possession is a message from the godhead. Any informant will solemnly and sincerely assert that it is so and marshal many wondrous case examples in which the diviner's prediction came to pass. But an intimate acquaintance with the culture reveals numerous instances in which the prediction went wild. These cases do not shake Kota faith, since the diviner may have been misunderstood or his words misinterpreted. Similarly, an observer can find occasions in which a diviner's message was utterly disregarded. When pressed to account for these, a Kota will answer somewhat in this wise: "Well, sometimes it is an evil spirit that gets into the diviner instead of the God, or else it may be that the God didn't really come to the diviner and he just speaks out of his own mind."

The crux of the matter is that the whole life behavior of the diviner determines the manner in which his supernatural speeches are received. Just as a minister in our society is accorded the show of respect due his office, while his prestige in the society—i.e., his ability to influence behavior—rests on his personal attributes, so among the Kota: the diviner must be treated with deference, but the compulsive force of his messages depends on his status and personality. It must be said that the official significance of this pattern usually coincides with its actual significance; the diviner's words are taken very seriously. But when a diviner is patently an eccentric or a dimwit, then the villagers, by a sort of tacit consent, rarely listen to what he has to say, in possession or out.

Such a person is Kusvain. Sulli scornfully epitomized his behavior:

> Kusvain's conduct is very bad. . . . His habit is this. He calls a woman over to him and when she stands before him he begins to shake as though possessed and says, "You have sinned, you have sinned." The poor ignorant woman, what does she know? She fears and says, "O God, O God," and she thinks, "O, the God knows what mistakes I have done." Then he says to her, while shaking, "If you come and lie with me tonight at such and such a place you will be forgiven." The woman promises and goes there. He lies with the woman and comes away. He is not a good worker; he seems just like mad.

Most Kota men have amorous adventures during the greater part of their lives, in which they secretly speak to a woman and cajole or threaten or use force to achieve their purpose. There is a bagful of stereotyped tricks available for these affairs, and a man who rings a change on an old trick gains a certain measure of fame. But Kusvain alone resorts to possession for this end, and to Kota men it appears as a scurvy trick indeed, a perversion of the sacred state for a very profane purpose. Little wonder it is that Kusvain is generally a personage of no account in the community.

The anecdote brings out a dominant note in Kusvain's personality. His way to personal power and ego satisfaction is attained by exercising his propensities for possession. He used these abilities in culturally approved situations, as when he first became a diviner. He also used them in situations not sanctioned by his society, as a means of getting women. Though he was officially barred from doing so, he used them again during the crisis situation of January 1925, when all were bewildered. He became possessed and revealed a new dispensation by which he could continue to follow his own road to personal victories.

A whole set of problems must be glossed over here. The psychological nature of possession among the Kota can be described only briefly and impressionistically. It is my feeling, from observing Kota diviners in possession, that the rapid movements help induce a state of dissociation in which the words which then tumble through the diviner's lips do not rise from a conscious level and are not later recognized by the speaker as products of his conscious thinking. It seems to me a diviner rarely fakes his performance, and that Kusvain himself probably thinks of his possessed states as being of supernatural origin. For lack of controlled data, these observations cannot be adequately documented.

The import of possession for Kusvain is clear enough. It is for him the prime means of self-assertion, of personal dominance. Less clear are the processes whereby the means of personal satisfaction for an aberrant individual came to attain social significance.

The condition which led to this socialization of an individual symbolism is to be found in the general disorientation of established societal values which came with the epidemic. Kota culture, like every other, has a set of basic behavior patterns to meet the exigencies of life. Each of these patterns has a certain potential of energy, so to speak. It may be more or less compelling than another pattern which might be used in the same life situation. When two patterns conflict, the one with the greater dynamic potency is translated into action. For example, when a man's child is ill, the first pattern to follow is that of coddling the child, keeping it warm, administering herbal remedies. If this course of action fails to work, another supersedes it. A Kurumba is sent for; he doctors the child magically. Now, a powerful maxim of Kota conduct is to have as little as possible to do with Kurumbas. Yet this principle is overridden when a person is gravely ill; the Kurumba sorcerer is invited into the village. Should the child die, or linger in pain, a father may have recourse to yet another socially recognized pattern—that of beating, even killing, the Kurumba thought responsible for the illness. Under ordinary circumstances a Kota will go far out of his way to avoid meeting Kurumbas, but personal fears may give way before the more compelling behavior of personal grief.

In this situation and in the countless number of major and minor crises that characterize the life of any human group the scale of values is socially calibrated. That is to say, any tribesman knows what values may normally be expected to have highest compulsive power in a familiar situation. Thus he can predict that no man in his senses will ordinarily molest a Kurumba, but a sorrowing father may deliberately pick a fight with one.

In the ordinary round of life, the general hierarchy of values is well known and consistently observed. The culture may be said to be well integrated. Conflict and strife do occur within such a society, but the existence of a recognized scale of values enables men to allay societal friction. The dockets of our legal system are crowded with trials and debates, yet the existence of a calibrated code of behavior, law, enables society to deal effectively with these conflict situations.

But when the scale of values has been undermined, when men are not sure about which patterns are most compelling and which less compelling, then such a society is full of stresses which are not relieved. It displays a lack of co-ordinated action, frequency of continued friction, a general disphoric state.

And the society is disorientated because the individuals

within the group are personally disoriented. Kolme·l society was dislocated because each villager had suffered the loss of many relatives and friends. Most men felt that the old set of patterns dealing with illness and death were suddenly inadequate. These patterns and the dynamic value which adhered to them were rarely questioned as long as the usual cycle of life and death prevailed. But when one's kin and companions keel over wholesale, then a man wants to find some new way of coping with death. He is not so sure of the authority of the priests or of the supernatural sanction of the diviners, and these doubts shake his whole scheme of evaluation and response. He is ready to accept some new way of behavior which can be evaluated as more puissant than the old. For the disruption of one's personal and social scale of values is a dreadfully uncomfortable experience. It blasts all security and ease out of the universe. Hence men seek a quick reinstallment of paramount values. Best of all is some fresh pattern of thought and action which will explain away all previous difficulties with one sweeping generalization. In short, many villagers were ripe subjects for conversion.

Just any explanation and new pattern will not do. New ideas may be rejected if they deviate too greatly from established modes or if the proffered pattern conflicts with an old pattern of great compulsive power. The Kolme·l incident affords an example of such rejection. While the villagers were standing before the temples in January 1924—before Kusvain went into his historic spasm of possession —a woman, Ni·ǰ, became possessed. She attempted to come forward to the temple pillar, and began to speak as diviners do about the sins of the folk and the desires of the deities.

Ni·ǰ, like Kusvain, is an aberrant personality. Kota women may not participate directly in the service of the gods. A sacred object touched by a woman becomes profaned; a sacerdotal personage who happens to see a woman during her period of catamenia becomes defiled; of all the phenomena of the universe the object most repugnant to the gods is a menstruating woman. Hence women may not become the vehicles of the gods, although they do become possessed with spirits of the deceased. Ni·ǰ had long been a pe·nbačo·l, a medium of communication with the beings of the afterworld—who are not as fussy as the gods themselves. But to have a god deliberately choose a defiling vessel was an intolerable concept. It would invalidate the most basic, the most compelling ideas concerning the relation of women to gods and men.

Thus it came about that when Ni·ĭ trembled and shook before the temple, stepped into a fire as diviners do, and uttered prophecies, Ma·ga·ly settled the matter. Ma·ga·ly was one of the headmen of the village, an ally of Ka·kn. Let me quote Sulli again:

> That was the first time I ever saw a woman shaking. All were astounded except Ma·ga·ly. He told . . . her to stop. She kept on shaking. He asked her, "If you are a true god tell me what I have in my hand." She didn't speak but kept on shaking. So he took a stick and beat her.

That finished the career of Ni·ĭ as a diviner for the gods. No one was disposed to listen to her since the concept of a woman diviner clashed with other concepts at too many strategic points. Ma·ga·ly's action summarily and decisively rejected this new avenue of behavior. It was too great a departure from previous patterns, too great a negation of established concepts.

Yet Kusvain's behavior also departed from previous patterns and established concepts. Some villagers have never become reconciled to his innovations. To say that the villagers were disorganized and ripe for the adoption of a new pattern is hardly a sufficient explanation of the event, since some of them proved impervious to the new idea. From the testimony of these men it is apparent that they too were beset by fears, they too had suffered and were not sure of the old values, but still they have refused to accept Kusvain's proposal. The reasons for acceptance by some and rejection by others may be brought out by a consideration of two more personalities, Sulli the advocate of the new, and Ka·kn the defender of the old.

Sulli has already figured in the narrative of the epidemic and its aftermath. He is now a man of about fifty, the teacher of the village school. His manifold energies and unique position make him a powerful influence in the community. He is the only member of the tribe who has learned to speak and write English; he is the only Kota who holds a government post; the only tribesman who has had extensive contacts both with Europeans and with Hindus.

Sulli's command of English—not a very firm command, incidentally—is a potent weapon in his hands. Whenever he is balked by others of the tribe, whenever he seeks to overcome resistance, he can cow his opponents by threatening to submit a petition to the British officials. The advent of the English did not of itself greatly affect Kota political and social organization, since their colonial policy refrains from unduly disturbing existing social mechanisms. But it did impose an ultimate authority above the tribal council which previously had been the court of last appeal. Since Sulli possesses something of a monopoly on communications with this higher authority, his words and desires carry weight.

He also fulfills some of the traditional requirements for a leader. From his teacher's salary, his agricultural activity, his trading pursuits, Sulli has acquired more wealth than most of his people, and Kota society accords social recognition to men of wealth. More important, he argues impassionately and fluently. A man who can speak effectively, who can quote an apt proverb at the right time, who can meet and master opponents in debate, is the man who swings the decision of a council. And Sulli is glib beyond most of his tribe.

This is not to say that the tribesmen meekly follow his lead. Despite his strategic social position and personal attributes, his opponents are many and the number of his devoted followers is small. For Sulli is a rebel and a reformer. He is everlastingly advocating change. He wants to alter tribal dress and diet, to abandon old occupations and take up new. He has scant respect for some of the most venerable taboos of the culture, and wants to abolish certain phases of social behavior which are now right and proper. Like men the world over, many Kotas resent gratuitous attempts to manipulate the established way of life. Hence they dislike Sulli's propensities for reform and refuse to follow his lead.

Sulli's easy flow of language lent itself well to the compilation of a life history, and the pages of the record of his personal career are many. Through all the material the dominant note of his personality is sounded again and again. He must always seek to deviate from the societal norm, and often attempts to induce others to adhere to his deviation. When he was just a boy, he ran off to a missionary and announced his desire to be converted. No Kota has ever become a Christian, and it took a mass raid by villagers to carry him away from the mission compound. This social recognition of his deviation evidently satisfied him, for there was no further talk of being converted. The very fact that he alone has gone through a long and painful process of schooling is another manifestation of his drive to depart from tribal custom.

The genesis of this compelling factor in Sulli's personality cannot be traced here. But it is interesting to note that Sulli's father and grandfather also flouted convention. His grandfather raised a quarrel, whose reverberations are still remembered, when he was the first to use tile instead of thatch as roofing material. Sulli's father, against strenuous opposition from his fellows, insisted on being the one Kota to own a horse. Roof tiles and a single horse may seem of little moment, but in this area such matters serve as insignia of group status. The adoption of these traits promised to affect intertribal relations. But parental influence alone cannot account for Sulli's perpetual itch to tamper with the setup of his society, because his two brothers who shared the same familial environment do not share his deviant desires.

Sulli's radical notions apply only to a few narrowly circumscribed aspects of Kota culture. He does not question most of the dominant themes of his society, and if they should be questioned by his non-Kota associates, he stoutly defends them. At the time of my stay on the Nilgiris, Sulli was moving heaven and earth in an attempt to keep a young second wife. He has only one son by his first wife, who is now beyond childbearing age. While a Kota with a single son is saved from social ignominy, to be truly a man one must have several sons. The difficulties Sulli encountered in keeping a second wife arose from the disparity between his and the bride's age and even more from the machinations of the senior wife. The troublous quest for a second wife was hardly motivated by sensuous considerations, because even when a marriage was contracted the elder saw to it that Sulli had little time for the younger spouse. And the second wife was known to have alliances with other men. These affairs did not disturb Sulli a bit, for he shares the prevailing Kota notion that biological paternity is of slight importance. He knows what store a European or a Hindu sets on being the biological father of his wife's children, but regards that view as one of the queer notions of alien peoples. Sulli is content to accept the greater part of the prevailing values of his society.

This in spite of the fact that he is culturally isolated beyond all his tribe. He has participated in ways of life foreign to Kota society. He has been exposed to cultural influences which have not yet seeped through to any other Kota. Whole complexes of behavior which are significant to present-day Kota life—behavior toward Europeans, literacy in English and Tamil—are carried only by him among the tribesmen. But even he does not resist the most pervasive and compelling modes of Kota behavior. He rings no discordant note on the great majority of the dominant themes in Kota life. Most of the ideas and attitudes which have a high rating in the cultural scale of values have also high rank in Sulli's personal scale.

Sulli's desire to deviate, to modify his culture, finds expression in his efforts to get his fellows to cut their hair, to give over the eating of carrion, to abandon music as a tribal vocation, to curtail or abolish the menstrual seclusion hut. Around these four issues Sulli's reforming campaigns are currently crystallized. The life-history data reveals that each of these issues has a different symbolic meaning for Sulli, and each strikes deep at fundamental precepts of Kota life.

The matter of a hair cut is a serious matter indeed to the tribe. Kota men wear their hair long, tied up in a bun at the nape of the neck. The knot of hair has ceremonial significance and is the hallmark whereby a man can be recognized as a Kota. This is precisely why Sulli wants the Kotas to cut their hair. He sees Kota status among the other tribes as lowly and mean, degrading and distasteful. Their carrion-eating habits and tribal occupations make them defiling and repugnant to caste Hindus. Sulli was often refused admittance to tea shops in the district because his hairdress made him immediately recognizable as a Kota. Only his bun of hair marked him, and he long had yearned to lop it off. But no Kota had ever worn short hair, and the pressure from within and without the tribe was great enough to keep Sulli from a barber until the end of 1936. In that year Dr. M. B. Emeneau began using Sulli as a linguistic informant. This intimate contact with a member of the white ruling class strengthened his prestige and determination until he mustered enough courage to cut his hair and face the criticism of his tribesmen and Badaga neighbors. Three young man of Kolme·l, egged on by Sulli, followed his example.

For all other Kotas there is nothing particularly mean in the tribal status, nor is their chignon a symbol of inferiority. If they may not enter the houses of other peoples, why, others may not enter theirs. They go to the weekly market, but feel no urge to enter a tea shop there where the food is queer and the surroundings uncomfortable and strange. They have not sampled of the extra-Kota world as has Sulli; they have no feeling of being barred from places and associations, since they have as yet no desire to seek out strange places and non-Kota associates.

The symbolic significance of long hair for Sulli is quite contrary to its meaning for his group. To him it is an irritating stigma of social inferiority; to them it is a comfortable part of the way of life. A similar differential in symbolic connotation occurs in the other issues on Sulli's agenda of reform. Sulli has learned from his Hindu acquaintances that musicians are lowly and subservient folk. But the other tribesmen tootling away at a Badaga or Toda ceremony feel a justified measure of self-importance in their music. They know that without it the ceremony could not go on. In the matter of meat-eating, there is less of a gap between Sulli's evaluation of the custom and that of his people. The strong antipathy to the eaters of flesh and carrion, held by Badagas and Todas as well as caste Hindus, has percolated through to the Kotas, and they are not too eager to defend the practice. Sulli's drive to abolish the menstrual hut—at least as a shelter for childbirth—is derived either from some unique personal experience within the village or from the influence of European hygiene. Hindus and tribesmen alike observe menstrual and childbirth seclusion. At any rate, the Kotas recognize no necessity for change in this as well as in the other issues.

These battles of Sulli's may be interpreted as overt manifestations of a trend discernible in his childhood, the drive to deviate from the cultural norm. The desire to deviate, as we have seen above, affects only selected aspects of the culture, but appears in the life history over and over again as a theme of high compulsive power. And for Sulli the advent of the new gods harmonized with his personal motif. They signalized the introduction of new elements to the pattern of Kota life, and since the new gods were Hindu deities, the direction of the change accorded with his own inclinations.

It is understandable, then, why Sulli adopted the new dispensation and urged its acceptance in spite of his contempt for Kusvain and his continuing loyalty to the old gods. It was one means of actualizing a goal, social change, that is of great importance to him. To most of the men who have accepted the new Trinity, the deed has no such symbolic significance. For them the new gods were a means of re-establishing the equilibrium of life, of abolishing uncertainty, of coping with new conditions. Fear and pain motivated their conversion. Fear played little part in Sulli's motivation. He had been inoculated against the disease by health officers; he believed firmly in the efficacy of Western medicine. His conduct during an epidemic of bubonic plague in 1937 confirms his relative coolness in an epidemic situation. His continuing efforts to induce all the villagers to take over the new deities are attempts to secure social recognition for a personal symbol.

Since the new religion complex did not bear the same symbolic force to other men as it did to Kusvain and Sulli, some of them abjured the worship of the new gods soon after the shock of the epidemic had passed. A coterie of vigorous older men, of which Ka·kn was one, refused to bow at the new shrines, and opposed the new rites. These men see the new complex as a dangerous thing, a symbol of the sinister influences which are attacking the established customs. The meaning of the new dispensation to this group may be gauged by a glimpse of Ka·kn's career.

While the record of Ka·kn's personal history is not as ample or as complete as is Sulli's, there is enough data to indicate the nature of his main avenue to personal satisfactions. Ka·kn is about ten years older than Sulli, bulky, mustachioed, aggressive. He is not a particularly good craftsman or agriculturalist, has never achieved notable successes with women, and though he shouts down opponents in debate by sheer physical vigor, his wit is not keen or subtle enough to win plaudits in council. But when complex funeral rites are to be held, or a ceremony performed, it is Ka·kn who directs the procedure and leads the participants. He has no official role to fulfill, being neither diviner nor priest, but he tells the diviners and priests what to do next. The mastery of ritual and authority in ceremonies constitute for Ka·kn the means to personal ascendancy. His stakes in life cluster around the old ceremonies.

From Ka·kn's recorded remarks it is evident that the introduction of a new ritual meant for him the ultimate displacement of the old and hence the blocking of his road to glory. He made little attempt to secure a dominating position in the service of the new deities, for their acceptance threatened to allow the influx of a host of new elements which would ultimately invalidate his position of competence. His refusal to tolerate the new religious complex can thus be understood as a refusal to tolerate a threat to his personal status.

The single event, the intrusion of a new worship, had opposite meanings for these two Kotas. To one, it was a useful instrument which helped him toward his goal; to the other, it was an inimical weapon which menaced his security. Each gave a different version of the affair, stressed different aspects of the situation, derived different conclusions from the episode both had lived through. The historical outline of the preceding pages has been winnowed from the testimony of a number of informants. But a comparison of Sulli's story with that of Ka·kn reflects their respective attitudes toward the new complex.

Sulli's tale begins with a statement of the epidemic and its severity, and goes on to tell of the council meeting at which he tried to persuade the elders to be inoculated and to bury the dead. His advice was disregarded, and on his own initiative Sulli petitioned the health officers to inoculate the villagers. When they arrived, only the younger men submitted to treatment. This narrative describes the ceremony of January 1925 when the congregated villagers prayed for a visitation from the gods.

At once the god came to Kusvain. "Yes, my people, you ask that priests and diviners be choosen as they formerly were. But first you must build three shrines at ke·rva·y [for the new gods] and I will choose three men for that place, and then I will choose your old priests and diviners."

The men asked, "We already have three gods, why should we have three more?"

"Those gods do not know about the modern rules. . . . I am going to leave the ma:mu:l, the old rules. Now I have made pudmu:l, new rules. . . ."

All the men said, "We want only the old ma:mu:l; why do you treat us in this pudmu:l?"

"See my people, in former times you were the only ones living here and you need not get new rules. After a while the Badagas came, but they had the same ceremonies and customs as you. So I let you live together as ma:mu:l. Now I won't let you do as before, for many different people have come from the plains and other places. You mix with other people, and now I want to change the old rule. You must obey me and build three shrines."

Sulli tells how the shrines were finally built, and a ceremony for the new deities performed. On this occasion the new god again spoke through Kusvain, saying:

"Why did I come here? I want to change the old customs of the Kotas. You Kotas have been senselessly killing buffaloes for your funerals. Till today you send the women to the te·lul [menstrual hut] for three to six months when they give birth. . . . Stop killing cows and buffaloes. Your ancestor Kitu·r-payk [the culture hero] tamed these wild animals for your use in milking and plowing. Or you may sell them and in that way become rich."

Sulli's version of Kusvain's speeches goes on at length to give an elaborate rationale for these reforms. Now it is quite certain that Kusvain's words simply commanded the new worship, gave a few details of the new ritual, and hinted at general modifications of tribal behavior. Sulli has apparently amplified these hints to include his pet controversies. Kusvain, in possession or out, is little interested in reform. When Sulli was asked about Kusvain's allegiance, his answer was: "When he has something to eat he is for me; when he needs food he is for the others." It is difficult to visualize Kusvain as being deeply concerned with social amelioration. Yet the main emphasis in Sulli's account of the event is on the long-winded program of reform and the reasons therefor which are cited as the words of the gods. From all the evidence it appears very unlikely that Kusvain ever uttered such harangues, and that the words, their interpretation, and the stress laid on them all stem from Sulli.

Ka·kn's tale, in turn, indicates the focus of his interest and desires. It begins with Kusvain's possession, and does not mention the epidemic. The new god insists that devotions be performed to him, else retainers for the old gods cannot be chosen. This account then goes on to tell how Kusvain became possessed on subsequent occasions. One time he ran through the brush to a swift-flowing stream several miles from the village. There he mounted a tree which had fallen across the stream, and ran along its length, crossing and recrossing the stream several times. This extremely dangerous procedure was halted when Ka·kn and others, who had followed, pounced on him as soon as they could and brought him back to the village. Then, says Ka·kn:

We waited for a few days. Meanwhile Kusvain was shaking even in his own house. One day Kusvain went to the smithy . . . and was hammering a piece of iron to make an ax. At that moment he became possessed. I and some others were looking on there. Kusvain grabbed the red-hot iron in his hand. "Now if you don't believe me," he said, "you come and grab this iron." Then I agreed to his word.

Although Ka·kn thus accepted the revelation—tentatively—he countered objections at every step. His story continues:

> I thought the shrine should be built at ponatgal, farther off, which is more convenient and cleaner than the ke·rva·y place which Kusvain had chosen. But Kusvain said, "I will punish you if you say that." In all other villages the shrines are built on a hill, so I thought that this temple also should be built on a hill. But they wanted the shrine at ke·rva·y and so I agreed.

The two other diviners of the new gods demanded, while possessed, that shrines be built for all three new divinities. Ka·kn thus met this demand:

> I refused that entirely and told them, "We can't build a temple to you here. Do you want us to leave our ma:mu:l gods entirely and build temples to you?" Then the Goddess said, "Unless you make three temples to us here, you will not be able to get diviners for the Kamaṭrayṇ [the old] gods." So we were forced to agree, because without diviners we cannot carry on the old ceremonies.

The shrines were built. The ceremony conducted before them followed closely the pattern of the old God Ceremony save for the introduction of coconuts and other lowland ritual traits. One part of the God Ceremony entails the making of new pots in which the ceremonial feast is cooked. When the newly made pots were fired on this occasion, they broke. Ka·kn's account continues:

> Then Kusvain became possessed and told us to bring those pots which we use for the ma:mu:l [the old] gods. I refused and told him that those pots cannot be used here. But the young men said, "If you do not like it, go. We are going to use the sacred pots—you know nothing." I told them, "Don't get angry; the ma:mu:l rule is ma:mu:l; don't spoil the sacred pots." So I did not give my sacred pots. Those who were on my side gave other pots, not the sacred ones. Those who were against me gave the sacred pots. . . . While they were preparing the

food, a big rain came. All were talking about it. I told them, "This is the punishment for using the sacred pots. If it were a true god, why couldn't the rain be averted?" . . . They were going to prepare the food with salt only [as is done in the traditional God Ceremony], but I told them to mix in curry powder also [as for ordinary foodstuffs]. Because I thought that if they make the food in the same way as they do for the Kamaṭrayṇ gods, then they will honor the new gods the same as the old. . . . They agreed to put curry-stuff in the food. By my talking I defeated those who wanted salt only. Then I thought, by the rain and by my winning in the matter of the salt, I know that the Kamaṭrayṇ gods are the true gods."

The wonders he had witnessed counted for so little to Ka·kn that a heavy rain and a skirmish in argument sufficed to cancel their effect. Kusvain's deeds, he decided, were inspired by evil spirits and not by genuine gods, and so he renounced the new worship. The dominant motif in his personality which impells him to cling to and preserve the ancient ritual led him to discount the force and influence of Kusvain's wondrous acts. Sulli, too, made little of these acts, but for another reason. In his story they are only of marginal interest because these new gods are a means toward his goal of social change, and Sulli accepts these means as useful without too searching questions as to their supernatural validity.

One last episode in Kusvain's career may be cited to demonstrate a situation in which both Sulli and Ka·kn share the same attitudes and values. When a priest and a full complement of three diviners had been selected for the new gods, Kusvain's deity again spoke through him. The god commanded the four newly chosen retainers to bedeck themselves in ceremonial raiment. They were told to go to a certain Badaga village to demand tribute for the Kotas and their gods. The men faithfully dressed in new waistcloths, wore shoulder cloths in the fashion of high-caste men, and painted on their foreheads the red and white trident of Vishnu. A sad fate awaited them among the Badagas. The temerity of these Kotas in adopting dress and symbols sacred to the Badagas and coming to levy tribute to boot so aroused the villagers that a mob intent on trouncing the four soon collected. When the crowd closed in, Kusvain, ever reliant on his single weapon, went into a fit of possession and was allowed to escape. But the other three received a mauling whose marks they still bear.

This debacle might have been a cause for rejoicing by the opponents of the new complex as an additional proof of the impotence of the new revelation. Actually they were highly indignant and took retaliatory measures against the culprits who had hurt their fellow tribesmen. The beating was felt by Ka·kn and his coterie as a blow against themselves as Kotas, and not as a well-deserved slap at the followers of the new faith. Their loyalty to their group overrode sentiments of hostility to a faction within the group. They decided to boycott the Badagas until a suitable fine had been paid in expiation. When they were next called to provide music at the Badaga village, all the Kolme·l men refused. The hot-blooded younger Badagas now felt that the Kotas were becoming obstreperous beyond all tolerance, and they systematically began to waylay and beat Kotas. The Kolme·l elders then invoked Sulli's aid. A petition was dispatched to the police, who put an end to the Badaga campaign of terror. A token fine was paid by a Badaga elder to smooth the ruffled Kota feelings, and amicable relations once again prevailed between the Badaga village and Kolme·l.

Manifest in this incident is the operation of a principle which spreads wide through Kota society and through many another society as well. The hostilities which were rife within the group were temporarily abandoned in the face of external aggression. Ka·kn's opposition to the new gods and their followers was subordinated to another impulse. The impulse to defend one's own people against the onslaught of an out-group, the Badagas, was paramount to the urge to discredit a hostile faction within the in-group. Once the Badaga trouble died down, the Kolme·l dispute flared anew.[2]

[2] It is probably safe to say that if the Badaga onslaught had continued, the dissension within Kolme·l would have been suppressed —at least for the duration of the larger conflict. But the inner an-

Both recorded and reconstructed history are replete with examples of the process noted here. Dissident factions within a group suddenly consolidate when the security of the larger group is menaced. Perhaps the principle may be stated most succinctly as: loyalty to a larger social entity is more demanding than loyalty to a smaller social entity. When the security of the total societal unit is in danger—or is thought to be in danger—then the members of that unit spring to its defense, and shelve the antagonisms and narrower allegiances which obtain among the lesser groups that comprise the whole.

Although principles of social behavior need not necessarily have logical basis, there is a measure of logic to this doctrine. For the dissolution of the greater unit would automatically wipe out all within its compass, would cancel both the strife and the solidarity of the lesser unit. Hence the larger group must be defended first. This may well be one of the ". . . culture patterns which tend to be universal, not only in form but in psychological significance. . . ." [3]

Furthermore, the reason for the ubiquity of this pattern among cultures and the basis for its dominance within a given society may be attributed to a drive for self-preservation. The collapse of the structure of the larger society means the collapse of every compartment within the general organization; therefore, each member must rise to the defense of the whole to preserve his own particular niche. This seems to hold true for all units of society down to the ultimate entity, the individual. The individual, too, forgets about internal conflict when his general status as a personality is endangered. Ka·kn evidently was just as much in a conflict situation during the epidemic as were the others, but when the new complex began to threaten his personal status, he relinquished any tendency to follow the new way and opposed it with might and main. It

---

tagonism would become dominant again when the extra-tribal pressure was raised—as did happen—or if the external hostilities so harassed the group as to undermine confidence in all established values, as may yet occur. In the latter case, the disintegration of the hierarchy of values would foster strife within the group and then the religious rivalry might well become the focus of civil violence.

[3] Edward Sapir: "Cultural Anthropology and Psychiatry," *Journal of Abnormal and Social Psychology*, Vol. 27 (1932), pp. 229–42.

looks as though he felt that his whole role in the drama of society would be cut out by the introduction of a new scene into the play. Here again one of Edward Sapir's observations is germane. "Personality organizations, which at last analysis are psychologically comparable with the greatest cultures or idea systems, have as their first law of being their essential self-preservation. . . ." [4]

The life situation that concerns us here includes phenomena we recognize as cultural and—as we have seen—personal, individualized aspects. The two are not mutually exclusive categories nor do they represent irreconcilable points of vantage. An understanding of Ka·kn's personal conflicts and reactions clears the way for an understanding of the behavior of others in his group. Kolme·l village still supported sectarian differences—really a cultural dichotomy—when the Kota field work was terminated at the end of May 1938.

The men belonging to the conservative faction, as Ka·kn's group may be called, are mostly older men. The meaning which the new complex bears for them is generally the same as its meaning to Ka·kn. Like him, they know the old ways, cherish them, feel comfortable within them. Though new circumstances make the old shoe of custom pinch a bit, they would rather keep it than chance a try with new gear. In the personal scale of values of each of these older men, the new complex is similarly rated, and it is no startling discovery to note that this congruence of evaluation and response constitutes cultural behavior.

The similarity of response by these Kota conservatives is, in large measure, a corollary of the similarity of their ages. An old Kota does not have the same value system as does a young Kota, and the Kota elder does not have the same scale of values he maintained when younger. Age in itself brings about a certain kind of shift in the personal dynamics of evaluation of an individual. This process operating in the personal career of each older man is largely responsible for the like response manifested by the members of the Ka·kn faction.

The age shift is a condition which occurs in the life experience of all individuals (save, perhaps, in some excep-

[4] Ibid., p. 242.

tional cases), which transcends the limits of any one society, which operates in all societies. It ensues from the very nature of the human materials which constitute a society. All men grow old. As each individual advances in age, his values change. The exact nature of the shift varies from individual to individual, and the range of the shift must be redefined for every culture, but the juxtaposition of values with advancing years is a process that must be taken into account in any thorough analysis of personal and cultural history.

The common denominator of age is not to be taken as a blanket explanation for the actions of all members of the conservative group. Young men also have repudiated the new complex. For them, any predilection for the new has been overridden by stronger considerations, such as filial loyalty or private symbolisms discerned in the new triad. Conversely, Sulli is getting on in years but is not a conservative. And Sulli's elder brother belongs to his party simply because he follows his brother wherever Sulli may lead. Behind the façade of this cultural expression there lie multiple personal meanings as well as the uniformity of evaluation and response which comes out of the common age alignment of values.

We may now supply certain answers to the questions asked above. The new complex could gain a foothold after 1924 because the old had lost compulsive value for some individuals. The value of a culture pattern lies in its relative power to be translated into action in a given situation. A pattern has compulsive value when an individual always brings it into play to meet a certain need, when alternative patterns of behavior are never used to meet that need.

A pattern is culturally compulsive if it has compulsive value for most individuals (or all individuals) within a given society. Prior to the epidemic, the way of the old religion was culturally compulsive in Kolme·l. It adequately met and fulfilled at least one basic need, the need for coping with death. After the epidemic, many villagers felt that it no longer met that need satisfactorily. For them the old pattern lost its compulsive validity, and they could admit a supplemental pattern of equal potency into their evaluation system.

The new pattern did not entail the same kind of value

displacement for its progenitor, Kusvain. For him it was largely a projection of a unique personal compulsion. Nor did it involve the same displacement for its chief sponsor, Sulli. For him the new worship was merely one pattern which could be nicely adapted to the actualization of a personal goal. These private meanings of the new pattern were factors which brought about the culture change no less than the general weakening of the old in the scale of values of many villagers. The origin and growth of a culture pattern must ultimately be referred to motivations and reactions within the individual.

The special connotation which the new complex had for Ka·kn and his adherents worked to block the change. Each of these men evidently felt that the new complex took away more than it might add to their personal security. For these individuals, therefore, the old religion still has compulsive value and continues to function as a cultural compulsion within their group. A graduated weighting of patterns, a hierarchy of values, is characteristic of the phenomena we call cultural, as well as of the behavior we term personal. The shape of a culture, when we probe into its essential nature, begins to look more and more like the structure of a personality.

Postscript: 1960

Eleven years after my first stay with the Kotas, and again twenty years after, I was able to revisit them. The visit of 1949 was of several months' duration; in December 1958 I had little more than a week, but it was enough for a fine reunion and it gave me some insight into the course of Kota life and lives in the intervening years.

Two of the three chief protagonists in the above account were alive in 1958. Kusvain was still a marginal and unimportant person in the community. He has never been steady enough to earn a man's living and he has not been able to keep any wife for long. When men gather to talk, he still sits on the edge and listens, or seems to. Younger Kotas see in him only a village eccentric, artless and shiftless. His moments of glory have long gone, and those who do recollect his part in the coming of the new gods give him no particular esteem for it.

Ka·kn died in 1947, his means and his health expended —so his widow told me—in his passionate fight against the reformists. There was much litigation; he spent much time and money trying to find his way in the world of courts and lawyers, a labyrinth he never came to understand. One great personal achievement was not denied him. A few months before he died, his wife became pregnant. His only son was born posthumously, but Ka·kn's name and memory are thus kept on among Kotas. However, in 1958 that son was in a government boarding school established to advance the Nilgiri folk by teaching their sons useful new ways.

Sulli flourishes. He was still hale and vigorous in his sixty-fourth year, content with his accomplishments but also full of plans to bring the Kotas even farther forward. I have sketched Sulli's life-history elsewhere ("A Reformer of His People," in *In the Company of Man*, Joseph Casagrande, ed. [New York: Harper; 1960]); his personality had not changed in the more than twenty years between our first meeting and our most recent discussions together.

One token of this is his continuing reinterpretation of the story of the coming of the new gods. In 1958 he mentioned a version I had not heard before. He told of a Kota man and his wife, dead some fifteen years, who had lived in the northernmost Kota village and who had differed from other Kotas in that they would eat no meat, on religious principle, like high-caste Hindus. Because of this man's piety, Sulli told, the traditional Kota gods appeared to him in a dream and vouchsafed a message of reform, the same program which Sulli had been propounding for many years. In Sulli's report of the dream, the gods advised that they were to be called by the new names and that they would appear in Kolme·l village to start the change because the people of that village were "bravest and wisest of all."

There was indeed such a couple, and others in their village were perturbed about their vegetarianism, which they thought unseemly for a Kota. I heard about this unusual man both in 1937–8 and in 1949, but no one mentioned anything then about his having had a revelation of reform. Sulli's present version sounds plausible because it links a Kota known to have adopted vegetarianism with the reforms in the direction of Hinduism.

In this and in other ways Sulli has been a consistent personality over two decades, just as Kusvain has not deviated from his own aberrant style of life, and Ka·kn, until his death, plugged away steadfastly in his own personal pattern. But though these three personalities remained constant, Kota society and culture have changed.

While some factional alignment remains in Kolme·l village, only a few of the older, conservative men still cherish the feud. Most men in the village both affirm their loyalty to the "old rule" and also take on the new traits espoused by the reformists.

Kotas have taken advantage, led by Sulli, of the special aid offered by government to disadvantaged tribes and castes. There is a new road to Kolme·l, a new school there, a new well, new houses built with government subsidy. Government land-conservation measures have improved Kota lands considerably, and some Kota land-owners get good rentals for their fields. The rapidly increasing population of the Nilgiris, especially among the Badaga cultivators, has created a great demand for land and good returns from leasing fields. While there has been no startling economic improvement, their economic lot is better than it was. Thus much more rice, in place of rough millet, is now eaten. Kotas have more dealings and more useful contacts with town and government than they did twenty years ago. In all, the Kotas have become less like a tribe and much more like another caste group of modern Indian rural society.

Yet this social adaptation has not precipitated any sweep toward cultural assimilation. The traditional cycle of Kota ceremonies is still performed, Kota marriage and family patterns have not been changed, and the triad of traditional gods is still paramount in Kota belief.

A fine temple for the new gods was built in the forties by Sulli and his party. Masons were imported from the plains to construct it in proper Hindu style, and it stands in the field where the first little shrine was put. The top of this new temple can be seen from almost every part of the village, and the priest and diviners of these new gods make offerings there daily. But in 1958 the new temple on the outskirts was in shabby condition, while the three old temples in the center of the village were kept spruce and clean and inviolate, as always.

When any villager feels in need of divine help, he always prays first at the old temple and then, if he desires to do so, before the new one. No ceremonies are performed only for the new gods; at each major ceremony the ritual is enacted in the traditional way before the old temples and then all the village men go in a body to worship the other triad. The priests and diviners for the old gods still dress only in the traditional manner and guard themselves zealously against pollution. They are given precedence, on every occasion, over the officiants for the new gods, who are not particularly different in dress and conduct from lay villagers.

Sulli is quite content with this state of affairs. He has succeeded in having the new gods accepted in the village and with them certain changes in what he considered to be the most degrading of Kota customs. Kotas no longer collect carrion or sacrifice cows. Few play at Badaga funerals; Kota men may wear their hair short or long, as they like. Sulli's plans for further improvement entail no great abolition of traditional custom or any desire to make the new gods paramount over the old. Most other villagers are of the same mind. They are satisfied that the way has been opened for certain changes, but they do not want to give up their old gods or try to become something other than Kotas.

A perceptive Badaga who knows Kolme·l village well gave this appraisal of the rising Kota generation. "For the last five years those boys who are growing up are taking Sulli's ways as good. In the course of time all the Kotas will come to Sulli's side and prefer his civilization. This is not because of his personal leadership or any personal advantage [which he can give them], but because they are going to town and they themselves are preferring to take on these new ways."

The new ways are so much with the tide of the times that even the most obdurate of the surviving conservatives have yielded to them in some degree. For a time, there was a possibility of fission in Kota society, through a process which has often occurred in Indian village life when the devotees of a new dispensation form themselves into a new endogamous group. But the reforms now seem quite right to most Kotas who have grown up in the past twenty years; and the integrative forces—including their apprehensions about the Badagas—are strong enough to avert any threatened split in the Kota community.

This generation of Kota householders has the same firm sense of their worth and rights as did their fathers. They feel themselves confronted by and continuously challenged by their vastly more numerous and powerful neighbors, especially the Badagas.[1] That only impels them to consolidate their ranks and to reinforce their Kota identity. In accepting the new gods, they are demonstrating (at least to themselves) that Kotas are respectable participants in a respectable form of Hindu worship. And in keeping steadfast to the ancient worship, they are reaffirming their traditional and continuing sense of the worth of things Kota.

They can happily worship two sets of gods because, like most peoples of India, they find no necessary contradiction in doing so, as long as their social practices and identity do not suffer thereby. And as has commonly happened in India, the new deities are being amalgamated with the older gods. Many of Sulli's fellows agree with him that the new gods are just the old ones who have decided to take new names, new forms, and to prescribe new ritual practices.

In the past twenty years, then, the new religious complex has come to take on similar meanings for most people in this village. They were first advanced by Sulli, who took advantage of Kusvain's temporary influence. They have been bolstered by the broad forces for change which have

---

[1] On the subject of Kota and Badaga views of each other, see the author's "The Kotas in Their Social Setting," in *Introduction to the Civilization of India.* (University of Chicago Press; 1957), pp. 288–332. On Kota views of themselves, see the author's "The World and the World View of the Kotas," in *Village India*, McKim Marriott, ed. (University of Chicago Press; 1955), pp. 223–53. On changes in Kota patterns, see the author's "Form, Variation, and Meaning of a Ceremony," in *Method and Perspective in Anthropology*, R. Spencer, ed. (University of Minnesota Press; 1954), pp. 60–102.

reached into most Indian villages, Kolme·l among them. And these meanings are posited on values—such as the easy acceptance of differing deities and creeds—which have long been shared, not only by older and younger Kotas, but by very many of the people of India.

THE
SOUTH
PACIFIC

THE SOUTH PACIFIC showing the approximate
locations of the societies described by Gregory
Bateson and Raymond Firth in the following pages.

A NOTE ABOUT THE AUTHOR

Gregory Bateson

GREGORY BATESON (1904–   ) is the son of the great English geneticist William Bateson. He was initially trained in biology at Cambridge University, where he was later a Fellow of St. John's College. Following his biological training, he studied anthropology under A. C. Haddon. Haddon enjoyed the distinction of having introduced field research into the study of social anthropology in England. In 1898–9 he led an expedition to the Torres Straits, which lie between Australia and New Guinea. Bateson conducted his first field research in New Guinea in 1927–9, and he returned to the field in 1931–3 and 1938–9. He based the study, *Naven*, from which the following selection is reprinted, upon field work among the Iatmul people who live on the middle reaches of the Sepik River.

The book takes its name from the *naven* ceremony performed by kinsmen to celebrate various accomplishments of a child. Although the ceremony may be performed in a variety of ways, it usually involves transvesticism. That is, men dress as women, and women as men. After briefly describing the *naven* ceremony, Bateson devotes the greater part of his book to the development of theoretical means for interpreting its meaning. In an epilogue written for the 1958 edition of the book, he wrote: "*Naven* was a study of the nature of explanation. The book contains of course details about Iatmul life and culture, but it is not primarily an ethnographic study . . . it is an attempt at synthesis, a study of the ways in which data can be fitted together, and the fitting together of data is what I mean by 'explanation.'" Our selection is taken from a section of the book in which Bateson described the ethos of Iatmul men and women; in later chapters he used the notion of a characteristic group ethos to interpret the *naven* ceremony.

Besides experimenting with a number of ideas in his book on the Iatmul, Gregory Bateson worked with Margaret Mead in developing a technique for describing a culture by analyzing photographic records. Mead and Bateson did field research together in Bali in 1936-8, and in *Balinese Character,* a book that they co-authored, Bateson wrote a running analysis of a series of several hundred ethnographic photographs.

Bateson's approach to anthropology has been based upon the notion that problems of social organization and the biological problems of organization and differentiation within the individual organism are fundamentally comparable. In recent years he has been engaged in teaching and research on the borderline fields of anthropology, psychiatry, and cybernetics at the Veterans Administration Hospital in Palo Alto, California. He is also part-time Visiting Professor of Anthropology at Sanford University.

❧ ❧ 6 ❧ ❧

A Selection from

*Naven**

by

GREGORY BATESON

If it were possible adequately to present the whole of a culture, stressing every aspect exactly as it is stressed in the culture itself, no single detail would appear bizarre or strange or arbitrary to the reader, but rather the details would all appear natural and reasonable as they do to the natives who have lived all their lives within the culture. Such an exposition may be attempted by either of two methods, by either scientific or artistic techniques. On the artistic side we have the works of a small handful of men who have been not only great travelers and observers but also sensitive writers—such men as Charles Doughty; and we have also splendid representations of our own culture in such novels as those of Jane Austen or John Galsworthy. On the scientific side we have detailed monumental monographs on a few peoples, and recently the works of Radcliffe-Brown, Malinowski, and the Functional School.

These students have set themselves the same great task, that of describing culture as a whole in such a manner that each detail shall appear as the natural consequence of the remainder of the culture. But their method differs from that of the great artists in one fundamental point.

* The following selection is reprinted from NAVEN, SECOND EDITION, by Gregory Bateson, with the permission of the publishers, Stanford University Press. Copyright 1958, by the Board of Trustees of Leland Stanford Junior University.

The artist is content to describe culture in such a manner that many of its premises and the interrelations of its parts are implicit in his composition. He can leave a great many of the most fundamental aspects of culture to be picked up, not from his actual words, but from his emphasis. He can choose words whose very sound is more significant than their dictionary meaning, and he can so group and stress them that the reader almost unconsciously receives information which is not explicit in the sentences and which the artist would find it hard—almost impossible—to express in analytic terms. This impressionistic technique is utterly foreign to the methods of science, and the Functional School have set out to describe in analytic, cognitive terms the whole interlocking—almost living—nexus which is a culture.

Very properly and naturally they have paid greatest attention to those aspects of culture which lend themselves most readily to description in analytic terms. They have described the structure of several societies and shown the main outlines of the pragmatic functioning of this structure. But they have scarcely attempted the delineation of those aspects of culture which the artist is able to express by impressionistic methods. If we read *Arabia Deserta,* we are struck by the astonishing way in which every incident is informed with the emotional tone of Arab life. More than this, many of the incidents would be impossible with a different emotional background. Evidently, then, the emotional background is casually active within a culture, and no functional study can ever be reasonably complete unless it links up the structure and pragmatic working of the culture with its emotional tone or ethos.

¶ EXAMPLES OF ETHOS IN ENGLISH CULTURE

Before describing the ethos of Iatmul culture, I shall illustrate the ethological approach by some examples taken from our own culture in order to give a clearer impression of what I mean by ethos. When a group of young intellectual English men or women are talking and joking together wittily and with a touch of light cynicism, there is established among them for the time being a definite tone of appropriate behavior. Such specific tones of behavior are in all cases indicative of an ethos. They are expressions of a standardized system of emotional attitudes. In this case the men have temporarily adopted a definite set of sentiments toward the rest of the world, a definite attitude toward reality, and they will joke about subjects which at another time they would treat with seriousness. If one of the men suddenly intrudes a sincere or realistic remark, it will be received with no enthusiasm—perhaps with a moment's silence and a slight feeling that the sincere person has committed a solecism. On another occasion the same group of persons may adopt a different ethos; they may talk realistically and sincerely. Then if the blunderer makes a flippant joke, it will fall flat and feel like a solecism.

The point which I wish to stress in this example is that any group of people may establish among themselves an ethos which as soon as it is established becomes a very real factor in determining their conduct. This ethos is expressed in the tone of their behavior. I have deliberately for my initial example chosen an instance of labile and temporary ethos in order to show that the process of development of ethos, far from being mysterious and rare, is an everyday phenomenon. The same group of intellectuals were at one time serious and at another witty, and if the blunderer had had sufficient force of personality, he could have swung the group from one ethos to the other. He could have influenced the evolution of ethos within the group.

But if, instead of such a temporary conversation group, we examine some more formed and permanent group— say an army mess or a college high table—whose members continually meet under the same conditions, we find the ethological position much more stable. In the more casual groups sometimes one sort of remark and sometimes another is inappropriate, but in any formed group we find certain types of remark, certain tones of conversation permanently taboo. The ethoses of the formed groups are still not absolutely fixed. The processes of ethological change are still at work, and if we could compare a college high table or an officers' mess of fifty years ago with those groups as they are today, we should no doubt find very considerable changes. Such changes are only very much slower in the formed groups, and enormously greater force of character or force of circumstances is required suddenly to shift the ethos.

Correlated with this greater stability of ethos, there is a new phenomenon present in the formed groups which was absent or scarcely recognizable in the unformed. The group has developed its own cultural structure and its own "traditions" which have grown up hand in hand with the ethos. At the high table (a group which is more familiar to me than is the army mess) we find such cultural developments as the Latin Grace, the dons' gowns and the silver presented to the College by former generations of Fellows. All these things have their effect in emphasizing and stabilizing the ethos of the group; and we cannot in any instance say that a given detail is due exclusively either to tradition or to the present ethos. The dons of St. John's College drink water, beer, claret, sherry, and port—but not cocktails; and in their choice they are guided both by tradition and by the ethos of the group. These two factors work together, and we may say that the dons drink as they do both because generations of dons have drunk on the same sound system in the past and because actually in the present that system seems to them appropriate to the ethos of their society. Whatever detail of the tradition we examine, the same considerations apply. The Latin Grace, the architecture of the college, the snuff after dinner on Sundays, the loving cup, the rose water, the feasts—all these cultural details constitute an intricate series of channels which express and guide the ethos.[1] The details were in the past selected by the ethos and are still preserved by it. The system is a circular one; and the very attitude which the dons adopt toward the past has been historically formed and is an expression of their present ethos.

This intimate relationship between ethos and cultural structure is especially characteristic of small segregated groups where the ethos is uniform and the "tradition" very much alive. Indeed, when we say that a tradition is "alive," what we mean is simply this, that it retains its

---

[1] Such metaphors as this are of course dangerous. Their use encourages us to think of ethos and structure as different "things" instead of realizing as we should that they are only different aspects of the same behavior. I have let the metaphor stand *pour encourager les autres.*

connection with a persisting ethos. But when we come to consider not isolated groups but whole civilizations, we must expect to find much more variety of ethos and more details of culture which have been separated from the ethological contexts in which they were appropriate and retained as discrepant elements in an otherwise harmonious culture. Nevertheless, I believe that the concept of ethos may valuably be applied even to such enormous and confused cultures as those of Western Europe. In such cases we must never lose sight of the variations of ethos in different sections of the community and the curious dovetailing of the ethoses of the different sections into a harmonious whole, whereby, for example, peasants with one ethos are enabled to live happily under feudal lords who have a different ethos. Differentiated systems of this kind may persist for generations and only break down when the scales of values are questioned; when the lords begin to doubt the ethics of their position and the serfs to doubt the propriety of submission—phenomena which are liable to occur when the differentiation has proceeded too far.

¶ The Ethos of Iatmul Culture: the Men

Compared with European ethology, the conditions among the Iatmul are remarkably simple, since their culture recognizes no differentiation of rank or class. Indeed, the only social differentiation we need to consider is that which exists between the sexes, and since the problems which we are studying are connected with transvesticism, it is the differentiation between the sexes which is most likely to afford clues.

From whatever side we approach the culture, whatever institutions we study, we find the same sort of contrast between the life of the men and that of the women. Broadly, we may say that the men are occupied with the spectacular, dramatic, and violent activities which have their center in the ceremonial house, while the women are occupied with the useful and necessary routines of food-getting, cooking, and rearing children—activities which center around the dwelling house and the gardens. The contrast between ceremonial house and dwelling house is fundamental for the culture and will serve as the best starting point for ethological description.

The ceremonial house is a splendid building, as much as 120 feet in length, with towering gables at the ends. Inside the building, there is a long vista from end to end down the series of supporting posts as in the nave of a darkened church; and the resemblance to a church is carried further in the native attitudes toward the building. There is a series of taboos on any sort of desecration. The earth floor must not be scratched or the woodwork damaged. A man should not walk right through the building and out at the other end; he should turn aside and pass out by one of the side entrances. To walk right through the building is felt to be an expression of overweening pride—as if a man should lay claim to the whole building as his personal property.

But the analogy between ceremonial house and church must not be pushed too far for many reasons: the ceremonial house serves not only as a place of ritual but also as a clubhouse where men meet and gossip and as an assembly room where they debate and brawl. Further, the ceremonial house does not stand to the natives as a symbol of their devotion, but rather as a symbol of their pride in head-hunting. Where we think of a church as sacred and cool, they think of a ceremonial house as "hot," imbued with heat by the violence and killing which were necessary for its building and consecration. Lastly, the ethos of behavior in the ceremonial house is as far removed from the austerity which we associate with certain churches as it is from the meek devotion associated with others.

Instead of austerity or meekness, there is a mixture of pride and histrionic self-consciousness.[2] An important man, on entering the ceremonial house, is conscious that the public eye is upon him, and he responds to this stimulus by some sort of overemphasis. He will enter with a gesture

[2] In my description of ethos, I have not hesitated to invoke the concepts of emotion and to use terms which strictly should only be used by observers about their own introspections. I have been driven to this loose phrasing through lack of any proper technique for recording and of any language for describing human gesture and behavior. But I wish it to be understood that statements of this kind are an attempt—crude and unscientific, perhaps—to convey to the reader some impression of the *behavior* of Iatmul natives.

and call attention to his presence with some remark. Sometimes he will tend toward a harsh swagger and overconsciousness of pride, and sometimes he will respond with buffoonery. But in whichever direction he reacts, the reaction is theatrical and superficial. Either pride or clowning is accepted as respectable and normal behavior.

In this community there are no steady and dignified chiefs—indeed, no formulated chieftainship at all—but instead there is continual emphasis on self-assertion. A man achieves standing in the community by his achievements in war, by sorcery and esoteric knowledge, by shamanism, by wealth, by intrigue, and, to some extent, by age. But in addition to these factors, he gains standing by playing up to the public eye; and the more standing he has, the more conspicuous will be his behavior. The greatest and most influential men will resort freely either to harsh vituperation or to buffoonery when they are in the center of the stage, and reserve their dignity for occasions when they are in the background.

Among the younger men whose standing is not as yet assured, there is rather more self-control. They will enter the ceremonial house soberly and unobtrusively and sit there quietly and gravely in the presence of their ranting seniors. But there is a smaller junior ceremonial house for the boys. Here they carry out in miniature the ceremonial of the senior house and here they imitate their elders in mixing pride with buffoonery.

We may summarize the ethos of the ceremonial house by describing the institution as a club—not a club in which the members are at their ease, but a club in which, though separated from their womenfolk, they are acutely conscious of being in public. This self-consciousness is present even at times when there is no specific formal or ritual activity taking place, but it is enormously more marked when the men are assembled in the ceremonial house for some debate or ritual performance.

Any matter of general interest may be disputed formally in a traditional manner. In every large ceremonial house there is a special stool, which differs from the ordinary stools on which men sit in having a "back," like a chair, carved into some representation of totemic ancestors. This stool is not used for sitting upon, and is indeed not casually touched if it be an old and sacred specimen. It is used solely as a table for debates. The speaker has three bunches of *Dracaena* leaves, or coconut leaflets. He picks these up at the beginning of his speech and with the combined bunches he gives a blow to the stool. He then puts down the bunches on the stool, one by one, as if they were a tally of his sentences. When all are put down, he again bunches them together and gives another single blow. This series of actions is repeated throughout his speech, ending with a final blow.

The tone of the debates is noisy, angry, and, above all, ironical. The speakers work themselves up to a high pitch of superficial excitement, all the time tempering their violence with histrionic gesture and alternating in their tone between harshness and buffoonery. The style of the oratory varies a good deal from speaker to speaker, and that of the more admired performers may tend toward the display of erudition or toward violence or to a mixture of these attitudes. On the one hand there are men who carry in their heads between ten and twenty thousand polysyllabic names, men whose erudition in the totemic system is a matter of pride to the whole village; and on the other hand, there are speakers who rely for effect upon gesture and tone rather than upon the matter of their discourse. Such a man will make a speech in which there is only the barest minimum of contribution to the issue— and that minimum something which has already been said by other speakers—but he will fill out his speech with assertions of his scorn and threats that he will rape the members of the opposition, accompanying the word with obscene pantomimic dance. Meanwhile the insulted will watch and smile a little, or laugh aloud and shout ironic encouragement to the insulting speaker. Besides these two types—the erudite and the abusive—there are also nervous and apologetic speakers whose contributions to the debate are despised. These men generally attempt the erudite style, but their memories are undermined by nervousness and their "howlers" are laughed at by the audience.

As the debate proceeds, both sides become more excited and some of the men leap to their feet, dancing with their spears in their hands and threatening an immediate resort to violence; but after a while they subside and the debate goes on. This dancing may occur three or four times in a single debate without any actual brawling, and then suddenly some exasperated speaker will go to the "root" of the matter and declaim some esoteric secret about the totemic ancestors of the other side, miming one of their cherished myths in a contemptuous dance. Before his pantomime has finished, a brawl will have started which may lead to serious injuries and be followed by a long feud of killings by sorcery.

The emotions which are so dramatically paraded in debate have their center in pride, and especially in individualistic pride. But hand in hand with this, there is developed a prodigious pride in the totemic ancestors of the clan; and most of the debates are concerned with the details of the totemic system. This totemic system has an obvious affective function—a very important one in this culture—of providing the members of every clan with matter for self-congratulation. But inversely the proud ethos of the culture has reacted in a curious way upon the system, and though we are not here concerned with the origins of Iatmul totemism, a description of the system is relevant as indicating the emotional background against which we are to see the *naven* ceremonies.

The totemic system is enormously elaborated into a series of personal names, so that every individual bears names of totemic ancestors—spirits, birds, stars, animals, pots, adzes, etc., etc.—of his or her clan, and one individual may have thirty or more such names. Every clan has hundreds of these polysyllabic ancestral names which refer in their etymology to secret myths. It seems that the effect of pride upon this system has been to corrupt the origin myths, so that today each moiety has its own phrasing of the origins of the world according to which that moiety's own importance is stressed at the expense of the other moiety. The same tendency extends to the clans. Groups of clans flatter themselves by secretly maintaining that they are not really members of either moiety but are the *fons et origo* from which both moieties sprang; and each group has its own secret mythology to support its secret claims. The debates about totemism are usually concerned with attempts to steal totemic ancestors by stealing names, and one of the most important features

of every Iatmul ceremony (except initiation) is the chanting of name songs, whereby the members of the clan are
reminded of the importance of their ancestors and the
system is continually memorized.

Actually, as a result of the overlapping mythology and
the stealing of names, the system is in a terribly muddled
state. In spite of this, the people are very proud not only
of the number of their totemic ancestors and their esoteric
exploits in the origins of the world but even of the
"straightness" of their song cycles. They feel that the
whole gigantic system is perfectly schematic and coherent.
Thus the prevailing pride which has led them to build up
this mass of fraudulent heraldry is still such that the
people regard the resulting tangle as rigid and coherent.

If we turn to the ritual connected with the ceremonial
house, we see the men, as a group, still vying with each
other, but in spite of their rivalry, managing to work
together to produce a spectacle which the women shall
admire and marvel at. Almost without exception the ceremonies of the men are of this nature; and the ceremonial
house serves as a Green Room for the preparation of the
show. The men put on their masks and their ornaments
in its privacy and thence sally forth to dance and perform
before the women, who are assembled on the banks at
the sides of the dancing ground. Even such purely male
affairs as initiation are so staged that parts of the ceremony
are visible to the women who form an audience and who
can hear issuing from the ceremonial house the mysterious
and beautiful sounds made by the various secret musical
instruments—flutes, gongs, bullroarers, etc. Inside, behind
screens or in the upper story of the ceremonial house, the
men who are producing these sounds are exceedingly conscious of that unseen audience of women. They think of
the women as admiring their music, and if they make a
technical blunder in the performance, it is the laughter of
the women that they fear.

The same emphasis on pride occurs in many other
contexts of the life of the men. Here it must be remembered that the ceremonial house is also the meeting place
in which a great deal of the everyday work of the men's
lives is organized. In it their hunting, fishing, building,
and canoe cutting are discussed; and these activities are

carried out in the same spectacular manner as the ritual. The men form parties in their big canoes to go fishing or hunting; or they go off together in big groups to cut trees in the bush. Such parties are called together by rhythms beaten on the great slit-gongs in the ceremonial house; and if the work is taking place close to the ceremonial house, the gongs are beaten to "put life" into the workers. Finally, the completion of every considerable task is marked by the performance of some spectacular dance or ceremony.

Thus it comes about that the ritual significance of the ceremonies is almost completely ignored and the whole emphasis is laid on the function of the ceremony as a means of celebrating some labor accomplished and stressing the greatness of the clan ancestors. A ceremony nominally connected with fertility and prosperity was celebrated when a new floor had been put into the ceremonial house. On this occasion the majority of informants said that the ceremony was being performed "because of the new floor." Only a very few men were conscious of, or interested in, the ritual significance of the ceremony; and even these few were interested not in the magical effects of the ceremony but rather in its esoteric totemic origins—matters of great importance to clans whose pride is based largely upon details of their totemic ancestry. So the whole culture is molded by the continual emphasis upon the spectacular, and by the pride of the male ethos. Each man of spirit struts and shouts, play-acting to convince himself and others of the reality of a prestige which in this culture receives but little formal recognition.

No account of life in the ceremonial house would be complete without some reference to the ethos of initiation. Here we might expect in another culture to find the men combining together with dignity and austerity to instruct the youths; and in the painful process of scarification we might expect to find them inculcating Spartan resistance to pain. The culture has many of the elements which would seem appropriate to such an ascetic ethos: there are days during which neither novices nor initiators may eat or drink; and there are occasions on which the novice is made to drink filthy water. Again the culture contains elements which would make it appear that the novice is passing through a period of spiritual danger. He must not touch his food with his hand and he is subjected to a drastic washing which suggests ritual purification; and so we might reasonably expect to see the initiators protecting the novices from dangerous contamination.

But actually the spirit in which the ceremonies are carried out is neither that of asceticism nor that of carefulness; it is the spirit of irresponsible bullying and swagger. In the process of scarification nobody cares how the little boys bear their pain. If they scream, some of the initiators go and hammer on the gongs to drown the sound. The father of the little boy will perhaps stand by and watch the process, occasionally saying in a conventional way "That's enough! that's enough!" but no attention is paid to him. The operators are chiefly interested in their craft and regard the wriggling and resistance of the novice as prejudicial to it. The spectators are rather silent with, I think, a touch of "cold feet" at the sight of the infliction of pain divorced from the normal setting of histrionic excitement. A few are amused.

When pain is inflicted in other parts of initiation, it is done by men who enjoy doing it and who carry out their business in a cynical, practical-joking spirit. The drinking of filthy water is a great joke, and the wretched novices are tricked into drinking plenty of it. On another occasion their mouths are opened with a piece of crocodile bone and examined "to see that they have not eaten what they ought not." They are not under any food taboos at this time, but the result of the examination is invariably the discovery that the mouth is unclean; and the bone is suddenly jabbed against the boy's gums, making them bleed. Then the process is repeated for the other jaw. In the ritual washing, the partly healed backs of the novices are scrubbed, and they are splashed and splashed with icy water till they are whimpering with cold and misery. The emphasis is upon making them miserable rather than clean.

In the first week of their seclusion, the novices are subjected to a great variety of cruel and harsh tricks of this kind, and for every trick there is some ritual pretext. And it is still more significant of the ethos of the culture that the bullying of the novices is used as a context in which the different groups of the initiators can make pride points against each other. One moiety of the initiators decided that the novices had been bullied as much as they could stand and were for omitting one of the ritual episodes. The other moiety then began to brag that the lenient ones were afraid of the fine fashion in which *they* would carry out the bullying; and the lenient party hardened their hearts and performed the episode with some extra savagery.

The little boy's introduction into the life of the ceremonial house is conducted on such lines as these and it is one which fits him admirably for the irresponsible histrionic pride and buffoonery which are characteristic of that institution. As in other cultures a boy is disciplined so that he may be able to wield authority, so on the Sepik he is subjected to irresponsible bullying and ignominy so that he becomes what we should describe as an overcompensating, harsh man—whom the natives describe as a "hot" man.

The natives themselves have summed up the ethos of initiation in a formulation which is especially interesting in view of the contrasting ethos of the two sexes. During the early period of initiation, when the novices are being mercilessly bullied and hazed, they are spoken of as the "wives" of the initiators, whose penes they are made to handle. Here it seems that the linguistic usage indicates an ethological analogy between the relationship of man and wife and that of initiator and novice. Actually, resort to such sadistic treatment only occurs in rather extreme circumstances in the case of wives, but it is perhaps true that the men would like to believe that they treat their wives as they do their novices. I think we may see a consistent cultural pattern running through the contrasting sex ethos, the shaming of the novices, the *wau* shaming himself by acting as the wife of the *laua*, and the use of the exclamation *"Lan men to!"* ("Husband thou indeed!") to express contemptible submission. Each of these elements of culture is based upon the basic assumption that the passive role in sex is shameful.

In fact, the initiatory situation is not a simple one from an ethological point of view but is essentially a contact between two ethoses, that of the initiators and that of the novices. The ethos of the former is clearly a mere exaggeration of that of men in the daily life of the ceremonial house. But the ethos of the novices is not so clear. To some extent, especially in the early stages of initiation, they play the part of women; and we may ascribe some of the exaggeration of the initiators' behavior to the presence in the ceremonial house of novices with an opposite ethos.

For the moment we are not concerned with how this contrast has arisen; but we may suppose that the little boys have to some extent imbibed the women's ethos in their early life and so come to their initiation with some of the emotional attitudes characteristic of women in this culture. This assumption I cannot definitely state to be founded on fact, because I did not study the children; but whether it is correct or not, it is certain that there is some vague idea of this sort behind the initiation rituals. The response of the initiators to this real or nominal contrast between the novices and themselves is to force the boys further into the complementary position, dubbing them "wives" and bullying them into expressions of the wifely role.

The end of all this is the adoption by the novices of the masculine ethos, but it seems that the first step in inducing this process is to compel the novices to behave as women, a sufficiently paradoxical method of setting about the business to force us to inquire more closely into the processes which it involves.

I believe that we may distinguish[3] four contributory processes:

1. A process whereby the novice becomes contra-suggestible to the female ethos. We have seen that the treatment of novices *qua* wives is a great deal more drastic and arbitrary than the treatment of real wives; and further that while the women grow up gradually into their ethos, the novices are suddenly and violently plunged into submission. These differences account, I believe, for the fact that while the wives accept a somewhat submissive ethos without too much difficulty, the novices become contra-

[3] The theory here presented to a considerable extent overweighs the facts upon which it is based. This analysis of the initiatory process is, however, intended as a sample of the ethological point of view and an indication of the sort of problems which this point of view raises, not as an exposition of proven hypothesis.

suggestible and rebel against it. It is certain that revolts and refusals to undergo further bullying sometimes occur among the novices. Such revolts may from our present point of view be regarded as symptoms of well-developed contra-suggestibility to the submissive role, and the sharp repressive measures to which the initiators have recourse do not, we may suppose, extinguish the resentment in the breasts of the novices.

2. A process whereby the novices become proud of the male ethos. We may suppose that the novices derive some feeling of superiority from their separation from mothers and sisters and especially from undergoing an experience from which women and smaller children are excluded. Certainly they begin at quite an early stage, even before their cuts have healed, to be proud of the scars. About ten days after the initial scarring the novices are taken out into the bush and are threatened with bamboo knives. When I saw this done, four out of the five novices shrank away and screamed with something approaching hysterics at the idea of further cutting and were excused, but the fifth novice, after a few moments' hesitation, submitted to the operators and proudly acquired extra scars without flinching.

After the first week of intensive bullying, the relationship between initiators and novices alters. The former are no longer described as "elder brothers" or "husbands" but are now known as "mothers" of the novices. Corresponding to this change of phrasing, the initiators turn their attention to making much of the novices. They hunt game so that their "children" may grow big with good feeding, they teach them how to play the flutes, and they undertake as communal tasks the making of various ornaments—pubic tassels, lime boxes, spear-throwers, etc., for presentation to the novices. Finally at the end of initiation the novice, decked in all this finery, is exhibited to the women as the hero of the occasion, and the completion of his initiation is celebrated with *naven*.

3. Reactions to the presence of later novices. The ceremonial end of his initiation by no means completes the assimilation of the novice into the group of the initiators. There are other younger boys who though too young for initiation are by descent of the same grade as the recently

initiated novices. Later, when these boys come up for initiation, the former novices will line up with them to be shown the flutes all over again. They will not undergo again the more drastic forms of bullying, but ceremonially they will be reckoned as novices. At all these ceremonies they are frankly bored. Only much later, when they themselves become initiators, will they begin to take considerable interest in the business of initiation. Then they react to the presence of novices by themselves becoming bullies, completely assimilated into the system.

4. Reactions to the presence of other initiators. The drastic bullying behavior of the initiators is not merely a reaction to the presence of novices, but is also promoted to a great extent by the feelings of emulation which exist between members of the rival initiatory groups.

One characteristic of the Iatmul men is very clearly exhibited in the contexts provided by the initiatory system. This is their tendency to "cut off their own noses to spite the other fellow's face." Whenever a serious situation arises in the initiatory enclosure, e.g., when a woman sees something of the secrets, or some disrespect is shown to the secret objects, or when some serious quarrel breaks out, the talk is always of "breaking the screens," throwing the whole initiatory system open to men, women, and children, showing everything to everybody. Much of this talk is of course mere shouting without any real intention of drastic action, but from time to time an impasse causes such a degree of exasperation and shame that the men carry out some self-humiliating act which may cripple the ceremonial life of the village for some years.

Such a case occurred in Mindimbit. The initiatory system in this village was getting feebler and feebler. The boys were going away to work on plantations, leaving the village too weak in numbers for any great ritual to be attempted; while those who returned to the village did so with a scorn of the initiatory crocodile. The ceremonial houses were full of boys with no scars on their backs, and one small ceremonial house had even been slowly invaded by women and was now deserted by the men, who left it to the women as a place where they might sit and gossip.

One day a party of Mindimbit natives were being given a lift on a white recruiter's schooner. In the basket of one of the young men was a small bamboo end-flute. This object was noticed by the man's wife, who picked it up and said "What is this?" An older man was present and saw the incident. He scolded the woman, and she was ashamed. Then he went to the ceremonial house and reported what had happened and abused and ranted against the carelessness of the young man who had allowed the accident to occur. The old man and the other members of the opposite moiety raided the young man's house and smashed his wife's pots. But still they were not satisfied, so they went to the *tagail* or junior ceremonial house and to the dwelling houses to collect all the small boys together. Even the small toddlers who could only just talk were included. Then, that night, they showed them everything, including the *wagan* gongs. The procedure was an extreme telescoping of the whole initiatory cycle, but was unaccompanied by any sort of scarification. This drastic event was regarded both in Mindimbit and in the scornful neighboring villages as the final utter shame and destruction of Iesinduma, the village "crocodile" of Mindimbit.

Another more violent but similar event took place in Palimbai some fifty years ago. The village was celebrating its *wagan*, a performance on the gongs very much more secret and serious than the earlier initiation ceremonies which only involve flutes, bullroarers, etc. In the *wagan* ceremonies the secret gongs are beaten continuously, day and night, for months on end, in the upper story of the ceremonial house; and during all this time there must be no noise in the village: no person may quarrel or shout or break firewood. The spears stand, ever ready, leaning against the outside of the ceremonial house and against the screens, to kill any man or woman who offends against the *wagan* by disturbing the peace. But in spite of this preparedness for killing, the spears are not often used, and the incident which occurred in Palimbai is still remembered vividly and is cited as proof that the spears are there for serious use.

The ceremony had proceeded without serious trouble, and it was time to prepare for the final spectacle in which old men, impersonating the *wagan*, perform a dance in front of the assembled women. The initiatory group who were producing the spectacle went out to get croton

(*Codiaeum*) leaves with which to ornament the giant representations of *wagan* sneaking secretly out of the village so that no women should know of the methods of staging the spectacle. They had collected the leaves and put them in string bags and were on their way back to the village. Some children were playing near the mouth of the water-way which leads in from the river to Palimbai village, shooting the straight stalks of elephant grass with toy spear-throwers. One of these missiles fell in the men's canoe and pierced the string bag in which the croton leaves had been put.

The men at once gave chase and speared the small boy who was guilty of this offense. When they got back to the village, a general fight ensued in which three (or four?) men were killed, all of them members of the clan Wain-ggwonda, "fathers" of the small boy.

Then the clan, Tshimail, which had taken a chief part in the killing, went into the ceremonial house and pulled down the *wagan* gongs from the upper story. They built a small screen around them in the dancing ground and then showed the gongs to all the women of Wainggwonda and handed over the sacred gong sticks to them, to keep in their houses.

In killing the boy, they had only acted according to the conventions of the *wagan* ceremony; but still, perhaps feeling they had gone too far, they were impelled to humiliate themselves, to preserve their pride. They did not hang *tambointsha* (tassels) on their lime sticks for these killings.

In the business of head-hunting, the masculine ethos no doubt reached its most complete expression; and though at the present time the ethos of head-hunting cannot be satisfactorily observed, there is enough left of the old system to give the investigator some impression of what that system implied. Lacking observations of actual behavior, my description must, however, be based on native accounts.

The emphasis here was not on courage; no better *coup* was scored for a kill which had entailed special hardship or bravery. It was as good to kill a woman as a man, and as good to kill by stealth as in open fight. An example will serve to illustrate this set of attitudes: In a raid on one of the neighboring bush villages a woman was killed and her daughter was taken by the killer (Malikindjin) and brought back to Kankanamun. He took her to his house, where for a while he hid her, thinking of adopting her into his household. But she did not remain there. He took her to the ceremonial house and a discussion arose as to her fate. She pleaded that she should be pitied. "You are not my enemies; you should pity me; later I will marry in this village."

One of the young men, Avuran-mali, son of her captor, cut into this discussion, and in a friendly way invited her to come down to the gardens to get some sugar cane. Accordingly he and the girl went down to the gardens together with one or two of the younger boys, among them my informant, Tshava, who was then a small boy. On arriving there, Avuran-mali speared her. (The duty of cleaning the skull fell to Tshava. An enemy skull must never be touched, and Tshava had some difficulty in detaching a ligament. He therefore discarded the tongs, seized the end of the ligament in his teeth and pulled at it. His father saw him and was very shocked; but Tshava said to me: "The silly old man! How was I to know?" —an attitude toward taboos which is not uncommon among the Iatmul.)

But in spite of the lack of "sportsmanship," the activity of head-hunting was to a considerable extent a "sport." There was no clear rule that you must have a grudge against a man before you killed him, or against a village before raiding it; though a majority of the killings were certainly regarded as vengeance. In general the fighting and killing was confined to the killing of foreigners, i.e., members of other villages, especially of villages against whom a feud existed. But even this rule was not too strictly interpreted; a woman, married into the village, might for purposes of head-hunting be considered a foreigner. I even came across one case in which a man wore a tassel for killing his own wife in revenge for a kill accomplished by members of the village from which she had come.

Two main motives informed this system: the personal pride of the individual, and his pride and satisfaction in the prosperity and strength of his community. These two motives were closely tangled together. On the purely personal side, the successful homicide was entitled to special ornaments and paints and to the wearing of a flying fox skin as a pubic apron; while the apron of stripped *Dracaena* leaves was the reproach of the man who had never killed. The homicide was the hero of the most elaborate *naven* and the proud giver of feasts to his *lanoa nampa* (husband people). Lastly, he was admired by the women; and even today the women occasionally make scornful remarks about the calico loincloths worn by the young men who should strictly still be wearing *Dracaena* aprons like those which were given them when they were little boys being initiated.

The association of personal pride with success in head-hunting and of shame with failure is brought out too in the behavior of those whose relatives had been killed. Their first duty was the taking of *nggambwa* (vengeance). The rings of cane worn in mourning for the killed individual may not be put aside until vengeance has been achieved; and a pointed reference to an unavenged relative is one of the most dangerous insults that one Iatmul can use in ranting against another—an insult which is felt to be specially aggravating now that head-hunting is forbidden.

Indeed, so serious is the condition of those who are unable to secure revenge that it produces *ngglambi* in the group and may lead to the sickness and death of its members.

This spreading of clan dysphoria resulting from the unavenged insult to the pride of the clan may be contrasted with the "sociological" phrasings of the benefits which successful head-hunting confers upon the community. Here, as is usual in sociological phrasings, the matter is expressed in tangled symbolism, but may be made clear by an artificial separation of the various components of the system:

1. The enemy body was, if possible, brought back to the village and was there ritually killed by a man wearing a mask which represents an eagle. Thus the kill symbolically became the achievement not only of the individual homicide but of the whole village.

2. The natives articulately say that the eagle is the *kau* of the village. *Kau* is a word which means "a raiding party," "a fighting force," "an expression of anger," etc.

The eagle is also represented on the finial of the ceremonial house and at the ceremony with which this eagle
is put in place, the bird speaks. He looks out over the
enemy country and sees them there as "birds preening
themselves" or as "fish jumping in the water"—ready to
be killed.

3. The natives say that prosperity—plenty of children,
health, dances, and fine ceremonial houses—follows upon
successful head-hunting.

4. Prosperity is also dependent upon the *mbwan*, those
ancestral spirits which are represented by standing stones.

5. The heads of the killed were placed upon the *mbwan*
and in some cases their bodies were buried under the
mbwan.

6. The standing stones are phallic symbols, e.g., in the
shaman's jargon the phrase for copulation is *mbwan tou-*,
"setting up a standing stone."

7. The male sexual act is definitely associated with
violence and pride.

Running through this plexus of cultural details, we can
clearly see the general position of head-hunting as the
main source of the pride of the village, while associated
with the pride is prosperity, fertility, and the male sexual
act; while on the opposite side of the picture, but still a
part of the same ethos, we can see the association of
shame, mourning, and *ngglambi*.

Closely linked with these emphases upon pride and
shame is the development of the spectacular side of head-
hunting. Every victory was celebrated by great dances and
ceremonial which involved the whole village. The killer
was the hero of these and he was at the same time the
host at the feasts which accompany them. Even the vanquished assented to the beauty of the dances, as appears
from a text collected in Mindimbit describing the typical
series of events on a raid:

(After the fighting) they leave off. Then he (the killer,
standing in his canoe and holding up the head which he
has taken from the enemy) asks "I am going to my beautiful[4] dances, to my beautiful ceremonies. Call his name."

---

[4] In this text the phrase which I have translated as "beautiful
dances, beautiful ceremonies" is of considerable interest. The native
word for "beautiful" is *yigen*, a common Iatmul word which is used
to describe an admired face or spectacle. The same word also occurs

(The vanquished reply) "It is so-and-so that you have speared." (Or the victor will say) "This one is a woman," and they (the vanquished) will call her name (and they will cry to the victors) "Go. Go to your beautiful dances, to your beautiful ceremonies."

¶ THE ETHOS OF IATMUL CULTURE: THE WOMEN

In the everyday life of the women there is no such emphasis on pride and spectacular appearance.[5] The greater part of their time is spent on the necessary economic labors connected with the dwelling house—food-getting, cooking, and attention to babies—and these activities are not carried out publicly and in big groups, but privately and

---

in the adverb *yigen-mbwa*, "gently," the opposite of *nemwan-pa*, "violently" (literally, "greatly"). The whole phrase is *yigen vi, yigen mbwanggo*, a poetical form built up out of the common everyday phrase *vi mbwanggo*, "a (triumphant) war dance." In this phrase, *vi* is the word for a particular sort of spear with many points, used in warfare, and *mbwanggo* is the ordinary word for any dance or ceremony. In the traditional diction this phrase is divided into two parallel phrases, a common trick of Iatmul poetic genius.

[5] There is some local difference in ethos between the Eastern Iatmul (Mindimbit, Tambunum, etc.) and the Central Iatmul (Palimbai, Kankanamun, etc.). Among the Eastern people the women wear large quantities of shell ornaments in their daily life, only removing them for such tasks as the tending of fish traps. These women have also a slightly prouder bearing than the women of Palimbai and Kankanamun, who normally wear very little ornament. This difference has probably some bearing upon the culture as a whole, and it is worth mentioning that among the Eastern group *iai* marriage, in which the initiative rests with the woman, is commoner than in Palimbai; and that it was in Mindimbit that I was shown a very interesting lime gourd. It is the custom there for men to scratch on their gourds tallies of their successful love affairs; but the gourd in question besides the ordinary tally had incised upon it a large representation of a vulva ornamented with geometrical designs. I asked whether it was carved there as an emblem of the mother moiety, but the owner replied with pride: "No, that refers to a woman. I did not want her, but she came to my mosquito bag and took the active role in sex."

In general there is the same sort of contrast between the ethos of the two sexes in both areas, but this contrast is most marked in Kankanamun, where the women are definitely shabby. They are a little smarter in Palimbai and markedly smarter in Mindimbit. The men of Palimbai are conscious of the difference between their women and those of Kankanamun, and attribute it to the better supply of fish which they get because their village stands on the banks of a lake.

quietly. In the very early morning before dawn the women go out in their tiny canoes to tend the fish traps in which they catch the prawns, eels, and small fish which form the staple supply of protein food. Each canoe is just big enough to carry a woman and perhaps her small child, and on the stern is a little fire in an old pot for the woman to warm herself by in the chilly dawn; for the business of examining the traps involves her wading about in water up to her breast, and she will be cold when the job is done. The little fleet of canoes, each with its column of smoke rising in the half-light, is a very pretty sight; but as they draw away from the village, each canoe separates from the others as each woman goes to the part of the river where her traps are set. In this work there is none of the excitement which the men introduce into their fishing expeditions. Each woman goes off by herself to do her day's work. When she has tended the fish traps, she will go and collect, for firewood, old dead stems of the elephant grass which lines the banks of the river. Then she will return to the village where she will attend to the cooking and the jobs of the house.

A single house is divided between two or three men related by patrilineal ties; and this division of the house is felt by the men to be very real, almost a matter for stiffness and formality. The man who owns one end of the house will avoid intruding upon his brother's or his son's residence at the other end although there is no screen or wall dividing the house, only the big sleeping bags in the center of the floor. But although typically the women of a house are not mutually related, they seem to be much less conscious of the divisions and will constantly bandy remarks the whole length of the house. Each woman has her separate cooking place with its fire basins set up close to the wall, and the different wives of one man carry out their cooking independently, but still there is more ease in their mutual relations and less self-consciousness than is the case among the men.

The women's life is regulated by a three-day week, the middle day of each three being a market day. The supply of fish and prawns is such that a quantity can be set aside, either kept alive in baskets immersed in the water or smoked. On a market day the women gather up these supplies and go off in their canoes to the bush villages where they barter the fish for sago. The market may be held actually in the bush village, but more often the women of the bush tribes come halfway along the road and the parties meet at some agreed spot. The chaffering is done easily and with a good deal of jolliness. The deals are small and there is very little haggling but a great deal of talk, not only about the matter in hand, but about the events of the last few days in the various villages. At these markets men may be present, but so far as I know, their presence has no quelling effect on the general ease of the women. I have, however, only attended markets at which men were present and so cannot state definitely what effect their presence has upon the women. The women's markets contrast sharply with the behavior of the men when they are engaged in their more serious negotiations. In buying a sleeping bag or a canoe, each party tries to outdo the other in a pose of critical taciturnity, and in the majority of cases no business will be done.

Compared with the proud men, the women are unostentatious. They are jolly and readily co-operative, while the men are so obsessed with points of pride that co-operation is rendered difficult. But it must not be supposed that the women are mere submissive mice. A woman should know her own mind and be prepared to assert herself, even to take the initiative in love affairs. In *iai* marriage it is nominally the woman who makes the advances and who, of her own accord and uninvited, goes to the house of her *ianan*. It is said in Tambunum that in such cases the chosen man has no right to refuse such a proposal.

The same pattern is often followed in less formalized marriages in which the woman has no such nominal right. A typical case will illustrate the extent of the woman's initiative: I had gone with my native servants to look at some ceremonies in the neighboring village of Aibom, a village of foreigners who are not regarded as true Iatmul but whose social system is very closely related to that of the Iatmul. On the day after my return from this expedition, a girl from Aibom arrived alone in Kankanamun. She inquired for members of her own clan and went to the house of one of my informants, who was her clan brother. She told him that she was in love with one of my cook boys. Her clan brother asked: "Which cook boy?" She ex-

plained that she did not know his name. So they went together to a spot where they could observe my domestic
staff, and the girl pointed out the cook boy whom she
loved and he was thereby identified. In the negotiations
which followed, the boy and girl modestly avoided each
other (so the cook boy told me), but her clan brother
acted as intermediary and she lodged in his house. The boy
was definitely flattered by the proposal and decided to accept it. He sent a series of small presents to the girl, which
she accepted. Very soon messages began to come from
Aibom demanding the bride price; and the cook boy was
not rich. There were delays, and after about a fortnight
the girl returned to Aibom. The boy then put on some
show of anger and demanded from her relatives some return
for the presents which he had given her. But this return
was not forthcoming.

The point which I wish to stress in this incident is the
extraordinary courage which the girl showed in coming
alone to a foreign village, and the clarity with which she
knew her own mind. Her conduct was regarded as culturally normal by the Iatmul.

As a further documentation of the respect which is paid
to women of strong and courageous personality, we may
cite here a traditional myth which was told to me in Mindimbit in explanation of the head-hunting alliance between
that village and Palimbai. Both of these villages have a
traditional feud with the village of Kararau, which lies between them.

> Kararau were killing us. They speared women who
> went out to get tips of wild sugar-cane, and women
> who went to get water-weed [for pigs' food], and
> women who went to their fish traps. And they shot a
> man, Au-vitkai-mali. His wife was Tshanggi-mbo and
> [his sister was] Au-vitkai-mangka. They shot him and
> beat the gongs [in triumph]. Au-vitkai-mangka was
> away; she was on the lake [fishing]. Au-vitkai-mali
> went to his garden and they speared him, and the
> sound of his gongs came [over the lake]. She asked,
> "Whom have they speared?" and [the people] said,
> "They have speared your husband."
> Then she filled up a string bag with shell valuables

and she [went to the ceremonial house and] said, "Men of this village, I have brought [valuables] for you." But they said, "No. We do not want them," and they were ashamed [because they had not dared to accept the valuables which she had offered as payment for assistance].

Then she went down into her canoe; she loaded the valuables into the canoe; she took off her skirt and put it in the canoe. Au-vitkai-mangka was in the stern and Tshanggi-mbo in the bow. The bag of valuables was in the middle of the canoe. She went up the river to Palimbai, because she had heard his gongs. The two of them went by night.

They sat leaning against the ceremonial mound [a place of refuge] in Palimbai, and they put the bag of valuables on the ground close to the mound. At dawn [the people of Palimbai] got up and saw [them]. They were sitting stripped of their skirts, with their skirts on their shoulders.

The men of Palimbai said, "They are women of Kararau"; and they were for spearing them. The women said, "Why will you spear us?" Kaulievi [of Palimbai] saw and said, "Don't spear them"; and he said "Come." Then he beat the gong to summon all the men of Palimbai, Kankanamun, Malinggai, and Jentschan. The men of the four villages came together, and the women told them to debate. The men said, "What women are you?"; and the women said, "We are women of Ienmali." [Ienmali is the name of the old site of Mindimbit.]

Kaulievi said, "Tell your story"; and Au-vitkai-mangka said, "That is [the sound of] my brother's gongs coming"; and the men said, "Who speared him?"

Au-vitkai-mangka then [calling the names of the totems of the four villages] appealed to Kankanamun: "You! Crocodile! Wanimali!"; and to Malinggai: "You! Crocodile! Kavok!"; and to Palimbai: "You! Pig! Palimbai-awan!"; and to Jentschan: "You! Pig! Djimbut-nggowi!" And she said, "I shall take away my bag of valuables."

She set out the valuables in a line; and the four

villages accepted them. That night they debated, "Already tomorrow we shall raid them." Each of the four villages [brought] a fleet of canoes. They formed into one fleet on the Sepik River.

They [the men] gave a spear to Au-vitkai-mangka and the men of Palimbai gave another spear to Tshanggi-mbo. They gave one canoe to the two, a swift canoe; and the two women were in the center of the fleet.

When they drifted down to the Kararau [reaches of the] Sepik, [the canoes took up formation]. The two women hid in the center. Then the men shot an eel. It said "War." [A favorable omen; and here my informant reproduced the grunting of the eel.]

The two women came out [of the fleet]. They [went forward and] sang dirges in midstream. They were smeared with clay [for mourning] and the people of Kararau came out to spear them. But [the women] were going down stream in a swift canoe. They went for the setting of Palimbai's battle [i.e., the women acted as decoys]. The Palimbai people killed the people of Kararau and they caught two men [alive] in their hands. Au-vitkai-mangka speared one of them. Tshanggi-mbo speared the other. They speared them all, every one of them.

They all went upstream together to Palimbai and there they beat the gongs. The two women beat the gongs. In the morning the men cut the women's hair and oiled them and presented valuables to them. Then they brought the women in a fleet of canoes to Ienmali, and left them. Kaulievi said, "Kararau are our enemies" and he came and set up a stone [in Ienmali, now removed to Mindimbit]. And so Palimbai took Kararau for enemies. That is the stone, here, and the name of the stone is Kaulievi, an ancestor of Kepmaindsha. That is why Kepmaindsha came here, and Tonggalus too. [Kepmaindsha and Tonggalus were two men who had left their own villages as a result of quarrels.] Later when the two women died, they made a song about them; the clan Mwai-lambu [to which Au-vitkai-mangka and my informant belonged] made the song.

In the household, too, a woman may have considerable power and authority. It is she who feeds the pigs and catches the fish; and it is upon these activities that her husband chiefly depends for the wealth which helps him to make a splash in the ceremonial house. When a man is haggling silently over a canoe or sleeping bag, he will withdraw before concluding the deal, in order to consult his wife. And, judging by the things which the wife is reported to say in such circumstances, it appears that wives hold the purse strings very tight. But the stubbornness of an absent wife makes a very convenient tool in the business of striking a bargain, and I doubt whether the wives are really as "strong" as their husbands report.

In a few households, however, it is definitely the wife who "wears the trousers," and in two such cases the sympathy of outsiders went to the wife rather than to the henpecked husband. It was the wife's misfortune to have married a weakling.

But, as against the occasional instances in which women take up an assertive role and even participate in warfare, the more habitual emphasis of the women's ethos is upon quiet co-operative attitudes. Though the woman may take the initiative in sexual advances, it is the activity of the male which is stressed in the native remarks about copulation, while the part played by the female is despised. In the Iatmul language the ordinary verb for copulation and the jocular synonyms which are used for it are, so far as I know, all of them transitive and in their active forms refer to the behavior of the male. The same verbs may be used of the female role, but always in the passive.

Thus, in our study of the women's ethos, we find a double emphasis. For the most part, the women exhibit a system of emotional attitudes which contrasts sharply with that of the men. While the latter behave almost consistently as though life were a splendid theatrical performance —almost a melodrama—with themselves in the center of the stage, the women behave most of the time as though life were a cheerful co-operative routine in which the occupations of food-getting and child-rearing are enlivened by the dramatic and exciting activities of the men. But this jolly, co-operative attitude is not consistently adopted in all contexts, and we have seen that women occasionally adopt something approaching the male ethos and that they are admired for so doing.

In the ceremonial activities of the women, the same double emphasis is present, and these activities fall into two distinct ethological groups according as one or the other emphasis is predominant. In general, the jolly, co-operative emphasis is most evident when women celebrate by themselves in the absence of men, while the proud ethos is exhibited when women celebrate publicly in the dancing ground of the village with men in the audience.

In the first group are the frequent dances held by women in the houses. These dances are very much resented by the men, who regard them with contempt and do all they can to discourage them. When the women's ceremonial demands that the performers shall keep taboos on sexual intercourse, the men do their best to cause them to break these taboos—and then boast to the anthropologist of the postponement of the ceremony. At such times the sex opposition—never far from the surface—comes to a head. Quarrels between husbands and wives are especially frequent, and the wives take their revenge by refusing to cook sago for their husbands.

I found a husband sitting sulkily in the ceremonial house. He had a lump of sago which he was roasting rather ineffectually, naked on the fire—for the men believe that the art of cooking pancakes of sago is one which they cannot learn. He said: "Yes, we copulate with them, but they never retaliate," a reference to the despised passive sexual role. Then he jumped to his feet and shouted this taunt across the village to the women in his house, from which he was excluded.

For, in spite of their contemptuous attitude, the men withdraw quietly enough when the dance is actually about to take place; and the women are left in complete command of the house. They remove all the sleeping bags, clearing the floor space for the dance; and a great crowd of women collects together from all over the village, all joking and in the best of humor. After a while the dancing begins and the gathering sounds very gay.

On one occasion I was sitting in the ceremonial house when these sounds reached us. The men greeted the sound with contempt; but I asked if I could go and look at the women's dance. The men told me that the dances were very silly and not worth my looking at, that they could not compare with the dances of the men. I said that Mindimbit was a poor, "cold" village; the men never performed any of their vaunted spectacles; and if I couldn't see any dancing, I was going to go to another village. Finally and very reluctantly a young man said he would take me to the dance, and we went together. We entered while the women were dancing around the floor in short, jumping steps and singing a rather catchy, quick tune. We sat down on stools in a corner of the floor in silence. My companion was acutely uncomfortable, and after a few minutes, he slipped away.

When the women had finished the song, they came crowding up to me and offered me areca nut and betel. I asked for lime. Most of them had never seen me chew betel, and my acceptance of the offer created some excitement, screams of laughter and noisy, screaming talk—like a flock of parrots. In the middle of this excitement two women started to dance in front of me. They stood face to face in a jumping dance, and at every jump one woman pushed her hands forward with palms pressed together, the other woman received the hands between her own. Between the beats the first woman drew her hands back only to push them forward again at the next beat. This dance was obviously a representation of copulatory action, but I was completely surprised when suddenly, in a single jump, the two women dropped to a sitting position on the floor, still facing each other and one sitting between the legs of the other, one of the standard positions for sexual intercourse. In this position the women went through the motions of copulation still in time to the beat of the song; and then, as suddenly as they had sat down, they jumped up in a single motion, and after a few more jumps, they broke off, giggling.

The mere description of what these two women did gives very little idea of the extraordinary naïveté of this "obscenity" and the contrast between it and the harsher obscenity of the men. Lacking a photographic record, I can only record my subjective impression of this.

After more joking, the crowd of women left me to continue their dancing around the house. The same jolly atmosphere continued, and I had no doubt that this was the regular tone of the women's dances in the absence of men. I think too that an analysis of the tunes, sung by women and men respectively, would show the same ethological contrast between the sexes which I observed in their behavior.

But this characteristic jollity is not carried over to those occasions when women celebrate publicly. Then they march in procession in the middle of the dancing ground before a mixed audience of men and other women; they are fully decorated and wear, among other things, many ornaments usually worn by men—a sort of mild transvesticism which will be referred to again in the theoretical analysis of *naven*. They march with a fine, proud bearing very different from their jolly behavior when men are absent, and different too from their quieter demeanor on everyday occasions when they are in the presence of men but are not decked out in finery. Their marching gait in these processions is indeed more closely comparable with their swaggering demeanor when dressed in full homicidal war paint for the *naven* ceremonies than with their patterns of behavior on other occasions.

A similar phenomenon to that which appears on ritual occasions may be observed fairly constantly under the experimental conditions produced by pointing a camera at an individual. When a woman is photographed, her response to the camera depends on whether she is wearing her finery or is in everyday dress. In her finery she holds her head high when the eye of the camera is on her; but in everyday dress she hangs her head and rather shrinks from the public appearance constituted by standing up alone before the photographer while her friends are watching in the background. When a man is photographed, whatever his costume, he tends to swagger before the camera, and his hand goes almost instinctively to his lime stick as if about to make with it the loud grating sound which is used to express anger and pride.

¶ ATTITUDES TOWARD DEATH

We have so far examined the behavior of men and women only in the everyday and the ceremonial contexts of their culture. But the contrast between the sexes is even more striking when the individuals are faced with events highly charged with emotion. To illustrates this, I shall describe the sequences of events after a death has occurred.

In Palimbai I was awakened at about 4:30 a.m. one morning by the sound of weeping in the house next to mine. I went to see what was happening and found that a young man, who had been sick for two or three months, had finally died. The corpse was stretched out straight and was naked. A circle of women were crouched around it, and the mother of the dead man had the head in her lap. A fire was burning close to the corpse, and gave the only light in the house. The women were quietly weeping and dirging, singing songs of the dead man's maternal clan— songs which might be used on gay and everyday occasions, only now the singing was slow and out of tune and broken with sobs.

From time to time there were pauses when all were quiet, and then one of the women would make some remark about the dead man. Some incident of his life was referred to, or some small possession of his mentioned with the suggestion that it should be buried with him. Then the songs and the sobs were resumed, set off by this recall of another facet of their personal loss.

There was one man in the house. He was sitting apart from the group of women, silent and embarrassed. When I went up and spoke to him, he greeted my intrusion with pleasure and was very ready to discuss the arrangements for the funeral—how the government had forbidden them to expose the corpse in a canoe till the floods abated; as it was, they would have to take the body into the Tshuosh country to find dry ground for the burial; they would measure the body in order to know how big a hole to make; and so on.

The women's weeping continued until after dawn, but it was no hysterical exaggeration of grief such as is recorded from other primitive communities. My feeling was that I was witnessing an easy and natural expression of sorrow at a personal loss.

The behavior of the man was in marked contrast to this. On the one hand, he quite evidently wanted to escape from his embarrassment into conversation about the funeral, and, on the other hand, he boasted: "We [Iatmul] are not people who only play at weeping," and when I asked whether it was not only the women who wept, he felt this remark as an aspersion on the men, and insisted that men also weep. Later in the conversation he turned his attention from the affairs connected with the death and started to lecture me on the East wind and its totemic position.

After dawn, we first waited for the rain to stop and then proceeded with the funeral, for the men say: "Tears are not found in the lake," meaning that the supply will not last long and therefore they must bury the body quickly. The men put the body in a canoe and took it over the fens from one piece of supposedly higher ground to another, but all were flooded. We were a party of eight of whom two were women, the mother and sister of the dead man. The mother sat immediately behind the corpse, sometimes dirging over it. Conversation on the journey was quiet and concerned with possible causes of the death. Our plan was to take the body to Marap village, but the men were impatient and on the way said: "No, Marap is a long way. Let us bury him on Movat Tevwi" (a piece of high ground in the fens): but in the end we had to go to Marap and arrived there in the late afternoon. The Tshuosh were not pleased to see us, but at last they permitted the body to be buried under a deserted house.

The men had some difficulty in digging a grave, and the site had to be changed twice because they came on other old bones when they dug. Finally the corpse was laid in the grave, and the portrait skull of the dead man's brother was deposited with him. A shilling was placed in each of his hands, and his string bag was placed in the grave. Since he was buried among the Tshuosh, the grave was oriented so that (on raising his head) the corpse would look toward the setting sun, as is the custom of the Tshuosh. In Palimbai the dead are normally buried with their feet toward the dancing ground, so that the corpse is not "looking into the bush."

The women retained their skirts throughout this burial, but I was told by an informant in Kankanamun that the mother, sister, and wife of a dead man would normally be naked while he was being buried. This nakedness is, no doubt, in some way analogous to the nakedness of the women when they lie down before the hero in *naven*, and with the nakedness of female suppliants.

The mother of the dead man stayed behind in Marap to mourn for a few days, but the rest of us returned that evening to Palimbai as a normally cheerful party, no longer an embarassed and silent group.

A second occasion on which I was able to observe the reactions of the men to a death was on the day after Tepmanagwan, a great fighter of Palimbai, had died. He died during the night and was buried in the early morning. I arrived in the village at about nine o'clock, after the interment, and found that the men had by then left the grave and gone to the ceremonial house. A few women were weeping at the graveside, and from the ceremonial house I could just hear the weeping of others in the house of the dead man.

I proposed going to the house, but the men hinted that I should not. They were just starting a debate in the ceremonial house. It was a scandal that Tepmanagwan had died without passing on his esoteric knowledge, and the debate was an inquiry as to whose fault this was. A few men sobbed while they were making their speeches, and I found it hard to judge whether these sobs were the result of genuine feeling bursting its way to the surface against resistance, or whether they were a theatrical performance staged in absence of strong feeling to give this impression. In any case, it was perfectly clear that the men's sobs were very far removed from the natural weeping of the women.

The debate reached no conclusion, and when it petered out, the men set up a figure to represent the dead man. The head of the figure was an unripe coconut, and the body was made of bundles of palm leaves. Spears were set up against the figure with their points stuck into it to mark where the man had been wounded in war, and other spears were stuck into the ground beside the figure for those which he had dodged. A series of vertical spears was set up in front of the figure according to his achievements. The figure itself was ornamented with shells, etc. Six sago baskets were suspended from its right shoulder to represent his six wives; a string bag was suspended on the left shoulder, representing his skill in magic. A number of sprigs of ginger in its headdress represented persons whom he had invited to the village so that other people could kill them. In the right hand of the figure was a dry lump of sago, because it was said that in his lifetime he had once killed a bird by throwing a lump of sago at it. A branch of *timbut* (lemon) set in the ground beside the figure was symbolic of his knowledge of mythology. Finally, on the ground at the feet of the figure were a broom and a pair of boards used for picking up rubbish. These objects were symbolic of the work which the dead man had done in cleaning the ceremonial house during his lifetime.

This figure was set up by members of the initiatory moiety of which the deceased was a member. It was a boast of the greatness of their moiety, and when the figure was completed, all the men of both moieties crowded around it. The members of the opposite moiety came forward one by one to claim equivalent feats. One man said: "I have a wound here on my hip, where the [people of] Kararau speared me. I take that spear," and took the spear set against the figure's hip. Another said: "I killed so-and-so. I take that spear," and so on till all the emblems of prowess had been removed.

Thus the men made, out of the context of death only a few hours old, an occasion for expressing the competitive pride of the initiatory moieties. They escaped entirely from a situation which was embarrassing because it seemed to demand a sincere expression of personal loss, an expression which their pride could scarcely brook. From this situation they took refuge in a cultural stunt. They rephrased their attitude toward the dead and expressed it satisfactorily in terms of spectacular pride, the emotional language in which they are at ease.[6] But such a handling of grief is, I think, still not adequate, and later a further compensation is added. It is my impression that when a man is asked about some past funeral, he will generally drag into his answer some reference to his own great weeping, in spite of the fact that at the time he wept but little

---

[6] In our own culture, of course, both these types of emotional patterns and many others are mixed and tangled together in our mortuary ceremonial. Culture contacts and the recurring instability of Western European societies have provided us with every sort of conflicting phrasing, and these phrasings have been preserved for us in script through the ages. But the Iatmul have a less confused culture.

and probably made a show of his resistance to womanly tears.

In the later mortuary ceremonies the contrast between the behavior of the two sexes continues. The skull of the dead man is exhumed and a portrait is modeled upon it in clay. This is set up one night as the head of a highly decorated doll which represents the deceased. Around this figure the men stage an elaborate performance of name songs and flute music. The ceremony, which is called *mintshanggu*, takes place in a dwelling house, and the women are present as audience. The flutes are played by men hidden under the platform on which the figure stands, where they have been secretly smuggled. Thus, though the ceremony takes place in a dwelling house and its context is a personal one, it is staged upon the same general principles as all the other performances staged by the men, a spectacle for the admiration and mystification of the women.

Later the women have a little mourning ceremony by themselves in the absence of men. This is called *yigen kundi* (quiet singing). It takes place at night in a house from which the men have withdrawn. A little food is hung up for the ghost to "eat," and the women sit in a circle by the firelight and softly sing the name songs of the dead man's mother's clan. The wife or mother of the dead may weep a little, but the general tone of the group is one of quiet sorrow rather than of passionate grief. The "quiet singing" goes on till late in the night, when the women disperse to their houses.

In the months or years which follow, the mother or wife of the dead man will occasionally, when she is alone, sing as a dirge one of the name songs of his maternal clan; these dirges may often be heard on the river, coming from some woman mourning as she paddles her canoe to her garden or fish traps. The men quite frequently caricature this musical effort, probably because the attitude of the women toward death is one which they themselves find distasteful.

Indeed, one of the most important phenomena which is brought to light by examination of ethological contrast is this distaste which persons trained in one ethos, their emotional reactions standardized in one pattern, feel for other possible ethoses. In the illustration which I gave, I mentioned how a remark which is out of tune with the temporary ethos of a group of Englishmen is received with silence, and in Iatmul culture we may recognize the same phenomenon in the distaste which the men feel for the ethos of the women. This phenomenon is extraordinarily widespread, and it affects even the anthropologist, whose task it is to be an impartial student of ethos. Every adjective which he uses is colored by and evokes the feelings which one sort of personality has about another. I have described the ethos of the men as histrionic, dramatizing, overcompensating, etc., but these words are only a description of the men's behavior as seen by me, with my personality molded to a European pattern. My comments are in no sense absolute statements. The men themselves would no doubt describe their own behavior as "natural"; while they would probably describe that of the women as "sentimental."

It is difficult too to describe a pair of contrasting ethoses without so weighting the descriptions that one or the other appears preferable or more "natural." The business of the scientist is to describe relationships between phenomena, and any ethos which he finds in a culture must be regarded not as "natural" but as normal to the culture. Unfortunately what is normal to one culture may well be abnormal to another, and the anthropologist has at his disposal only the adjectives and phrases of his own culture. Thus it has happened that English people with whom I have discussed Iatmul ethos have sometimes remarked that the women appear to be "well adjusted," while the men appear to be "strained" and "psychopathic." My friends forget that the values assigned by European psychiatrists to various mental conditions are either *cultural* values based upon European ethos or estimates of the fitness of the individual for life in a European community.

The pride of the men, when seen in contrast with the women's ethos, may appear to my readers somewhat angular and uncomfortable. I found it also splendid. I have not stressed this aspect enough, and therefore I shall conclude the description of Iatmul ethos with a free translation of a story which illustrates how a man should behave when his own death stares him in the face:

A man went with his dog to hunt for wild pigs in the

sago swamps. When they had killed a pig, the man went to wash its guts in a lake. While he was doing this, a giant crocodile (Mandangku, an ancestor of Tshingkawi clan) seized him by the instep and held him fast.

The man said to the dog: "Go home and sniff at my feather headdress, and sniff at my armbands and all my ornaments."

Then the dog went home, and when the man's wife saw the dog sniffing at the ornaments, she took them and put them in a basket, and the dog led her and her child back to where the man was, still held fast by the crocodile on the lake side.

When he saw them, the man said: "My child, my wife, I am lost," and then he said: "Give me my things."

He put on his legbands and his shell girdle. He put on one of his armbands and then he put on the other. He hung his mother-of-pearl crescent around his neck. Finally he put on his headdress of parrot skins and bird-of-paradise feathers. Then he said to his wife and child: "Come close and wait."

The crocodile began to pull him down into the water. He took off his legbands and threw them ashore. The crocodile pulled him farther, and he took off his shell girdle. The crocodile pulled him farther till the water came level with his armpits, and then he took off his armbands and threw them ashore. The crocodile pulled him farther, and finally he took off his mother-of-pearl crescent and his feather headdress and threw them ashore. He said: "It is done," and then he said: "Go! my wife, my child, go! What is become of me?"

Then there was the sound of splashing, the crocodile waved its tail, and bits of leaf and grass were stirred up from the bottom of the water.

A NOTE ABOUT THE AUTHOR

Raymond Firth

As a boy growing up in New Zealand, Raymond Firth (1901–   ) read early accounts of the Maori and other Polynesian peoples, and nourished what he later called "the faint hope that it might one day be my own fortune to see something at first hand of a Polynesian folk who had barely come into contact with civilization." He realized this hope in 1928–9, when he conducted field research on the remote island of Tikopia. At that time Firth was the only white resident of Tikopia, and the people were "almost untouched by the outside world." Raymond Firth returned to Tikopia in 1952, this time accompanied by James Spillius, one of his students at the London School of Economics. Together they studied the changes in Tikopia society wrought by increasing contact with Western civilization. *Social Change in Tikopia*, published in 1960, reports their findings.

"The Fate of the Soul," reprinted in the following pages, was the Frazer Lecture for 1955. In it Raymond Firth examines a subject of central importance in the anthropology of folk religion by drawing upon his field experiences in Tikopia. In a two-volume study, *The Work of the Gods*, Firth has described the seasonal cycle of ceremonies, which he calls "the crowning point" of the social life of Tikopia. That study is the only thoroughgoing description in the literature of an elaborate Polynesian ceremonial cycle, based upon field research in the manner of contemporary social anthropology.

But Raymond Firth's most distinctive contributions to modern anthropology have been in the areas of kinship and economic organization. *We, the Tikopia*, published in 1936, is one of the most impressive studies of kinship in the anthropological literature. And Firth established the study of primitive and folk economies as a viable field of anthropological research in a series of monographs which began with his doctoral thesis under Malinowski: *Primitive Economics of the New Zealand Maori* (1929: Second edition; 1959); *Primitive Polynesian Economy* (1939); and *Malay Fishermen, Their Peasant Economy* (1946).

At the present time Raymond Firth is Professor of Anthropology at the University of London. He has received many honors in recognition of his contributions to anthropological scholarship: he is a Fellow of the British Academy; in 1939–40 he was Leverhulme Research Fellow; he was elected President of the Royal Anthropological Institute for 1953–5; and in 1958 he became the first British anthropologist to receive the Viking Fund Medal in General Anthropology of the Wenner-Gren Foundation in New York.

7

The

Fate of the Soul*

by

RAYMOND FIRTH

We are assembled here to do honor to James George Frazer. More than any other man of his time he was responsible for the general development of public interest in anthropology in this country. Yet he is not merely the laymen's anthropologist. Not only the breadth of his learning and the grace of his writing, but also his perception of basic motives in human thought and endeavor have given him an enduring place in anthropological science.

Frazer collected and examined a great mass of evidence on concepts of the fate of the soul—primarily in Oceania —in lectures delivered between 1911 and 1922, and published in his three-volume work, *The Belief in Immortality and the Worship of the Dead*. This massive work is full of fascinating data. The coverage is encyclopaedic, and the occasional generalization—as, for instance, about the Maori belief in immortality as a sanction for private property and for the status of chiefs—anticipates much modern treatment of social relations. But Frazer was primarily an ethnographer interested in the accumulation and classification of social facts. Personally a most reticent man, he was averse to much theoretical construction—or to what

* The following essay is reprinted by permission of the author and of Cambridge University Press. It was first published as: Raymond Firth, THE FATE OF THE SOUL: AN INTERPRETATION OF SOME PRIMITIVE CONCEPTS, Cambridge at the University Press, 1955.

he recognized as such. Hence to the modern social anthropologist, who is avid of theory, revels in abstractions, and is highly sensitized to the influence of personality upon material, Frazer offers no clear lead. One can read him with profit—but one must supply one's own framework.

My framework in this lecture is for the most part that common to all social anthropologists. But in dealing with such a delicate subject as ideas of the soul, about which there is such diversity of view, my approach must be to some extent a personal one.

Goethe, in 1834, expressed the keynote of many human ideas on this subject when he said that he had a firm conviction that the human spirit is a being that cannot be destroyed. Just a century ago, in a general review of the natural history of man, James Cowles Prichard, who may be described as a proto-anthropologist, said more cumbrously: "There is nothing more remarkable in the habitudes of mankind, and in their manner of existence in various parts of the world, than a reference, which is everywhere more or less distinctly perceptible, to a state of existence to which they feel themselves to be destined after the termination of their visible career." [1]

Prichard was concerned here as elsewhere with evidence to demonstrate the common origin of mankind. But granting an almost universal interest in life after death, it is the variation rather than the uniformity in such beliefs which seems so striking. E. C. Dewick (in a book on primitive Christian eschatology some forty years ago) has pointed out that primitive peoples, as contrasted with civilized, are concerned with individual eschatology rather than cosmic eschatology. It is the fate of souls in their own society, not the fate of the world which interests them. Even within this sphere there is much further variety, as Tylor, Boas, and Frazer himself have helped to show. In all this there are several points of special interest that I want to make.

The first is that in most primitive communities it is continuity rather than immortality that is assumed. In some societies, like the Manus, there is provision for termi-

[1] *History of Man.* Fourth edition. Revised by E. Norris, Vol. II (1855), p. 661.

nation of the soul. In most, it is believed to endure, but there is no positive notion of eternity as such.

Secondly, as a rule the fate of the soul is not associated with any concept of rewards or punishments after death. The doctrine of retribution on a moral basis after death is generally lacking. In this there is a strong contrast to the beliefs of followers of most of the major religions. Most primitive peoples are like the Tongans, of whom Frazer has pointed out that they do not appeal to another life to redress the balance of justice which has been disturbed in this one. Their pagan faith does not rest its ultimate sanction for conduct on what Frazer has called "the slippery ground of posthumous rewards and punishments." [2] It is a common view that moral sanctions are discoverable in ideas about the future of the soul only insofar as they repose on the belief in such retribution. I regard this view as incorrect, and later shall show why.

The third point is that, like many people who belong to the more sophisticated religious systems, members of most of the primitive communities have no great *concern* about the fate of their own souls. Their ideas may be formulated in terms of a general problem of knowledge. Each individual does not worry in advance about the personal problem of his future life. This does not mean that such people have a poverty of religious ideas in general. In those societies which, like the Nupe of Northern Nigeria, have few developed concepts of the persistence and fate of the soul, there are nevertheless elaborate ideas about the existence and actions of spirit beings or powers of other orders, and elaborate practices for constraining or propitiating them to promote the ends of man.[3]

The fourth point is that primitive beliefs about the fate of the soul are usually not polarized, as they are in the great religions. The field is more open. Not uncommonly, there is wide variation of belief, or at least of statement, about the possible fate of the soul, even in a single community. A. R. Radcliffe-Brown has pointed out that in every Andamanese tribe there are alternative and inconsistent beliefs as to the place where spirits go—up to the

[2] Op. cit., Vol. II, pp. 146–7.
[3] S. F. Nadel: *Nupe Religion* (London; 1954), pp. 34–5.

skies, beneath the earth, out to the east where the sun and moon rise, or into the jungle and the sea of their own country.[4]

One thing, he says, is clear—that the Andamanese ideas on this subject are "floating" and lacking precision; they have no fixity or uniformity of belief. One might speculate about the reasons for such lack of precision. I suggest three possibilities. One is that different destinations of the soul are structurally determined, being associated with different group alignments. Another is that obscurity in itself in such a matter has a social function, allowing dispute and differences of interpretation according to existing committal of interest. The third possibility is that this doctrinal sphere is one in which "a free vote," so to speak, is possible; that a crystallization of dogmatic terms is not relevant because it offers no particular social advantage.

These alternatives cannot be tested on the Andamanese material. But I mention them here because they foreshadow some of the lines of my own analysis.

A fifth point is that most primitive eschatology is dynamic, with plenty of social interaction. Unlike the Western view, in which the departed soul is effectively depersonalized in favor of group dependence upon the Divine, the primitive gives departed souls a field of concrete social activities. First, they interact with one another and, secondly, with the world they have left behind. In the West, we have reduced the volitional field of the departed soul. We have given the soul after death a direction but no magnitude. We have removed from our dead and our ancestors the ability to make choices, to participate effectively in the society of the living. As Le Van Dinh has pointed out in comparing Western beliefs with the cult of the dead among his own Annamite folk, we in the Occident "liquidate the past" as far as our dead are concerned. In the light of our emphasis on the importance of the individual this might seem surprising, were it not for the inference that it is the individual freedom of the living that demands the annihilation of the exercise of decisions by the dead. But of course the difference is one

[4] A. R. Radcliffe-Brown: *The Andaman Islanders* (1922), pp. 168–70.

of procedure rather than of principle, since in the primitive system, one may argue, the dead are merely the living in another guise. In particular, in an ancestor cult they are a means of expression of social obligations, and an important element in the process of decision-taking, by an indirect route.

From this you see that my problem is not that of the ethnography of the soul—of exploring concepts of the fate of the soul descriptively to see the range of ideas of which man is capable in conceiving this subject. It is concerned with these beliefs in terms of their social functions—the way in which they have been expressed and their correlates in social action. I am interested, too, in relating such expressions to the structure and organization of a society where a change of religious system is taking place.

Let us examine further some primitive notions of the soul or human spirit.[5] By soul in this context I mean a symbolic extension of the human personality, invisible, believed to be responsible for supra-physical activity and for the most part to be capable of survival after physical death. Lack of primitive interest of any intense kind in the fate of the soul after death does not mean a corresponding lack of interest in what Frazer has called "the perils of the soul" during life. Most primitive peoples have quite elaborate theories about the souls of the living and their liability to attack. They may even believe in the existence of multiple souls—several such personal entities of different types all attached to a single human individual, and each sensitive in different ways to environmental influences. Again, the distinction is commonly made between the soul of a living person and his soul after death. At the death of the body the soul undergoes a radical transformation, or there is a substitution of per-

[5] I am tempted in view of the vagueness of terms in this field to adopt the following distinctions: *soul* for an immaterial entity which represents the survival personality of the human being both before and after the death of the body; *spirit* for an immaterial entity which may include the category of soul but also other categories in which the human connection is minimal or imprecise in emphasis; *ghost* for the survival personality of the human being after death, in apparitional or manifestational form. But though such distinctions would be useful, they would seem too artificial in comparison with current usage.

sonality in which one type of soul takes over, as it were, from another the spiritual continuity of the man. Such different types of soul have usually different names, giving rise to semantic problems for the anthropologist.[6]

For primitive peoples even more perhaps than for civilized, there is a sharp recognition that death is what Gustav Fechner has called "the great climacteric disease" which the spirit of man as well as his body has to go through. But what is the implication of this recognition and emphasis? Is it that once the body of man has passed beyond our care, concern for his personality reaches out beyond the grave to promote his future well-being? In some cases this may be so. Attention is focused on an invisible object, the personality of the departed. He is held to endure in some immaterial form and to be cared for by the appropriate actions of those he has left behind, such as funeral rites and offerings. Is it again that the emphasis upon continuity of the soul after death is one form of protection of the personality; an assertion that man's will to survive has reality and not merely yearning? This wish-fulfillment type of explanation has a wide currency far beyond the primitive field. I take at random (from *L'Ecole des Vacances*, a novel by André Bay, a translator of Lewis Carroll and of Swift into French) such *obiter dicta* as "every kind of faith is a protection against death" or that "the ideas of the continuity of the soul are part of the barrage that life invents against death." These have an important element of truth. But I hazard a hypothesis here. It is rather as a framework for activity in *this* world and for positive experience in *life* that concepts about the continuity and fate of the soul are developed, rather than as protection against death. In the ritual behavior where crude fear of the dead seems to be the salient theme, the concern for freedom of action of the *living* is most marked. But apart from this highly negative reaction, there are more positive

[6] C. von Fürer-Haimendorf has pointed out in an earlier lecture in this series the confusion resulting from the common failure of Western observers to make this distinction between types of soul when writing about Indian tribal beliefs. He also gives an interesting example of the way in which one Indian tribal people, on abandoning their own dialect for Telugu, have fallen into the same semantic confusion ("The After Life in Indian Tribal Belief," J.R.A.I., Vol. LXXXIII [1953], pp. 37–49).

and more subtle aspects. In many primitive religious systems, it is true, the soul of a dead person is regarded at times with fear and horror. But this is only part of the reaction. On other occasions it is looked upon with respect, even affection, and is held to be in frequent welcome contact with the living. It is difficult to accept literally Ralph Linton's statement that in some societies death is regarded simply as a transfer comparable to that from child to adult, and that—as with the Tanala—the dead remain an integral part of the clan, merely surrendering one set of rights and duties and assuming another.[7]

Even in the traditional ancestor cults of the Annamites and the Chinese the dead are "members" of the social group in a very different way from the living. But there is an important point made in this statement in its emphasis on the way in which the concept of the behavior of the souls of the dead is used as an instrument of social control of living human behavior.

In placing the weight of interpretation of primitive eschatology on its social functions, I do not intend to deny other highly significant elements. In the ideas of the fate of the soul, intellectual and rational components are easily perceived. The early history of Christianity in Western Europe has demonstrated how important is the theoretical problem of where the soul goes after the death of the body, and why it goes to the destination appointed. Here are two vital questions. On what principles is the fate of the soul determined? Who are the agents who activate or operate these principles? Such questions have their parallel in the less sophisticated form in primitive religious systems although they tend to be implicit, not explicit. But however they are framed or implied, they do represent an attempt to handle a difficult and puzzling problem in terms of reasoned relations and not merely in terms of emotional solutions. In this respect the approach of Edward Tylor has tended to be undervalued. It is easy in the light of the work of the psychologists over the last century to point to Tylor's failure to recognize the importance of emotional construction in primitive religious phenomena. But while the religious premises may be basically emotional, the associated argument may be mainly rational. At times

[7] Ralph Linton: *The Study of Man* (New York; 1936), pp. 121–2.

indeed it may be intellectualistic, even metaphysical. What one must acknowledge in any primitive series of concepts about the fate of the soul is that there is some logical relation seen and explainable between the condition in which the soul of the dead finds itself or manifests itself at any given time, and some particular social circumstance. What is usually lacking in the primitive field is the retribution theme of drawing this social circumstance from the past behavior of the living person whose soul is now active after his death. What is, on the other hand, very manifest in the primitive field is that the social circumstance is drawn from the behavior of other living persons here and now.

In much of the primitive material about the fate of the soul there are also aesthetic elements. In many primitive religious systems, institutionalized spirit mediumship brings back to the living in word or in deed the presence of the dead. Often the words attributed to the soul of the dead are in descriptive or narrative form, with much use of imagery. They may tell of how the living man met his death, and his soul released has come to notify his kin. Or they may tell of adventures dramatic, ludicrous, erotic, or simply mundane, of the soul among other spirits in the afterworld. As with the visions of medieval Christianity, the narrative sequence of plot and incident and the stimulus of the imagery of color and harmony undoubtedly give outlet for aesthetic creation and for aesthetic satisfaction.

Such intellectual and aesthetic elements are subtly intermixed. The anthropologist often collects material about the fate of the soul in descriptions of a generalized kind through set interviews with informants. The stories therefore are often robbed of their social context and full meaning. This meaning is more clearly demonstrated in an oral recital of experiences by some subject who tells the story of a vision or a dream about the afterworld or describes some ordeal of ghostly visitation which he has undergone. Here the eschatological evidence may be more closely linked with a personal satisfaction of a meaningful kind. The author of visions or other accounts of the afterlife and the fate of souls may be seeking confirmation for personal decisions, standpoints, relationships. He may be expressing in a roundabout way the dilemmas or solutions of some personal problems.

In the primitive world such accounts take the place of the literature to which we in the West owe far more than we realize of our notions of the hereafter. In such literary recital the element of direct subjective experience varies greatly. On the one hand, there are men writing down what they themselves have felt they experienced of visions of the fate of souls—or, like St. Catherine of Genoa, describing Purgatory by personal analogy. On the other hand, there are the obvious literary devices of a Virgil, of a Dante, or of the composer of the Buddhist Lotus Sutra, which reveal to us the scenes of Heaven, Hell, and their ancillaries. Yet now that, to quote Tylor, "the dead have been ousted by geography from any earthly district, and the regions of heaven and hell have been spiritualized out of definite locality into vague expressions of future happiness and misery," [8] the role of such literature as information is much less important. (This is all the more so now that modern astronomy on the one hand and space fiction on the other have pushed the limits of the accessible or conceivable universe still farther back.)

Now that Sartre has replaced Dante as our eschatological authority, each statement about the hereafter becomes more than just a piece of descriptive material about another world. It expresses even more strongly a personal attitude about action in this world.

A word more about Hell in our immediate context. Primitive peoples have in their pagan religion no idea of Hell. Nor have they usually any doctrine of the Last Judgment as satisfying the demands of perfect justice. Only recently through Christianity have such notions come to them. Now, the importance of the idea of Hell as a direct moral sanction has often been emphasized. What has been less clearly noted is that sociologically the idea of Hell is a very useful defining element for a religious system. Unequivocally, it separates those who belong to the religious body from those who do not, by carrying the boundary fence into the hereafter and preserving the moral differentiation. As Franz Cumont has shown for the

[8] E. Tylor: *Primitive Culture*, Vol. II, p. 101.

Orphics of the Greco-Latin world, Dewick for the primitive Christians, and, quite recently, Maquet for the Banyarwanda Ryangombe sect, the pains of Hell were the distinguishing fate for those unpurified by initiation into the special cult.[9] Hell then was the ritual defining factor for the system. Belief in Hell is in modern times possibly less of a negative personal moral sanction than of a positive social reinforcement—part of the ideological structure supporting the integrity of the churches that maintain it and the uniqueness of their members.

I give this example as a pointer to the situation in primitive religious systems.

Let me now take an example for more detailed analysis and outline the main ideas about the fate of the soul after death in an Oceanic community, Tikopia—an island in Frazer's field. First there are the traditional ideas of pagan Tikopia. (The ideas of Christian Tikopia I shall mention later.)

The Tikopia have no theory of multiple souls. They believe that in life a person has a single vital principle or soul, as we may call it, variously termed *mauri* or *ora*.[1] This may go away from the body during dreams[2] and have other experiences. Some time after death there is a change of terminology with change of function; the soul now comes to be referred to as *atua*, not *ora*. This implies its

[9] Franz Cumont: *After Life in Roman Paganism* (New Haven; 1922), pp. 170 *et seq.*; E. C. Dewick: *Primitive Christian Eschatology* (Cambridge; 1912); J. J. Maquet: "The Kingdom of Ruanda," in *African Worlds, Studies in the Cosmological Ideas and Social Values of African Peoples* (International African Institute; 1954), pp. 171, 183–4. According to S. Angus (*Mystery Religions and Christianity* [1925], p. 152), only the "lower and popular" Orphism stressed Hell in order to exact fees from the initiates.

[1] Most Tikopia I consulted asserted that the *mauri* and the *ora* were the same thing—that is, they referred to a single entity. A few said they were different, but were not able to give any clear criterion of differentiation. Certainly the two terms seem to be used interchangeably in practice.

This usage is different from that of the traditional Maori, who have three terms for human vital principles—*mauri*, *wairua*, and *hau* (apart from *ora*, meaning life)—and do seem to have differentiated between them to some extent. (See Elsdon Best: "Spiritual and Mental Concepts of the Maori," *Dominion Museum Monograph*, No. 2 [Wellington; 1922]; Raymond Firth: *Primitive Economics of the New Zealand Maori*, pp. 268–71.)

[2] Raymond Firth: "The Meaning of Dreams in Tikopia," in *Essays Presented to C. G. Seligman* (London; 1934), pp. 63–74.

emergence as an entity in its own right, no longer in direct association with its body.

Its relation to the body is interesting and needs a brief linguistic discussion. The Tikopia soul is what Tylor called an ethereal image of the body. The proof of this is that the soul is always expected to be recognized by its friends and kin by its appearance. But the Tikopia here play a kind of three-card trick, which is not uncommon in eschatology. They distinguish the body, called *tino* when alive and *penu* (husk or shell) when dead, from the soul, called *mauri* or *ora*—the immaterial essence, the ethereal image. But they also have a third entity in between, a kind of symbolic body—perhaps "etheric body"—which is regarded as physical or not according to circumstances. This is the *ata*, the semblance. Now ordinarily the *ata* is the shadow, or the reflection. But in certain circumstances a wandering ghost can get into the dead body of a person and walk abroad in his shell. Yet here comes the problem. On the one hand, the Tikopia will say it is the corpse that is animated; on the other, they will say that the corpse is still in the grave, and that it is only in the semblance of the dead man, his *ata*, that the foreign ghost appears. Of course this question—when is a body not a body?—involving a subtle transition from the physical to the symbolic sphere is a problem not confined to the primitive. As the sophisticated arguments of theologians, from Athenagoras to Karl Barth, about the exact nature of the bodily resurrection have shown, there is grave difficulty here.

The Tikopia soul at death, though it leaves the body, does not immediately set out on a journey to the afterworld, but remains in the vicinity until after the burial, or later, until conducted away by the ancestral spirits of its mother's patrilineal kin group. In some versions the soul must pass a barrier or test—walk over a slippery stone which turns under its feet and projects it down to annihilation if certain conditions have not been complied with. But in most accounts, the soul passes without hindrance to its first destination.[3] This is a pool in the afterworld, guarded by two grim spirits, with a curious function. The newly

[3] According to the Ariki Taumako in 1952—son of my informant of 1929—the slippery stone (*fatu sekeseke*) is encountered at a later stage. But this would not easily fit into the sequence.

arrived soul is lowered into the pool by its mother's gods or ancestral spirits. The two guardian spirits then devour, or rather chew up, the soul, mumbling its substance between their gums so that its essence, described as "blood," runs down into the pool. This blood is then collected by a female deity in a gourd, in which it begins to assume once again human form, growing arms, legs, head, etc., and finally taking on full human shape, but of spirit character. This process of maceration is not regarded as victimization. No Tikopia expresses any abhorrence of it. It is looked upon as a necessary procedure in the conversion of crude souls with the taint of mortality still upon them into refined spirits capable of taking part in the life of the afterworld. In the early stage, indeed, before this grim refinement, the soul is known as the "living man" (*tangata ora*) by other spirits. Now it is the *tama furu*—the "cleansed child," an *atua*. Then comes another curious procedure, in typical Tikopia idiom. The re-created spirit of itself is a weak thing, of no particular capacity. It is therefore fitted out with special powers. These are known as its "swiftness" (*vave*) and enable it to travel with speed through the skies. But they also enable it to perform superhuman deeds. In particular, this "swiftness" is exemplified by and in a sense identified with, thunder. Thunder is a phenomenon clearly outside the human field; in Tikopia view it is made by spirits. The ability to make it, in common with other weather phenomena, is a mark of the more powerful spirits. The equation of *speed* with *power* is itself an interesting one. But here again, the spirits of the mother's patrilineal kin group (*paito*) play their role; it is they who endow the newly re-created soul with his "swiftness." They do it by the concrete act of sticking at the back of the soul's waist cloth a tuft or spray of leaves in the form of a dance ornament. This does not just symbolize the "swiftness": to the Tikopia it bears or is the swiftness. So we have the equation in different contexts, or at different levels of abstraction of: *spray of leaves* = *spirit swiftness* = *spirit power* = *thunder*. Into this elaborate system of thought comes yet another element of a structural kind. The various major kin groups have each a particular type of plant or shrub which they and they alone are properly entitled to use in this spirit investment.

Hence the re-created soul goes off decorated with the particular emblem of his mother's group, a fact which is significant in various kinds of linkage and identification in many other ritual and secular contexts.

Thus equipped, the soul goes off, making various visits of observation and courtesy to his ancestral and other spirits. But sooner or later he settles in a dwelling place (*noforanga*). There are very many of these; I have the names of at least two dozen, each under the control of a lineage god or other spirit of rank, and there are many more spoken about without being named. Some are in the ocean, some in the mountains or elsewhere in distant lands, but many are in the skies. Those in the skies are known as *Rangi* (Heavens), a term affiliated with that for sky, *vaerangi*, and are said to be similar to the clouds floating above. These *Rangi* have a complex and not entirely consistent structural order. Firstly, as a most general statement, there are often said to be ten of them in horizontal layers, and number from top to bottom, in their names as "First Heaven," "Second Heaven," and so on. In the topmost heavens live the senior gods and most important ancestors, with lesser gods and spirits in the lower strata. (The lowest heaven, number ten, is also known as the Heaven of the Turnstones, because this migrant wading bird, like a small curlew, is believed to wait up there during the winter season until its time comes to descend and be seen again.) Rather ill-fused with this schematic numbered arrangement (which, incidentally, is very reminiscent of that in other parts of Polynesia) is another, rather less systematized, but more elaborate. There is a directional allocation. The Tikopia of course traditionally had no compass points, but they divided the circle of their horizon up into something very like it, in the form of wind points —the directions from which the major winds come. Each of these major wind points, of which there are four, is the home of a major deity of the Tikopia, who is a prime clan and lineage god. He controls the wind and weather from that particular direction. (The prime god of Kafika controls the west, of Tafua the northwest, of Taumako the south, and of Fangarere the southeast.) Each of these quarters, as we may call them, is in spirit terms made up of a number of *Rangi*. Names are given to these heavens, according to their various characteristics. They are arranged in layers, but in fact when these names are counted, in any quarter there may be more or less than ten. (One reason for this I will explain in a moment.) In the topmost division lives the deity who is known as the Post or Stay of the Heavens, the controller, who presides over his whole set of heavens. Below him live the "small gods," as they are sometimes called, and the souls of ordinary men. These heavens can be identified with the tenfold scheme mentioned earlier, but in practice no one seems to bother to do so unless asked by the anthropologist.

Some of these heavens are peculiar. One, belonging to a particular lineage, is a Heaven of the Halt, or the Lame; spirits who limp have that as their home. Another is the Heaven of Cannibals, spirits who eat flesh and who have only one nostril, one ear, one leg, one arm, etc., apiece. Other heavens are sloping, others still unstable. I have an account of heavenly doings, telling how a spirit may be standing on a sloping, unstable heaven, to the irritation of the owner spirit. He is annoyed; he wants the other to leave. So he gives his heaven a tilt and slides the other spirit off, making him take flight to another heaven. He goes off, flying like a bird, because of the "swiftness" of the dance ornament at his back. Unmarried women have their own heaven, as do married women, married men, and bachelors. But the rules of abodes in the hereafter are elastic; as in Tikopia, there are fixed dwellings determined by social affiliation and by status in sex and marriage, with additional provision for physical defects. But choice among these dwellings and visiting from one to another are free. The lame spirits and the rest, like the gods, go strolling about as they wish. In the heavens there is eating and drinking, and some spirits go and work in the cultivations. But the great occupation is dancing. In many ways it is a pagan South Seas version of the Elysian fields—or of Marc Connelly's *Green Pastures.*

But what does it all amount to? What does it mean? To some degree it is just sheer fantasy. The notion of a heaven for the lame, or one-eyed, or of a spirit playing a malicious joke upon another by tilting up his heaven and sliding him off, or many of the erotic adventures described for some souls have no deep social roots. They are embroideries, more or less socially accepted, on the main themes.

But we accept the view that Tikopia eschatology is not just fantasy. To what does it correspond? In psychological terms there are various aggressions symbolized in the images of spirits chewing up the souls of the dead so that the blood flows, or wish fulfillments in spirits flying with speed. But in social terms there are other points to be made.

Firstly, it is of the character of religious belief that it must bear some relation to the state of society in which it is held. These statements about the destination and the fate of souls are restatements of social structure, at a symbolic level. The hierarchy of gods and spirits in the heavens parallels the principles of rank on earth. The names of the heavens relate to significant social differences. Not only this—the souls of the dead retain their earthly status when they arrive in the afterworld. The system of clan dwellings, the special position of chiefs and ritual leaders, the particular assignment of married and unmarried—all broadly follow Tikopia alignment.

Here comes a second point—that the reproduction of this social structure is not just an imaginative simulacrum of the world below; that one important function is its expression of the *continuity* of the structure. It is reassurance that not merely the personality, but also the society, goes on. When the society is not threatened by external forces, this aspect is not so significant. But if it is so threatened, then the emphasis of the eschatology upon continuity may become critical.

But the fate of the soul is not a simple reflection of the structural positions of the living. Firstly, not all human elements of the structure are catered for. In the Tikopia world of souls there are no guardians of public order corresponding to the executive officials (*maru*)—the "policemen," they call them—on earth. Again, there may be a compensation mechanism. It is true that primitive eschatology knows little of the *ubi sunt* principle—"where are the kings and emperors, the great ones of the earth? . . . They are now as common men. . . ." Unlike the overt egalitarianism of most of the great religions, those of the small-scale societies usually place the soul in the situation ascribed to the individual in life. But occasionally some souls do rise in the hierarchy higher than their human status would seem to have entitled them. However, this is rare.

But the fate of the soul offers material for manipulation. The spirit mediums and other charismatic leaders are able to use the material dealing with the fate of the soul to bolster up their own authenticity and confirm their powers. In the course of their recitals of doings in the spirit world, they use a great deal of creative imagination. They give adventures to the soul. They enlarge the geography and social structure of the spirit world. They introduce the names of heavens, some new to the listeners. This is the reason why the number of heavens, and the spirits who live in them, is not always identical and clear. The spirit mediums can do this because the souls of the dead are regarded as active. In Western belief, souls of the dead are not in action—except to a limited extent, as in the cult of Saints. They remain at a distance—wherever that may be. In Tikopia it is not so; they are in social movement.

But support to position of spirit mediums and other ritual leaders does not in itself throw much light on the firmness of belief the Tikopia have in this general picture of the fate of the soul, and the intense interest they have in detailed accounts. As a general proposition, I have said that this belief and interest seem to be less oriented toward their own ultimate individual fate than toward current concerns. What is the relationship? In essence it is that the pronouncements of spirit mediums, ritual elders, chiefs, and the frequent other references made to the afterworld and the fate of the soul relate directly to practical and personal issues of weather, food supply, sickness, accident, the fate of kinsfolk abroad, and many other daily affairs.

Here comes a further hypothesis, that in all this the implicit moral bearing is very important. For instance, the Tikopia stress the theme of the soul being carried by the gods and ancestor spirits of its kin to its spirit home.

Not to be carried is a terrible thing. The soul must wait until some other spirit takes pity upon it and bears it away. This is a powerful restatement in symbolic language of the moral role of kin.

The moral aspect appears in the relation between funeral ritual and ideas of the fate of the soul.

Some form of rite for "speeding the soul" is very common in primitive religious systems. It is often said that the reason for this is to stop the soul from afflicting the living by remaining in the vicinity of the corpse and being tempted to interfere with the affairs of the survivors. This interpretation often seems to be correct. But there are more complications and rather different reasons in some cases.

Many of the funeral rites seem to be essentially associated with ideas of completeness of sequence in human affairs. That relations with the person who has died physically may be properly terminated socially needs formal recognition. This termination of social relations is acknowledged, as it were, by being notched in memory by a specific rite. In the last resort this notion may perhaps be reduced to aesthetic criteria.[4]

The analogy here is quite close with the ordinary ceremonies of farewell. But when there have been strong emotional attachments to the dead person, the rites of speeding the soul then represent not so much a formal emotional severance as a formal emotional shift from the *vital personality* associated with the body to what may be called the *survival personality* associated with the spirit.

But there may be other forms, too, indirectly concerned with the fate of the soul. As part of the funeral rites the Tikopia have a custom called "pressing down the grave mat." This is partly a technical operation of firming the sandy soil after the burial and partly a ceremonial operation of covering the grave mat—plaited from coconut fronds—with aromatic leaves. This helps to protect the body of the dead person, now empty of its soul, from wandering spirits. If this is not done, a wandering ghost may enter the corpse and walk abroad in it in the sem-

[4] See also Raymond Firth: *Elements of Social Organization* (1951), pp. 63–4.

blance of the dead person. Apart from the protective physical barrier of the aromatic leaves, there is a spirit barrier. The spirits of the family of the mother of the dead person are expected to sit by the grave side and keep watch, chasing away any alien wandering spirit that approaches.

One of my friends in Tikopia, a spirit medium, described to me in 1929 a dream he had had after he returned home from several nights' watch by the grave of a dead kinswoman. He said: "I had a dream last night. I was asleep in my house and two men came in with two women—spirits of the grave mat which I had pressed down. They came and said to me: 'You, there, abandoned the mat and came home, why did you not stay and ask for coconuts to be broken and to be put on the mat for us to drink? Here we have come to tell you to return where we were; we have abandoned the mat, we are hungry.' Thereupon I spoke to them. 'What is to be done? The earlier nights [i.e., the first phases of the rite] are finished.' Then they called to me: 'Why did you not stay to add on the later nights to complete the affair?' Then a little child came running and called to me: 'Father, Father, come and let us go to the mat of my mother, the mat has been deserted by the guardian spirits, the corpse of my father's sister will be entered, come and have a look at it, Father' [he was our son from among the spirits], and I woke up. This was my dream."

The expression of this dream shows some anxiety and guilt for his not having stayed longer by the grave side, although in fact he had completed his normal duty. There may have been some element of accusation for the omission of libations of coconut milk because the people concerned were Christians. But I do not think so, since my friend behaved in all matters as an ordinary spirit worshipper and such coconuts were offered on other occasions to spirits as appropriate. In other words, this was not a culture-conflict dream of the kind which I later collected in 1952. What it does show is the Tikopia conception that there is some relation between proper completion of the sequence of funeral rites and the appearance of a semblance of the dead person to the living immediately afterward. This point is relevant for our later discussion, in regard to ghosting by souls of the dead and not only by alien spirits.

In terms of kinship also the perpetuation of very marked family affection is thought to endure among the spirits of the dead. A sick person will say to his mother, his brother, or his son: "I shall be buried by you under your sleeping mat, I shall lie below while you live above, at the place where my head lies to sleep. I shall go among the spirits, and look down at you sleeping on my mat." There are many such informal ways in which the nostalgic sentiments of Tikopia spirits for their kin are shown through statements about the fate of souls. Apart from this, the formal procedures of conveying the spirit to the afterworld, cleansing it from its taint of mortality, equipping it with its spirit power, and assigning it to its permanent home, all are expressed in kinship terms. Particular weight is laid on the role of the ancestor spirits and gods of the mother's patrilineal kin group. It is they who are crucial in the proper care for the new soul, just as they are crucial in care of the person throughout life.

Tikopia statements and actions concerned with the fate of the soul involve, then, to a very large degree statements and actions about the rightness of social relations in their own society. Accounts of the journey of the soul to the afterworld and of its treatment in the afterworld are, *inter alia*, affirmations and extensions of the operation of basic moral principles of Tikopia social structure.

In saying all this, I do not mean to imply that in traditional Tikopia eschatology there is anything of the specific didactic kind which one meets, for example, in accounts of medieval visions of the Christian afterworld. When the thirteenth-century Essex peasant Thurcill had his vision of the brilliantly lit cathedral with the foetid smoke of Hell swirling up outside its walls, he was told by his guide (St. Julian) that the coughing of unhappy souls in this smoke was caused by the tithes they had unjustly retained. The brilliant light in the cathedral, on the other hand, was due to the tithes that the just had rendered. When Thurcill unfortunately happened to cough twice from a whiff of the smoke, his saintly guide suggested that he must have been remiss in paying his tithes. Thurcill admitted this, pleading poverty, to which the saint replied that the giving of tithes increases the fertility of the soil, so that it would have been more profitable for him to have paid up. Such didactic details in the visions were used in local medieval sermons, we are told.[5] But little of this plain speaking occurs in pagan Tikopia accounts. The story of the test barrier of the slippery stone has sometimes been given with a moral connotation—those who have not done their duty by the Kava rites miss their footing and are precipitated down no one knows where. But this story and its implications have no wide currency.[6] What is much more common, however, is for spirits of the dead to appear in dreams to the living, or in the trances of spirit mediums, and complain that they have not had proper attention paid to them. Here the tone *is* definitely one of moral application to the survivors, and this is recognized by the living Tikopia, who are spurred on by the belief that if they do not do what is asked, the spirit will afflict them with illness or death.

As Tylor has pointed out, the retribution theory is far from universal among mankind. Unlike the sophisticated religions, primitive religions make few distinctions between good and bad in the afterworld. What is weak in the pagan Tikopia eschatology is an overt moral judgment of a *generalized* kind, differentiating the fate of the soul by reference to the moral condition of the person in life. What they do give fairly fully is indirect or tacit moral approval to conditions in *this* world by their mere way of stating conditions, structural alignments, activities, in the *next*.

In brief, one may say that statements about the fate of the soul are in many respects symbolic affirmations of moral judgment about human action in society. In primitive religions these statements are moral expressions as much as moral sanctions. But looking at them from this point of view raises a question of the extent to which behavior in human society is likely to correspond to the approved line of treatment of the soul. In many cases human behavior is likely to be unaffected by the moral view ex-

[5] A. B. Van Os: *Religious Visions: The Development of the Eschatological Elements in Mediaeval Religious Literature* (Amsterdam; 1932), pp. 3, 75, etc.

[6] In 1929 the Ariki Taumako told me this. He also told me that people who have lived properly and not killed or committed theft go to their heaven without trouble. Those who have slain men or stolen

pressed through statements on the afterworld. A woman who dies in childbed and whose soul therefore goes to a different spirit home cannot be influenced in her situation in advance by the knowledge that some souls have this fate. It is doubtful if a warrior, whose soul will go to an undesirable spirit home if he is killed in battle, is likely to be stimulated to much greater warlike energies thereby. A status of an ascribed kind such as that of chief cannot be normally changed, despite the fate that awaits the soul of the office-holder. Even where, as in the major religions, the rewards and punishments allocated to the soul vary according to the behavior of the person among the living, the evidence as to just how effective these notions are as sanctions is ambiguous and contradictory. It seems as if the ideology of the fate of the soul operates rather as an inert or latent factor called into operation by some special *other* experience or controlled by some countervailing principle—such as that the expediency of the action saves the soul from a bad fate, or that some final and all-embracing act absolves one from the moral quality of previous actions.

A further test of some of these proposals is given by the behavior of people who, having previously been pagan, have now joined a major religion. Examples of this are many Tikopia, some of whom were Christian when I first knew them in 1928–9, and some who became converted from paganism to Christianity in the intervening time before I visited them again in 1952.

The tenets of the Christians about the fate of the soul are formally those promulgated by the Melanesian mission. I asked the Motlav priest, who had been in charge of the Tikopia Christians for many years, what he taught about the souls of the dead. He said that when God created Adam, He blew into him the breath of life. This is the soul. When man dies, his body gives jerking spasms

do not. But he said that this information was generally not known, nor did he have any clear idea of what happened to such evildoers. I noted at the time that this was not a current ethical concept, and regard it as a personal gloss due probably to the unconscious effect of mission teaching, and the desire to represent pagan knowledge as at bottom no less ethical. There was no evidence in other contexts that the chief paid attention to such a belief.

and the breath leaves. It returns straight to God, who gave it, just as does the soul. This is in the case of people who have behaved properly. Those who misbehave have their souls go straight to Hell. I asked about the ideas of the pagan Tikopia. He said: "They do not know. They think the dwellings of spirits are in the world of men." I asked him then, what about the spirits who walked abroad as ghosts; why was it they had not gone straight to God? He said: "Oh, no, they don't walk." Then I reminded him of an experience he had told me twenty-three years before, of an apparition of his dead father-in-law which he had seen in open day on the path. He said: "Oh, you remember it?" and he went over it again in clear, exact detail, almost identical with what he had told me a generation before. He said that this was the only time that he himself had seen such a spirit. But he gave me examples of other people who had seen ghosts, the spirits of dead people, recently. The priest then said to me: "We say that the soul goes straight to Heaven, but then we see people standing there. We don't know if it is their soul or not, it is not certain"—and he turned to me and asked: "What do you think?" I said, too: "It is uncertain."

The views of the more sophisticated Tikopia Christians follow those of their priest. For example, one man who had himself been a mission teacher discussed the Christian attitude toward suicide. Each man's soul belongs to God and each man should await the time of his death, "following the will of the Lord." Hence the man who commits suicide does not go to Paradise; he goes to Satan. The reason for this is that the Bible says it is wrong for a man to take his own life. If a person should commit suicide, then it is for the priest to make the proper prayers at the altar of the church so that the soul of the man may go to the proper place. The family of the person cannot themselves perform this service or intercede with God in any way—only the priest can do this. Normally the family of a suicide does not make any special inquiry about his fate. But if they do worry about the situation, they may go to the priest and ask him for special prayers, and they substantiate their request by presenting to the priest a pandanus mat. But, it was added, "once a man is in the ground, people do not worry about him or think too much of him unless he starts to 'walk.' " [7]

This question of the "walking" of the soul of the dead as a ghost is a crucial one in modern Tikopia eschatology. In the Western world we have a long history of ghost belief, and traces of this still remain in some popular notions and in humorous references. But it is no longer fashionable or necessary in Western Europe or the United States, for instance, to see ghosts. In Tikopia it is an accepted experience, and there were several cases during my visits. Psychologists have shown how greatly perception and memory may be conditioned by social circumstances. So it is not surprising that the Tikopia see their apparitions as Tikopia, as persons known to them, and in the forms of dead kin. Some are attributed to alien spirits who impersonate the dead, others to the actual souls of the dead revisiting for various reasons the human scene. This formerly was regarded as a matter to be treated with caution, likely to make people afraid. But on the whole, there was little structural interpretation or moral emphasis attached to it. Now it has become a matter of heightened interest and with some moral overtones.

I wish to examine the history of a couple of cases which were almost notorious in 1952.

The first was that of a young man, unmarried and a pagan, who fell from a high cliff while climbing to net birds nesting on the rock face. His spirit appeared on various occasions, causing talk and some fright. But the attitude of Tikopia to such apparitions is often very matter-of-fact. The lad was regarded as having lost his life through foolhardy tempting of his skill, and judgment on this comes out in the spirit encounters. A friend of mine told me how the lad appeared in spirit form to one of his kinsfolk who was awake in his house at night. He

[7] These observations were collected by J. Spillius from Pa Raroifi. In 1929 the same man, then known as Pa Motuangi, gave me the traditional account of the fate of the soul. He said nothing about going to Paradise, but told me that on death he would go first to the heaven of his mother's brother to be decorated and equipped with speed; then he would go to either Maunganefu, the cloud-capped mountain of Vanikoro, or to Tarafare in the ocean, both spirit homes of his own kin group. In the intervening generation he had evidently adopted the conventional Christian view.

called out "Brother," and the living man recognized the voice of the dead. He replied in a curse. "Here you are coming and calling out to me—I excrete in your gullet." Then the ghost went away. "What was the ghost's idea?" I asked. "His affection, it might have been," was the reply. Another of his kinsfolk had a similar experience when the ghost opened the door of his house. He called out something that, freely translated, was "You fool, what have you come peering in here for? It was your own stupid fault that you went and fell off the cliff." Rebuffed again, the ghost then went on to the cookhouse of his father's dwelling, and, finding his father absent, he apparently began to wail and was hea d crying by people. He is said to have pulled aside the c ors of several houses. It was not known if the father had seen his son after death or not. My informant had not seen him, but he told me that another man had seen him by day in an orchard up the mountain, and ran from him. He explained that only recently had the soul of the dead man been caught by the guardian spirits. He pointed out that a person who dies on a bed of sickness is all right; the spirits take his soul to the realm of the spirits and then they return it later to listen to the funeral rites and the wailing. But when a person is killed by a fall from a cliff, his body crashes down and his soul rises and floats about like a petal alighting on tree branches and wailing at its fate, but not perceived and secured by its spirit guardians. This is what had happened to the dead young man, who had been heard wailing in various orchards near where he fell.[8]

But why should such a spirit walk? Partly, it may be, in Tikopia belief, the result of his own choice. When a young man dies, "he is angry with his friends." He knows that other young men and maidens are still going about

---

[8] When a person falls and lives, his soul is collected by spreading out bark cloth near the spot and beating the bushes around with sticks until a petal or an insect alights on the cloth. This is then wrapped up, brought back, and opened on the body of the man, to allow the soul to re-enter its habitation. Cf. J. G. Frazer: *Belief in Immortality*, Vol. ii, p. 206; Margaret Mead: *Social Organization of Manua* (Honolulu; 1930), p. 101.

Note that in Tikopia this ceremony is never performed when a body is lost at sea or a person killed by accident on shore; it is only done in the case of injury. If it is not performed, the person goes into delirium because his soul has not been reunited with the body.

among the living. So he is annoyed and "walks" to object and disturb them. Or he wishes to make contact with his kin, from whom he has been so suddenly wrenched. One explanation given (to J. Spillius) was that the soul newly parted from its body by death is confused, does not know where it is, does not know that it can no longer communicate with them in the normal way, and so approaches them. On the other hand, older people, it is said, are content to be dead.

But to some degree the walking of ghosts is regarded not as a matter of choice, but as a reflection of the present divided structure of Tikopia religion.

The dead boy in the first case was a pagan. To Christian Tikopia the "walking" of his ghost was a sign of the inadequacy of his faith. Now, the stereotyped Christian view is that souls of Christians who have been given proper burial do not "walk" (i.e., appear to the living immediately after death), because they go to Heaven. But even the Christian priest admitted that there are cases to explain. One of these is the sacond example I wish to discuss.

The name of the young man concerned was Samuel. Soon after death, he was seen not only by mission teachers but also by other people. One of the teachers, for instance, had seen the recently buried lad standing by the seaward side of his father's house, clapping his hands and making the sound "Wo, wo, wo . . ." as if dancing. The teacher said to him: "You don't frighten me; I am on my way to our Father the priest," and, feeling protected by his ritual mission, went on quietly. When he arrived at the priest's house, he said nothing. A little later a son of the priest, also on his way home, saw the ghost too, was afraid, and ran. When he got to the priest's house, he told what he had seen, whereupon the other man told his story, too. Innocently one day I asked the dead man's father about the stories that his son was "walking." He replied hotly: "It is just untrue; people are lying; he was buried in the Faith." He added that the story was one put out by people of another district and that no one in their district had seen him. When I said that in fact it *was* by someone of their district, he replied: "Well, no one in our village has seen him, no one in this village, the one which buried him." He added again: "It's lies." But he had heard rumors of these stories, obviously, and he changed the subject quickly. His difficulty was that the dead are common property; other people cannot be stopped from seeing their ghosts. Whereas the family of the deceased, knowing that he has been buried with proper rites, may strenuously deny that he is "walking," others see him and report. The implication is disturbing to them. It suggests an insecure status, perhaps moral condemnation.

When I first talked about these matters in 1952, the Christians I saw told me that only pagan souls walked. Later this opinion was controverted by both Christians and pagans. An old friend of mine who had become a Christian recently, when I asked him if it was true, said: "They've been lying to you—those that are walking there are baptized people, they have been rejected by the gods."

When I asked a Christian lad who had been baptized as a child what caused the spirits of the dead to "walk," he answered: "A person who is correct with the spirits does not walk, but a person who is not correct with the spirits returns among men to walk about. So it has been from of old. The person who is correct is not discovered among men [i.e., his apparition is not seen]. He who walks has not been carried by the spirits." When I asked: "Are those who are given Christian burial also liable to be seen as apparitions?" he said: "A person who is buried with prayer can walk. There are many of those buried with prayer who have walked." Then he added: "Because this land rejoices—it rejoices in the work [i.e., Christianity] —the people oppose the things of the chiefs."

My old friend Pa Fenuatara and the Ariki Taumako also denied strongly that only unbaptized spirits walk. Pa Fenuatara was very definite. "People of the gospel who die, it is terrible. They stand midway in the sphere of man and of spirits. The reason is that they have opposed the gods and are rejected by them. Hence they are left to wander until the judgment day. Some Christian souls sleep peacefully—the reason is that they have given adherence to the gods. Baptized folk who have acknowledged that the gods are true are cleansed, but the man who denies the gods is rejected by them and not cleansed." In other words, in Tikopia belief Christian spirits walk because of the present spiritual situation. It will be remembered that the souls of pagan Tikopia are carried off, cleansed by their maternal kin's spirits, and then go to their ancestral gods. But under the new dispensation, ancestral gods are antipathetic to the Christian God. Hence it is believed He will not allow the souls of the baptized to pursue their traditional pagan course. So, there is danger that they will be rejected by their ancestral gods and neglected by their maternal kin spirits. So left, they wander about on the borders between the human world and the spirit world. And in this condition of uneasiness they are wont to come as apparitions, until in the end they are carried off out of pity.[9] To Christians this is a matter of regret, to pagans a matter of some pleasure and scorn. This is the plight of Christians as seen by pagans, and it is one of the few sanctions that the pagans can still use. But it is shared by Tikopia Christians in that they themselves are still confused about the immediate fate of the soul. They have no consistent theory about it. Moreover, they have no purgatory which could take care, in part, of their complicated loyalties.

Note that the fate suffered in pagan eyes by the souls of Christians who have denied the gods is assimilated to that of pagan Tikopia who have not supported the Kava ceremonies. An implicit morality has become converted to an explicit morality. In former generations, when Tikopia was completely pagan, it must have been rare for any man to have consistently absented himself from the Kava ceremonies of his chief. Hence there must have been only minimum grounds for interpretation of the walking ghosts in such terms. But in modern times, when a person can refrain from attending the Kava without necessarily being a Christian, the net effect is the same and the punishment in afterlife is therefore equated.

So much for the immediate facts of Tikopia belief; what is our further interpretation?

[9] Some people, Christian rather than pagan, apparently try to avert this fate by making a treaty with a spirit medium. Traffic with such mediums is, strictly speaking, not approved of by the Church, but many Christian Tikopia resort to them. Pa Motuata told me: "Nowadays, whoever may behave well to spirit mediums, give them tobacco, and the makings of betel (the food of the spirits is tobacco and betel), then the spirit will speak to him thus: 'You, when the time comes for you to die, I shall await you'—to carry off the soul."

The appearance of ghosts in Tikopia is a facet of the interpretation of physical experience. Certain untoward happenings occur: as a person is passing along a path at night, a cool breeze from nowhere suddenly blows upon his body, or to his nostrils comes a strong smell—of turmeric or of putrescence.[1] Or else he is startled by a sudden sound. These things need explanation, and they find it within the general framework of Tikopia belief in the mobility of spirits, including those of the dead. The sight of a ghost needs more complex explanation. But the Tikopia seem prone to interpret in human shape visual experiences of some uncertainty, and most of such statements about seeing ghosts refer to dusk or other conditions of poor visibility. There is no reason to doubt their sincerity; there is much other evidence for crediting them with a lively imagination.

There is plenty of skepticism. One young man said to me: "A spirit who walks will appear to one person but not to another person—and so the person who did not see him will deny it. When he appears to a person, he does not just appear: he chases him. It is not certain the reason why he comes to chase a man." About one particularly pervasive ghost there was much affirmation and denial, but as one man said to me: "If a person goes about a great deal and does not see it, he denies that it has come. For instance, I denied because I had not seen it. This is the custom of this land—who has not seen it denies, but the people who have seen it say so."

So, denial of any specific appearance is regarded as reasonable; it is the obvious reaction of people who have not seen the apparition in question; it is denial not about *ghosts in general* but about *particular* cases.

The question of identification is interesting. How is it that it is known that the apparition is indeed that of the dead person? There are various signs for this. Usually

[1] The curious odor, the stink, which the soul of the newly buried bears with him is termed *namuelo*. This is not to be confused with the ordinary physical products of decomposition. It is the soul that smells because of the recent death of its body. It is the taint of mortality from which it is later cleansed. "An ancient spirit when we look at it we are not certain whose it might be, but a new spirit, from a death of recent days, when we look at it we know at once because it has died that day and still has its stench."

someone who has seen it will describe it in reference to the clothing and ornaments with which the body is known to have been buried (sometimes a person who has been abroad at the time of the funeral will, on his return, see the apparition, which he cannot identify, and describes it in such terms as the relatives immediately recognize).

But granted that the Tikopia believe what they think they see, let us look at the social correlates for the experiences described.

The first concerns the attitude of the survivors to the death of a member of their group. There is first the direct emotional interest of members of the family in someone whom they have lost. In this respect the Tikopia practice concretely the more abstract formulation of Gustav Fechner, restated by A. E. Crawley—that when they think of a person who is dead, his image is not a mere inward semblance; it is the very self of the dead consciously coming into the personality of the living.[2]

But the manifestation of the dead may not be a simple response to yearning for a loved one. It may involve resentment at the rejection by a loved one who has gone away in death. This is the theme which is borne out by Tikopia linguistic expressions at death, accusing the dead person of having abandoned the living. But this in itself is not a simple reaction. It may embody elements of horror, of neglect, and even of the waste of a life carefully nurtured by members of the deceased's family. Aspects of all of this emerge in the reaction of people to an encounter with a ghost. Sometimes they run away, sometimes they curse, sometimes they object to the ghost's meddling, sometimes they accuse him of selfishness. The seeing of a ghost can be both the cause and the product of emotional disturbance.

But this emotional disturbance is not simply an individual matter; it is dependent upon the position of the person in his family and kinship circle. As Morris Opler has shown for the Apache, and Clyde Kluckhohn for the Navaho, ghosts may be understood as projections of the largely incon-

---

[2] On Life after Death, from the German of Gustav Theodor Fechner, by Dr. Hugo Wernekke, 1937 ed. (Chicago and London; 1914), pp. 102, 103; A. E. Crawley: The Idea of the Soul (1909), p. 212.

sequential hate and distrust that the living have felt toward dead members of the intimate family circle.[3]

But these explanations alone may not be adequate. In Tikopia the appearance of ghosts is in part an indication of structural strains in the society. Pagan ghosts seen by pagans indicate a temporary breakdown of the system of care for the soul. Pagan ghosts seen by Christians represent an index of the inadequacy of pagan eschatology to secure the peace of the soul. Christian ghosts seen by pagans indicate the results of abandonment of the traditional faith for a new one. Christian ghosts seen by Christians indicate the incompatibility between the two faiths and an uncertainty as yet unresolved as regards their absolute correctness.

This is, of course, an oversimplification for any single case. But the interest caused by the stories of ghosts seen in Tikopia was not merely due to bits of exciting gossip, or to the personal interest of those who encountered them and of members of the ghost's family. It also had an undertone of challenge and demonstration linked with the antagonism between the rival faiths. By contrast with this was the view of both Christians and pagans about the fate of the souls of chiefs. It was agreed by everyone with whom I spoke that the souls of chiefs did not walk; they went through the traditional procedure straight to their ultimate spirit home.[4] This unity of the Tikopia about the fate of the souls of chiefs, Christian or pagan, is in line with the full political and social support which they give at the present time to their chiefs, irrespective of religious affiliation. Chiefs, no matter what be their faith, have a religious status and a value as social symbols sufficient to

---

[3] C. K. M. Kluckhohn: "Conceptions of Faith among the South Western Indians," *Divinity School Bulletin* (Harvard University; 1948), pp. 5–19.

[4] They might later decide to roam about. In a seance purporting to be with the spirit of my old friend Pae Sao, he told me how he and the late Ariki Taumako died on the same day and how after the rites had been performed over them for five days their souls went together to their mothers' guardian spirits. Then the Ariki Taumako said to Pae Sao: "Let's go shooting about the skies," so they went rushing about the heavens. Then Pae Sao divided his principal home of Rangitorioro to give a dwelling to the Ariki Taumako, while the latter gave Pae Sao a dwelling in his home of Ngarumea.

ensure their proper treatment. They are not as ordinary men; they do not return to walk as ordinary ghosts. In Tikopia, conversion to Christianity means change of belief in the fate of the soul from a complex eschatology of status to a simple eschatology of nonstatus—but a special allowance is made for chiefs. This re-emphasizes that in such a system statements about the fate of the soul are in many respects symbolic affirmations of moral judgment about the social order and the position of persons in that order.

I have not tried here to present a general theory of primitive eschatology. But I hope to have shown by analysis of the material from one primitive society the possibility of certain social correlates.

My argument may be summarized as follows. The framework of ideas about the fate of the soul is in many respects a framework of ideas about the state of society. But this need not be completely so (e.g., even for an isolated primitive society, and still more when that society is affected by a religious ideology of an external, more sophisticated group, an egalitarian principle is apt to come into play as an offset against the traditional differentiated status structure). Again, in many primitive societies the eschatological beliefs appear to be variable, differing views being put forward by different people. This variation may be simple vagueness, an outcome of lack of interest. But the offering of alternatives is socially valuable, or at least socially significant. It may be associated with social position, and be a structural variation. A strongly marked ancestor cult of lineage type may offer one correlate. Or it may have specific moral associations. However, in such a variant eschatological system, difference of the fate of the soul on a theory of a moral retribution is secondary; destination of the soul in terms of social-group home is primary. To operate both together fully would lead to inconsistency if there is only a unitary soul concept. (The Chinese, for example, keep their clan and lineage interests, and also maintain their moral emphasis on the fate of the soul by operating spirit homes in terms of ancestral temples and spirit kingdoms—but with a multiple soul concept.)

With change in the major religious system comes also an eschatological change, a simplification of the spirit-home alignment, and the introduction of a specific moral criterion as a basis for differentiation.

But lack of a specific moral criterion in many primitive eschatological systems does not mean lack of all general moral interest. Statements about the fate of the soul are not simple projections of human personality into the future. They do not arise from a simple longing for immortality or even continuity. They are also expressions of contemporary human problems. They give views on what is thought to be right or wrong about the state of things and on the behavior of people and groups. They are judgments on social action of a more diffuse kind than the specific theory of individual moral retribution. They give opportunity for manipulation of affairs and for the expression of social linkage and cleavage. Their metaphysical implications offer a field for some of the most refined, wide-sweeping, and noble speculations about the destiny of man and the bases for his right conduct. But eschatology is also an instrument in human organization.

To conclude in the words of Dewick, and in the spirit of Frazer, in primitive eschatology ". . . simple ideas akin to those of primitive man probably underlie much of our own more developed language. . . . There appears to have been no break in the continuity of thought, and the great problems of life have remained the same." [5]

*   *   *

EDITOR'S NOTE: This Frazer Lecture, delivered in Cambridge on March 7, 1955, by Raymond Firth, F.B.A., Professor of Anthropology in the University of London, was published in 1955 by the Syndics of the Cambridge University Press, and printed at the University Press, Cambridge (Brooke Crutchley, University Printer). A modified presentation of this theme was also given as a public lecture in the Department of Anthropology, University of Chicago, in May 1955.

[5] E. C. Dewick, op. cit., p. 10.

THE
NEW WORLD

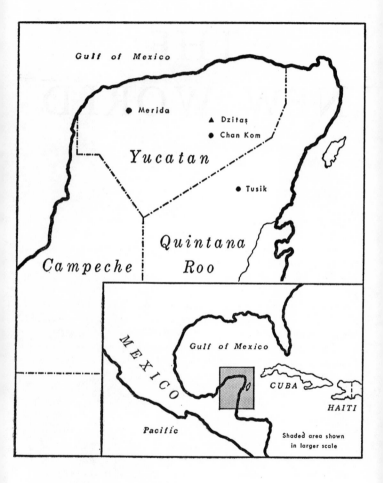

MEXICO AND THE CARIBBEAN showing the
approximate locations of the societies described by
Robert Redfield and Alfred Métraux in the following pages.

Robert Redfield

THE SON of a Chicago attorney, Robert Redfield (1897–1958) received a J.D. from the Law School of the University of Chicago in 1921, and practiced law before turning to anthropology as a career. This early training accounts, in part, for the close attention to the relationships between concepts and facts, and the elegant reasoning that characterized his work. He was not, however, a polemicist. In his Gottesman Lectures at Uppsala University, published in 1955 as *The Little Community*, Redfield examined the array of "viewpoints" contemporary anthropologists use to describe and compare whole communities. Many anthropologists would have made this an occasion for advocating a particular methodology and for disparaging others, but Redfield was a pluralist, and wrote in his conclusion: ". . . understanding is increased and the needs of mankind are met by any and all honest descriptions, responsible to the facts and intellectually defensible."

Redfield's first field research was in 1926–7 in the village of Tepoztlán, near Mexico City. In 1930 he became a Research Associate of the Carnegie Institution of Washington and began a series of investigations in Yucatan and Guatemala. The most ambitious volume that resulted from those studies was *The Folk Culture of Yucatan*, from which a selection appears in the following pages. The volume was, and remains, unusual among anthropological works because in it Redfield used a theory of ideal types of folk and urban societies to compare different communities. He was not so much interested in the particular cultural traits of these communities as in the ways similar elements of culture acquired different meanings as they entered into different social contexts.

In recognition of his distinguished contributions to anthropology, Robert Redfield received the Viking Fund Medal in 1954 and the Huxley Memorial Medal in 1955. Between 1934 and 1946 he was the Dean of the Division of Social Sciences at the University of Chicago, and in 1953 he was appointed Robert Maynard Hutchins Distinguished Service Professor at the same university. Gracefully written as well as closely reasoned, Redfield's books have greatly influenced the course of anthropological thought. His later works include: *A Village That Chose Progress* (1950); *The Primitive World and Its Transformations* (1953); *The Little Community* (1955); and *Peasant Society and Culture* (1956).

❦ ❦ 8 ❦ ❦

A Selection from

The Folk Culture

*of Yucatan**

by

ROBERT REDFIELD

Yucatan, considered as one moves from Merida south-eastward into the forest hinterland, presents a sort of social gradient in which the Spanish, modern, and urban gives way to the Maya, archaic, and primitive. This volume results from a study of four communities chosen to represent points, not too unevenly distributed, along this gradient. These four are: Merida, the only large city; Dzitas, a town situated on the railroad; Chan Kom, a peasant village; and Tusik, a tribal village of semi-independent Maya in Quintana Roo.

Dzitas, Chan Kom, and Tusik are in that order increasingly distant from Merida, where social change, for Yucatan, originates and from which social and political influence emanates. Merida is the hub of the railways, the terminus of all modern lines of communication; Dzitas is located at a junction on one of the radial rail lines; Chan Kom is connected with other communities only by paths through the bush, but its people not infrequently visit the towns; the Quintana Roo villages lie in deep forest, cut off from northwest Yucatan by a wide uninhabited zone. Merida publishes the newspapers of Yucatan and reads most of them; Dzitas receives about one copy for every hundred inhabitants; Chan Kom occasionally sees a single copy of a newspaper which only two or three in the village can read; no one in Tusik ever reads a newspaper. The people of Merida are well aware of their leadership and look down on rustics outside the capital; the more educated people of Dzitas seek consciously to be like the city dwellers and are much like them; the people of Chan Kom, understanding far less of the ways of the city and town, strive nevertheless to take over the techniques and practical advantages of the town; the Quintana Roo Indians are suspicious of outside influence and seek to maintain their independence and to be allowed to follow their old ways. The people of Merida exhibit a wide range of education, class, and some variety of ethnic origin; Dzitas includes city-trained people of largely Spanish culture as well as Indians from villages in the bush; the people of Chan Kom are all of Maya Indian race and are derived from similar villages, but recent differences in education and in response to influences from the towns have brought about notable differences among the natives; while Tusik, left alone for many generations, exhibits in its population the highest degree of uniformity.

¶ SPANISH AND INDIAN: THE TWO HERITAGES

I

The people of Yucatan, even including those of Merida, carry on many ways of life that are derived from native Maya tradition. The Indian far outnumbered the Spaniard; also, he was the established occupant with a manner of livelihood adjusted to the habitat. Therefore, many of his ancient ways have persisted into modern times. On the other hand, the Spaniard was the conqueror; some of his tools and customs announced their own advantages, and many of his ways, especially those of religion, he imposed upon the Indians by force and persuasion. Therefore, even the Quintana Roo Indians carry on a mode of life that is in great part Spanish in origin.

One would expect to find the Maya tradition strongest in Tusik and weakest in Merida, to find the situation reversed with respect to the relative importance of the European heritage, and to find Dzitas and Chan Kom occupying intermediate positions in these regards. These expectations are in general met by the facts. But there are important qualifications.

The comparison may begin with a consideration of the distribution of elements traceable to the native Indian tradition. As Tusik is compared with Chan Kom in this regard, one encounters many aboriginal elements which are present in Quantana Roo but absent in Chan Kom. Many of these (marked with an asterisk in the following list) are remembered to have existed in the customs of the Chan Kom people a generation or two ago. The tribal organization, with its patrilineal "companies," its dual government of priest and chief, and its architectural expression in temple, community house, and five company houses, must be in some important degree a heritage from pre-Columbian times, however much its character has changed in response to later events. In kinship terminology, while Chan Kom keeps only the three brother-sister terms and a tendency to classificatory use of certain of these, Tusik not only extends the classificatory use of these, but uses the same term for mother and mother's sister and the same term for a woman's child and her sister's child, and employs reciprocal terms for uncle-aunt and niece-nephew relationships. In Tusik the boy earns his bride by living with her parents and working for them;* some degree of brother-sister avoidance is practiced; the sacred images are housed not in the dwelling but in separate shrines;* the dead are not buried in cemeteries but in the village itself; earrings are worn as symbols of authority; the intercardinal directions are recognized in the four crosses guarding the public buildings at X-Cacal, and when food is carried in a procession at ceremonies and offered, it is first deposited at each of these intercardinal points; cotton is still raised and spun;* copal is burned;* a special vessel, equipped with arched branches, is used for certain ritual food;* articles of personal use are buried with the dead. It is possible that the custom of selecting the godparents before the child is born,* practiced at Tusik but no longer generally at Chan Kom, may go back to some Indian custom of selecting sponsors.

The largest group of clearly native elements is provided by the body of beliefs and practices attending the deities of the rain, cornfield, bush, and village. While a few of the elements that have been noted are apparently Christian (communion with a special liquor in a chalice marked with a cross; the use of candles and the cross; the names of God, the Virgin, and certain saints; perhaps table altars and kneeling), nevertheless so much of this complex corresponds with what is known from other Indian groups, and is so opposed to the spirit and practices of Christianity, that the complex can as a whole and in much detail be recognized as pagan and Maya in origin. Taken as a whole, the complex is strongly present in both Chan Kom and Tusik. Both have an important communal rain ceremony (*cha-chaac* in Chan Kom, *okot-batam* in Tusik); both have an individual first-fruit ceremony (*primicia* or *holche*), a periodic individual ceremony to assure the agriculturalist good crops (*u-hanli-col*), and minor ceremonies at planting and burning. Chan Kom has a special ceremony (*x-thup-nal*) for quick-maturing maize which is not present in Tusik; on the other hand, in Tusik there is a special annual ceremony (*tupkak*) which is lacking in Chan Kom. There is some reason for saying that the pagan agricultural ceremonies are more strongly present in Tusik than in Chan Kom: in Tusik both the communal rain ceremony and the individual *u-hanli-col* are performed annually, whereas in Chan Kom they are performed more rarely as conscience or fear dictates.

The core of ideas and practices represented in the agricultural ceremonies is the same in Tusik and in Chan Kom. It includes the following elements: spiritual beings associated with the rain, the cornfield, the bush, and the cenotes, and protectors of these, occasionally seen in the form of old men; the notion that these beings are hierarchically organized; rain deities (that ride on horseback) pouring rain from an inexhaustible calabash; the notion of waters that meet under the earth; a quadrilaterally conceived cosmos with deities, associated with colors, at the four corners, and therefore protecting crosses at the four corners of the village; the east as the direction from where the deities arise; ceremonies involving invocation of the deities, preparation and dedication of special breads of maize and squash seeds cooked in an earth oven, of broth of fowl, and of special sacred liquor; use of oriented altars for these offerings; use of certain ritual plants; corn meal prepared without lime (*zaca*) as a ritual offering; invocatory and dedicatory prayers; purification of domestic fowl before offering; divination by looking into a crystal; supernatural protectors of the deer (*zip*). The expected conservatism of Quintana Roo, as compared with Chan Kom, is in fact represented by certain Maya elements present there but absent in Chan Kom: the dance with a gourd rattle, around a table at the annual fiesta of X-Cacal; the occasional lustrative retreat (*loh*) of the shaman priest; performance of a ritual symbolic of fructification by a coati-impersonator perched in a ceiba tree; the ceremonial kindling of new fire with a fire drill.

On the other hand, the ceremonies and beliefs at Chan Kom include many pagan elements which those of Tusik and X-Cacal lack, and in these respects the expected intermediate position of Chan Kom with respect to indigenous features is not realized. The entire group of ceremonies attendant upon the bees and the beehives is lacking at Tusik. So also are the exorcistic and curative ceremonies known as *kex* and *santiguar* (although these ceremonies are known in certain other villages of Quintana Roo). The agricultural rituals lack the following elements, assuredly pagan, which those of Chan Kom possess: the impersonation of lightning or rain gods and of animals associated with the rain; the bringing of "virgin water" for use in the ceremony; the construction of a roadside earth oven for cooking the first ripe new ears; the use of bark beer (*balche*) and the sacrifice of fowl by pouring *balche* down their throats; the naming of four men (who are called by the name of the rain gods) to hold a fowl as it is sacrificed; the special ceremony for early ripening maize; and probably ceremonial continence. The practices at Chan Kom, as they were carried on during the years of the investigation, provide as much material for a reconstruction of the aboriginal village ceremonies of the field and the hives as do those of Tusik and X-Cacal.

Why should so many elements of indigenous religious

practice be present in the progressive village of Chan Kom and yet be absent in conservative Tusik and X-Cacal? The principal answer lies in the fact that these ceremonies depend upon the particular shaman priest who is available to carry them on. If there is no *h-men* to use them, they are lost. These elements are not "present in Chan Kom" so much as they are present in the *h-mens* who are used by the Chan Kom people. The knowledge possessed by any two *h-mens* is likely to differ considerably. A *h-men* does not teach his special knowledge to everyone, but to a disciple only. The Tusik people lack the elements enumerated because the Tusik *h-mens* do not know them. The people of the Chan Kom area feel free to call in renowned *h-mens* from distant villages to function in the local ceremonies. The very isolation and self-sufficiency of the X-Cacal subtribe tends to simplify the pagan rituals through obsolescence. There are only two *h-mens* in the entire subtribe. Warfare and the serious smallpox epidemic of 1915 may have removed *h-mens* and interrupted the ceremonial tradition. A third reason for the absence of many elements in the pagan rituals of the X-Cacal group may exist in the great importance attained by the Nohoch Tata. The *h-men* actually has a more subordinate role in Quintana Roo than in villages of the Chan Kom area. The two X-Cacal *h-mens* would be mere apprentices in Chan Kom. This in turn is an aspect of the fact, to be emphasized at the close of this chapter, that Catholic and pagan elements are more closely united in the peripheral communities.

At any rate, it is the details of ceremonial practice that are lacking in Tusik, not the spirit which lies behind them. Each beekeeper makes an offering at the opening of the beehives; if the *h-men* knew the full rituals, they would no doubt be performed. Divination with maize grains is not practiced at Tusik, but the *h-men* has some knowledge of the technique. When the Tusik *h-men* found out that Villa knew the *kex* and *santiguar* rituals (as he had learned them at Chan Kom), he arranged to have Villa instruct him in the manner in which these are conducted, so that his repertory might be enlarged.

It is difficult to carry the comparison with reference to the presence of indigenous elements into the materials from Dzitas, because in that town there is such a range of interest and practice. Among the least sophisticated *mestizo milperos*, especially those who have moved into Dzitas from hacienda settlements, there is no doubt present much of what is characteristic of Chan Kom, at least in knowledge and memory. In the field investigations no search was made for such extremely marginal individuals, but instead materials were collected solely from people born in Dzitas, with attention to the range of conservatism or progressiveness among these native townsmen. These materials indicate a great diminution of the indigenous elements of custom and belief and a great reduction of their importance, as compared with Tusik and Chan Kom. The relation of this dwindling of the pagan beliefs and practices to the secularization of life in the town will be dealt with in a later chapter. Here it may be said briefly that the communal rain ceremony in Dzitas becomes an occasional ritual performed for a group of *milperos* by an imported shaman priest rather than by the *milperos*; most of the special individual rituals disappear; bee ceremonies are entirely unknown; the pagan deities are confused with one another and treated with skepticism; the ideas as to the protectors of the deer and of the cattle are gone; the exorcistic ceremonies are still practiced but more rarely; and the system of cosmological and religious ideas which support and invest the pagan rituals practically disappears. And in Merida, as is more fully discussed in Chapter ix, only a very few of the semirural inhabitants on the edges of the city ever have occasion to be concerned with the pagan ceremonies; the pagan deities and rituals are vaguely known and are associated with a rustic life which the city man looks down upon as inferior to his own.

II

Attention may now turn to the distribution of elements of European origin in the four communities. It has already been indicated that the Spanish conquest spread many tools and customs over the entire peninsula. A few, which must have been introduced in the first years by the Spaniards, have not yet become a part of life in the outer periphery. Thus, the custom of riddling (in the Maya language) is known in Chan Kom (and, of course, in

Dzitas and in Merida). But no riddles were collected in Tusik. Rabbit stories, and other folktales of Spanish type, flourish in Dzitas, are more moderately represented in Chan Kom, and form only a trifling part of the folklore collected in Tusik. The first Spanish missionaries required the Indians to bury their dead in walled cemeteries; today this is the general practice, except in Quintana Roo, where the dead are buried in the villages among the houses. The system of divining the weather for the year by observing the weather prevailing during January is probably European in origin. It is used in Dzitas and Chan Kom but plays no role in Tusik. The distribution of such elements of culture as these represents the converse of that which on the whole characterizes elements of Indian origin. Similarly, many elements of recent invention or development fall off as one goes from Merida out to the periphery, as one would expect. Dzitas is familiar with baseball and moving pictures; Chan Kom with the former but not the latter; Tusik has no familiarity with either. Examples of this obvious situation could be multiplied.

What does strike the attention, as one compares the customs of the four communities with reference to the relative importance in each of elements of European origin, is the presence in Quintana Roo of so many features of Catholic ritual which are absent from the popular customs of the other three communities. The comparison here is with reference to the popular beliefs and practices only. It is, of course, true that in the city, and to a less degree in the town, there are educated, orthodox Roman Catholics, who are directly responsive to the teachings of the Church as expressed by the priest and in written works. Such persons are excluded from this comparison. With the decline of the influence of the Church in recent years, and with the restrictions laid upon her activities by government, the number of these, even among the urban sophisticates, has been much reduced. At any rate, the point to be made here is that it is in the peripheral communities, to some degree in Chan Kom, and to a much greater degree in Tusik, that elements of Catholic ritual are incorporated into the popular practices, so as to characterize the conventional behavior of everyone, or nearly everyone, in the community. The contribution of Catholicism to popular religious practice, as it appears today, is greatest, not least, in Tusik.

The natives of the Quintana Roo villages, and they alone of the four communities studied, observe daily recitation of Catholic prayers. Only there is it required that every adult be able to recite six certain prayers constituting "the doctrine." Independent of control by the Church, these natives celebrate masses on festal occasions, recognizing a distinction between high and low Mass and making appropriate changes for each. Special communion bread is used, and also a communion liquor (of honey and water); and Spanish names used for these in Roman churches ("oxdias" = hostia; caliz) are applied to them. These people recognize not only the more frequently observed days of the Church calendar but also less important saints' days—St. Mark, St. Bernard, St. John the Baptist—which, on the whole, pass unregarded by popular custom in the other communities. They preserve, furthermore, an observation of Lent and Holy Week in accordance with the uses of the Church which cannot be matched in Chan Kom or Dzitas. These observances include Palm Sunday, Ash Wednesday, abstinence on the last days of Holy Week, especially Good Friday, and the kindling of new fire on Saturday of Glory. Only in this community is the ritual distinction between white and black candles fully recognized in practice. Only here is it customary, at certain festivals, to perform a devotionary act by approaching the shrine on one's knees.

The tenor of this comparison—that elements of Catholic ritual are best represented on the periphery—is supported by a consideration of the situation in Chan Kom. As compared with Tusik, Chan Kom carries on much less Catholic ritual. The elements mentioned in the preceding paragraph are absent in Chan Kom or very weakly represented. Yet, as compared with Dzitas, there is more of Catholic practice that has been incorporated into popular custom and is still maintained there: the professional male chanters with their knowledge of Catholic prayers, the frequent recitation of rosaries, and the ringing of the Angelus.

The conclusion is that Quintana Roo villages are not only the most pagan, with respect to their religious practices, but are also the most Catholic. It seems plain that this situation results in large part from the retention on the periphery of elements received by instruction from priests of the Church—elements which have been lost in the other communities. Older people in Chan Kom remember the observance there in former days of Catholic practice now obsolete, and similar memories exist in Dzitas. The isolation of Quintana Roo has favored the retention of sixteenth- and seventeenth-century modes of life, including both elements which the missionaries taught the natives and those elements of indigenous practice which the missionaries were unable to destroy or which they did not know existed. While modern influences have reduced the hold of religion and the authority of the Church in city and town, these influences have failed to penetrate the extreme hinterland. Out in Quintana Roo the sacred images are paraded in processions through the streets; the Mexican law prohibiting such processions does not reach that far, any more than do skepticism and disbelief.

It may be repeated that the comparison here is with reference to popular custom. The orthodox practices of the Church described for Quintana Roo are, of course, also to be found in town and city when the priest is present and his immediate influence is felt. But in Quintana Roo there has been no direct contact with the Church for at least three generations. Yet it turns out that Catholic practices are more fully and popularly represented there than they are in Dzitas, where the priest comes several times a year, or in Chan Kom, where many of the older people have attended Mass celebrated by an ordained priest. It is only out among the primitive pagans of the hinterland that Catholicism has been thoroughly naturalized. There the practices belong to all the people—all know the principal prayers, all participate in the rituals, all in turn prepare the sacred breads, and all together consume them. Only in Quintana Roo has the liturgy of the Church been taken over completely by popular administration, so that masses and marriages are celebrated by a native functionary unconsecrated by the Church. The leader in these rituals and teacher of moral doctrine is a native. The Nohoch Tata, at once priest and pope, local leader and supreme authority, grew up among and out of the people themselves, is one of them, and is maintained by them in his holiness and prestige. He had his esoteric knowledge from his father and his grandfather. He is no member of the Roman hierarchy. Quintana Roo Catholicism is independent of the Church of Rome, as the entire little local society is (largely) independent of the great society outside.

It is the "naturalization" of Catholic practice out in the periphery that is to be emphasized, rather than the mere presence there of recognizably Christian ritual forms. Elements of European origin do not merely exist or persist out there; they invest the whole body of popular custom and belief so that each part is consistent with other parts and with the whole. The whole is made up of aboriginal elements, of elements taught by the Spanish priests, and of elements of popular secular Spanish lore. What impresses the investigator of the parts played by the two heritages in Yucatecan custom and belief is that the interweaving of Spanish and Indian threads to form a single web is most complete in the isolated peripheral communities. Catholic ritual elements are present in greatest number in Quintana Roo, but these elements are also most altered there from what must have been their original natures, and the alterations have been such as to present the investigator with a single system of conceptions and practices. If an investigator with no knowledge of either Indian or European Catholic customs were to be confronted with the religious ritual of the Quintana Roo villages, it is doubtful if it would occur to him that this ritual had been derived from two very different heritages. If the investigator should begin his investigations with the situation in Chan Kom, or with Dzitas, the idea would be more readily suggested to him.

The extent and character of the alterations which Catholic elements have undergone in Quintana Roo can be appreciated from a study of the materials as they have been presented by Villa. An illustration is provided by the practices and beliefs attending Holy Week in Tusik and X-Cacal. The Mass held on Palm Sunday is called "perfect offering" (*matan dzoc*). The Nohoch Tata blesses twelve palm leaves and places them on the altar. On the following day these are distributed to the worshippers, who make small crosses of them and place these over the doorways of their houses to keep out evil. Seven leaves are kept on the altar, to be burned on Ash Wednesday the following year, when crosses with these ashes are marked on the foreheads of the celebrants. No meanings in connection with the Christian epic attach to these acts. For the native the significance of the ritual lies in the opportunity to be purified through application of the ashes. On Holy Thursday the inner altar of the church at X-Cacal is covered with a leafy curtain made of the boughs of certain trees. This is called "shade" (*booy*); it represents the woods that covered the Teacher (Most Holy Lord; *Cichcelem Yum*) when he sought shelter during his pursuit and persecution by the Jews. Prayers are recited in the morning, and again at noon, the hour when the *Cichcelem Yum* was struck in the side by a sword, during the time he was on the cross, and at the moment when he died. At this time seven dishes of corn meal, made without lime (*zaca*), are placed on the altar in commemoration of the *zaca* given the *Cichcelem Yum* by a generous *milpero* who stopped his maize planting to help the fleeing Lord. A story is told of the punishments experienced by the first two *milperos* who ungenerously refused the Lord their aid. In the evening boiled beans and tortillas are offered and eaten. On Holy Friday (when other prayers are said) the women take off their earrings and gold chains lest the jingling of their jewels should identify them with the metal-loving Jews, enemies of God. On Saturday a ceremony called "Virgin Fire" is held: new fire is kindled with a fire drill by men who are supposed to have a special power or "fluid." All domestic fires are first extinguished; and after the new fire has been lit, each householder strives to keep his fire until the next year. The fire is made in commemoration of the ascent of the *Cichcelem Yum* to Glory, when, after dying on Thursday, he was born again on Saturday, at which time the Jews were condemned to live forever underground in Hell. The road to Glory was long and the way was cold, and the Lord stopped from time to time to light a fire with a fire drill to warm himself; therefore, the new fire is made each year on Holy Saturday in commemoration of these events.

The modification of Christian teaching in the course of

the centuries is apparent here, as is the contribution made to this body of ritual and belief from native sources and probably from Spanish folklore. What is more to be emphasized, as the situation in Quintana Roo is compared with that in Chan Kom or in Dzitas, is that ritual and belief are present, are deeply established in popular custom, and are so related to each other that the ritual expresses the belief and the belief is made manifest in the ritual. In Chan Kom Holy Week rituals are not performed. In Dzitas popular custom recognizes Holy Week much more simply. If the priest is there to celebrate masses, only part of the people participate, and few understand fully the relation of the Church ritual to the Christian epic. But in X-Cacal everybody takes part in acts which for everybody are expressive of sacred stories about a principal symbol of the moral order. It is not so much that Catholic— or that indigenous—elements are present in the rituals and beliefs in X-Cacal as that elements from all sources have been modified and woven together into a consistent structure of idea and practice. It is the peripheral communities that provide us with interrelated bodies of ritual and belief. This is the fact to be stressed. It may be illustrated equally well from rituals prevailingly European in origin or from those rituals, chiefly pagan, attending the agricultural deities.

It is only in the Quintana Roo villages that the distinction between two cults—one carried on by a Christian priest for the God of Heaven and the other by a shaman priest for the beings of the rain and the cenotes—almost disappears. But there it does almost disappear. In Merida the pagan cult is something very distinct from the rituals of the Church with their popular concomitants. The latter alone is found in the city; the cult carried on by the *h-men* is known about, but it is something uncanny, a little diabolic, carried on somewhere outside of the city on the cornfields of the ignorant and countrified. In Dzitas the pagan rituals are carried on with the participation of members of the community. The same man who takes part in the festival of the patron saint, and whose wife marches in the processions of the religious sisterhoods to escort the candles to be burned before the saint, may also go, upon occasion, out to the fields to kneel beside the *h-men* and eat the sacred maize bread of the *chaacs* and *balamob*. But the *h-men* is not a townsman, and the cult he maintains is not a part of the public life of the town. It is seclusive and surreptitious, while the cult of the saints is open and official. In the worship of the individual agriculturalists the two bodies of thought meet: he kneels and offers his prayers and his *zaca* to the Lord God and to the *yuntzilob*, the protectors of the fields and the woods. But the cults, as cults, in Dzitas do not confront each other and are never publicly joined.

In Chan Kom, however, the two cults are equally part of public worship. They are complementary ways of dealing with the supernatural. They are separate aspects of what the native feels to be a single body of pietistic practices. No priest of the Church reaches Chan Kom; the prayers of the Church are recited by native chanters. The chanter and the *h-men* are equally respected; each participates in the rituals led by the other; and the same congregation follows each. Each cult is as respectable and as powerful as the other. But they are separate cults. The chanter (*maestro cantor*) has his repertory of prayers, all derived from Catholic liturgy. In reciting these prayers, he may use a rosary. He performs his rites indoors, either in a private house or in the church. Women take the lead in preparing the altar. *Atole* is the suitable food to place on the altar, and the appropriate flowers are *Plumeria* and *Caesalpinia*. The prayers of the *h-men*, on the other hand, are in Maya and, although they include mention of saints, are addressed to the pagan deities. His rites are performed out of doors and certainly never in the church. No image of a saint is present (although a cross is always used). Men prepare the offerings and the altars (except as women assist by cooking food in the houses to be carried to the field), and the offerings are different: *zaca*, breads of maize and squash seeds, bark beer, sacrificed fowl. A different group of plants is used to adorn the altar. An emergency may occasion the celebration of a ceremony, first from the one cult and then from the other. The same people participate in both, but there is no doubt when the chanter is through and the *h-men*, at a different place, takes over.

In Quintana Roo the two bodies of ritual are so intimately associated that it is almost true that a single cult results. At several points the two cults co-operate in what is felt by the natives to be a single ceremony, and there are occasions upon which the *h-men* and the chanter (or the Nohoch Tata) perform simultaneously, at the same place, as coleaders of the same congregation. The annual ceremony held to assure the coming of rain (*okot-batam*) provides such a situation. In X-Cacal the ceremony called "*oxdias*" corresponds with the *novena* of Chan Kom and, like it, involves the recitation of Catholic prayers, led by a chanter, with laymen participating, and concludes with the distribution of special foods that have first been placed on the altar of a *santo*. In Chan Kom nine (or fewer) such evenings of prayer may be held, before the patron saint, to ask for rain. As such they are independent of the pagan rain ceremony (*cha-chaac*). But in X-Cacal and in Tusik the corresponding *okot-batam* is characteristically held as the ultimate night of a series of seven prayers of which the first six are *oxdias* and the seventh is the *okot-batam*. The entire series is felt to be one whole. On the last day the *h-men* sets up the altar to the pagan deities inside the church itself. Entirely contrary to the practice in Chan Kom and in Dzitas, this is the usual practice in Quintana Roo. Meanwhile, the Nohoch Tata (in X-Cacal) or the civil leader ("Corporal"—as representative of the Nohoch Tata—in Tusik) attends to the altar at the back of the church on which the *santo* (a wooden cross) is kept. The breads of maize and squash seeds are made in an earth oven, not outside the village, but within it, near the church. When they have been cooked, some are placed on the altar made by the *h-men*, and some—again contrary to practice in Chan Kom—are placed on the altar of the *santo*. A ritual drink, a mixture of honey and water, substituting for the older bark beer, is sometimes offered to the pagan deities and is sometimes placed on the Christian altar. Women are admitted to the church and kneel on one side, while the men kneel on the other. Then two sets of prayers rise simultaneously: the *h-men*, beside his altar, addresses the pagan deities, while the Nohoch Tata, or the civil leader, kneeling beside the other altar at the back of the church, recites Catholic prayers. At their conclusion, both religious leaders participate in the distribution of food and drink; the *h-men* passes out the holy sweetened water (*caliz*), while the other leader distributes the concentrated breads (*oxdias*). The worshippers attend a single ceremony with dual leadership.

¶ THE DECLINE OF THE GODS

I

The decline and disappearance of the pagan gods and ceremonies as one goes from Tusik to Merida may be regarded most obviously as the supplanting of indigenous culture by European, but it may also be recognized as an aspect of the relatively more secular character of life in the town and city. In the villages the gods of the forest, the cornfields, and the hives are close at hand, plainly defined and distinguished, and are worshipped in fixed ritual. The *chaacs* are closely identified with the rain; when the rain clouds gather, the native may announce that "the *chaacs* are riding the sky." The *balams* that guard the *milpa* and the village are heard in the whistlings and rustlings of the forest by night. The *kuilob-kaaxob* (spirits of the wood) are probably more vaguely conceived than are the other two principal classes of deities associated with aspects of nature; but any mature native will distinguish them from the other *yuntzilob*, and at the time of felling the trees for new *milpa* it is these beings that receive propitiation. The cosmogonic notions sketched in the fifth chapter provide for the native of the village a sort of topography of the unseen world. The unseen side of nature, the "beings of wind" that are felt in animals and trees and in the godlike spirit copies of the animals they protect —deer and cattle, peccary and turkey—are frequently recognized and are always to be treated with circumspection. The Yucatecan Maya does not have an intensely religious personal life; he does not have characteristically mystical, let alone ecstatic, experiences. Yet his life is religious in the sense that there are unseen beings close about him to whom he must constantly appeal. He may sometimes circumvent them by the use of "secrets," those magical charms which gain man's end directly without mediation of supernatural wills. But he is frequently in awe of these beings, and their propitiation, while it is in large part prudence, is in a large degree piety. In the villages one would not scoff; uncertain and uncanny results, it is felt, would follow.

In Dzitas those who scoff are not lacking. The differences in beliefs as to the pagan gods are wide. Some hold the *chaacs* to be the powerful rain gods recognized in the villages. Others are skeptical, saying that "other people say" that they are gods of the rain but that they must be, like all things, "of *Dios*." Others are disbelievers. "Of course, it is only the wind. It is the wind that brings the rain; it whirls the water up from the sea and rushes it across the sky and pours it on the land. . . . In books it explains that the lightning is electricity." The situation for conflict among these various attitudes is presented in the occasions of agricultural ceremony, when a group of *milperos* cultivating adjacent lands participate, according to the prevailing sentiment, in a joint ceremony. Then various shades of belief are present. "When I go to the *u-hanli-col*, of course, I have to say 'Yes' and 'All right,' and I don't argue with them. Because many of them believe what the *h-men* tells them. They are my friends— I bring the rum and the other things they need. Sometimes they say that the lightning will strike me. But the lightning won't strike until one's hour has arrived." Another man said: "When I am with the others, poor creatures, my mouth is one way and my heart is another. They say the offering is for the *kunku* [great rain god], but they eat it all themselves! It is not true. The *zaztuns* [divining crystals] of the *h-mens* are just bottle tops."

On the whole, the pagan religion has in Dzitas much less influence over the agriculturalist's life. The difference lies partly in the disappearance of conceptions as to the supernatural world and partly in the lessening of the awful or sacred qualities of such beings as are still recognized. This has been briefly stated in Chapter vi. The townsman does not know as much as the villager about the gods of the rain and of the bush, and such beings as he does know about are to him not so tall or so terrible. They become blurred, while they shrink from gods to goblins.

No one in Dzitas among those who discussed the matter with the writer could give the meanings of the figurative expressions used in the prayers of the shaman priest. The "doorway in the clouds" (*holhuntazmuyal*), through which the *chaacs* are supposed to emerge, could not be identified. Few people can identify the four directional rain gods with colors or with the proper directions, although it is generally felt that there are four or five of these gods. Nor can people give the names of the special *chaacs*. The *balams* are confused with the *kuilob-kaaxob*, and the bee-gods and specialized guardians of the cattle and the deer are not recognized at all by these same natives of Dzitas, or they are barely known.

Especially are the *balams*, *chaacs*, and *kuilob-kaaxob* confused with the *alux*. The *alux* (goblin-like little beings) are properly the animated form of the ancient idols and effigies, mischievous little terrestrial creatures rather than gods controlling nature. To the agriculturalists of Dzitas the confusion of the *alux* with the *yuntzilob* is such that it is the former rather than the latter which are foremost in their minds when they feel fearful at night in their *milpas* or when they set out the *calabash* dishes filled with corn meal and water. The materials abundantly support this statement. "The *balams* watch over everybody. The *alux* guard the *milpa*." "The *alux* say, 'If you don't pay me, I don't work.' And that's fair, isn't it?" "The *aluxes* are like little children. They stay in the *milpas* where the bush is high and protect the *milpas* so no one can rob them. That is why, when new ears are ripe, you must perform *loh*" [ceremony of lustration and appeasement]. "We do not make offerings to the *balams*, but to the *alux*." The association of the *yuntzilob* with the evil winds is, in Dzitas, more often than not converted into an association of the *alux* with these winds. "If you pass a place where an *alux* has just been, often the *alux* has left a wind there, and it gets into you, and you suffer an attack. That is why there are *yerbateros* [*h-mens*]; so they may drive out the winds. They do it with their Maya prayers. But we do not know how." From being the dwelling places of the gods, the *milpas* become the lurking places of mischievous fairies.

A corresponding change occurs in Yucatan on the side of ritual. The agricultural ceremonies are performed in Dzitas, but with less fullness, regularity, completeness, and consistency. Only the most conservative put out any

offering at the time of burning the *milpa* or at sowing.
When the ears are ripe, most *milperos* leave first fruits in
the *milpa*, "for the *balam*" or "for the *alux*," but there is
no group ceremony of *pibil-nal* under the leadership of a
h-men. In the villages the *cha-chaac* is a ceremony performed by all the men of the village collectively on occasions of threatening drought. In Dzitas the ceremony is
frequently performed, but by small groups of *milperos*
cultivating certain lands particularly endangered. Some
agriculturalists have never participated in a *cha-chaac*. In
Chan Kom *u-hanli-col* is a ceremony to be regularly performed by each agriculturalist to maintain good relations
with the *yuntzilob*. In Dzitas it tends to be regarded as a
ceremony necessary to certain lands if they are to produce
a good crop.

This is the essential difference in emphasis. In Chan
Kom the agricultural rituals are to a marked extent acts
of piety. In Dzitas they tend to be acts of safeguard. In
Chan Kom and in Tusik the relation of the ceremony is
not only to the land; it is also to the person of the native.
If he is sick, the *milpero* calls the *h-men*, who probably
tells him that his illness comes from his failure to make
the proper rituals to the gods. He must atone for the
wrong he has done by making a more expensive ceremony
to the *yuntzilob*. In Dzitas, on the other hand, the *h-men*
is rarely called in for illness. But if the land does not
yield a good crop, and no simple explanation appears, the
milpero may ask the *h-men* to perform a ceremony, "to
fix up the land," so to speak. "Two years ago Filomeno
Dzul made *u-hanli-col* at his *milpa* at Popola. That was
because his *milpa* was not growing properly, and the animals were eating the corn. . . . You don't have to make
it always, but only on lands that are accustomed to it.
Some are, and there you have to make it or the corn
doesn't grow or is eaten by animals. Especially where
there are *alux* you have to make it." "There is a place
not far from here where there is a stone like a horse.
It is a horse of the *chaac*. The man who had the *milpa*
there one year felled the bush and let the trees fall on it;
then he burned the bush. After that no one was ever able
to get a crop on that land. Now for six or seven years they
have been making *u-hanli-col* on that land, and at last

it is beginning to yield a harvest again." The personal security of the *milpero* is here not involved; there is little thought of danger to his body, let alone his soul.

The *loh* ceremony, which is lustrative of the evil winds rather than a prayer to the *yuntzilob*, is not infrequently performed in Dzitas. A man will have it done as another elsewhere would put fertilizer in his field or would spray a crop with insecticide. It is simply a prudent precaution. The postmaster at Dzitas, a sophisticated *mestizo vecino*, had the ceremony performed in his cattle pen. His uncle, also a *vecino* but himself a simple agriculturalist, urged him to. The postmaster's account of what took place is characteristic of the attitude of the more sophisticated townsman:

> It was very nice. All night long and all day that fellow [the *h-men*] sat at the door of the corral and didn't sleep. He kept praying in Maya. I couldn't understand anything he said. He asked me to answer several times, but I didn't know what to answer. It was all in Maya, but said backward. He didn't put up any table in the corral. He did put a table in the house—I think there were four dishes of *zaca* on it. In the four winds [i.e., corners] of the corral he planted crosses of wood, and he put lime leaves with each. It was just praying and rum. . . . The bad wind gets into the ground and you have to get rid of it.

Thus the contrast between the field rituals of the villages and those of Dzitas is expressed in the contrast suggested by the terms "religion" and "magic." Certainly the performance of the rituals of the *milpa* in the villages has a "magical" component in its motivation to the extent that they are performed as a technique to assure a good crop. On the other hand, much if not all of the moral and religious meaning of the rituals that is present in the villages is lacking in Dzitas. The loss of religion in these rituals is probably due to a number of interacting factors. There can be no doubt that the example of urban non-believers and the effects of education in which natural phenomena are rationally explained play a considerable part. Some of the skeptics in Dzitas offer as disproof of the rain gods rational explanations of astronomical and meteorological phenomena. The prestige of the city man and hence of his ideas favors a growing disbelief. The fact that some neighbors do not perform the ceremonies and yet are successful agriculturalists at least raises questions as to the importance of the ceremonies.

My cousin Fernando has a *milpa*. And he never puts out *zaca*; even at harvest he doesn't. He says it is foolishness. But he doesn't get any harvest. Last year he planted forty *mecates*, and got only ten *cargas*. He doesn't believe in it. But he has been making *milpa* only two years. Goodness knows what will come of it. None of the storekeepers make *milpa* except Bernardo, and he just began. He says he never made *milpa* before, and he is beginning here And his *milpa* burned beautifully this year. It is strange.

The emphasis, it may be noted, is upon efficacy rather than moral or religious virtue. The doubter does not ask: "Is it wrong?" He asks: "Does it work?"

This year my uncle Pepe did not put out *zaca* when he made his *milpa*. He always did before. I don't know why he didn't this year. I did, and my *milpa* burned well. But he didn't, and his burned well too. I guess maybe it isn't necessary to put it out at the burning. But what *is* necessary is to put out *zaca* at the sowing and at the harvest.

It does not appear that the group of Evangelical Protestants constitute an important center of skepticism with regard to the pagan gods and ceremonies. As a whole, the Protestants pay relatively little attention to the *yunt-zilob*, yet many of these men make offerings and some take part in the group ceremonies with other agriculturalists. The evangelical missionaries direct their proselytism against the Catholic faith rather than against paganism.

In looking over the materials from Dzitas, the writer forms the impression that indirect factors are as important as the direct influence and example of nonbelievers in bringing about a decline in the pagan religion. It seems to him that the simplification and obsolescence of the ceremonies is not only a result of the loss of faith but is also a cause of it. People cease to believe partly because they cease to understand and cease to participate in those once dramatic gestures of the group by which the nature of the gods is proclaimed. They do not perform the rituals or do not perform them with such understanding for the principal reason that in Dzitas the shaman priest is not a member of the local community. In such villages as Chan Kom there is likely to be at least one *h-men*, a relative and a close neighbor, who talks in the evenings with his fellows about the *yuntzilob* and about the significance of the ceremonies he performs. When the ceremonies are carried on, a group of men who truly represent the local community take part. They are all agriculturalists and all are equally concerned with matters of the *milpa*. But in Dzitas there is no *h-men*, nor has there been for many years. The *h-men* is a fellow with uncanny powers brought in from a more rustic settlement to do something which ought to be done lest harm come to the harvest. The Dzitas people are unaccustomed to his liturgical language, and few of them understand it. "The *h-men* prays in Maya, but we don't understand it. That's because he talks the true Maya, and the Maya we talk isn't the real Maya." The postmaster, in the instance cited above, felt a little foolish when he could not make the responses the *h-men* required of him as owner of the land being purified. "It was all in Maya, but said backward." Even the cardinal numbers above five, expressed in Maya in the prayers, are not understood by many participants whose usual Maya makes use of Spanish words for these quantities. For certain of the ceremonies that in the villages are performed with the leadership of the *h-men*, as that in which new ears of corn are offered to the *yuntzilob*, the townsman substitutes the mere leaving of new ears in his *milpa*—for whom? The many times repeated invocations of the *h-men* are not there to remind him.

This is also one of the reasons why the *alux* tend to become the principal objects of propitiation. The *yuntzilob* are everywhere—Tusik, Chan Kom, or Dzitas—approached chiefly through the shaman priest. The *h-mens* know the words to use and the acts to perform. But the *alux*, while they are included in a few of the rituals maintained by the *h-men*, are not his specialty. Anyone can hear them, occasionally see them, and often seek to propitiate them. One deals directly with the *alux*. But the tall gods become less accessible when their mediators are not present.

A related circumstance contributing to the weakening of the religious faith in the *yuntzilob* lies in the fact that in the town the ceremonies, if held at all, are less likely to occur at moments of genuine crisis. This needs little explanation in the case of the principal rain ceremony (*cha-chaac*). Every instance of the performance of this ceremony reported in Chan Kom and in Tusik corresponded with the culmination of a season of drought and involved the participation of every man in the village. The sense of common cause among the villagers is, naturally, much more intense in the village than in the larger and more heterogeneous town. In Dzitas the *cha-chaac*, as already stated, is a ceremony brought about by a small group of *milperos*. Many of their neighbors are disinterested or ignorant of what is going on. The ceremony, therefore, is a relatively minor episode in the town, while in Chan Kom and Tusik the entire community—and the women, too, for they are busy preparing part of the offerings—devotes itself simultaneously to the appeal to the pagan gods. A similar observation may be made about the lesser ceremonies which are effected at the instance of a single *milpero*. In Dzitas, where the *h-men* is not ordinarily called in to treat a sickness, the explanation for the sickness in the failure of the patient to perform a ceremony is rarely given; therefore, the lesser ceremonies are not so often made coincident with the anxiety of sickness. In Chan Kom a man performs the ceremony because he is prudently and piously regular or, alternatively, because he believes that his relations with the gods are unsatisfactory, and thus he is experiencing some personal distress. Since in Dzitas the regular offerings are usually without the benefit of the illuminating and explanatory formalisms which relate them to the moral life of the individual, they are less often than in the villages made on occasions of personal emergency. They are acts directed more immediately to the practical end: a successful crop. They tend to become part of the technology—of the nonrational technology—in another word, of the magic, of the agriculturalist. To a less extent do they provide expression for that critical state of mind conducive to prayer. So a man in Dzitas will merely say, for example, that "when you are taking out the honey, it is a dangerous [*delicado*] time when winds might strike you"—without making any ceremony and without very definite conceptions as to deities. Or he will set out the corn gruel at time of planting without prayers, just to be sure that the crop will turn out all right.

When we turn from the villages and the town to Merida, it may almost be said that we leave the pagan gods behind. They are associated in the minds of residents of the capital with the backcountry, the bush, and *milpa* agriculture. Only a few of the semirural inhabitants of the periphery of the city who cultivate maize with some regularity ever have occasion to be actively concerned with pagan ceremonies. A fair number of other persons have seen one or more of these ceremonies on the invitation of friends or relatives who live in the country. But they understand little of what goes on, and they can be characterized better as sight-seers than as participants. The great majority of people know only what they have learned through listening to accounts of rituals to bring rain, of fields delivered to the care of supernatural guardians, and of the ill fortune that befalls those who offend the guardians by attempts at theft.

Among the peripheral Merida agriculturalists one hears reports of many of the ceremonies described for Chan Kom. But it is difficult to get any details or to find out how general the observances are. Such practices are secret. An individual does not confide even to his neighbor, unless he feels certain that the neighbor is friendly and sympathetic, for fear of being ridiculed or denounced before the city authorities. For important ceremonies a *h-men* is brought in from a village. There is, however, in at least one suburb a man who sometimes officiates in *milpa* ceremonies. But he devotes most of his time to curing sickness and working black magic. He is usually, and properly, called a curer rather than a *h-men*. His functions are more those of a practitioner in folk medicine and a sorcerer than those of a shaman priest.

Knowledge of the pagan gods is more vague and confused than in Dzitas. Most people connect the *chaacs* with the rain in some way, but ordinary rains do not seem to be thought of seriously as the work of the *chaacs*. Other beings of bush and field are rarely differentiated at all. They are commonly referred to collectively as *dueños del monte* or *dueños del cerro*, or simply as *vientos*. The use of this last term reveals a disposition to identify them with the "winds" that operate in disease and black magic. Caves and artificial mounds are dangerous because disease-producing *vientos* are likely to reside within them. These places are suggested as the special habitations of the *dueños* as well. But the confusion is not complete. There are many who insist that the *dueños* are less malevolent than are other kinds of winds; that they do no harm, beyond a little mischief, unless they are provoked. Nevertheless, nobody seems quite sure, and "winds" of any sort are to be treated with caution.

The association of the pagan deities with black magic was made explicit by the suburban curer mentioned above. He says that he calls on the *balams* for aid in curing sickness and that in one instance he employed the help of nine *balams* to bring about the death of a *milpa* thief who had insulted him. The same man defined the *alux* as figures of clay *or wax* which are found *or put* in the fields to protect the crops. The identification of the *alux* with a well-established technique of sorcery would have been complete in this case, except for the fact that the curer went on to explain that some *alux* inhabit the bush permanently without having been placed there.

The general attitudes and beliefs of urban residents regarding the pagan cult vary widely. A part of the small number of agriculturalists who live in the city believe sufficiently to induce them to keep up some of the agricultural rituals. Their attitudes in doing this are probably similar to those described for Dzitas. Large numbers of the less sophisticated members of the lower class, though they have had no direct experience with the pagan cult, are credulous nevertheless. Many of them vouch for the efficacy of rain ceremonies and show respect for guardians of the *milpa*, even after they have begun to question some of their other folk beliefs. Their position seems to be that the Indians, especially those in faraway places, are closer to the ancient people and preserve better their secrets and magical powers

—secrets and powers that have been lost in the life of the city. The more sophisticated tend to look upon pagan practices as unfortunate superstitions of rustics. It is they who favor education and repressive state action to put a stop to such folly. Then, there are a few who interpret the cult as interesting local folklore and who collect and publish stories on the customs of the Indians.

From the foregoing it is evident that, with the exception of an insignificant number of *milpa* cultivators, the inhabitants of Merida do not consider the pagan cult a part of their own existence, no matter what beliefs they hold concerning its reality or efficacy. It is separated from the city in space and is identified with a kind of people and a way of life that are regarded as inferior. When people of Merida think of the cult at all, they look outward or backward toward the hinterland—and downward.

II

In this chapter it is being said that religion plays a relatively larger part in the peripheral societies than in the town and in the city. What is sacred in the villages tends to appear as more secular in Dzitas and Merida. The reader has already been told that many elements of Catholic belief and ritual exist in Quintana Roo which are not now present in the other communities. What is now in addition to be said is that the elements of Catholicism common to all the communities are relatively more sacred in the peripheral communities than in the others. The symbols of divinity and the rituals that attend these symbols are more highly sacred in Tusik than in Dzitas or in Merida. The secularization of life that is to be noted in the progressive comparison that is now familiar to the reader is not confined to the pagan gods and ceremonies but extends also to the cult introduced from Europe. This might not have been said had the comparison been made a hundred years ago, or even seventy-five years ago, but the influence of an anticlerical government and the effects of recent mobility and other changes in the towns and the city have altered the Catholic practices and conceptions of the people. Today the most religiously minded communities, taking them as wholes, exist farthest from the episcopal authority.

The objective symbols of sanctity in Yucatan are chiefly crosses and images of saints. The *yuntzilob* are, since the Conquest, without effigy representation. In the Quintana Roo communities there are very few effigies of saints, but wooden crosses receive the greatest attention and worship. This is probably due in part to the fact that the Quintana Roo people are largely cut off from the wood carvers of religious images, but the extreme emphasis upon the worship of the cross in the outlying region may be a result of emphasis placed on that symbol of the early missionaries and may have roots in an ancient worship of some analogous pagan symbol. In the Chan Kom area, villages and families have wooden *santos* where the Quintana Roo people have crosses. Both groups of people also recognize in their prayers, and in certain beliefs, particularly named saints appropriate to certain activities or human needs. If one looks at the way in which these two conceptions—effigy and named saint—enter into the activities of the people, it appears that the conceptions, while related, are distinct. The saints appealed to in special connections—St. Mark in connection with agriculture and St. Isidore in connection with hunting deer—receive appeals without the necessity of the presence of any effigy, and even independent of an effigy of St. Mark or St. Isidore that may exist in some village. They are beings of special interests or functions existing in Heaven or in the woods. But the patron saint, whatever his name, is the symbol of the group of which it is patron, village or family as it may be, and of all the needs that that group may experience. He exists in the village or family shrine in the form of an effigy which in itself has power and sanctity. You cannot honor the patron without the presence of the effigy. One might distinguish the saints from the *santos*. If the matter be looked at in this way, then it appears that both in Quintana Roo and in the Chan Kom area there are both saints and *santos* but that in Quintana Roo the *santos* are crosses, not images of saints.

What is to be recorded in connection with the subject of this chapter is the loss of sanctity, especially of the *santos*. At least it may be declared that it is the crosses of Quintana Roo that are attended with the greatest veneration and awe. The Most Holy Cross, kept in X-Cacal for the respect and worship of the entire *cacicazgo*, is so sacred that few of its votaries are allowed to see it. Kept in a special precinct behind a screen, it is constantly protected by an armed guard. A worshipper may not himself place a candle before it; the candle is handed to the priest to place on the altar. Its power is expressed directly: if it is displeased with a votary, the cross indicates the fact by causing the flame of the candle to go out. It expresses its particular wishes by writing letters, and in former times it spoke with a human voice. No effigy in any other of the communities has this degree of awful power. Some of the same sanctity attends the other crosses of the Quintana Roo people. The village and family crosses are too sacred to be taken out of their chapels and carried about in procession; instead, equivalent substitute crosses are provided for the purpose. In Chan Kom, while the patron *santo* is venerated as greatly miraculous, it is maintained in a little oratory accessible to anyone, without guard. While in Quintana Roo it is thought wrong to keep crosses in the houses where people carry on everyday affairs, in Chan Kom many *santos* and crosses are kept there, although it is remembered that years ago all effigies were kept in special oratories. Nor do the *santos* of the Chan Kom area rule their people by any such direct method and explicit instructions as characterize the Most Holy Cross of X-Cacal. Except in the Quintana Roo villages, the sacred effigies are kept in ordinary dwellings and moved about as it seems convenient. If a man wishes to make a novena for a certain *santo*, he may in Chan Kom or in Dzitas or in Merida borrow it from a neighbor. It even occurs that a *santo* not properly suited to the occasion may be used "as if it were" the right *santo*: in Dzitas a small Virgin is borrowed from an individual and used as *La Concepción*, the original La Concepción having been destroyed during the Revolution.

Throughout Yucatan the *santos* retain much sacred quality. But it is the few widely recognized *santos* of especial potency that receive the attentions of the faithful. Most notable are the Three Kings, patrons of the town of Tizimín. The annual fiesta in their honor is attended by thousands of people, coming from as far away as Campeche. Many stories are told of the miracles these effigies perform. A miracle, as often as not, is the expression of supernatural power in the form of punishment of the unbelieving or the impious. A man, for instance, treats the fiesta lightly and is visited with sickness or blindness or other trouble. By some it is thought difficult even to gaze steadily upon these images because of the awful power they exert. Copies of the Three Kings are on hundreds of household altars in various communities throughout Yucatan, and on January 6 many people who are not at the fiesta in Tizimín dedicate celebrations to them at home. Somewhat similar prestige formerly attached to *La Concepción* of Izamal, but of late its reputation has declined sharply with the decay of its fiesta. Indeed there is in Merida something akin to fashion in the concern with *santos*. A few years ago San Nicolas was popular. Today he is almost forgotten; an image of the *Virgen de Perpetuo Socorro* has emerged from relative obscurity and may almost be said to be "the rage." In addition to these *santos*, associated with specific communities and certain particularly efficacious images, there are a few outstanding *santos* whose popularity is manifest chiefly by the fact that their effigies are to be found in an unusual number of homes and receive an unusual number of individual and family devotions. The main examples of this class are the *Niño Dios*, San Antonio, and the *Niño de Atocha*.

While a genuine religious feeling attaches everywhere to all *santos* and especially to certain of them, at the same time the general trend of change as one goes from the remoter villages toward the city is one of secularization. The unbelievers, from none at all in Tusik, become in Merida perhaps more numerous than the believers. In Tusik everyone attends to the great and supernatural authority of the Most Holy Cross. In Chan Kom the power of the patron has already been challenged by the coming of Protestantism. In Dzitas, while stories of the power of the patron, Santa Inez, abound, there are many people who from one year to the next never burn a candle before her. In Merida many of the inhabitants of the city, or of one of the *barrios* of the city, do not even know which *santo* is the patron of their local community. The prestige of the *santos* is in the city corrupted not only by competing cults (Protestantism, spiritualism, theosophy, and naturism) but also and more importantly by the anti-Catholicism associated with the political liberalism of recent times. The city includes the few very Catholic conservatives who follow all the ways of the Church and identify themselves with her interests, the great number of partial or nominal Catholics, and a large minority of frankly dissident or disbelieving cultists or other individuals. The lower class in Merida, in Hansen's words, "seems to be drifting toward a situation of no important or effective religion."

Of the special aspects of the general trend there is to be recorded in particular the progressive individualization of the *santos*. By this is meant the change wherein the *santo*, from being the universal and necessary religious symbol of all members of the group becomes a private and adventitious symbol of divine power. The number of *santos* known to any one person increases as their average sanctity declines; and as their number increases, their attachments to particular people become more variable. In Quintana Roo there is a hierarchy of crosses closely corresponding to the organization of society. At the top there is the Most Holy Cross, representing the entire subtribe, then the village crosses, then the familial crosses, and finally the crosses each representing an adult man and his wife and children. Thus everyone knows from childhood just what symbols of sacred power are of consequence for him, and the order of their relative consequence. One is born to one's gods; one does not elect them. Furthermore, everyone who belongs to one's lineage, or one's village, or one's tribe, attends to the same symbols of divinity. There is no choice. The *santos* reflect the structure of society, not the predilections of the individual. In Chan Kom, as in Quintana Roo, the *santos* on the whole express the collective attitudes of the people rather than individual preference. It is to the patron, to the *Niño Dios*, or to the Holy Cross that people make their prayers. All the villagers address themselves to the same *santos*, and these are all *santos* felt to belong to the local community. But, as there is no tribal organization in the Chan Kom area, there is no tribal god corresponding to the Most Holy Cross at X-Cacal. There is, to be sure, a vague feeling that the cross—not any particular cross—appertains to the *mazehua*, and that the Day of the Holy Cross (May 3) is a sort of ethnic festival. But there is no defined group more comprehensive than the village that might be marked by its own symbol of divinity.

On the other hand, in Chan Kom certain tendencies toward the individualization of society are reflected in some small changes taking place in the religious symbols. It will be recalled that in Quintana Roo there are familial crosses. Every family has the same kind of religious symbol which is a simulacrum of the village and tribal symbols. Furthermore, every family has such a symbol, and still further all the familial crosses are brought together at the occasion of the important village ceremonies so that no individual or family is unrepresented in the chief collective rituals. In Chan Kom, on the other hand, the familial symbols are not so regularly and systematically distributed according to the division of the community into family groups. Some families have *santos* and some do not, while there is no custom, as there is in Quintana Roo, that upon marriage every man secure his own cross and house it in some suitable oratory. The few private or familial *santos* that do exist in Chan Kom are effigies of different saints, involving different days of recognition. There is, in Chan Kom, some room for individual choice. If you want a *santo*, you may buy one from an image seller.

In Dzitas, and still more in Merida, the inclinations of the individual have still greater opportunity, and the relative predominance of the community patron is still further reduced. One man may have half-a-dozen *santos* on his domestic altar and observe the name day of each of them by novena or by simple burning of candles, while his neighbor may have no *santos* at all. Still more important, in the towns and the city it is common for an individual to make an attachment to a *santo* that is particular to him and that does not involve his family or his community. A woman may go to the fiesta at Tizimín, become convinced of the miraculousness of the *santos* there, and bring back a picture of them. She may then privately ask the aid of these beings without causing other members of her family to take part in the supplication. In both Dzitas and Merida, men, or more usually women, make vows to saints other than the patrons of the community, especially to the Niño of Atocha or to the Three Kings of Tizimín. While in Chan Kom seven or eight households have *santos* which are not regarded as patrons of the community, in Dzitas and in

The New World : 368

Merida the community patrons if not actually unknown are very unimportant in the galaxy of *santos*, and the elements which chiefly determine the *santo* to which the individual in town or city directs his prayer are the widespread fame of miraculous images in communities other than Dzitas or Merida and the separate attachments formed by chance and preference between the individual and such images. The high degree of instability in the relation between a person and the *santo* to which he is devoted reflects the mobility and disorganization of life in the city.

The essential facts are these: in the peripheral village the symbols of European form and apparently European origin have a sanctity recognized by all members of the group to which each symbol pertains and are worshipped in a series of ceremonies which are carried on either by small families, by lineages, by the village, or by the subtribe. These ceremonies involve all members of the group concerned, and all share common religious attitudes. In the city the degree of sanctity attached to these symbols varies between wide extremes as one individual is compared with another; and the ceremonies which involve them tend to be more individual and less collective and more secular and less sacred. The foregoing paragraphs have summarized the facts about the *santos* so far as they contribute to this general conclusion. The generalization may also be approached through a review of the rituals of Catholic form.

Throughout Yucatan prayers are recited in the presence of *santos* or of equivalent crosses as forms of appeal or as expressions of gratitude or of propitiation. The prayers are in part learned through oral tradition and in part (Quintana Roo excepted) are read from books. The principal prayers recited are the Our Father, the Hail Mary, the Creed, the General Confession, the Salve, and the Act of Contrition. Especially in Quintana Roo these six prayers are referred to as "the doctrine" (*payalchi*). Except in Quintana Roo, where it is usual to recite these six prayers successively, there is knowledge of the combination of certain of these prayer in fixed symmetrical groups (rosaries). In the more sophisticated communities these prayers, known to most people, are combined with various anthems and litanies which are less generally known. It is recognized that on the more important occasions these prayers are to be led by persons (*maestros cantores* or *rezadoras*) specially qualified by their knowledge of the less widely known elements of liturgy. The recitation occurs before altars including the effigy of the *santo* and is followed by the distribution and consumption of food and drink; this consumption is itself in some part a religious act, although it may be largely secular. It is generally understood that these prayers are to be recited on the days appropriate to the saints honored in the Christian calendar, but that they may also be held on occasions which are suggested by the interests or needs of the persons who bring about their recital.

Such is a formal statement of the formal resemblances among the Catholic rituals in the four communities studied. The interesting points of difference appear from a consideration of the varying functions of the Christian cult in the various communities. In Quintana Roo the Catholic cult is most elaborate and is expressed in the most specialized ceremonies. Both the community and the individual (or small family) are provided with rituals for both calendrical and occasional celebration. On the vespers of the days appropriate to the "great saints," the entire village holds a ceremony called "*oxdias*." The ceremony includes the recitation of the usual prayers under the leadership of a *maestro cantor*, with all laymen of the community participating. Every family must make a contribution of food, and to each person of prestige in turn falls the duty and privilege of preparing the special ritural breads (*oxdias, hostias*) from which the ceremony takes its name, and of which everyone partakes. A series of six *oxdias* is held when the village is threatened by drought (and is followed by the pagan ceremony called "*okot-batam*"). The *oxdias*, therefore, expresses the worship of the entire community, either on those days fixed in the calendar which tradition has sanctified or on those occasions when the community is collectively in greatest need. The celebrations of calendrical festivals are without exception community matters.

Oxdias and *okot-batam*, being community matters, are held in the village temple. The rituals of Catholic form which serve the individual and his family are held in the familial chapel. Two kinds of ceremonies are distinguished. *Edzcunah gracia* is performed whenever it is thought appropriate to maintain good relations with the crosses. The occasion may be the sickness of a child, concern over the crops, or the corresponding situations when a benefit has been received or thanks are to be given. This ceremony is also held—but in such cases in the chapel of the individual and before the substitute crosses—to assure harmonious relations with the spirits of the deceased relatives, especially the parents, of the individual. The *edzcunah gracia* requires no participation from outside the family. The votary and his wife prepare ritual foods; he himself places them on the altar or the table specially prepared; he himself kneels and prays "the doctrine" three times. After the offerings have been left for a time on the altar, they are eaten by the votary and his family. The other private ceremony, *chen rezar*, or *rezo*, is performed only when the shaman priest has declared that an illness has resulted from the anger of the souls of the dead relatives of the sufferer. The ritual asks pardon of the offended souls and of God as a means to the restoration of health. This ceremony takes place in the familial chapel and requires the help of the *maestro cantor*, and it differs from the *edzcunah gracia* also in that the food offered on the altar is afterward in part distributed among members of the man's great family and among his neighbors.

There should be added to this list of Catholic rituals in Quintana Roo the prayers recited on the Day of All Souls and on the Day of All Saints (*hanal pixan*) and the annual or biennial festival of the patron saint. The latter, as it occurs in different communities in Yucatan, will form the subject of a succeeding chapter. What is here to be emphasized is that in the exercise of the Catholic cult in Quintana Roo there is, on the one hand, a worship in which the entire community is engaged, and, on the other hand, private or small-family worship which occurs when a feeling of unease suggests it. The *oxdias*, held in the village church, requires the chiefs and *h-mens* of the settlement, as well as the *maestros cantores*, to perform special roles. Leadership, as in all public and ritual matters, is in the hands of the men, but both men and women kneel and pray and partake of the food of communion. The *oxdias* may be calendrically determined or it may follow from a general need, but in any case it is a common simultaneous expression of piety by the whole community. The individual, on his part, holds private ceremonies when there is a special reason to pray. The *edzcunah gracia* and the *chen rezar* (*rezo*) are also genuine expressions of piety, and their occurrences coincide with states of mind appropriate to prayer.

In Chan Kom it is usual to employ the word "novena" for any ritual recitation of Catholic prayers, whether on one afternoon or evening or on nine successive evenings. (As the prayers recited always include a rosary, the ceremony is sometimes called a *rosario*.) Only the prayers for the souls of the dead are distinguished as "*rezos*." The terminological distinction made among novenas is that between "name-day novenas" and "open-the-month novenas." The former are those held on the calendrical day appropriate to the *santo* honored and so correspond in function to the calendrical *oxdias* of Quintana Roo. But, as there are a few individuals in Chan Kom who have special *santos*, there are a few novenas, held on the responsibility of individuals, that are calendrically determined. Yet the most important name-day novenas are those held for the *santos* recognized by the entire community: San Diego, God, and the Holy Cross. These are usually full novenas of nine nights (distinguished as *novenarios*), while (with rare and recent exceptions) a man who has a private *santo* recognizes its name day with only a single night of prayer.

It is the *novenas de promesa* that are most common in Chan Kom. They are held whenever a man wishes to express thankfulness for a blessing received or to pray for a benefit sought. Thus they correspond to the *edzcunah gracia* of Quintana Roo. It may once more be emphasized that the object of supplication or the recipient of gratitude, though not a familial cross as in Quintana Roo, is in Chan Kom always one of the local *santos*, or is God, or is the Holy Cross—beings to whom all members of the community similarly appeal. "Outside" *santos* are not involved. It may also be pointed out that the novena functions in Chan Kom, as does its corresponding ritual in Tusik, chiefly as an expression of a genuine and occasional impulse of recognition of divinity. Although the novena is in large part social entertainment for the participants, the people who give the novena do so because they thank the *santo* or appeal to the *santo*. The calendrical novena is an obligation that goes with ownership of a particular effigy. The owner knows he has to recognize the *santo* on the appropriate day and feels that misfortune might follow if he failed to do so. But the day is fixed by the round of days; it is not one selected according to the immediate religious impulses of the worshipper.

The Chan Kom novena initiated by an individual is more of a neighborhood function than is the *edzcunah gracia* of Tusik. (It will be noted that in this respect an institution is more individualistic in Tusik than in Chan Kom.) It is the custom for persons outside the family to attend. A man's closest kinsmen will know that they are welcome, and they are likely to attend. Members of the family may speak of their plan to hold a novena and invite others to come. The people who attend are themselves performers of the ritual, for many of the prayers are known to all, and everyone joins in some of the responses. At the same time it is customary (as it is not in the case of the *edzcunah gracia*) to get one of the local *maestros cantores* to lead in the recitation and chanting of prayers and anthems; the occasion is, therefore, dignified by the presence of one of the men looked up to in the community for their religious knowledge. Men and women join equally in these village novenas; husband and wife are jointly votaries and hosts; and men friends attend as freely as do women.

The *rezo* of Chan Kom is similar in function to ceremonies of the same name in Quintana Roo. *Rezos* are held at certain intervals after the death of a member of the family or when one is sick by reason of the anger of the soul of such a close kinsman to whom not all the expected ceremonies have been made. In the latter sort of situation the *rezo*, like the *edzcunah gracia* and the *novena de promesa*, is a religious ritual occasioned by immediate needs. In Dzitas the prayers for the dead are held only in commemoration of the death on days fixed by the date of the death. The *h-men* is not there to tell a sick person that it is the souls of his kinsmen who are bringing the sickness upon him as a punishment for his failure to perform the rituals. So the occasional *rezo*, an expression of propitiation and of wish to be well, does not occur in Dzitas or in Merida; at least, no word of such a *rezo* was heard by the field investigators.

But there are more important respects in which the relatively more secular character of the Catholic ceremonies in Dzitas is evidenced. With the exception of the annual festival of the patron, the ceremonies held in the church on behalf of the entire town are far less inclusive of the people of the community than are the corresponding ceremonies in the villages. A small minority of the population attend masses on those exceptional occasions when the priest is there to perform them. When the priest is not there, a simple rosary is held; very few people attend. When the priest is not present on the important saints' days, novenas are held in the church. This may occur on the day of the Three Kings, on that of the Virgin of Guadalupe, and on Chrismas Eve; the last is a full *novenario*. But it is a few families of the town that take the lead in these novenas, and a great many people take no part whatsoever. A large part of the population is indifferent.

The situation with regard to individual, or familial, novenas is the reverse of that in Chan Kom in that the large majority of novenas held are name-day novenas, while *novenas de promesa* are relatively uncommon. (Some of the name-day novenas are referred to as "*novenas de promesa*" because it is remembered that an ancestor who had the image vowed to make the novena annually. But in cases known to the writer the reason why the vow was made has been forgotten; they are in substance like any other calendrical novena.) Because some people have many *santos*, and have different *santos* from their neighbors, there results a calendar of special obligations to perform novenas: it is known that so-and-so has a *santo* of San Isidro and therefore makes a one-night, or perhaps a nine-night, novena on his name day, while another man has a San Pedro and makes a novena at a different time. When these private *santos* are celebrated with full *novenarios*, relatives and friends are asked to take nights, providing the hospitality and food for that evening. Although the situation was different a generation ago, nowadays men take little part in novenas, either those of the Church or those held in private houses. Occasionally in a list of *devotos* a man's name will appear, but the man himself will rarely take active part; the night is listed in his name merely as an acknowledgment of his authority in domestic matters. Men will remain outside the house until the praying is over and then enter to enjoy the refreshments. Furthermore, the reciters of the liturgies appropriate to particular saints are, in the town, women, not men. The *maestro cantor* of the village has the prestige of his sex and also of a permanent and appreciated office in the community. But a *rezadora* is just a woman who knows the prayers. Thus a number of circumstances contribute to reducing the religious importance of the Dzitas novena: the atmosphere of indifference toward or even disbelief in all saints and *santos*; the fact that the occasion of a novena is a date in a calendar of little importance to persons not having the corresponding *santos*; the absence of a prayerful motive in most novenas; the fact that the *santos* honored are in most cases not the important symbols recognized by everyone but more special beings; and the deprofessionalization of the functions of the prayer leader. After this citation of easily verifiable points of difference, the writer may be permitted to record also the impressions of the field workers who have participated in these Dzitas novenas that they are not characterized by any strong religious sentiment and that they do not evidence any strong neighborhood solidarity. This is in distinct contrast, of course, to behavior in the villages.

Although the statement may not hold for the more rustic *indios milperos* of Dzitas, it is otherwise true that agricultural interests do not there play any important part in the motivation of the *novenas de promesa* The cases of *novenas de promesa* that the writers have from Dzitas are few at best, and among them is none with a motivation that arose from concern for the harvest. In the village the novena is certainly much more closely integrated into the predominant concern of the people—agricultural success; in the town, if the novena is not wholly secular and social, its motives are various and conform less to a pattern. Some cases from Dzitas followed vows made to a saint as conditional upon recovery from illness. One occurred because a mother wanted to ask a saint to reveal to her who had got her half-witted daughter with child. There is a certain magical or divinatory flavor to many novenas, clearer in the town than in the villages. "Some think it is good to have novenas for the sick. Some think it is bad and that then they die more quickly. It is the same way with confessing when one is sick. Some people think it makes them feel better, but others say, 'No, as soon as I confess I will die.'"

Merida presents one important general difference from the other communities with regard to Catholic ceremonies. The fact that it is the seat of ecclesiastical authority means that the ordained functionaries of the Church play a more important role there than elsewhere. This is especially true since the advent of anti-Catholic legislation. Priests are permitted to conduct regular services in only nine churches in the state of Yucatan; four of these churches are in Merida. It follows that it is chiefly in the city that an individual has the opportunity of attending ceremonies carried on by the official clergy. At the same time he can direct his devotions to the *santos* on his household altar and offer prayers for his dead relatives in his own home, as do the people of Dzitas and Chan Kom.

These two kinds of religious activity are distinct in many ways. It is common, especially among the lower class, to think of the formal church organization as belonging to the clergy. The rituals the priests provide tend to be accepted as a matter of course. They have always been available and presumably they always will be, unless the government interferes. The ordinary individual needs to make no contribution or to feel any responsibility. The organization seems to function independent of him. A person's household *santos*, on the other hand, are his *santos*, and the novenas he offers them are his novenas. He knows that only his continued interest and effort will keep the ceremonies going. Also, it may be noted that when an individual attends Mass, he is among strangers with whom his contacts are casual and secondary. In a novena he is surrounded by his friends and relatives. Another difference is that participation in official Catholic activities is urged upon people by the established ecclesiastical leaders, using every device at their command. Although the priests must have implanted the cult of the household *santos* in Yucatan in the first place, at present they give it no encouragement. The sole authority that now supports it is the authority of tradition. Tradition, however, is documented with a large number of stories that point out how the *santos* punish people who fail to honor them with the appropriate celebrations. It is significant that no corresponding myths were encountered depicting the rewards and pains that come from faithfulness to or neglect of the official Church, except for a few which illustrate the necessity of baptism. A further distinction derives from the circumstance that novenas held at home to which one invites one's relatives and friends are primarily a lower-class institution. It is not uncommon for pious lower-class persons to express their religious devotion by diligent attention to the images on the family altar, while they are rather lax in going to Mass and in carrying out their other obligations as members of the Church. In contrast, pious upper-class people tend to participate fully in the program of formal Catholicism and to limit their religious behavior at home to simple acts of worship performed individually and privately.

It is even possible to observe some signs of antagonism between these two aspects of Catholicism. Persons who are deeply attached to their *santos* think of themselves as being good religious people, though they may be quite negligent with reference to Mass, confession, etc. It is not that they really question the formal cult. They look up to the clergy and accept the things the clergy does as entirely right and proper. Their attitude appears to be that they want the church available to be used as and when they wish, but that the *santos* are nearer and the ceremonies addressed to them are more meaningful. When a priest exhorts them to greater faithfulness to the formal institution, they listen politely and respectfully. They agree and make promises, which they often fail to keep. But if they are urged too much, they are likely to feel annoyance instead of contrition. In the conversations of lower-class people who consider themselves to be good Catholics, one hears certain priests criticized for their zeal in trying to induce their parishioners to discharge all their duties to the Church. Other priests who are more tolerant of partial participation are commented upon approvingly. Among the clergy and among devout upper-class Catholics there is a disposition to disparage the traditional cult of the household *santos*.

Novenas are described as profane celebrations of little or no religious value. More often than not, according to these critics, the prayers are a mere excuse for a party. The only real religion, they hold, is that offered by the Church, supplemented by private devotions of pure prayer. It is their view that worship should be a specialized activity, unmixed with entertainment. They would certainly deny the right of an individual to call himself a good Catholic who did not fulfill all or most of his obligations to the formal organization. Aside from strictly religious considerations, novenas tend to be looked down upon because they are associated with the lower class. Everybody knows that the Church derives its most loyal support from the old upper class. The prestige of this class is identified with its characteristic mode of religious behavior in some degree, thus raising the rating of the formal Catholic cult and setting it off in contrast to the cult of the household *santos*.

We can return now to a consideration of novenas in Merida as compared to the other communities. But first it may be well to record that, as in Dzitas, prayers for the dead (called *"rosarios"* in the city rather than *"rezos"*) are held at fixed intervals determined by the date of the death of the person they commemorate. Much that has been said of novenas in Dzitas applies equally well to Merida. There is the same diversity of *santos* from household to household. *Novenas de promesa* are rare and, when given, are likely to be simple affairs involving only the immediate family. For full *novenarios* friends and relatives are invited to take nights. The arrangements are almost entirely in the hands of women, and the women alone do the praying, led by a *rezadora*. Other similarities with Dzitas could be cited, but we are more concerned with differences which reveal the greater secularization of these rituals in the city.

It is necessary to glance at the past of a generation or two ago to see one evidence of secularization that was more apparent then than now. At that time novenas played an important role in the lower class as means through which families could express their social status. As one family vied with another, the nonreligious features of novenas became very elaborate. On the final night the guests sometimes numbered more than a hundred. The house and lot would be decorated. There would be a *jarana*, provided with the best orchestra that could be afforded. Instead of the simple refreshments in vogue today, for the "better" novenas these would consist of chicken and turkey or perhaps barbecued pig. It was customary for the owner of the *santo* to entertain the *nocheros* (leaders of the eight previous nights of prayer and festivity) of the first eight nights and their families throughout the last day in order to repay them for their contributions earlier and to have their assistance in preparing for the final night. Certain families acquired fame for the splendor of their novenas. Since these were distributed throughout the year, they might be described as constituting the "events" of lower-class "society." With all this elaboration of the more secular aspects of the celebration, the part concerned directly with the *santo* remained relatively modest. The altar was highly adorned, and the leader of the prayers was often accompanied by one or two chanters and by a person playing a portable organ, but that was all. Although the foregoing refers chiefly to a few outstanding novenas, they represented the pattern that many people formerly sought to emulate, and they exhibited characteristics that have little in common with the domestic religious practices of Chan Kom and Tusik.

The novenas one finds in Merida today are generally much simpler than they used to be. There are other sources of entertainment and more effective ways to gain prestige. The guests do not often exceed thirty or forty, and the usual refreshments are sweetened rice water or commercially produced soft drinks, with some small edible delicacy. If there is a dance, a phonograph or a radio frequently suffices for music. Sometimes the affair is shortened to one night, which is definitely felt to be an inferior substitute for a full *novenario*. The more elaborate pattern of the past does have enough validity, however, to induce some people to cease giving novenas entirely in preference to making a show so modest that it might give rise to adverse comment among the neighbors. Reflecting the nature of social relations in the city, novenas are purely invitational. To attend without being specifically asked would be construed as "crashing the party." The guests come from anywhere in the city the host happens to have friends. Conse-

quently, novenas have little of the character of neighborhood gatherings. Modern dancing has completely replaced
the *jarana*. This means more than a mere change of style.
The *jarana* had a certain amount of religious connotation
due to its long association with religious festivities. In fact,
it persisted in connection with novenas after it had ceased
to be popular entertainment indulged in for its own sake.
Modern dancing, on the other hand, is entirely secular. A
few conservative old people even suggest that it is an offense to the *santo* for dancers to embrace in its presence
as they do today. A further sign of secularization is the
almost universal practice of requesting the male guests to
contribute to the cost of the orchestra, if there is one.
This is a direct violation of the traditional conception of
the function of the social enjoyment that went with a novena. The *santo* was thought to be pleased by the festivity
as well as by the prayer. Both were offered to honor the
santo, and both were part of the obligation of a person who
undertook to give a novena. By collecting from his guests,
the owner of a *santo* is escaping some of his duties. Moreover, it was the traditional idea that anyone who contributed in any way became to a degree a devoto, a participant in honoring the *santo*. Investigation disclosed that
the men who help pay for the music for a modern dance
are not considered devotos in any sense. Everybody with
whom the matter was discussed agreed that they are merely
paying for the privilege of dancing. Ordinarily this practice
of charging the guests serves only to make a novena a
better party and to reduce the expenses borne by the
host. But one case of outright commercialization was encountered. The novena in question had been given annually for a long time and was always an elaborate affair.
Over the years it acquired a reputation for gaiety that
made it very popular. During the period of study full advantage was being taken of the opportunities it presented.
To increase the attendance, four or five hundred printed
invitations were distributed throughout the city. There
were several dances in addition to the one on the last
night. All of them were organized by the owner of the
santo, not by the *nocheros*. The *nocheros* provided only
the prayers, in which few people participated, since
most of them came just for the dances. At other novenas it

is usual to collect from the guests informally during the course of the evening while the dancing is going on. In this instance, admission was paid at the door. Even the refreshments were sold, and, to increase the revenue, hard liquor was included. All in all, the novena returned a net profit. It may be observed that in this case the arrangements were not left to the women of the family; the male head himself was in active charge. What had happened can be summarized by saying that the *santo* had become the excuse for a celebration, the owner of the *santo* an entrepreneur, and the novena a business enterprise.

In addition to the apparent secularization of such novenas as are still maintained in Merida, the fact is to be reported that novenas are becoming less common there at a rate which suggests that the whole institution may be dying out. There are two partial exceptions to this picture of decline. They are the novenas offered to the Infant Jesus and to the Three Kings at Christmas time. Although they, too, show some signs of weakening, they have suffered far less than have other novenas. The reason for their continued popularity is that they are established features of the general holiday celebration; that is, they are the customary Christmas parties. Their association with this important holiday provides them with a kind of support no other novena has. Even people who are quite indifferent to the *santos* and to religion generally still feel that it is appropriate for Christmas parties to have a slight religious flavor, a result which can be achieved by following the traditional practice of organizing them as novenas to the Infant Jesus or to the Three Kings. Owing to the special factors operating in these two cases, they should be considered exceptions and omitted from a discussion of the decline of novenas. Leaving them out of account, then, we may begin by observing that, outside of the lower class, novenas are already practically extinct. Within the lower class one finds family after family reporting that it used to give them but does not now. Often a statement is added to the effect that the last novena was held four, five, or perhaps eight, ten, or fifteen years ago. An estimate of how far this trend has gone would be little better than a guess. But it seems perfectly safe to say that not more than one family in five still gives novenas to which outsiders are invited; and one in ten would probably be nearer the truth. Moreover, an observer get the impression that the majority of novenas are kept up by the older generation and that they are rare in families founded within the last two decades. After people stop giving novenas, they may retain their interest in the household *santos* and express it by burning candles and reciting prayers individually or in company with other members of the domestic group. Or they may pay almost no attention to the images on the family altar either because they have become unconcerned with religion in any form or because they are content with the religious experience provided by formal Catholicism or some alternative cult.

The factors undermining novenas in the city are many and varied. The most obvious is the antireligious propoganda maintained by the government, which is stronger here than elsewhere in the state. Although it is often discounted because of its political source, it does show, nevertheless, that some people can attack the *santos* openly with no apparent evil consequences to themselves. Moreover, every individual has friends and relatives, persons he knows intimately, who ignore the *santos* more or less and yet enjoy health and prosperity. Faced with a growing number of such cases, all but the most faithful question the efficacy and necessity of novenas. The old stories that point out how forgetting the *santos* brings misfortune are not told so frequently or so widely as they used to be. People do not have time to listen; they are too busy "going places" and "doing things." When the stories are recounted, it is usually an older person who tells them; and age today has no great authority or prestige. They are either frankly disbelieved or are rationalized into ineffectiveness by those who are somewhat credulous. It is said, for instance, that if a person lacks money for a novena, he is accustomed to give, or if he diminishes his attention to the *santo* little by little instead of all at once, the *santo* will understand and not take offense. Probably the abandonment of a novena in itself contributes to a further loss of interest and faith. As long as it is kept up, even though it be quite secularized, the very effort it requires tends to reaffirm whatever concern its sponsor still feels. At the same time it serves as a kind of public announcement that he feels something.

One suspects that many of the families who have substituted simple acts of devotion performed in private for the traditional celebrations in honor of the *santos* may be on the way toward a more complete neglect of them. The simplicity and privacy of these rituals may make them less capable of sustaining the individual's interest, particularly in a world where numerous and varied stimuli press upon him and compete for his time and attention. Finally, it will be recalled that participation in formal Catholicism is proclaimed as a form of religious expression superior to that provided by domestic ceremonies; superior because it is pure religion, uncontaminated by profane elements as are the traditional rituals addressed to the household images. In a similar way, though less directly and explicitly, new kinds of purely secular diversion strike at the entertainment features of novenas. Without being told, most people judge novena parties to be second rate as compared to the movies and the dances of social clubs. Their sole function is to divert, and they are deliberately designed to be glamorous and exciting.

III

The subject of this chapter was been the secularization of Yucatecan life. More specially it has dealt with the decline in religious faith and the reduction in sanctity of the acts and images in which faith is manifest. But the facts do not allow one to deal with this general trend apart from others that have been urged upon the reader in earlier chapters. Apart from the aspect of secularization, the differences in such an institution as the *santos*, as these are revealed by a comparison of the several communities, contribute to the documentation of other propositions set forth in this volume. The cult of the *santos* presents materials on individualization; it demonstrates the fact that the individual is in the villages less free to act independently of his family or settlement. It presents material on the disorganization of culture, for it shows that the interdependence and consistency of customs and belief are most marked in the peripheral communities. In Tusik and Chan Kom the *yuntzilob* express matters of universal and paramount concern: the rain, the bush, and the *milpa*. In Dzitas the *yuntzilob* still stand for these things, so far as they stand for anything, but these are not the paramount concern of those townsmen who are not thinking about crops but rather about their stores or their jobs. In Quintana Roo the crosses are not only objects of sanctity but they are also objectifications of the hierarchy of groups which make up the social organization. The *santo* of the city man expresses, in many cases, chiefly his own personal and private experiences in fixing upon that *santo* as helpful to him. Both *yuntzilob* and *santo*, in Dzitas, are less well integrated into a system of interdependent ideas. The separation of the novena from agriculture and the fact that in the towns the *yuntzilob* are less regarded as the causers of disease by way of punishment for moral wrong are instances of the way in which the network of meanings breaks apart, here and there. Connections that existed in the village, so that one realm of thought and practice offered justification for another, disappear in town and city. May it be that secularization is in part a result, simply, of this loosening of the web of meanings? Where the cross one prays to is the cross addressed by everyone in one's family, or one's village, or one's tribe—where, in other words, the symbols to which one points one's prayers remind one by their very arrangement and manner of treatment of the form of the society in which one lives, and where there are many other institutions about one that declare the rightness of that form of society, may it be that the political and social institutions thereby contribute to the sanctification of the religious symbols, and vice versa? And perhaps when the connections with social organization *are* gone, the *santos* become less sacred, just because those connections are gone. In the villages a man thinks of the *yuntzilob* when he plants his corn, or harvests it, and also when he has become sick and the *h-men* has told him that the *yuntzilob* have punished him with sickness. The townsman may or may not still be a farmer, and so concern himself with the *yuntzilob*, and it is not customary to attach to sickness a meaning involving the *yuntzilob*. There is at least one less source of support and justification for the divinity of the *yuntzilob*. It seems to the writer not unlikely that, even if there were no schools and no urban skeptics, religion, both pagan and Catholic, would decline with the appearance of specialized occupations or with the moving away of the *h-men* because those are circumstances that disorganize the culture. It seems probable that the loss of tribal independence by the X-Cacal Maya will, even without other contributing causes, bring about a decline in religious faith among that people. There will be no subtribe for the Most Holy Cross to stand for.

Returning to the subject, the decline of the gods, and reviewing what has been said in this chapter, the writer notes the instances in which the summary of differences has amounted to saying that what is religious in the peripheral communities becomes merely magical in the town or the city. The awful beings of the sky and the bush, the *yuntzilob*, are displaced by little goblins, the *alux*. The ceremonies from the *yuntzilob*, from being "acts of piety," become "acts of safeguard." From praying in the *milpa*, one hires a man to say some spells that "cure" the land. The *edzcunah gracia* of Tusik is a form of prayer. The corresponding *novena de promesa* in Chan Kom is more prayer than party. In Dzitas it is more party than prayer; and indeed, in so far as it is not secular entertainment, it is something that is done because it would be unlucky not to do it. People raise the question as to whether or not it is lucky to perform this or that novena or to leave it unperformed. Even the *santo*, religious symbol that it does remain for the true Catholic and the religiously minded individual in the town or the city, becomes for many a mere charm. One wears the image in the town, or puts it on the autobus one drives in the city, along with other luck symbols.

It appears that under the circumstances that prevail in Yucatan, magic, while it is present everywhere along with true piety and worship, is a sort of intermediate station on the road to complete secularization. When an object is sacred to a man, he will not tolerate a critical or rational exposure of its nature. For him it is protected by an uncertain, emotionally rooted aura. It has qualities that move him and that may not be explained away; he will resent it if you try. If, moreover, it is a religious object, it embodies and often personalizes qualities that are ultimate moral goods. These he seeks in the object, relating it to his own person in prayer, propitiation, and appeal. The *yuntzilob* cease to be gods; they leave religion; yet the woods remain uncanny. The old acts that once attested the *yuntzilob* are not to be given up entirely. One's neighbor perhaps disbelieves in the *yuntzilob*; so one doubts—but it is better to be on the safe side. Not to do anything at sowing is to feel uncomfortable. One is not entirely matter-of-fact when dealing with the bush and the uncertain rain. There is so much luck about the results. Maybe to do the act will help to bring a good crop. So the ritual is done, now not as worship but as a spell or charm. The *santo*, too, takes on this magical quality. It is not a chair or a hat; it has qualities which are not rationally to be dealt with. You may not have much faith in it as a supernatural person, but it might be unlucky not to perform a novena on the name day. The concern is no longer with the propitiation of a being that cares for one if one remains virtuous. The attention has shifted to the luck of the field or to uncertain mishaps that might occur if one did nothing. The object cannot be entirely explained away; it still has power. If the right words are said, it can be made to work.

Catholic and pagan elements in the religion exhibit this disposition to become more emphatically magical (once more speaking of the comparison in terms of a trend or change), while they are separating from each other and moving apart. In the villages there is, to the native, no paganism to be distinguished from Catholicism. Only an outsider, with knowledge of history, would make such a distinction. Indeed, in Tusik it would not represent the native's point of view to speak of religion as something distinct from the rest of life. There are the proper ways to do things; and included are prayers and offerings, just as are included work and behavior toward chiefs and kinsmen. To say that one is a Catholic, if it is said at all, is about the same as saying one is a proper human being of one's own world of affairs. In Chan Kom and villages like it, where there are Protestants, there are, for the first time, so to speak, Catholics. And being a Catholic rather than an *Evangélico* does not set either in contrast to paganism. Paganism, in the villages, is not recognized as a cult in opposition to anything else. *Evangélicos* do not believe in the saints, while Catholics do; but everybody makes the rain ceremony. It is in the towns that paganism begins to separate out, as it were. It is seen as a cult of value to the agriculturalists in the community or to some of them. It is in some disrepute. At least the leaders of the community, the men who have prestige, tend to be detached from it or to treat lightly such connection as they have with it. The cult of the *yuntzilob* becomes a useful magic—a little humorous, a trifle embarrassing. Beyond that, in the city particularly, it becomes a superstition. It is something somebody else mistakenly believes. And finally, if detached from all moral judgment, the ideas as to pagan deities become only folklore, quaint stories and beliefs which can be enjoyed by adults or told to children. Then secularization is quite complete; all the uncanny power has been drawn; the gods have become figures in fairytales.

Paganism simply fades away. It leaves almost no institutions in the life of the city. It is connected with all the rustic and backward elements of life which a spreading, dominant urban viewpoint depreciates. It is frowned upon by the state and condemned by the established churches. Its leaders, the *h-mens*, are suspect to city authority. So it retreats to the forests or shrinks to almost nothing.

Catholicism, of course, remains. The Christian elements in the religion of Yucatan have been supported for centuries by a vigorous organization and by the approval of the elite. They have long been identified with the sociologically superior. Yet the trend of secularization affects them, and piety declines. At the same time Catholicism appears as a distinguishable body of thought and practice. In Chan Kom there are, as there are not in Tusik, Catholics who are in opposition to *Evangélicos*. In Dzitas the opposition is more marked: the Protestants are more set apart; they maintain their own chapel; they are looked on by Catholics, who now feel themselves as something different, with distaste or fear. And in Merida the Catholics are fully recognizable as a special interest group in rivalry with other interest groups.

It is in the city that there is to be recognized a separation within Catholicism itself. On the one hand, there is the cult of the *santos;* on the other, is the formal Church. The cult of the *santos* is a kind of folk Catholicism. It is local, is without formal organization, is sanctioned by a body of folklore, and is carried on by ordinary persons with the assistance of a few individuals from among their neighbors who possess some knowledge of prayers not shared by everyone. It flourishes in a situation where a need is felt for supernatural aid in the course of daily existence and where the common experiences of all members of the community reaffirm the efficacy of such aid and the rightness of seeking it. In the city, as the crises people face grow more diversified and as secular attitudes come to characterize larger and larger areas of behavior, concern with the supernatural becomes less constant and less urgent. The cult of the *santos*, therefore, tends to disappear, since it is dependent on the active interest of common people. The decline is hastened by antireligious propaganda, by disparagement from the Church and from the elite, and by the multiplication of things to do, places to go, and ways to spend time and money that characterizes the city.

At the same time the Church, with its followers of orthodox faithful, exists as a semisecular institution in competition with other groups and institutions for the attention and support of the people. It is part of an international organization. It has specialized, full-time leaders. It survives in the urban environment, defending itself against competitors, self-consciously proclaiming vigorously and insistently the value of its program, and modifying its program as necessary to give it greater appeal. In doing this, it is transformed into an interest group which functions to provide certain people with a ready means of religious expression that tends to become a specialized segment of their lives.

In the remote villages, where conceptions we may regard as Catholic are generally held by everybody, there is no Catholicism as something set apart from or opposed to something else. In the city, where Catholicism takes on some of the characteristics of a political party, many people are relatively indifferent to the conceptions supported by the Church.

The principal differences among the four communities with regard to religion, including both pagan and Christian elements, may now be briefly summarized. In Tusik there is a single body of beliefs and practices, in which everyone participates; religion is not distinguished from the rest of life; and, of course, therefore, there is no distinction between Catholicism and paganism or between

Catholicism and anything else. In Chan Kom the integration of pagan and Christian elements is less nearly complete than in Tusik; religion is still an important concern of everyone and is still integrated with the rest of life. Catholics here appear, because there are some Protestants. In Dzitas, religious activity is less well integrated with the rest of life; religion is recognized as a distinguishable interest or activity; paganism occupies the attention of only part of the population and is in disrepute among the "better" people; and Catholics and Protestants are well-defined groups. In Merida paganism is practically gone; it is associated with the back country and is viewed as superstition or as quaint folklore. A division appears in Catholicism. The traditional cult of the *santos*, carried on by the common people, decays. The Catholic Church remains, competing with Protestantism and other cults and struggling to maintain itself against antireligion and indifference. Even for those who continue faithful, religion has lost much of its connection with the rest of life and is to a considerable degree a separate and specialized division of behavior. One is a member of a church rather than a participant in a society and a culture.

A NOTE ABOUT THE AUTHOR

Alfred Métraux

ALFRED MÉTRAUX (1902–   ) first visited Haiti in search
of archaeological sites and remains of the occupation by
the French pirates and buccaneers. He later wrote: "I
had scarcely disembarked in Port-au-Prince before I heard
of the campaign being waged by the Catholic Church
'against superstition.' It was at Croix-des-Bouquets, near
Port-au-Prince, that I was given a glimpse of the vigour
with which African cults had spread in Haiti: an enormous
pyramid of drums and 'superstitious objects' towered high
in the court of the presbytery, waiting for the date on
which there was to be a solemn *auto-da-fé* . . . The
scale of this offensive against Voodoo, and the brutality of
the measures taken against its devotees, suggested that its
days were numbered; and so I conceived the desire to
study it before it was too late." *Voodoo in Haiti*, from
which the following selection is reprinted, is Métraux's
most comprehensive publication on the subject.

Métraux has engaged in field research in Polynesia,
South America, and the West Indies, and he has written
numerous articles and monographs on the ethnology of
these areas. He is perhaps better known as an ethnologist
than as a social anthropologist. Although the two fields
overlap, the social anthropologist as a rule is concerned
with developing theoretical analyses of human societies,
while the ethnologist is more interested in recording materials which he considers to possess intrinsic historical
value. Métraux's publications on Easter Island are authoritative sources of information about that intriguing outpost
of Polynesian civilization, and he contributed greatly to
the *Handbook of South American Indians*, an encyclo-
pedic seven-volume ethnography edited by Julian Steward.

At the present time Alfred Métraux is a member of the Division of Social Sciences of UNESCO in Paris. His career has been remarkably international. Born in Lausanne, Switzerland, and educated in France and Sweden, he is a naturalized American citizen. Between 1928 and 1934 he was Director of the Institute of Anthropology at the National University of Tucumán, Argentina. In 1936–8 he was a Fellow of the Bernice P. Bishop Museum in Honolulu, and from 1941 to 1945 he was a member of the Bureau of American Ethnology of the Smithsonian Institution.

Métraux first studied Oriental languages, receiving a *Diploma* from the Sorbonne in 1926. He received a *Doctorat-ès-lettres* in anthropology from the same institution in 1928. He has been a President of the American Folklore Society, and a Fellow of the Guggenheim Foundation.

A Selection from

*Voodoo in Haiti**

by

ALFRED MÉTRAUX

Certain exotic words are charged with evocative power.
Voodoo is one. It usually conjures up visions of mysterious
deaths, secret rites—or dark saturnalia celebrated by
"blood-maddened, sex-maddened, god-maddened" Negroes.

In fact—what is Voodoo? Nothing more than a con-
glomeration of beliefs and rites of African origin, which,
having been closely mixed with Catholic practice, has
come to be the religion of the greater part of the peasants
and the urban proletariat of the black republic of Haiti.
Its devotees ask of it what men have always asked of
religion: remedy for ills, satisfaction for needs, and the
hope of survival.

¶ THE SOCIAL FRAMEWORK OF VOODOO

Voodoo is essentially a popular religion. The greater
part of its adherents are recruited among the peasants
who form ninety-seven per cent of the total population
of the country. As to the city dwellers, they have remained
faithful to it in whatever measure they have kept up their

* VOODOO IN HAITI *was published in Great Britain, Canada, and
British Commonwealth countries by Andre Deutsch, Esq. The follow-
ing selection is from* VOODOO IN HAITI *by Alfred Métraux.* © 1959 *by
Alfred Métraux. Reprinted by permission of Oxford University Press,
Inc., New York, and by Andre Deutsch, Esq.*

rural roots. The practice of Voodoo, along with the exclusive use of the Creole language, is one of the characteristics which sociologists have kept to distinguish between the masses and the small class of educated people who enjoy a certain material ease and call themselves the "élite." The members of this élite, who are mostly Mulattos, adhere with the utmost tenacity to Western modes of life and thought, and hold the country people in the greatest contempt. Between these two classes the cleavage is so pronounced that the élite has been termed a "caste," and one American sociologist, Leyburn, has gone so far as to describe them as two different nations sharing the same country. In fact the differences have been very much exaggerated. The élite is not a caste since it is open to those who succeed in raising themselves, either by talent, luck, or politics from the masses. Even in the subject which concerns us here, the contrasts are not so marked as one might think. Most of the élite children are brought up by servants who come from the *mornes* (mountains) and carry with them the terrors of "African Guinea." All Haitians, whatever their social status, have trembled in their youth at stories of *zombi* and werewolves and learned to dread the power of sorcerers and evil spirits. Most of them, under the influence of school or family, react against such fancies, but some give in to them and consult a Voodoo priest in secret.

On this point I will quote the evidence of a bishop who unfortunately must remain anonymous. "Superstition is so widespread and deep that it could be said to touch everyone. The best, even those who don't practise it, have to fight against the feelings they experience when faced with certain facts, certain signs which recall superstition to them." Even a Haitian priest once confessed that he was prone to such feelings. "The whole of one's being is impregnated with them, right to the bottom of the soul; the smallest detail of existence is dominated by them." And beside this testament we can quote an excerpt from a conference held by Monseigneur Kersuzan in 1896. "A *bocor* [sorcerer] crosses our streets. We know him. Everyone spots him. Where is he going? You might think to some poor person who cannot afford doctor or chemist. But no. He is going to a superb house where he will operate on the father of some family in the highest rank of society."

The political and social frameworks peculiar to the African tribes from whom the Haitians of today are descended were pulverized by slavery. Even the family did not survive that dissolution; only in haphazard fashion was it reconstituted on the fringe of plantation life, and in the first years of the country's independence Toussaint Louverture, Dessalines, and Christophe had all intended to maintain the system of huge properties on which the peasants would have lived as serfs. History decided otherwise. It was the peasant small-holding which triumphed in the end. The families which divided between them the lands of the State regrouped along lines which, though not strictly speaking African, yet recalled the organizational forms common to Africa and Europe. Not very long ago the social unit of the Haitian countryside was the extended family consisting of the head of the family, his children, married or unmarried, and his grand-children. Each *ménage* had its house and field. The whole group of conjugal families, all closely related, was called the "compound" (*laku*), and its houses and granaries often made up a hamlet. Its members were further bound together by worship of their common root-*loa* (*loa-racines*), that is to say, of the gods and protecting spirits of the extended family which were inherited just like property. The compound head kept a little sanctuary or *humfo* for his gods, and there, in the presence of his kin, he officiated. A *hungan* (priest) and *mambo* (priestess) were only called upon in the event of serious illness or to "feed" the family gods.

Today the compound is tending to disintegrate. Families are being dispersed by the carving up of land and weakening of the kinship ties. The cult of ancestral spirits with its attendant obligations continues to assure a measure of cohesion between the members of a scattered kin group: when the gods and spirits demand food, the whole family must be present and share the costs. Nevertheless, Voodoo as a domestic cult is losing importance daily to the profit of the small, autonomous cult groups which grow up around the sanctuaries.

People who regret that Voodoo is, in fact, the religion

of the people of Haiti forget how hard is the life of the average peasant and worker. Isolation, economic stagnation, administrative fecklessness, ignorance—all help to explain the misery which is to be found among the masses. At the source of that poverty stands the familiar curse of so many underdeveloped countries: overpopulation on ever less fertile land. Haiti has the highest density of population in the Western Hemisphere—250 people to the square mile. Beneath a gay and optimistic exterior the peasant conceals a chronic anxiety which is, unfortunately, only too well justified. Seldom does he own enough land to escape the dearth which occurs at the slightest caprice of weather. Usually he is in debt, in possession of doubtful title deeds, and can neither read nor write. Unable to speak French, as do the townfolk, he feels an easy prey to their cupidity. And then to all these causes of anxiety is added the dread of illness. Tuberculosis, malaria, and hookworm are endemic, and their threat is always present in addition to that of the accidents which may ruin him. Voodoo reflects these cares. What the faithful ask of their gods is not so much riches and happiness but more the removal of the miseries which assail them from every quarter. Illness and misfortune seem to them divine judgments which must somehow be mitigated by offerings and sacrifice. It is unjust and naïve to reproach the peasants for wasting much of their meager resources on pagan ceremonies. As long as medical service are nonexistent in the country districts, so long may the Voodoo priests be sure of a large clientele. Voodoo allows its adherents to find their way back to a rudimentary form of collective life, to show their artistic talents, and to have the exalted feeling of contact with the supernatural. At Marbial, where Voodoo has been more or less suppressed, a wretched depression has settled over the valley, and life for the peasants has lost all point.

We have seen that Voodoo exists in two forms—one domestic, the other public. It is this last which mainly concerns us here. Most of my observations were made at Port-au-Prince, where the sanctuaries are numerous and prosperous and where the ritual is full of refinements and subtleties which are lacking in the rural cults. People are prone to suppose that the purest and richest traditions are to be found in the remotest valleys. The little I was able to see of rural Voodoo convinced me that it was poor in its ritual compared to the Voodoo of the capital. Simplicity of rite is not always a guarantee of antiquity. It is often the result of ignorance and neglect. No doubt some African characteristics are better preserved in the backwoods than in the faubourgs of Port-au-Prince, but the purity of the African heritage only moderately concerns us. Voodoo deserves to be studied, not only as regards the survival of Dahomean and Congolese beliefs and practices, but also as a religious system born fairly recently from a fusion of many different elements. It is the dynamic aspect of Voodoo always evolving before our eyes which is more to our purpose than the rich material it affords to the erudite, possessed by a craving for the search for origins.

¶ VOODOO CLERGY AND CULT GROUPS

Voodoo has preserved one of the fundamental characteristics of the African religions from which it is derived: worship is sustained by groups of adherents who voluntarily place themselves under the authority of a priest or priestess whose sanctuary or *humfo* they frequent. The faithful who have been initiated in the same sanctuary and who congregate to worship the gods to which it is sacred form a sort of fraternity called "the *humfo* society." The importance of this cult group depends to a great extent on the personality and influence of the priest and priestess who preside.

This complex religion with its ill-defined frontiers may perhaps be more easily approached through a study of its social and material frameworks. It is the priests and their numerous acolytes who have, out of widely different beliefs and rites, formed a more or less coherent system.

Spirits incarnate themselves at will in the people they choose. Any devotee can therefore enter into immediate contact with the supernatural world. Such intimacy, however, does not involve communication or dialogue with the god, since the person possessed is mere flesh, a receptacle, borrowed by the spirit for the purpose of revealing himself. If you wish to get a hearing from the spirits—

particularly when health and fortune are at stake—it is better to have recourse to the skills of a priest or priestess: *hungan* and *mambo*, less commonly called *papa-loa* and *maman-loa*. The word *gangan*, used as a synonym of *hungan*, carries with it a nuance which is respectful or depreciatory, according to the region.

Although *hungan* and *mambo* are often closely linked with each other, they are by no means part of a properly organized corps. They are the heads of autonomous sects or cult groups, rather than members of a clerical hierarchy. Certainly the prestige of a *hungan* may spread and affect sanctuaries served by his disciples, but there is no subordination, as such, of one *hungan* to another. The profession has its grades which correspond with the various degrees of initiation, but a priest only has authority over those who voluntarily offer themselves as servants of the spirits worshipped in his sanctuary.

There is the greatest variety of types in this profession, ranging from the ignorant, inspired peasant who puts up an altar near his little house and invokes the *loa* on behalf of his neighbors, to the grand *hungan* of the capital, cultivated in his own way, subtle and tinged with occultism, with a sanctuary full of artistic pretentions. Some priests enjoy a reputation which goes no further than the limit of their district, and others attract crowds of clients and are known all over the country.

Some *hungan* and *mambo* even cut a figure in the world of fashion. Their *humfo* is frequented by members of the *bourgeoisie* who are not afraid to rub shoulders with artisans and workmen. Some years ago a *mambo* of Croix-des-Bouquets who was getting ready to celebrate a grand ceremony for her guardian *loa* sent out printed invitation cards to her many relations in the town. The evening was a great success. An elegant gathering, which included several high-ranking members of the government, crushed into her peristyle. The *mambo* led them through the rooms of her sanctuary, replying graciously to the naïve questions which were put to her, and while the *hunsi* were possessed by perfectly mannered *loa*, she had refreshments served. Indeed, she was the perfect hostess, and the impresario of an exhibition which convinced the most prej-

udiced that Voodoo was obviously a wholesome and pic-
turesque entertainment.

All sorts of fantastic stories about the powers of *hungan*
may be heard. Atenaïse, a woman in Marbial who claimed
to be a *mambo*, often spoke to me about her grandfather,
a *hungan* well versed in all the lore of Africa who could
"change people into animals and, what is harder still, into
Guinea grass!" The power of remaining several days under
water is attributed to many *hungan* and *mambo*. Madame
Tisma, who was nonetheless a well-balanced and intelligent
woman, told me in the most normal tones that she had
spent three years at the bottom of a river where she had
received instruction from water spirits.

The gift most prized in a priest is second sight. To some
hungan it has brought fame which merely increased after
their deaths. A certain Nan Gommier acquired such a
reputation that even today a soothsayer will say as a boast:
"What I see for you, Antoine Nan Gommier himself
would not have seen." This *hungan* is reputed to have
known a long time in advance who was going to come and
consult him, and if it were a person of importance, he sent
a horse to meet him. With Nan Gommier questions and
explanations were superfluous. He read people's thoughts
and replied before being asked.

Voodoo adepts use the word "knowledge" (*connais-
sance*) to describe what we would define as "supernatural
insight and the power which is derived therefrom." It is
in degrees of "knowledge" that various *hungan* and *mambo*
differ from each other. In addition to this power, which
depends more or less on supernatural gifts, *hungan* and
mambo must also acquire a more technical kind of education: they must know the names of the spirits, their
attributes, their emblems, their various special tastes, and
the liturgies appropriate to the different kinds of ceremony. Only those who have mastered this lore deserve the
title *hungan* or *mambo*. To do so requires perseverance, a
good memory, musical aptitude, and a long experience of
ritual. A good *hungan* is at one and the same time priest,
healer, soothsayer, exorcizer, organizer of public entertain-
ments, and choirmaster. His functions are by no means
limited to the domain of the sacred. He is an influential

political guide, an electoral agent for whose co-operation
senators and deputies are prepared to pay handsomely.
Frequently his intelligence and reputation make him the
accepted counselor of the community. Those who frequent his *humfo* bring their troubles to him and discuss
with him their private affairs and work. He combines in
his person the functions of *curé*, mayor, and notary.
Material profit is not the only attraction of his profession:
the social position which goes with it is such as to interest
all who feel they have enough talent and application to
raise themselves above manual labor. To become a *hungan*
or *mambo* is to climb the social ladder and be guaranteed
a place in the public eye.

A psychological study of *hungan* and *mambo* would
perhaps reveal that most of them shared certain characteristics. My experience in this subject is not wide enough
to allow me to generalize. Many *hungan* whom I knew
seemed to me to be maladjusted or neurotic. Among them
were homosexuals—impressionable, capricious, oversensi-
tive, and prone to sudden transports of emotion. On the
other hand, Lorgina, with whom I had a long friendship,
was a perfectly normal woman. She did occasionally "go
off the deep end"—with the violence of a cyclone—but
she calmed down so quickly that these frightening outbursts never struck me as being completely sincere. Madame Andrée, another prominent *mambo*, was remarkable
only for her intelligence and cunning. In spite of her
peasant origin she became a complete bourgeoise in her
tastes and behavior. Of the *hungan* I knew, there was one
whose name I shall withhold who acquired a certain reputation among intellectual circles by his intelligence and by
his readiness to put himself at the disposal of anthropologists. He was rather a disturbing person, sickly, perhaps
a drug addict and gifted with a rather odd imagination.
To strengthen the effect of his services he made innovations which he subsequently justified by bold and naïve
theological speculation. Beneath a genial exterior he con-
cealed a morbid vanity and sensitivity. When I refused to
pay the costs of a ceremony which he had wanted to
organize in my honor, he revenged himself by inviting me
to his *humfo* to take part in a fete. Pretending to honor

and to doctor me, he in fact made me expiate my crime with all kinds of small cruelties.

Most of those who choose the profession of *hungan* or *mambo* do so at the impulse of a motive in which faith, ambition, love of power, and sheer cupidity are all inextricably mixed. Priestly vocation is nonetheless interpreted as a call from the supernatural world which cannot be disregarded with impunity. Suspicion and censure weigh heavily on those who are accused of having "bought" their patron spirits, for if they have indeed done this, then it is because the "good *loa*" rejected them as unworthy, and the mercenary *loa*, to whom they applied in despair, accepted them. Those who have done such a thing can only be *hungan* "working with both hands" (*travaillant des deux mains*)—that is to say, the kind of sorcerer known as *boko*. The amount of power put into the hands of a *hungan* lays him open to great temptations, though his profession—like that of medicine, with which it has much in common—has its ethic. Unhappily this is often violated. Have not certain *hungan* been accused of showing themselves to be in no hurry to cure their patients and even of aggravating an illness in order to make it more fruitful of fees? It has even been suggested that they get together with the sorcerers who have cast a spell on their client in order to learn the secret of the spell which caused the disease. The two accomplices then share the profits from the treatment. Against this kind of extortion the faithful are powerless or, more exactly, they have no other refuge than the moral sense of the *loa* themselves. Spirits do not like to see their help abused. Sometimes they punish the guilty *hungan* by withdrawing their patronage and depriving him of his "knowledge." Their punishment can even go as far as subjecting him to prison or to some other humiliation.

Spirits who have chosen a man (or a woman) as vessel for supernatural powers and have decided to keep him in their service make their will known to him either by the utterances of the possessed or by a symbolic dream. Before one man, Tullius, became a *hungan*, he often saw, in dreams, a gourd containing the beads and snake bones covering the sacred rattle (*asson*), symbol of the priestly profession. To say of someone that he (or she) has "taken the *asson*" means that person has become a *hungan* or *mambo*.

Anyone singled out by the *loa* could only avoid the summons at risk to himself. Some time after he had dreamed the dream which we have just mentioned, Tullius became seriously ill. He believed he had been struck down by the *mystères* who had grown tired of his inability to make up his mind. He felt all the more guilty since *loa* had announced, at his birth, by means of various miracles, that he was predestined to serve them: his mother, fleeing from a cyclone which had burst on the region, took refuge in a church and was there gripped by the first pangs of childbirth. She then distinctly heard the noise of drums and religious chanting: this was the sound of her guardian spirits Ogu-balindjo, Linglessu, and Mistress-Mambo-Nana, who were coming to her assistance. She had her baby in the porch, to the dismay of the *curé*, who would have liked to rush her to the hospital. Finally—another omen of an exceptional career—the baby came feet first.

The case of a famous *mambo* of Port-au-Prince, Madame L., affords another example of a person not daring to resist a supernatural vocation. She was a zealous Catholic, proud of belonging to the Société du Sacré-Coeur. She was covered with pious medals, and her certificate of baptism was framed on the wall of her parlor. In spite of her repugnance, the *loa* insisted on her becoming a *mambo*, and she gave way only because she was afraid of their "punishment." In return, they helped her to set herself up and contributed to the success of her treatments. They did not require her to give up her Christian duties, and that is why, on her altar, a prayer book stands cheek by jowl with the playing cards and rattle of the seer.

The call of the spirits is sometimes heard by people who seem in no condition to comply with them. I was told the extraordinary story of a peasant who became a Protestant after the death of his son: he wanted to get his own back on the *loa* who had disregarded his prayers. In fact, he bore them such hatred that he had sworn never again to have anything to do with them. Then, one evening, when he was returning from a gathering at the church, he met three mysterious beings on the road. He distinctly heard one of these say "No—it is not he . . ." whereupon he lost consciousness. A few days later, waking from a deep sleep, he found on his chest the emblems of a *hungan*: two "thunderstones" and the pack of cards of a soothsayer. Realizing his danger, he took the hint. He gave up Protestantism, went back to the bosom of the Catholic Church, and became a *hungan*. It is said that he brings about remarkable cures and that his predictions always come true.

The profession of *hungan* can be hereditary. Naturally a father likes to hand on the secrets of his art to his son, and train him to take his place. The mere fact that the sanctuary and the spirits which live in it form part of the inheritance entails a responsibility for the heir from which he can only escape with difficulty: on the one hand, the *loa* and the clientele of the *humfo* constitute a sort of capital which a family does not lightly give up, and on the other, the abandoned, famished spirits may turn on the person whose duty it is to feed them. The struggle which takes place in the soul of the man who finds the profession of *hungan* repugnant and who, in spite of this, is pushed into it by his family soon takes on the nature of a personal conflict with the ancestral *loa*. He feels they are threatening him. He attributes every illness, every disappointment to their hostility, and so, weakened by fear, he often gives in to what he imagines to be a supernatural appeal. Sometime the very opposite happens. A son wishes to succeed his father, but the spirits are against it and put every obstacle in his path.

Most candidates for the priesthood go through a course of instruction lasting several months or even several years with a *hungan* or *mambo* who wishes to take them on. They learn the technique of their profession by passing through all the "grades" of the Voodoo hierarchy, serving their master successively as *hunsi*, *hungenikon* (choirmaster), *la-place*, and *confiance*. The master's fame is reflected on his pupils, and these, when they become *mambo* or *hungan*, talk with pride of their apprenticeship.

Some priests say they got their education directly from the spirits. Among the *loa*, Ogu, Legba, Ayizan, and Simbi regard themselves as proper *hungan* and undertake the instruction of certain novices, selected by them. A man who has received his *asson* from the "mysteries" will pretend to be proud of it—in order to conceal a feeling of inferiority, for he who claims supernatural patronage has never had the advantage of a proper training and so tries to say as little as possible about his "knowledge." He is known as a *hungan-macoutte*, a name which bears a disparaging nuance. Similarly, it can happen that priests who want to make innovations in ritual without offending their terrestrial masters attribute the novelties to the fuller instructions which they say they have got from the *loa*.

The transmission of "knowledge" can be effected through a magic object. A *hungan* of Port-au-Prince, who had set himself up in Marbial, was gifted—so people said—with such extraordinary powers of second sight that he managed to amass a fortune which was estimated at more than 10,000 gourdes (i.e., $2,000). On his deathbed he gave his *soeur baptême* a piece of silk which he always wore around his waist. As soon as the girl girdled herself with it, she was possessed by a *loa*, and inherited, on the spot, her brother's gifts. She followed in his steps and became a *mambo*.

When a candidate to the priesthood has completed his apprenticeship, he must pass through an initiation which is surrounded by the greatest secrecy. The *hungan*-to-be is shut up in one of the sanctuary rooms for nine days. He lies on a straw mat with his *asson* by his side. His head rests on a stone under which a pack of cards has been placed. He may only sit up for a few minutes. His dreams during his confinement are extremely important: they are the means by which the gods—particularly the local ones—convey to him their instructions. The formal enthronement of the *hungan* is called "lifting" (*haussement*) because the main rite consists of raising the candidate three times in an armchair amid the cheering of all present. "Lifting" is also practiced whenever a community member achieves a new grade in the Voodoo hierarchy.

The gift of clairvoyance which earns a *hungan* the title of *divino* (seer) is obtained at the end of a special ceremony, "the gripping of the eyes" (*la prise des yeux*), which is looked upon as the highest degree of priestly initiation.

The Dignitaries of the Humfo

Initiates, men or women, who regularly take an active part in ceremonies and who help the priest in his functions are called *hunsi*, a word of Fon derivation meaning "the spouse of the god." Together they make up a little court around the *mambo* or *hungan* or, more exactly, a society sworn to the worship of the *loa* and made up usually of more women than men. Hence we shall speak of the *hunsi* as feminine, although the title is common to both sexes.

There are many different reasons which prompt people to belong to a society. They might join simply because they live in the neighborhood of a sanctuary or because a member of their family is already part of it. Others attach themselves to a priest (or a priestess) because they have been treated by him or simply because they admire his style or have a high opinion of his "knowledge." Equally a devotee might tend to visit a sanctuary where his own *loa* took precedence over others.

Hunsi who agree out of piety to serve the *loa* in some chosen sanctuary are tied down to many duties. They must be prepared to spend whole nights dancing and singing beneath a peristyle and to be possessed by spirits. A *hunsi* is committed, not only to offer sacrifices to the *loa* of the *humfo*, but also to devote herself to the humblest tasks, without hope of any reward beyond the friendship and protection of the *loa*, as well as living in dread of divine punishment should she prove negligent. The singing and dancing can be a satisfaction in themselves, but the same could scarcely be said of the down-to-earth chores such as cooking food for the *loa*, cleaning the peristyle, collecting and making ready the sacred objects—in short, fulfilling the role of "spouse of the god." Moreover, the *hunsi* can only do their job adequately if details of ritual are familiar to them. The initiation of the *kanzo*, during which they receive proper instruction, rounds off the religious training acquired by assiduous attendance at the *humfo*.

Zeal, devotion to the *hungan* or *mambo*, and obedience are the main qualities expected of a *hunsi*. She must be as deferential to the *mambo*, whom she calls *maman*, and to the *hungan*, whom she calls *papa*, as she would be to her own parents. The good name of a sanctuary depends much on the discipline and *esprit de corps* of its *hunsi*.

It is high praise to say of a *hungan* that he keeps his *hunsi* in good order; the negligence or lax behavior of a *hunsi* upsets the serious atmosphere which should obtain when *loa* are expected. Naturally the occasional mischief and inattentions of the *hunsi* are resented by *hungan* as personal slights. Lorgina, whom illness and old age had made suspicious and touchy, was always complaining of her *hunsi*. She found them idle, irresponsible, and, above all, *radi* (*hardi*—brash and disrespectful). When possessed by a severe *loa*, she seized the opportunity of lecturing and sometimes chasing them with a whip. Once I saw her beat an unfortunate *hunsi* in fury and then take her on her knee to comfort her. Of course *hunsi* punished like this could not complain, since it was the *loa* who had chastized them—without Lorgina knowing anything about it. . . .

The misbehavior of *hunsi* weighed on Tullius, too. One day, when he had got Guédé-*fatras* into his head, he lectured his *hunsi* at length on the theme of obedience and, to edify them, told the story of the young woman who, having been whipped for making some mistake in procedure, not only bore no grudge against her *maman*, but came and sang to her:

Salânyé onaivo	Salânyé onaivo
M'respèté hûngâ mwê	I respect my *hungan*
M'respèté mâmbô mwê	I respect my *mambo*.

For his part, the *hungan* has responsibilities toward the *hunsi*: he is their counselor and protector, and if they find themselves without means of support, through no fault of their own, he houses, feeds, and clothes them until he has found them a job. When they are ill, he looks after them as though they were members of his family.

The *hungan* unloads part of his responsibilities on the most devoted and zealous of his *hunsi*. She who is promoted to the rank of *hungenikon* or "queen chorister" (*reine-chanterelle*) is mistress of the choir during ceremonies. The standard of the liturgical singing depends upon her. It is she who, with arms dramatically uplifted, sings out in a full, strong voice the first notes of the hymns, and she who subsequently scolds and chivvies the *hunsi* if they sing feebly. Finally, it is she who, shaking her rattle (*chacha*), breaks the rhythm of the singing, which she wishes to stop. It is she also who identifies each *loa* as it appears, who chooses the songs to be sung in its honor, and stops them after the approved number of couplets or at the order of the *hungan*. During fetes the *hungenikon* work themselves silly night after night, all night long, never sparing themselves and without even seeking the relaxation and rest which is to be found in the dizziness of trance. For a *hungenikon*, no less than a drummer, must remain in possession of her faculties and attend to what is happening; otherwise chaos would bring the ceremony to an end.

The head storekeeper, also called the *hungenikon*-quartermaster, is a man or woman appointed to be in charge of the offerings. The *la-place*—abbreviation of the commander-in-chief of the city (*commandant général de la place*)—is the master of ceremonies. His emblem is a saber or a matchet with which he juggles in an elegant manner. He marches in front of all processions and controls their movements. He is also responsible for keeping order during ceremonies. Last of all the personages of importance, we must mention the confidant (*le confiance*) —the right-hand man of the *hungan* and the "beast of burden" or major-domo who takes care of the administrative chores of a *humfo*.

The staff of a *humfo*—*hunsi*, *hungenikon*, *la-place*, *drummers*, etc., as well as people who have been treated there—*pititt-feuilles* (small leaves)—or who have become regular attendants—*pititt-caye* (children of the house)— make up what is known as the "*humfo* society." This sometimes assumes the character of a mutual-assistance association. The "support society" (*société soutien*) is not always the same as the *humfo* society, although it would be difficult to draw a boundary between them. As its name suggests, the *société soutien*, by means of its subscriptions, helps toward the maintenance of the *humfo*, defends its interests if they are threatened, and helps the *hungan* to organize the "big feastings of the gods" which he is bound to give. These societies have been most aptly compared to the parish councils of the Catholic Church. Hence the *hungan* try and stiffen them with influential politicians or prosperous tradesmen, whose moral or financial support could be of use.

Associations like these, which grow up around a *humfo*, are often modeled on the co-operative work groups which are to be found everywhere in the Haitian countryside. They comprise a whole hierarchy of dignitaries whose rolling titles flatter the vanity of the members. The "ranks" are conferred in the course of a "lifting" ceremony, and they turn the little groups into a parody of the State—with a President, a full-fledged Minister, Secretary of State, Senators and Deputies, Generals, Government Commissioners, etc. Women are not left out of this generous distribution of titles and lofty functions. There are the "flag-queens" (*reines drapeaux*), the "silence queens" (*reines silence*) whose job it is to enforce complete silence during ceremonies, the "empresses of Dahomean youth," the "directing ladies," and even the *agaceuses*, who incite people to drink. The *humfo* society itself always has some fine name like Gold Coast, God First, Polar Star, Who Guides, The Flower of Guinea Society, Remembrance Society, etc., which is written up proudly on the façade of the main *caye-mystère*.

Certain priests do without a society. They content themselves with the appointment of a *père-soutien* or *mère-soutien* to whom they apply in times of financial emergency. The only compensation available to the bearer of such a title—and such a burden—is the honor of "keeping up" the *humfo*.

¶ Possession

Relationships Between Spirits and Men

The explanation of mystic trance given by disciples of Voodoo is simple: a *loa* moves into the head of an individual having first driven out "the good big angel" (*gros bon ange*)—one of the two souls that everyone carries in himself. This eviction of the soul is responsible for the tremblings and convulsions which characterize the opening stages of trance. Once the good angel has gone, the person possessed experiences a feeling of total emptiness as though he were fainting. His head whirls, the calves of his legs tremble; he now becomes not only the vessel, but also the instrument of the god. From now on it is the god's personality and not his own which is expressed in his bearing and words. The play of his features, his gestures, and even the tone of his voice all reflect the temperament and character of the god who has descended upon him. The relationship between the *loa* and the man seized is compared to that which joins a rider to his horse. That is why a *loa* is spoken of as "mounting" or "saddling" his *chual* (horse). Possession being closely linked with dancing, it is also thought of in terms of a spirit "dancing in the head of his horse." It is also an invasion of the body by a supernatural spirit; hence the often used expression: "the *loa* is seizing his horse."

The symptoms of the opening phase of trance are clearly psychopathological. They conform exactly, in their main features, to the stock clinical conception of hysteria. People possessed start by giving an impression of having lost control of their motor system. Shaken by spasmodic convulsions, they pitch forward, as though projected by a spring, turn frantically around and around, stiffen and stay still with body bent forward, sway, stagger, save themselves, again lose balance, only to fall finally in a state of semiconsciousness. Sometimes such attacks are sudden, sometimes they are heralded by preliminary signs: a vacant or anguished expression, mild tremblings, panting breath, or drops of sweat on the brow; the face becomes tense or suffering.

In certain cases trance is preceded by a sleepy condition. The possessed cannot keep his eyes open and seems overcome with a vague languor. This does not last long: it suddenly gives place to a rough awakening accompanied by convulsive movements.

This preliminary phase can soon end. People who are used to possession pass quickly through the whole range of nervous symptoms. They quake, stagger, make a few mechanical movements, and then, suddenly—there they are: in full trance. Even as much preamble as this may be dispensed with when a ceremony is in full swing and demands instantaneous entries on the part of the gods.

The intensity of this crisis varies according to the character of the spirit who is seeking incarnation. The great and terrible *loa* rush into their fleshly envelope with the violence of a hurricane. Those of a gentler nature spare their mount. The nervous attack also varies with the ritualistic status of the possessed: the less experienced he is, the more he will throw himself about. As long as his head has not been washed—that is to say, as long as his *loa* has not been formally installed in his head—he behaves wildly. His chaotic leaps and gestures are like the bucking of a wild horse who feels the weight of a rider on his back. Is not initiation the breaking-in which prepares the faithful as mounts for the deities? The horse which at first rears becomes accustomed to its master and at last scarcely moves when ridden and guided by an invisible hand. Such metaphors are not out of place in a system which continually makes use of equestrian terminology.

The possessed are protected from the possible effects of their own frenzy by the crowd which surrounds them. They are prevented from struggling too furiously and if they fall, arms are ready to catch them. Even their modesty is shielded: a woman rolling on the ground, convulsed, is followed by other women, who see to the disorders of her dress. This sympathetic concern on the part of the crowd for the gambols of the possessed certainly provides an atmosphere of moral and physical security which is conducive to total abandon in the state of trance.

Sometimes—though not often, it is true—the person possessed seems unable to come out of his stupor. I remember one woman, seized by the *loa* Agassu, who remained a long time on her back with eyes closed, her arms flung out like a cross. She might have been thought to have fainted, had she not thrown her head from side to side and had her body not been subject to mild spasms gradually reaching her shoulders, which she shook rhythmically. With great difficulty she managed to kneel. She then opened her eyes: they were fixed and estranged. She kissed the earth and got up with the heavy movements of a person weighed down by pain. Like a sleepwalker she went and kissed the *poteau-mitan*. Tears rolled down her cheeks. Losing balance, she fell to the ground, where she resumed her previous position. The *hungan*, rushing up to her, alternately cajoled and entreated her gently. She wiped her tears, got up, and went and sat on a seat where she remained motionless, her face fixed in a sad, farouche stare.

A person emerging from trance remembers nothing of what he did or said while possessed. Even if the trance seemed obviously "put on," he will deny it categorically. No possessed person is supposed to know that he has been the receptacle for a spirit, unless he has learned as much from someone else. Many, when informed, seem to disbelieve the account of their words and actions. A woman whose dress had been torn while she was in trance came and asked me the reason for the damage, by which she was much vexed. Her pained surprise radiated good faith.

Such amnesia, or more exactly reserve, does not embrace the initial stages of trance. Some informants say that before darkness engulfs their brain, they feel pins and needles in their legs or a strange heaviness which glues their feet to the earth. Some compare the first inrush of the spirit to a blow on the nape of the neck. Then all sense of time vanishes.

Possession may last any time; and sometimes, when the subject is what is known as "saoulé," that is to say, slightly dazed, it only lasts a few seconds. This state of drunkenness results from any contact with a spirit or a sacred object. Thus, a possessed person may cause mild intoxication in others if he spins them around as a gesture of courtesy. The priest who carries the necklaces of the *hunsi* staggers as if overcome by the sacred energy contained in these ornaments. It is then said that they have been brushed by the *loa* whom for a moment they approached.

With some people trance lasts several hours or even whole days. I was told of a woman who was ridden by Ezili for fifteen days in succession. Throughout this time she wore the clothes of the goddess and remained powdered and made-up. From time to time the goddess gave up her seat on her *chual* to her friend the Siren. A person visited by a *loa* for as long as this usually experiences difficulty in sustaining the condition of trance. Oversights and omissions betray his weariness and obscure the personality of the god incarnate in him. Unless warned, a visitor may fail to realize the situation and so address the possessed as though he were in his normal condition. The unrecognized *loa* then takes offense and scolds. To avoid such confusion, *loa* usually have the good grace to withdraw their essence if their minions forget to establish their identity for them. Mistakes of this kind are more excusable when a god deserts his "horse" in mid-conversation. A visitor imagines he is talking to a god . . . and finds himself face to face with a man or woman, who listens gaping with astonishment.

Such mix-ups are rare. Uusually signs of fatigue in the subject give clear indication that trance is ending. He loses momentum, and if he does not collapse in a corner, he falls semiconscious on the knees of spectators. Motionless and dazed for a few minutes, he at last opens his eyes and looks around him with the astonished air of a person waking in unfamiliar surroundings. Often out of respect for the departing god, the face of his "horse," during this phase, is covered with a cloth.

Once the acute stage of the crisis has passed, the footwear, necklaces, rings, hairpins—in short, any form of dress or adornment that could get broken or lost, or might put the *loa* off and so "stop" him—are removed. When a subject has difficulty in mastering his convulsions, a priest goes up to him and soothes him by shaking his rattle softly, close to his ear. Sometimes, too, if the subject is rolling on the ground, the officiating priest will keep him still by straddling and gripping him.

The frenzy of the *criseur* wears off gradually. Suddenly a new person takes shape: it is the god. At once his attributes are brought to him—hat, sword, stick, bottle, cigars—or if he has to be dressed up, he is escorted to one of the sanctuary rooms used as a dressing room. The spirits, whatever their sex, incarnate themselves in men or women as they please. Subjects must indicate by dress, or simply manner, whatever change of sex may have taken place in them. In the chapter devoted to mythology we tried to characterize the principal *loa* by the dress or behavior of their "horses." We must here take the liberty of referring the reader to those descriptions. But let it not be forgotten that such impersonation is achieved with degrees of success which vary according to the imagination or resources of the *hungan* or the *mambo* concerned.

The appearance of a *grand loa* is greeted by a special rhythm called *aux champs* (flourish): singers, men and women alike, burst out with redoubled enthusiasm. The god is fanned and his face is wiped free of sweat. If he is one of the accredited guardian spirits of the sanctuary, he is given an escort with banners in front. Such adulation does not exempt him from observing strict Voodoo procedure. Admittedly the "ground is kissed" in front of him— but he, in his turn, prostrates himself before the resident priest or priestess, before the drums and before the *poteau-mitan*. Usually he dispenses small favors among the on-lookers—clasping both hands of some rather roughly, anointing the faces of others with his sweat, or shaking their clothes to bring them luck. He lifts in his arms those whom he wishes to favor, or he wriggles between their open legs. He is expected to effect cures, so he must touch the sick and improvise treatment. This can miscarry —as when a man possessed by Agwé tried to cure Lorgina of rheumatism . . . and bit her cruelly in the leg.

The possessed—or, to be more precise, the gods— prophesy, threaten sinners, and gladly give advice. What is more, they give advice to themselves, for often a *loa* will ask the spectators to tell his "horse" to behave differently or follow his advice. These messages are faithfully transmitted to the person concerned as soon as he is in a fit state to receive them.

A description of one of the many possessions which I witnessed will give a clearer picture of this essential aspect of Voodoo than any amount of general observations. The following passage is from notes taken on the spot. "The *hunsi*, with red cloths around their heads and colored dresses, dance in honor of Ogu. At the very first dance, *mambo* Lorgina is possessed by this god. In spite of her age, her infirmities, and her weight, she dances nimbly in front of the drums, hands on hips, shaking her shoulders in time to the music. She then fetches a saber and jams the hilt of it against the *poteau-mitan* and the point against her stomach. Now, by pushing with all her strength, she bends the blade. She repeats this dangerous practice, this time basing the hilt on the post's concrete plinth. A *hungan* sprays rum from his mouth on to her stomach and rubs her legs. Lorgina, in a sudden frenzy, fences with the *la-place*, he, too, being armed with a saber. The ceremonial duel degenerates into a real fight, so that spectators, fearing an accident, have to intervene. Lorgina is then seized by another wave of bellicose frenzy. She hacks the *poteau-mitan* with her saber and chases the *hunsi* who flee in terror. She is on the point of catching them when prevented by the shafts of the sacred flags which two women cross in her path. At once she becomes calm— and thus will it always be whenever Lorgina-Ogu gives way to an attack of rage. A priest comes up to talk to her, keeping prudently in the safety zone of the banners. The *mambo* winds up by going back to the *hunsi*, whom she beats violently with the flat of her saber; and this outlet has a soothing effect upon her. Suddenly all smiles, she salutes everyone present and overflows with politeness in every direction. She has a cigar brought to her which she smokes in a nonchalant way. Then she gives orders that the meat safe hanging on the *poteau-mitan* should be placed before her. She eats heartily and distributes what is left among the *hunsi*. She calls up a trembling and excited little girl whom she has already spanked hard with the flat of her sword: she gives her a long lecture on her future behavior and foretells a terrible fate for her unless she takes the warning to heart. Having forced the little girl to prostrate herself before her, Lorgina—still in the tones of Ogu—lectures her *hunsi*, giving them detailed advice on dress. Then, speaking of herself in the third person, she boasts of her own labors, and tells how she managed to save up to build the sanctuary. The *hunsi* listen with respect. Shortly afterward the god leaves the *mambo*, who then returns to herself.

A *hunsi* is possessed. She begins by tottering and then flounders doubled-up, strikes her forehead, and twists her arms. Very gradually, almost insensibly, her movements fall into rhythm, become more supple, more harmonious until they can only be distinguished from those of the other dancers by a nervous quickness. She comes out of the trance by imperceptible stages.

Two young girls are possessed by Ogu-balindjo. At the mere sight of this event Lorgina bursts out laughing and with a pretence of impatience chases them from the peristyle. The two women jump into the pool, where they romp like children. They come back streaming, and the public greets them with gibes and laughter. Proud of their

success, they return several times for a bath. Finally
Lorgina orders them back into the sanctuary where they
will be given a change of clothes, since, says she, "the
horses of Ogu must not catch cold."

Every possession has a theatrical aspect. This is at once
apparent in the general concern for disguise. Sanctuary
rooms serve to a certain extent as the wings of a stage
where the possessed can find all the accessories they need.
Unlike a hysteric who shows his own misery and desires by
means of a symptom—which is an entirely personal form
of expression—the man who is ritually possessed must
correspond to the traditional conception of some mythical
personage. The hysterics of long ago who thought themselves the victims of devils also certainly drew the devilish
part of their personality from the folklore in which they
lived, but they were subject to influences not entirely comparable to those felt by the possessed in Haiti.

Adepts of Voodoo make a very clear distinction between
possession by *loa*, which is sought after and desired, and
possession by evil spirits, which is frightening and morbid.
In Voodoo there is nothing comparable to the dialogues
between the two personalities of the demoniac. With the
ritually possessed, consciousness is entirely obliterated, at
least in appearance, and the individual obeys the *loa*—
perinde ac cadaver. As soon as he has chosen the personality which the folklore mystique suggests to him, or, to
speak in Voodoo terms, as soon as the *loa* has, at his own
wish, or in response to a call, descended into him, the
subject fulfills his role by drawing upon the knowledge
and memories which have accumulated in the course of a
life frequenting cult congregations. The amount left to
his own whim will be governed by his relations with other
people. He can be benevolent if he wishes, or, on the
contrary, he can be angry with certain people; but he
cannot alter the characteristics or the appearance of the
divine personage he incarnates. Some, in the eyes of spectators, succeed better than others in representing such and
such a god. That is why you hear in Voodoo circles statements such as "You should see her when she's got Ezili
in her head."

Similarities of this kind, between possession and the
theater, must not obscure the fact that in the eyes of the

public a possessed person is never really an actor. He does not play a character part; he *is* the character as long as the trance lasts.

And yet, what else can it be called except "theater" when the possessed turn the simultaneous manifestation of several gods in different people into an organized "impromptu"? These impromptus, which vary in style, are much appreciated by the audience, who yell with laughter, join in the dialogue, and noisily show their pleasure or discontent. Take an example: someone possessed by Zaka appears under the peristyle in the get-up of a peasant. By canny movements he mimes the anxiety of a countryman come to town, and who fears to be robbed. Now another possessed person joins him, one might almost say "comes on." It is Guédé-*nibo*, of the Guédé family, which watches over the dead. Zaka is clearly terrified by the presence of his gloomy colleague and tries to propitiate him, inviting him to have something to eat and to drink some rum. Guédé, who is making a show as a townsman, exchanges courtesies with him, trying to tease him. He asks him: "What have you got in your bag?" He searches it and examines the contents. Alarmed, Zaka cries "Stop, stop." The bag is returned to him only to be surreptitiously lifted off him while he is examining one of the sick. Zaka, in despair, calls for cards and shells in order to discover the thief by means of divination. The audience chants: "Play, Zaka, play." Zaka: "I have come to complain about Agau-*wèdo*." "Play, cousin Zaka, play." The objects he has called for are brought.

Several people are suddenly possessed by Zaka and provoke what in Haiti is so aptly termed "a scandal" (*youn escandale*). One of them accuses a woman of having stolen certain objects which had been left in her keeping. Protests from the woman—screams, temper, and backbiting. It is Zaka who is at last accused of thieving. He has not got an easy conscience and is on edge whenever anyone goes anywhere near his precious bag.

The following anecdote is also indicative of the theatrical nature of possession. During Voodoo ceremonies each divinity is honored in turn by three dances accompanied by songs; the order of the dances is laid down and cannot very well be changed. During one of them, consecrated to

Ogu, a priest was suddenly seized with a *loa*. At first it was thought to be the expected god. So there was general astonishment when it turned out to be Guédé, making a premature appearance. A priest addressed him and asked him kindly to go away and come when it was his turn. Guédé refused and demanded his paraphernalia. Priests and other dignitaries returned to the attack. From prayers they passed to threats. Guédé laughed at them. Weary of strife, they sent for his clothes. He proceeded to dance gaily, took the liberty of a few farcical jokes, and then collapsed on a chair. The possession was finished. Returning to his senses, the possessed was disconcerted to hear songs and drum beats which in no way corresponded with the normal order of events. He became angry and sharply reproached the *hunsi* for this breach of discipline. It was in vain they told him the only person to blame for the deviation was Guédé, who had possessed him. He would not hear of it. In fact he had his work cut out insisting, as do all people possessed, that he knew nothing of what had taken place.

Some of the possessed have a considerable repertory of tricks. Their talent is particularly evident when they are possessed several times in succession and have to change their identity without intervening pause. They can, like a *hungan* I saw one evening, become successively Ogu-balindjo, a shrill god who sprinkles his head with well water, and then on the spur of the moment turn into Guédé-*fatras* and carry out an acrobatic dance which in its turn gives place to transformation into Petit-Pierre— a gluttonous and quarrelsome spirit who, to the joy of the gallery, tries to pick a quarrel with the audience. Another time it was a woman who, prey to the goddess Veleketé, racked her body into strange shapes with her tongue hanging out and her neck twisted. She had managed to distort her body in the most terrible manner when suddenly she stopped incarnating the hideous Veleketé and became a blithe and frolicsome divinity.

Whenever a depressing atmosphere develops as a result of the violence of possessions, then Guédé appears, puckish and obscene. He sits on girls' knees and pretends to be about to rape them. The congregation revels in this sort of fun and laughs heartily.

Ritual trances pose a fundamental problem: are they genuine dissociations of the personality, comparable to those found in certain cases of hysteria, or are they entirely simulated—merely part of the traditional cult and obedient to ritualistic imperative? To put it differently, when a man becomes the vehicle of a god, has he lost all sense of reality, or is he simply an actor speaking a part? This question can only be answered by firmly establishing the basic data relevant to the problem. First and foremost it is essential to realize the part played by possession within the social and religious system which has attached so much importance to it.

Trance usually occurs during religious ceremonies, private as well as public. Spirits must take part in the homage which is paid to them and must themselves receive the sacrifices offered. Their appearance is expected and takes place at the desired moment. When the feast is being celebrated in a private sanctuary, the spirits only "enter into" the members of the family. If a stranger went into a trance, it would be thought bad taste and he would be asked to remove himself. As a general rule, it is the same people who are visited by the same spirits each year. Possessions are as arranged as the details of family "services."

But when a public sanctuary organizes a dance or a grand ceremony, possessions are not restricted to office-holders of the cult, *mambo, hungan,* and *hunsi.* Many spectators, mere visitors, are abruptly picked upon by a god and for a few moments take part in the dances and rites.

The confusion caused in the smooth working of a ceremony by successive possessions is more apparent than real. Only very seldom is the arrangement of worship disturbed by *epiphanies.* The main rites are always accompanied by possessions, since it is desirable and even necessary that the main *loa* concerned should take part in them. They usually go into the person officiating and also into the man or woman who is paying for the ceremony. In showing themselves, they give an earnest of their goodwill and guarantee the efficacy of the ceremony. If the gods kept away, it would be a sign of their indifference, or worse, hostility. When a present is brought for the *loa,* the priest, who will be the only real beneficiary, is careful not to thank the donor. Marks of divine gratitude will be shown later during a feast when the god incarnates himself in the priest or some other person.

Collective possessions take place without fail whenever in the course of a ceremony the crowd gets worked up by some spectacular effect such as the leaping flames of alcohol burned in honor of Ogu, or when the *zin* (sacred pots), coated with oil, suddenly catch fire, or when small charges of powder are detonated to greet a god. Moreover, some connection may be noted between possessions and certain drum rhythms: the musicians seem to be capable of inducing trance by redoubling their effort. They themselves, then, seem subject to delirium; though they are seldom genuinely "mounted." *Hungan,* too, know how to overcome the resistance which certain people put up against the god. They dance in front of them, staring at them all the time and making certain gestures which seem to have the suggestive power of hypnotic passes. On the other hand, people who are subject to "attacks" of possession but who, for one reason or another, do not wish to give in to them make use of various magic procedures to "moor" the god where he is. Sometimes they do their hair in a certain way or sometimes they carry in a corner of their headcloth some ingredient effective against an attack of *loa,* such as wax. Spirits who have been "moored" can do no more than make a person "tipsy"; their passage is quick and has only a moderately inebriating effect. To avoid being mounted, a person can also remain seated with arms crossed and wearing a forbidding cast of countenance.

Possessions also occur in ordinary daily life. In fact, it is in lay surroundings that the psychological function of possession becomes clear. Trance sometimes amounts to an escape mechanism in the face of suffering, or simply fatigue. Dr. Louis Mars witnessed an attack of *loa* which took place in someone undergoing an operation; it broke out at the very moment when the pain was at its sharpest. On another occasion he saw two people became possessed just after a motor-bus accident in which they had been involved.

People who have to make some exceptional effort sometimes ask a spirit to help them—in other words, they hope their task will be made easier if attempted in a state of trance. Stories are told of shipwrecked sailors who were able to reach land thanks to the god Agwé entering into them. In the course of a pilgrimage to the Balan cave, in the neighborhood of Port-au-Prince, *mambo* Lorgina, who was moving over stony ground slowly because of rheumatism, was suddenly possessed by Legba: instead of limping and pausing every few seconds, as she had been till then, she went on her way with a resolute step and without apparent weariness. Apart from this sudden access of energy the possession had no other effect upon her.

It was freely said in Port-au-Prince that the dancers who had taken part in a dance marathon were all "mounted by a *loa*." *Hungan* and *mambo* who had "doped" them as an inoculation against the nostrums of their rivals took care that their possessed condition was not too apparent. But the malicious and uncontrollable Guédé could not contain themselves. In the very middle of the competition the nasal voice of a Guédé cried out: "*Sé mwê Papa Gédé —mwê fò*" ("It's me, Papa Guédé, I'm strong.")

The characteristics of a *loa* can be very useful to the person in whom they are temporarily vested. A thief who has Damballah within him can slide through the narrowest openings like a snake. He can also climb with the utmost speed, and even if he falls from the top of a telegraph pole, he suffers no ill effects because "nothing is impossible for a person possessed by a *loa*."

Trance does indeed make strange exploits possible. Mme Mennesson-Rigaud witnessed the most appalling gluttony on the part of the *loa* Guédé-*cinq-jours-malheureux* (Guédé Five Days Unhappy), who had revealed himself at the end of a big *manger-loa* (food offering for the spirits). Dragging himself along on his knees and elbows, he moved among the offerings, all of which he gobbled, only pausing to distribute occasional handfuls to the children. Having returned to his normal state, the possessed complained of hunger and asked for food. He was given a plateful which he cleaned up as though he had an empty stomach.

Trance can provide a person with a means of escape from an unpleasant situation. One of the ordeals of initiation obliges novices to beg in public places. Some are ashamed to do so. They ask the *hungan* to call down a spirit into them. Once possessed, they need not feel embarrassed, since it is not they but the *loa* who stretches out his palm.

The individual in a state of trance is in no way responsible for his deeds or words. He has ceased to exist as a person. Someone possessed can express with impunity thoughts which he would hesitate to utter aloud in normal circumstances. It is an observed fact that the possessed hold opinions or give free rein to aggression which can only be explained by repressed grudges. Their indiscretion is sometimes shocking and throws the whole crowd into a flutter. People show their disapproval and implore the god to shut up. Possession in this respect has much in common with drunkenness in America, which often excuses outbursts of frankness in the same way.

The state of possession gives weight to advice which a priest, or anyone else, wishes to give the congregation. How often have I seen *mambo* Lorgina transformed into one of the mighty *loa*, scolding her *hunsi* or exhorting them to be obedient and grateful to the good Lorgina.

Certain *hungan* hide behind their *loa*, protesting to their clientele that it is not they who care for and counsel them, but the spirits of which they are merely the servants. Lorgina attributed the success of her medical treatments to Brisé, the "master of her *humfo*." Possession allows a spirit to take the place of his "horse" and assume his functions. Some *loa* have a liking for the profession of *hungan* and incarnate themselves in those who are officiating in order to control the ceremony in their place. This was done, it seems, by Guédé-Achille-*piquant*, who finished up by being regarded as the true master of the *humfo* of a certain Dieudonné, who, not being a *hungan*, always performed the offices with this *loa* in his head.

Possessions sometimes occur in the middle of the market at Port-au-Prince. A prospective buyer may suddenly perceive that the woman behind her stall is saying the most preposterous things to him in a nasal tone. He need not be surprised. It is Guédé who is "riding" her and indulging in a bout of frankness, just to cheer everyone up.

Some possessions satisfy obscure cravings which have a masochistic tendency. The possessed, in fact, sometimes hurls himself to the ground as though flung there by some power greater than himself, or bangs his head against a wall. In certain exceptional cases, rare it is true, women have ripped up or burned expensive clothes. These acts are interpreted as punishments for some ritual fault which the "horse" has committed. The vengeance of a *loa* can also take other forms, scarcely less cruel. He will come down into his "horse" in the middle of church, at the Elevation of the Host, and so cause a distressing scandal.

Loa who wish to humiliate their "horses" put them in a dangerous or ridiculous position or abandon them suddenly, to such effect that the person possessed, becoming aware of and pained at his plight, suffers for it. M. Marcelin told me that during one ceremony a woman was possessed by Damballah and climbed up a tree where she prepared to hang by the legs from a bough which might have broken beneath her weight. The congregation became frightened and did not know what to do. An old woman traced out a *vévé* in the middle of which she put some sweetened water and an egg. She then sang: "Damballah-*wèdo* everyone is perfectly happy. It's you who are in a bad temper. If you see Damballah, give him a caress from me." When she saw the offering, the possessed woman came down from the tree, drank the water, swallowed the egg, and immediately returned to her normal state.

Last but not least of the functions of possession is the pleasure which it gives to poor souls ground down by life. They are able, by virtue of such a mechanism, to become the center of attention and play the part of a supernatural being, feared and respected. Histrionics and exhibitionism undoubtedly do play a large part in the phenomenon of possession, just as they do in the case of genuine hysterics.

Voodoo adepts say that spirits prefer to come down into people who resemble them. In other words, there would seem to be a correlation between the character of the god and that of the devotee who represents him. Gentle people are inhabited by calm and friendly gods, while the violent harbor fiery and brutal spirits. It is true that the practice of Haiti, unlike that of Dahomey and Brazil, allows one person to be "ridden" by several different divinities. The analogy of a *loa* and his "horse" should only be applied therefore to the *loa-tête*—that is to say, to the spirit who first possessed the subject and became his official protector. Not uncommonly, however, devotees are possessed by *loa* whose character is the very opposite of their own. Trance, then, acts as a form of compensation.

This last aspect of trance suggested a Freudian interpretation to Professor R. Bastide. In his view, possession allowed the repressed personality to come to the surface in a symbolic form "in a jovial, festive atmosphere without any of the sinister colouring which Freud gives it." It was "a confessional which was played not spoken, a physically active cure—based on the muscular exaltation of dance instead of on a horizontal, disguised couch, in clinical half-darkness." The comparison is slightly forced and attributes too much to individual pressures, when very often trance is a ritualistic reflex. We are also entitled to ask just what are the repressed drives which a person "exteriorizes" through the medium of trance. Apart from the cases mentioned above, a subject's behavior is rigorously laid down by tradition, and far from expressing *himself*, the possessed tries to personify some mythological being whose character on the whole is foreign to him. Most of the possessed apparently get nothing more out of their condition than does an actor who lives his part and gains applause. And the approval of the congregation is measured merely by the amount of attention it devotes to his words and actions.

Too often people imagine that a crowd exalted by mystic enthusiasm is the usual setting for Voodoo possessions. In fact, those who attend ceremonies as spectators only cast an occasional absent-minded glance at the goings-on. They gossip on the edges of the peristyle, smoke cigarettes, or nibble at *tablettes* (pralines). At no time is the crowd subject to collective delirium, or even to a degree of excitement propitious to ecstasy. The traditional dances of Voodoo—*yanvalou, doba, Dahomey, petro* —all carried out with great seriousness, a subtle sense of rhythm, and admirable suppleness, are far from being Dionysian. Only at certain ceremonial moments does the degree of excitement reach enthusiasm.

Ritual possessions are often attributed to nervous disorders of a hysterical nature. Twenty-odd years ago Herskovits

had already refuted that explanation by drawing attention
to the stylized and controlled nature of the phenomenon
and its frequency in a society in which it was the normal
means of communicating with supernatural powers. The
number of people subject to possession is too large for all
of them to be labeled hysterics, unless the whole population of Haiti is to be regarded as prone to mental disorders.

If trance is suited to an innate disposition in Haitians,
then we may well wonder what mutation can account for
the fact that the same faculty has disappeared from regions
with the same ethnical composition, but where African
religious tradition has either disappeared or been preserved less faithfully.

Possession could hardly be explained entirely in terms
of psychopathology. Such an explanation is probably only
valid for a limited number of people who are unquestion-
ably true neurotics, people subject to what has been called
dissociation of the personality. Is hysterical anaesthesia to
account for the impressive performance of those men and
women who, while inhabited by a god, handle red-hot
bars of iron without apparent discomfort? In ceremonies
which I attended the possessed brandished plenty of *pinces*
(bars of iron) reddened in fire, but they contrived to hold
them by the very end. The *hunsi* who danced in the fire
jumped prudently on logs which the flames had spared. All
the same, I have no reason to doubt the word of those
who have seen the possessed grasp red-hot bars with wide-
open hands. It is difficult for me to give an opinion of
feats such as may be found in other religious manifestations, and among sects which practice an extreme form of
asceticism. As for those Haitians who, while in trance,
munch glass—their performance is of the same order as
that of our own traveling showmen. According to Voodoo
logic, the "horse" should not suffer for actions initiated
by the god on his back.

Apart from chaotic preliminaries, there is in most cases
of possession a theatrical element which unavoidably suggests a certain amount of simulation or at least of inten-
tional delusion. We are entitled to doubt the authenticity
of possessions which come, so to speak, on request the
moment ritual requires. The loss of consciousness, without
which, from an absolute standpoint, there can be no pos-

session, is at most partial with many subjects, if not actually nonexistent. Take the woman who, when wearing a new dress, is possessed by Damballah. She avoids throwing herself on the ground in case she spoils it, although the serpent god normally requires his "horse" to wriggle along the ground. Take the person who refers to events or matters which she could only know about if she has remained in full possession of her memory. Take another, finally, who too obviously uses his divine immunity to give vent to his spite or his greed. How often, when talking to someone posssessed, I have learned that the god I was hoping to meet is none other than himself! More than one person posssessed has been guilty of such give-aways and lapses. Here are a few examples: one day Lorgina, who was supposed to be possessed by Brisé, nevertheless begged for help from this very *loa* and praised him just as if she were merely his "servant" and not Brisé himself. Her attitude would have made sense if the god had in fact left her, without warning, and without anyone noticing; but Lorgina then sprinkled her speech with oaths—of which Brisé is prodigal—and this showed that she had forgotten her role and, becoming aware of it, was trying to recoup.

Organizing the details of a fete, which I wished to offer Guédé, I found the *mambo* and her acolytes, who were allegedly possessed by Guédé, became only too human when the question of money arose. Once the discussion was over and agreement reached, they again remembered their roles and behaved like true Guédé. I remember one possessed who completely forgot she had a god inside her the moment I gave her news of a woman from her own village.

Thanks to imperceptible signs, it is sometimes possible to foresee when a person intends to fall into a trance. When I was on the sailing boat which was taking me back from the Islets where we had been sacrificing Agwé-taroyo, a *hunsi* asked me to jump into the water. Feeling that she was going to be possessed, I replied that I thought it wiser to stay with her and prevent her from jumping into the sea should a marine god suddenly visit her. I had scarcely finished speaking when she closed her eyes and began breathing heavily. Two men seized her, but she managed to break free and threw herself writhing into the lowest part of the boat. There it was possible to over-power her. She grew calm and of her own accord went and lay down on a mat. She had been possessed by Agau, who is a "diving" god, which explains the efforts made to keep her from the side. The insistence with which this woman pressed me to jump into the sea suggests that even then she was intending to identify herself with Agau.

The obviously stylized behavior of people possessed does not in itself allow one to be sure whether the origin of possession is voluntary or not. Only very rarely you see a subject genuinely fight against trance and be overcome in spite of himself. I remember seeing a well-dressed woman in a crowd which was admiring the dances of people pos-sessed by Simbi. She was certainly a member of the Port-au-Prince *petite bourgeoisie*. She seemed ill at ease and was looking at the dancer with an abstracted expression. Suddenly she shut her eyes, and her face contracted as though she were in pain. She began to sweat profusely; her shoulders and arms became stiff. In a few moments she was shaking all over and then was violently convulsed. The *hungan* came to where she was swaying, quicker and quicker, from side to side on her chair. From his closed fist he stuck out a thumb and pressed it into her forehead as though he was driving in a peg. With face still convulsed she close her eyes as tight as she could, but in less than a minute her trembling came to an end. She looked round about her and her sweating eased off. She seemed relaxed and remained seated as though nothing had happened.

Song, or, more often, drumming, has an undeniable effect on certain subjects. The *hungan* Tullius, during an audition in Paris, was listening to the tape recording of a ceremony which he had himself conducted, when he was suddenly seized with dizziness at the exact moment when he had been possessed during the "live" recording. There and then, dancing on a Parisian stage, he was properly "ridden" by the god Damballah, much to the annoyance of his colleagues.

That possessions can occur during ceremonies which formally rule them out affords another proof of the sugges-tive nature of the phenomenon. One evening, during the rites which celebrate the seclusion of initiates—rites from which gods are carefully kept away—three people showed signs of possession. Two calmed down of their own accord, but the third had to have his forehead pressed by the *mambo* before he returned to his senses.

The preliminary crisis has a contagious effect, particularly upon people who are nervous and unstable. That is why the sight of a possession often has the effect of provoking others, not only among the *hunsi* who are ready to be ridden by the gods, but also among the spectators who have come as visitors or out of curiosity. In Voodoo circles, among the masses, a nervous crisis is not regarded as cause for shame or even anxiety. There is nothing mysterious or abnormal about it; on the contrary—it is a mark of divine favor. It would seem that those who have once been affected by and given in to suggestion become gradually more and more likely to succumb to trance. Their crisis, which is at first incoherent, ends by attaining the stylized behavior which I have tried to describe.

Among the apparently stylized possessions which are presumably spontaneous, it is impossible to distinguish between those initiated by psychic infection and those which reflect a private impulse on the part of the subject. We may well wonder whether the convulsive and trembling phase may not be for many—I was on the point of saying for most—devotees of Voodoo, a sort of physical technique which induces the "delusion" of divine possession. This of course is merely hypothetical, yet is it not possible that such a simulation of a nervous attack might actually assist the evacuation of the real personality in favor of a borrowed personality? Might not the exaltation and dizziness consequent upon such frenzied agitation create a mental climate propitious to a certain amount of auto-suggestion? If this were so, then possession would engulf the senses in the wake of the heralding symptoms.

When watching some of the possessed, it is tempting to compare them to a child who is pretending to be, perhaps, an Indian or an animal, and who helps the flight of his fantasy by means of a garment or an object.

Adults are the accomplices of this waking dream by supplying helpful disguise. The possessed then move in an atmosphere which is even more propitious than that of the child: the public does not *pretend* to believe in the reality of their play, it does believe in it sincerely. Among the poorer people and even in certain circles of the Haiti *bourgeoisie* the existence of *loa* and their incarnations are articles of faith. Anyone possessed shares this conviction. Having undergone or simulated a nervous crisis, his state of tension is such that it is not so easy for him to distinguish between his own self and the person he has been representing. He plays his part in good faith, attributing it to the will of a spirit who got inside him in some mysterious fashion. In short, it would seem that merely for a person to believe himself possessed is enough to induce in him the behavior of a person possessed—and that without any intention of trickery. Filliozat compares possession to a "suggested state" and explains it as "a momentary forgetting either of intentions based on normal activities, or of any real sensation of one's actual condition," all of which results in a person "acting against his normal will or believing himself to be in some other state than the actual one."

The "forgetting" of the possessed is not always a piece of crude mystification. For a person to admit that he remembers what he has said or done as a god is to admit that he was not genuinely possessed—it being impossible to be oneself and a *loa* at the same time. Better convince himself that he has forgotten everything than admit that he pulled the wool over the eyes of everyone present, and of the divinity, too. Whoever puts himself into a trance must keep up the pretense right through to the end. To simulate possession does not necessarily imply a skeptical attitude. The *hungan* Tullius, whose possessions were often "done" to oblige, was haunted by fear of the *loa* and took very seriously—even tragically—the threats and warnings which he received from the mouths of other people possessed.

The state of possession can be explained, therefore, by the extremely religious climate which obtains in Voodoo circles. The ubiquity of the *loa* and their incarnations are the object of beliefs so profound and so unquestioned that possessions are received with less fuss than the arrival of a friend. If a woman rolls on the ground or writhes, the spectators merely say "she has a *loa*." This faith is contagious: it is shared by part of the Haitian clergy who naturally see in this phenomenon the work of the devil. A few cultured Whites accept possession as a supernatural manifestation and take an interest in Voodoo which borders on faith. The frequenting of sanctuaries demands from the detached and polite observer the use of expressions which in fact amount to an acceptance, by him, of the authenticity of possession. Indeed, it is impossible to mention the behavior of someone possessed without attributing it to the god who has gone into him. It would be improper to make the "horse" responsible for the actions or utterances of his invisible rider.

The following story gives an idea of the conviction to be found among the possessed themselves. A young woman "ridden" by the goddess Ezili had danced during a ceremony with a young man to whom she afterward accorded her favors. While still in a state of trance, she gave the young man a hundred dollars—all her savings. In this she conformed to the generous nature of the goddess. Next day, no doubt regretting her gesture, she pretended she had been robbed and would not accept the explanation of her friends—who said simply that she had no memory at all of what really happened. She brought an action against the young man. When the judge was informed of the circumstances he ordered the young man to give the money back; but the girl was at once seized with fear and refused to accept it. She was rightly afraid of going back on the divinity who had guided her while she was supposed to be unconscious.

¶ Voodoo and Christianity

"To serve the *loa* you have to be a Catholic . . ." These words—of a Marbial peasant—deserve to stand as epigraph to this chapter, for they express very precisely the paradoxical ties between Voodoo and Christianity. The peasant who sacrifices to the *loa*, who is possessed by them, who every Saturday answers the call of the drums, does not believe (or did not believe fifteen years ago) that he is behaving like a pagan and offending the Church. On the contrary—he likes to think of himself as a good Catholic and contributes to the salary of his *curé* without hesitation. This "idolater" would be wretched if he were excluded from the Communion or if he were forbidden to marry or baptize his children in church. Not always for truly Catholic reasons does he adhere to such rites, but because he attributes magic virtues to them and fears that if he were deprived of them, he would lose his respectability. Even while scrupulously observing Catholic rites, the Haitian peasant has remained little touched by the spirit and doctrine of Catholicism; chiefly out of ignorance, since such religious instruction as he may have received is rudimentary, to say the least. He knows little of the life of Jesus or those of the saints. Besides, he feels more at ease with gods and spirits which maintain friendly or hostile relationships with him, in the same way as he does with neighbors. Voodoo is for him a familiar personal religion, whereas Catholicism often shares the cold nature of the cement chapels which crown the crests of the hills. Once when I asked a fervent Catholic whether he had finally finished with Voodoo, he replied that he would always be faithful to the Catholic Church, but nothing could make him give up the worship of *loa* who had always protected his family. The *hunsi* of Lorgina saw nothing wrong in attending Mass after dancing all night for the *loa*. It takes a white man's mentality to be shocked that a *hungan* or *mambo* can march beside a *curé* at the head of a procession without a trace of shame.

The equivocal reputation which Voodoo has acquired is in fact due to just this very syncretic quality by which it mixes together, in almost equal proportions, African rites and Christian observances. All who have concerned themselves with Voodoo have been pleased to list the many things it has borrowed from Catholicism. The clergy has denounced these same things as so many abominations, but no systematic attempt has been made to define, with any precision, the connection between these disparate elements or the way in which they integrate themselves in the whole system of Voodoo religious values. In other words, no one has raised the question of whether the Voodooist ranks the beliefs which he holds from his African ancestors on the same level as those he has derived from the Whites. An example usually cited of the fusion of the two cults is the identification of African gods and spirits with Catholic saints. Authors drawing up lists of *loa* have taken care to mention only the saints which correspond with the most important of the spirits, and have never tried to pin down how this phenomenon works, or establish its real significance. This was a mistake, for in most cases there has been no real assimilation or common identity. The equivalence of gods and saints only exists in so far as the Voodooist has used pictures of saints to represent his own gods.

The walls of *humfo* and sanctuary living rooms are plastered with posters printed in Germany, Czechoslovakia, Italy, or Cuba showing various saints equipped with their attributes or in the act of living some key episode of their legend. Merely by being pinned up in a place sacred to the cult of Voodoo, these personages lose their identity as Catholic saints and become *loa*. But this mutation does not happen in an arbitrary way. It proceeds from some resemblance, in certain particulars, of the picture to the conception which the Voodooists have formed of their *loa* and his attributes.

Often it has needed a mere detail—to our eyes an unimportant one, though important in the context of Voodoo mythology—for a poster to be selected as a representation of this or that African divinity. For instance, the snakes chased out of Ireland, which are seen at the feet of St. Patrick, have suggested a link between him and Damballah-*wèdo*, the snake god. In the same way, Our Lady of the Sorrows has come to represent Ezili-Freda-Dahomey because the jewelry with which she is decked and the sword transpiercing her heart evoke the riches and love which are the attributes of the Voodoo goddess. Saint Jacques le Majeur, James the elder, who is shown as a knight encased in steel, has naturally been identified with Ogu-*feraille*, the blacksmith and warrior god. On the same poster the person armed from head to foot is for some Ogu-*badagri*, for others one of the Guédé because of his lowered vizor, which vaguely recalls the sling put under the chins of corpses.

The cases of common identity which we have just given are, in the apt phrase of Michel Leiris, "concrete puns." The same poster can represent different *loa*, according to whatever detail may have struck the attention of the faithful, or, reciprocally, the same *loa* can be represented by several different pictures. Thus the name of Legba is applied not only to Saint Lazarus but also to Saint Anthony the Hermit, who in Catholic iconography is traditionally shown as an old man. Agwé, the great sea god, has for long been borrowing the traits of Saint Ulrich because on one poster the latter is shown with a fish in his hand. In the war years, when this picture became rare, it was replaced by that of Saint Amboise. Certain pictures which are completely unreligious in character have been put to the same use. Thus sometimes in a *humfo*, among the sacred pictures you come upon a poster depicting the sad fate of a debauche—a caved-in young man in evening dress. On account of his dark clothes and rather sinister expression he has sometimes been taken for Baron-Samedi or some other member of the Guédé family.

The Catholic clergy seem at first to have had no inkling that the holy pictures and crosses which they were required to bless were to be used as idols. Finally the truth dawned on them. During the antisuperstition campaign, which we will discuss later, the *curés* felt no qualm of conscience when they burned every picture they could lay their hands on in sanctuary rooms—although these were the same pictures as were being put up in Catholic churches and chapels for the adoration of the devout. In a report written a few years ago Monseigneur X denounced the abuse by Voodooists of sacred pictures. "They worship the pictures of the saints and one might say no saint in the calendar is excepted from this attention unless it be those whose likenesses have not been imported into the country. In the people's minds the picture they worship does not represent a saint at all—but the pagan divinity which they have substituted for him and which, from then on, constitutes the identity of that particular picture."

Although we cannot really talk of a true assimilation of *loa* to Catholic saints, it remains nonetheless true that Voodooists have not failed to notice analogies between their respective functions. When they wish to defend or explain their beliefs, they like to lump *loa* and saints together and say: "All the saints are *loa*, which is not to say all *loa* are saints." In the north of Haiti *loa* are called "saints," which certainly underlines the homology. All the same, even if the two groups do resemble each other in exercising similar powers, they still stand apart and belong to two entirely different religious systems. Whereas all *loa* reveal themselves in possessions, no one to my knowledge was ever possessed by a saint. In the same way *loa* do not borrow the attributes and characters of the saints to whom they are supposed to correspond. It is, as we have seen, the other way about: the saint, stripped of his own personality, takes on that of the *loa*.

The difference in origin of saints and *loa* is explained in a myth which I picked up in Port-au-Prince. "When He had created the earth and the animals in it, God sent down twelve apostles. Unfortunately they behaved too stiffly and powerfully. In their pride they ended by rebelling against God. He, as a punishment, sent them to Africa where they multiplied. It is they and their descendants who, as *loa*, help their servants and comfort them when they are unhappy. One of the apostles who refused to leave for Guinea [Africa] gave himself up to sorcery and took the name of Lucifer.

"Later God sent twelve more apostles who this time behaved like dutiful sons and preached the gospel. They and their descendants are what we call the saints of the Church."

One of those who provided Simpson with information explained to him that because God is too busy to listen to the prayers of men, *loa* and saints have fallen into the habit of meeting each other halfway between Heaven and earth. There the *loa* inform the saints of the wishes of the faithful. The saints then transmit the requests to God, who grants them or not, as He chooses.

The assimilation of *loa* and saints is very much more superficial in Voodoo than it is in the Afro-American cults of Brazil. The one and only example of a Catholic saint being substituted for an African god in Voodoo is given us by Herskovits *a propos* St. John the Baptist, who, in the north of Haiti, has taken the place of Sogbo and Shango in the role of storm god. In this context there is a story which, under a Christian exterior, still savors of Africa. "On a given day of the year God permits each saint to have control over the universe. St. John the Baptist, however is so irresponsible, and his rage so violent, that God fears the consequences if he were allowed to exert his power on his day. By plying him with drink the day before, he is therefore made so drunk that when he falls asleep he does not awaken for five days. When he is told his day has already passed, his rage is so terrible that great storms flay the earth, and it is a commonplace in Mirebalais that this day is marked by thunder and lightning storms of almost hurricane proportions. Though he can do some damage, his power is now limited, however, to his own sphere."

Saint Expedit, once included in the Catholic calendar thanks to a pun, has now in Haiti become a great sorcerer —thanks to another pun.

Then again, the title "saint" is sometimes used to express animist representations which are not out of place in Voodoo. On certain occasions, rare it is true, prayers are addressed to "Saint Earth," "Saint Thunder," "Saint Sun" (identified also as Saint Nicholas), and to "Saint Moon."

Voodoo ritual has borrowed heavily from Catholic liturgy: it is customary for most services to *loa* to be preceded by thanksgiving (*action de grâce*). Standing in the middle of their *hunsi* before an altar covered with candles, under a panoply of lace decorated with pictures of saints, priest or priestess recites Paters, Confiteors, and Ave Marias followed by hymns to the Virgin and to the saints. The famous "African prayer" (*prière Guinin*) which opens the most solemn ceremonies begins with Catholic prayers and interminable invocations of saints: the *loa* are only summoned afterward. In giving a Catholic *cachet* to ceremonies which are not Catholic, Voodooists are in no way trying to pull the wool over the eyes of authorities or Church: rather is it that they are in fact convinced of the efficacy of Catholic liturgy and therefore wish their own religion to benefit from it. The singing, prayers, and kneelings, which precede a service, are said to "stir the *loa* up": in other words, help to attract their benevolent attentions.

Voodoo has also appropriated the use of holy water, with which its devotees are sprinkled from a leafy branch. Father Labat, at the end of the seventeenth century, had already noticed that slave converts used it for magical ends. "All the Christian Negroes have a great devotion to, and a lively faith in blessed bread and holy water. They always carry blessed bread about with them. They eat it when they are ill or when they fear some danger. As for holy water—whatever quantity may be prepared on Sunday morning for High Mass, seldom a drop is left by the end of the service; they take it away in little calabashes and drink a few drops standing up, thinking they will thus guard themselves against any spell that may be cast upon them. However hard I tried I was unable to discover who had inspired them with this faith: even the elders and most reasonable among them could say no more than that they learnt it from their fathers and handed it down from one to another and found it good."

The profanation of the Host is one of the most serious charges which the clergy have lodged against the devotees of Voodoo. "One of the most painful revelations," wrote Monseigneur X, in the memorandum quoted above, "was that people were often sent to the Holy Table to steal the Host. To obey a *bokor* people are prepared to submit to any conditions, pay any price, undergo any ordeal: they had to get their Holy Communion. But the catechism which they have been taught has changed nothing in their hearts. It is a formula required of them by the priest and which must therefore be learnt." The bishop is, however, wrong not to make clear that it is only the magicians who feel the need to procure the Host—for themselves. No Voodooist, unless he is a sorcerer, would think of committing such a sacrilege.

The symbiosis of Catholicism and Voodoo has resulted in a very close parallelism between their respective calendars. *Loa* feasts often coincide with those of the saints who have been identified with them: the day of Kings is kept for ceremonies in honor of the Congo *loa*; throughout Lent, Voodoo sanctuaries are shut and no service is celebrated in them; sometimes even—in Holy Week—cult accessories, such as pitchers containing spirits, *loa* stones, emblems of gods, are covered over with a sheet, as are the images in Catholic churches; at All-Hallows the Guédé spirits of the dead overrun the countryside and towns, clad in black and mauve, and people possessed by them may be met not only in the sanctuaries but also in the markets, public places, and on the roads. Christmas night is the moment when Voodoo ritual takes wing, as it were, in its full plumage.

Catholic clergy finally came to realize that some of the patron saints' days were attended by many more Voodooists than true Catholics. The grand pilgrimage of Saut-d'eau and Ville-Bonheur, which was started fairly recently, gives us a classic instance of syncretism. The Tombe River, having crossed a green and laughing plain, hurls itself in one leap into the void. All the mysterious charm of tropical forests which have today disappeared survives in that dense grove where the falls gleam like jewels, darkly cased. An iridescent mist crossed by tiny rainbows rises from the foaming water, bedews the ferns, and blurs the luxuriant foliage of the giant trees, whose roots break the moist ground into humps and valleys. This oasis of coolness is the home of Damballah-*wèdo*, Grande-Bossine, and other aquatic deities. Toward the middle of July it is invaded by thousands of pilgrims from all parts of the Republic. As soon as they reach the foot of the cascade, they merge their prayers and hymns with its level roar; and they hasten to expose their bodies to the violence of the healing, saving water. They roll about, frolic, and feel at the same time excited, happy, and a little afraid to be in the vicinity of spirits. From time to time a bather shaken by tremblings staggers like a man drunk; his neighbors hold him up so that he shall not sink into the deep pool which the waters have worn away. It is one of the spirits of the falls, usually Damballah-*wèdo*, who has "mounted" him. The possessed man reaches the bank, flickering his tongue, eyes upturned, and making the characteristic "*tétététété*" of the god. The pilgrims crowd around him, speak respectfully to him, squeeze his hand, and ask those small favors which the *loa* dispense among those they love.

A huge fig tree which rears up beside the falls is the resting place of Damballah. Among its roots the pilgrims put little candles and attach their bodies to its branches with strands of wool. Some take pinches of earth from around the tree and store them away in a handkerchief.

The aquatic gods of Saut-d'eau are no longer the only masters of the river. Today they share their domain with Saint John and the Virgin. Notre Dame du Carmel appeared on top of a palm tree in a little sacred wood, not far from Ville-Bonheur and some few miles from the falls, and from then on the palm also became an object of devotion for the pilgrims and cured the sick who came in their hundreds to petition Notre Dame du Carmel. A zealous *curé*, scenting idolatry, had the miraculous tree cut down.

Then, when he found the faithful merely transferred their veneration to the roots, he had these torn out. But the Virgin punished him for his sacrilege, for, I was told, he soon lost both his legs in an accident. Faced with the persistence of devotees who, having bathed in the falls, came to pray to the Virgin and Saint John, the clergy made the sacred wood an official place of pilgrimage. On the eve of the Festival of the Virgin of Saut-d'eau, brightly painted charabancs bring devotees into the center of Ville-Bonheur. They spend the night in the grove lit by thousands of candles. The bush priests recite prayers; herb doctors rub the hands of the sick with oil from the lamps which have burned in front of the sacred trees, and with the water of springs in which medicinal plants have been left to soak.

In the town many peasants make merry, dance to the sound of jazz orchestras, and exchange spicy sallies with the prostitutes, of whom there is always an influx. Penitents sport their motley costumes and distribute food to the poor, hoping by this act of Christian charity to appease the *loa* whom they have offended.

On the actual day of the fete an enormous crowd crushes around the church built in honor of the Virgin. Those who cannot enter accumulate outside. After the service the statue of the Virgin is tied to the front of a truck and taken around the main square followed by a publicity car blaring out hymns to the Virgin through a loudspeaker. The crowds of faithful who at dawn bathed in the waterfall of the aquatic spirits watch her go by with their hands lifted in adoration and their faces transfigured.

The Church must certainly have tolerated many of these "popular superstitions" in the hope of eliminating them slowly, without violence or outrage. In 1,500 years it has surely acquired some experience in the art of transforming practices and beliefs which could not be supplanted at once. Yet in Voodoo the clergy found themselves faced with a different problem, which was formulated very concisely by the bishop just mentioned. "It is not we who have got hold of people to christianize them, but they who have been making superstitions out of us." This veritable seizure of Catholicism by Voodoo is nowhere better illustrated than in the sacrilegious use it makes of the Holy Sacraments.

Since the Colonial period the Haitian peasants have attached great importance to baptism. Moreau de Saint-Méry had already pointed this out. "Since the Creole Negroes who have been baptized pretend, on this account, to a great superiority over those newly arrived from Africa, whom they call *bossals* [a name used throughout Spanish America], then the African Negroes, who are also slightingly referred to as "horses," hasten to get baptized. At certain days such as Holy Saturday and Whit-Saturday, when adults are baptized, the Negroes turn up at the church and too often without any sort of preparation and no concern for anything but the provision of a godmother or godfather who are sometimes allotted to them on the spot, they receive the first Christian sacrament and thus guarantee themselves immunity from the insults addressed to the non-baptized: although in the eyes of the Creole Negroes, they remain always those who were 'baptized standing up.'"

The haste shown by these slaves in getting baptized cannot be entirely explained by their desire to become assimilated to the Negroes born in Saint-Domingue. Other writers tell us they tried to get themselves baptized several times over. This zeal, whatever people may say, was not based on hope of small presents, but sprang from magico-religious motives. At the first treaty between the runaway slaves of the west, and the French authorities of Saint-Domingue, it was laid down that the rebels who had waged guerrilla warfare for eighty years in the woods should be allowed to go and get baptized at Neybe and that they should retain the liberty they had won with their blood.

Baptism has been adopted by Voodoo as a consecration rite. Not only are men baptized, but also *loa* and all objects used in the cult. The ceremony is celebrated with a degree of solemnity which varies according to whether the object baptized is a sanctuary, drums, necklaces, clothing, or any other object—but it is always carried out in conformity with Catholic liturgy. The officiant recites prayers, sprinkles the object with holy water, and gives it a name chosen by a godmother and a godfather, who remain beside it and who afterward call each other jokingly *commère* and *compère*.

Catholic communion is considered by certain Voodoo priests as a sacrament which increases their powers; sometimes they recommend it to their clients. Even further: some *loa* are regarded as Catholics and by virtue of this fact must communicate from time to time. This is notably the case with Damballah-*wèdo*; when the god feels the need to approach the Holy Table, he tells one of his servants, who then prepares himself, as a good Christian, to take the sacrament, and when the day comes, putting a stone sacred to Damballah in his pocket, he goes and kneels before the altar; at the very moment of taking communion he is possessed by Damballah, who communicates in his place. A woman of Jacmel who was more or less a Voodooist told me that one Sunday during Mass she noticed signs of strange excitement in one of her neighbors. She watched her and realized that she had Damballah in her head. This woman went up to communicate, and it was only at the moment when she got back to her place that she frankly abandoned herself to trance. While she was being removed from the church, the *loa* inside her kept calling out: "They were saying I couldn't communicate: well, I have."

The marriage sacrament serves to unite a human being with a *loa*, thus assuring the former the protection and favor of the latter. In order to obtain forgiveness from an offended *loa*, Voodooists also practice various forms of external, typically medieval, Catholic penitence. The penitents, usually women, wear garments made of gray, so-called siamese, cloth or a kind of harlequin dress made of bits and pieces which correspond in color to the various different *loa*; the clothes must be blessed by the bush priest. Having sung a Mass, burned some candles, and said prayers to the saints, the penitents offer their friends and relations a grand farewell feast. Then they go out, all over the countryside, visiting in turn all the main places of pilgrimage—Saut-d'eau, Vierge du Mont Carmel, Alta Grecia, Saint Dominique—and live on public charity and on the food distributions which certain pious people dole out to acquit themselves of debts to *loa* or saints. They frequent the markets where they are sure to get a few sous and at least some fruit and vegetables. When they think that by their suffering and weariness they have expiated their sin in the eyes of their protecting *loa*, they go home and resume their normal life.

At Marbial market I met a penitent who said she had incurred the wrath of the *loa* Champagne-*miofré*, of the Ogu family. This divinity had inflicted various illnesses upon her, but, fearing worse, she was trying to placate him with the spectacle of a painful and wandering life. She devoted part of the alms she received to the saying of Masses for the dead.

Some devotees, on orders from a *hungan*, take food to people in prison, who in Haiti are usually very poorly fed. Others give food to the poor, not in any spirit of Christian charity, but to obtain the favor of a *loa*.

Voodoo borrows from Catholicism unevenly: whereas the main elements of the liturgy have been indissolubly mixed in with ritual of African origin, the sacraments and funeral rites have not been similarly absorbed. Only partially integrated with Voodoo, and occupying a rather marginal position, they stand outside the competence of *hungan* and *mambo* and fall within the province of the *pères-savane*, who have become, to a certain extent, established as the official representatives of the Catholic Church in the bosom of paganism. They are entrusted with the conduct of all rites—baptisms, communions, marriages with *loa*, funerals—all of which should, if it were possible, be celebrated by a *curé*. These personages are catechists or sacristans on the loose—men who know how to pray and sing in Latin and French with the correct gestures and intonation. They are called in whenever a Voodoo ceremony has to include a Catholic intermediary. Often it is they who carry out the thanksgiving which precedes the invocation of *loa*—the latter being always the responsibility of a Voodoo priest.

All the *pères-savane* I knew seemed to me good-for-nothings who took their functions very lightly. It is hardly surprising. Are they not marginal people who, having learned to despise the beliefs of their brothers, have yet failed to become good Christians? I was somewhat surprised that their off-handedness and buffoonery shocked no one. In actual fact the Catholic sacraments and liturgy incorporated in Voodoo lose part of the religious significance which they have in their rightful context, in a proper church. Voodooists therefore draw a very clear distinction between sacrament administered by a *curé* and the more or less faithful imitation as practiced by the *pères-savane*. How can Voodoo communion be taken seriously when you see the absent-minded and amused way in which the servants of the gods kneel down before the bush priest, who crams into their gaping mouths crustless lumps of bread soaked in wine?

In other words, we are here faced with a counterfeit which easily explains the indifference and even the irreverence of the participants. Sometimes the bush priests and the devotees overdo it: then parody turns to farce. Proof of this lies in the "catechism of the Guédé," which would doubtless be regarded as sacrilege by the Voodooists themselves if they thought it was their own doing; but since it is the Guédé themselves who are fooling, then nobody need be shocked: everyone knows that the spirits of the dead are roguish and rather obscene. I witnessed this game or play—as you please—at the conclusion of a fete which I had offered in honor of the Guédé. A goat had been sacrificed to them with all the usual circumstance, and the sacrificial meal had put them in a good mood. Most of the *hunsi*, possessed by various Guédé, were dancing with gusto, rolling their bottoms and behaving like so many clowns. Suddenly the drums stopped, and a *hungan*, himself possessed, ordered the Guédé to form up in one rank. He told them he was going to make them undergo an exam. Stationing himself before the leader of the file, he intoned the first question of the catechism. "Are you a Christian?" The Guédé questioned assumed an idiotic expression, crooked his knees, and bleated: "I am a Christian—yes," firmly emphasizing the "yes." The examiner went on. "What is a Christian?" to which, still in the same tones, the Guédé gave the first response of the catechism. Questions and answers followed until the moment the possessed man, affecting an ever more stupid manner, finished by singing in an urgent, pressing rhythm a song which described coitus in the crudest terms possible. The *hungan* heard him out with enjoyment, congratulated the candidate, and awarded him the rank of "colonel of the Haitian armed forces," a promotion which was greeted by shouts of joy and capering. The examiner passed to another Guédé, who distinguished himself by his understanding of the catechism and the *brio* with which he sang an obscene couplet—a feat which earned him the rank of general. Each Guédé in turn received some prestigious title borrowed from the military, ecclesiastical, or political hierarchies. A fat girl with a jolly nature was proclaimed "pope." At the announcement of this high distinction the "popess" let out roars of triumph and, despite her size, skipped about like a little girl whose success in school has gone to her head.

We would be wrong to look upon this burlesque interlude as a sacrilege. The *hunsi* possessed by the Guédé put no malice into their performance. They amused themselves just as did our ancestors, who, however devout, saw no harm in taking off the rites and sacred personages for whom, in another time and place, they showed the greatest respect. The *curés* of those days, more tolerant than the *curés* of Haiti, knew what was not important and cast no anathema on games which, when all is said and done, were quite harmless.

The Attitude of the Catholic Church to Voodoo

The Church is, to a certain extent, responsible for the survival of African cults in Haiti. In the eighteenth century the instruction of slaves in the religion to which they had been compulsorily admitted by sprinklings of holy water was entirely neglected. Priests who wished to convert the Blacks came up against the indifference, or more often the hostility, of owners who cared little if their beasts of burden, were or were not, dignified with the status of Christians. Then the struggles for independence and the civil wars which followed each other, practically throughout the whole of the nineteenth century, were scarcely propitious to the diffusion of Christianity. The Concordat of 1860, still in force, provided a formula which was acceptable to national pride but which was to prove obstructive to the establishment of Catholicism. What the Haitian country districts needed were not *curés* working parishes organized on the pattern of those in France, but missionaries who would have taught the masses and fought idolatry. Even today, when schools are beginning to multiply and peasants are no longer cut off in the mountains, I have heard *curés* say their task should have been approached in the spirit of mission work. Most Catholic priests in Haiti come from Brittany, where there is a seminary specially to train them. When they find themselves confronted, not by good Catholics who dabble in a few harmless superstitions, but by parishioners who are visited by—and maintain familiar relationships with—spirits, they feel bewildered and helpless. Neither the milieu in which they have lived nor their training fits them to face up to such a state of affairs. Far from pitying the ignorance and credulity of their flock, most of them, whether they are French or Haitian, look upon Voodoo as the work of the devil—a demonic manifestation against which they must fight with every means at the Church's disposal. In this context one *curé* said to me: "Judging by what I have seen with my own eyes, I have to admit that the *loa* are very real beings. Is it not true that there is a devil? The people of this country are truly possessed by the Fiend, for it is by our prayers that we manage to deliver them. Before going into a seminary, I witnessed many strange happenings. For instance, a woman bending a bar of iron made red hot. Do you suppose such a thing would be possible without supernatural intervention? Was she not possessed by the devil?"

The catechisms used in the country districts give a clear picture of the clergy's attitude toward Voodoo:

31. Who is the principal slave of Satan?—the principal slave of Satan is the *hungan*.

32. What are the names given by *hungan* to Satan? —The names given to Satan by *hungan* are *loa*, angels, saints, *morts*, *marassa*.

33. Why do *hungan* give Satan the names of angels, saints, and *morts*?—*Hungan* call Satan after saints, angels, and *morts* in order to deceive us more easily.

34. How do men serve Satan?—In sinning, casting spells, practicing magic, giving food offerings, *manger les anges, manger marassa* . . .

37. Are we allowed to mingle with the slaves of Satan?—No, because they are evil doers; like Satan himself, they are liars.

Even more precise is this definition, copied into a manuscript catechism which was going about the Marbial Valley. "A *loa* is a wicked angel who revolted against God and for that reason is in Hell."

The only divergence of opinion between the pastors and their flock on this point turns on the very different character which they attribute to supernatural beings. To those who tell them the *loa* are so many minor "satans," they reply that since God created them, *loa* can hardly be bad, and that anyhow there is no shortage of proof of their goodwill and compassion. It is true certain spirits are prepared to help wicked people and make themselves feared for their violence and cruelty, but they alone deserve the name of *diab*: nice people have nothing to do with them, and their victims should try and appease them, without, however, stooping to crime. No more than man does God approve the carry-on of "bad *loa*" and "bought *loa*" employed by sorcerers to further their evil designs.

In 1941, given a strong hand by the more or less open support of the government, the clergy determined to intensify its campaign against the outer manifestations of Voodoo and to bring the peasantry as quickly as possible to an undiluted form of Catholicism.

The first official attempt on the part of the Church to combat Voodoo dates back to 1896. The Bishop of Cap Haitien, Monseigneur Kersuzan, launched against "superstition" a campaign of conferences, gatherings, and sermons which resulted in the creation of the "League against Voodoo," an organization which in the parishes was to work through the *curés*—but the success of this league was apparently moderate. In a synodical address, Monseigneur Kersuzan complained of not being supported by the authorities, although the President himself had assured him of his support. He added: "In certain places even intelligent and educated people are siding with fetishism and this is leading the common folk astray."

In the same breath as he denounced the evils of Voodoo, Monseigneur Kersuzan threatened Voodooists with serious sanctions. Those who took part in a ceremony were deprived of the right to communicate, *hungan* and *mambo* could not become godfathers or godmothers, and for their absolution they had to go to the diocesan bishop. In 1913 the Episcopate returned to the attack. The "monstrous mixture" became the target of a collective pastoral letter.

These first skirmishes resulted in very little and were quickly forgotten. The real battle between the Church and Voodoo was only joined in 1939, during the presidency of Elie Lescot. Monseigneur X tells us the campaign was set off by "the discovery, in truly providential circumstances, of the existence of the 'mixture' [le mélange] and above all by the discovery that this abomination was not only the way of one isolated person but the current practice of the whole body of converts."

The tardiness of this "discovery" shows a fine indifference on the part of the Haitian clergy to all that had been written about Voodoo long before it became aware of the existence of this abominable mélange. Perhaps they can scarcely be blamed for having ignored the brilliant study which Melville J. Herskovits devoted to the interpenetration of African and Catholic cults in his book In a Haitian Valley, but it is impossible not to be amazed by their blindness when one thinks of the daily opportunity of country curés to become acquainted with Voodoo belief and practice.

The "discovery" referred to by Monseigneur X thus hardened the will of the clergy to combat the paganism of their flocks at all costs. The extremely vigorous campaign which it was to undertake to root out Voodoo had, as its precursor, a man of the people called Ti-Jules (whose real name was St. Giles-St. Pierre) who lived in the neighborhood of Trou d'Eau near Hinche. Like all Haitian peasants, he was a convinced Voodooist. Three of his children being ill, he took them to a hungan. At first he strictly adhered to whatever the healer prescribed: his house became full of "knotted strings," "indigo crosses" had been painted everywhere, and he gave his children "ill-smelling baths" (basins sentis) to turn away from them the fury of the wicked spirits. However, he was experiencing certain scruples in preferring all this magical cookery to the protection of Almighty God. One morning, rising from prayer, he suddenly began to destroy and throw away, not only what the hungan had introduced to his house, but all that the hungan had ever touched; tables, chairs, plates, cups—all was sacrificed to his virtuous indignation. To his dejected family he explained: "We must rid ourselves of every trace of Satan so that God will take care of us." The subsequent recovery of his children confirmed him in his rebellion against the *loa*. He became a lay preacher and began exhorting his neighbors to serve God "without mixture." A vision soon gave his mission divine sanction: he saw two "*péres*" who came into his hut with radiant faces, made him sit down, and told him in the name of God he must "guide people from magic and put them on the true path." They explained to him the truths and the prayers he must teach to all who came in search of him, and the means of giving up the *loa*.

News of this miracle spread, and a great many people came in search of Ti-Jules to learn how to serve God "without mixture." He made them kneel, crossed himself, and, having made them say a few prayers such as the Credo and Confiteor, asked them to destroy their sanctuaries and cut down their sacred trees (*arbres reposoirs*). He then made them repeat a text in which, as repentant Voodooists, they renounced all service of *loa*. This ended with the phrase: "*Ak pitit ak travo, m'détaché, m'ataché, m'rénôsé*" ("With my children with my work, I detach myself, I attach myself, I recant").

Those who declared their intention of renouncing, from then on had to fulfill their religious duties punctiliously, get married if they lived in sin, and avoid all contact with Voodoo.

Ti-Jules's success was so great that thousands of peasants of Artibonite and the north went as pilgrims to Trou d'Eau and returned home changed beings. Ti-Jules was soon to know the fate of all prophets. His neighbors, jealous of his ascendancy, and offended in their beliefs and traditions, denounced him to the *curé* as a heretic "so blinded by his own pretensions as to have invented a new religion." The *curé*, before whom Ti-Jules was brought, found nothing very reprehensible in his behavior or in what he said. The *hungan* and *boko* then got at the civil authority and described Ti-Jules as a magician who "turned people's heads" by means of "cabalistic words and instruments" and who, at his home, "organized meetings dangerous to the security of the State." The reformer was arrested, thrown into prison, and, although acquitted by the court, nevertheless had to pay out a considerable sum of money.

But the persecutions visited upon him merely increased his reputation. The faithful came in ever greater numbers to be freed from the grip of *loa*. On the advice of the archdiocese, Ti-Jules was asked to refer his penitents to the *curés* of their respective parishes. Thus started the movement of those who were called the *rejetés* (rejectors). Among these a certain Simon, who had been seven years under *boko* for treatment, distinguished himself by his zeal. He accompanied the *curés* on their rounds, and his words were given greater weight by his habit of accusing himself of those very sins from which he wished to preserve his compatriots.

The Catholic chroniclers of this antisuperstition crusade made no bones about the pain and general disturbance caused by these violent accusings and threats of eternal punishment for all who refused to give up the cult of *loa*. This general *crise de conscience* resulted in a revelation—to the clergy—of the number of "converts" who had remained faithful to Voodoo. "All converts or *devotions*—that is to say, all the faithful—were deep in superstition. Even the directors of chapels whose duty it was to catechize others were no exception. In nearly every dwelling there was to be found a little *loa*-house [*maison-loa*] and all the other objects of superstition. Astonishment gradually turned to stupor, but before such an array of facts there could be no more argument: henceforward it was established that nearly all our converts were practicing "the mixture."

The Church then took a step which was to provoke profound indignation even in those quarters from which it might have expected most support. The clergy decided to insist upon an antisuperstitious oath—to be taken by all the faithful. Here is the text of this oath—the oath of the so-called rejectors.

I before God, stand in the Tabernacle, before the priest who represents Him and renew the promises of my baptism. With hand on the Gospels I swear never to give a food-offering [*manger-loa*] of whatever

kind—never to attend a Voodoo ceremony of whatever kind, never to take part in a service to *loa* in any
way whatsoever.

I promise to destroy or have destroyed as soon as
possible all fetishes and objects of superstition, if
any—on me, in my house, and in my compound.

In short I swear never to sink to any superstitious
practice whatever.

[For married persons] I promise moreover to bring
up my children without exception in the Catholic
and Roman religion, outside all superstition, submit-
ting myself fully to the teaching of this Holy Church.

And I promise that with God's help I shall abide
by my oath until death.

Members of the "elite" and even of the middle classes
were outraged they should be required to take an oath
which suggested they were suspected of sharing peasant
beliefs and practices. Their indignation knew no limits.
In vain the *curés* told them that it was precisely because
they were good Catholics that they were being asked to
make a show of solidarity and separate themselves from
those who practiced *le mélange*. It was no good: they still
saw in this measure nothing but humiliation and persecution. The fact that it was imposed upon them by white
priests increased their resentment. It confirmed their suspicions that the foreign priesthood looked upon them as
so many savages. Sermons, conferences, reunions, home
visits—nothing was neglected in the effort to make them
see that the oath was necessary. But in a parish which
included some 2,000 regular churchgoers, no more than
a few dozen agreed to take the oath. In the whole of the
Gonaïves diocese only 3,000 were sworn in. The bishops
attributed this set-back not to hurt vanity but to the
attachment of so-called Catholics to Voodoo, and to
their refusal to break with "superstition." In my opinion,
priests, thinking thus, had rushed from an excess of optim-
ism to one of pessimism. If indeed it be true that a great
many of their parishioners preferred to be deprived of
the right to communicate rather than desert their *humfo*,
then many others certainly regarded the oath as a shameful
admission, incompatible with their personal dignity.

The disillusion, which the clergy confess they felt, was largely compensated by the mass conversions of Voodooists who, seized by a vague collective enthusiasm, "abjured" in large numbers and came flocking to the priests, asking them to destroy the ritual objects which they possessed and to "free them from the impossible obligations which had been imposed upon them." The "obligations" which Voodoo imposes on its devotees explain in many cases the ease with which many of them abjured and the enthusiasm they showed—probably to cover secret misgivings. Finally, peasant populations are easily carried away—sometimes as briefly as violently. It would be as unjust to deny the spontaneity of some conversions as to pretend there was no coercion. From the Catholic point of view, very serious sanctions were taken against all who attended or took part in, actively or passively, any Voodoo ceremony. The mere wearing of an amulet entailed six months' penitence. Fearing they would be deprived of the sacraments, to which they attached the greatest importance, many Voodooists promised to break with the *loa*. Up to this point the Church kept within its rights. Now it changed its tactics and secured the support of the secular arm: on the demand of the clergy, President Lescot ordered the army to co-operate with the *curés* in their hunting down of all objects to do with the Voodoo cult.

Strengthened by the more or less open support of the government, the *curés* had the *humfo* shut up or destroyed, and thousands of sacred objects were burned in veritable *auto-da-fés*. I was in Haiti in 1941 and I remember seeing in the backyards of presbyteries vast pyramids of drums, painted bowls, necklaces, talismans—all waiting for the day fixed for the joyous blaze which was to symbolize the victory of the Church over Satan.

The peasantry whose sanctuaries had been pillaged and who could no longer *battre tambour* (beat their drums) to summon the *loa* of Africa finally began to express their resentment more or less openly—in some regions by staging religious strikes. In addition, both Press and public opinion disapproved the often immoderate zeal of certain priests. The government, aware of the hostility of the *bourgeoisie* and people for the clergy, withdrew its support. On February 22, 1942, shots were fired in the church of Delmas, near Port-au-Prince, just when a Haitian priest was saying a Mass which was to inaugurate a new week of preaching against superstition. The Catholic newspapers let it be clearly understood that this affair was an act of government provocation—alleging that police disguised as peasants had been sent to Delmas. The fact is the government did immediately seize on the affair as a pretext for curbing the anti-Voodoo campaign. Monseigneur X himself relates how, after the earlier enthusiasm for the *renonce*, there was now a massive swing back to "superstition."

With great honesty he admits that "the greater part of that mass which had rejoiced to be delivered from its slavery, now, once more, took up their chains." Voodoo sanctuaries opened again, and little by little the faithful gathered again around *hungan* and *mambo*. Under the government of President Estimé (1946–52), Voodoo emerged completely from semiclandestinity. Many black intellectuals who supported the new regime professed to admire Voodoo as an expression of the popular soul. It was natural for a government which claimed to be sprung from the masses and to represent the *authentiques*—that is to say, Haitians of pure Negro stock—to show itself tolerant of, and even kindly disposed to, the popular religion. In spite of the economic distress which afflicted country districts, the presidency of Estimé was marked by a revival of Voodoo. Many adepts had been nourishing the desire to regain the favor of the *loa*, whose worship they had only neglected out of fear of *curés* or police.

The *renonce* has had a very definite effect on the Church's idea of its task in Haiti. The clergy had understood that it was high time the masses received a more solid Christian grounding. An attempt is now made to guarantee clerical influence by means of catechists who are chosen from among the "rejectors." These receive training which makes them useful auxiliaries of the country *curés*. On the other hand, the war declared on Voodoo by the Church has awakened the peasants to the very real opposition which exists between the cult of *loa* and official Catholicism. The *curés* of today are much more strict on the question of orthodoxy, and they are not allowed that lenience which in the past made it possible for the Voodooists to use the Catholic liturgy for pagan ends.

Selected Bibliography
on Folk Religion

There is a vast anthropological literature on folk and primitive religions. The following bibliography is a selection from the outstanding books and monographs published over the past twenty-five years in the English language. It also contains a list of the major professional journals which frequently publish articles and book reviews on the anthropology of folk religion.

Andersson, Efraim: *Messianic Popular Movements in the Congo.* Uppsala, Sweden: Studia Ethnographica Upsaliensia, Vol. XIII; 1958.

Barnett, Homer G.: *Indian Shakers: A Messianic Cult of the Pacific Northwest.* Carbondale, Illinois: Southern Illinois University Press; 1957.

Barton, R. F.: *The Relgiion of the Ifugaos.* Menasha, Wisconsin: Memoirs of the American Anthropological Association, No. 65; 1946.

Bascom, William R.: *The Sociological Role of the Yoruba Cult-Group.* Menasha, Wisconsin: Memoirs of the American Anthropological Association, No. 63; 1944.

Bateson, Gregory: *Naven: A Survey of Problems Suggested by a Composite Picture of the Culture of a New Guinea Tribe Drawn from Three Points of View.* Second edition. Stanford, California: Stanford University Press; 1958.

Bellah, Robert N.: *Tokugawa Religion: The Values of Pre-Industrial Japan.* Glencoe, Illinois: The Free Press; 1957.

Belo, Jane: *Bali: Rangda and Barong.* New York: American Ethnological Society Monograph, No. 16, J. J. Augustin; 1949.

——: *Bali: Temple Festival.* New York: American Ethnological Society Monograph, J. J. Augustin; 1953.

Berndt, Ronald M.: *Djang; ıwul: An Aboriginal Religious Cult of North-Eastern Arnh m Land.* Melbourne: F. W. Cheshire; 1952.

——: *Kunapipi.* New York: International Universities Press; 1951.

Codere, Helen: *Fighting with Property: A Study of Kwakiutl*

Potlatching and Warfare, 1792–1930. New York: American Ethnological Society, No. 18, J. J. Augustin; 1950.

Elkin, A. P.: *Studies in Australian Totemism.* Sydney: Oceania Monograph, No. 2, Australian National Research Council.

Emmet, Dorothy: *Function, Purpose and Powers: Some Concepts in the Study of Individuals and Societies.* New York: St. Martin's Press; 1958.

Evans-Pritchard, E. E.: *Nuer Religion.* London: Oxford University, The Clarendon Press; 1956.

——: *Witchcraft, Oracles and Magic among the Azande.* London: Oxford University, The Clarendon Press; 1937.

Fauset, Arthur Huff: *Black Gods of the Metropolis: Negro Religious Cults of the Urban North.* Philadelphia: Publications of the Philadelphia Anthropological Society, Vol. III, University of Pennsylvania Press; 1944.

Firth, Raymond: *The Work of the Gods in Tikopia.* Two volumes. London: Monographs on Social Anthropology No. 1 and No. 2, London School of Economics and Political Science; 1940.

Forde, C. Daryll, ed.: *African Worlds: Studies in the Cosmological Ideas and Social Values of African Peoples.* London: International African Institute, Oxford University Press; 1954.

——: *The Context of Belief: A Consideration of Fetishism among the Yakö.* Liverpool, England: University of Liverpool; 1958.

Fortes, Meyer: *Oedipus and Job in West African Religion.* Cambridge at the University Press; 1959.

Fortune, Reo F.: *Manus Religion.* Philadelphia: Memoirs, American Philosophical Society, Vol. 3; 1935.

Geddes, W. R.: *Nine Dayak Nights.* Melbourne: Oxford University Press; 1957.

Greenberg, Joseph: *The Influence of Islam on Sudanese Religion.* New York: Monographs of the American Ethnological Society, No. 10, J. J. Augustin; 1946.

Geertz, Clifford: *The Religion of Java.* Glencoe, Illinois: The Free Press; 1960.

Gluckman, Max: *Rituals of Rebellion in South-East Africa.* Manchester: Manchester University Press; 1954.

Goode, William J.: *Religion among the Primitives.* Glencoe, Illinois: The Free Press; 1951.

Hallowell, A. Irving: *The Role of Conjuring in Saulteaux Society.* Philadelphia: Publications of the Philadelphia Anthropological Society, Vol. II, Brinton Memorial Series, University of Pennsylvania; 1942.

Harley, George W.: *Masks as Agents of Social Control in Northeast Liberia.* Cambridge, Massachusetts: Papers of the Peabody Museum of Harvard, Vol. XXXII, No. 2; 1950.

Herskovits, Melville J. and Frances S. Herskovits: *An Outline of Dahomean Religious Belief*. Menasha, Wisconsin: Memoirs of the American Anthropological Association, No. 41; 1933.

Hsu, Francis L. K.: *Religion, Science and Human Crises; A Study of China in Transition and its Implications for the West*. London: Routledge and Kegan Paul; 1952.

Hultkrantz, Ake: *The North American Indian Orpheus Tradition: A Contribution to Comparative Religion*. The Ethnographical Museum of Sweden, Stockholm Monograph Series, Publication No. 2; 1957.

Kluckhohn, Clyde and Dorothea Leighton: *The Navaho*. Cambridge, Massachusetts: Harvard University Press; 1946.

La Barre, Weston: *The Peyote Cult*. New Haven, Connecticut: Yale University Publications in Anthropology, No. 19; 1938.

La Farge, Oliver: *Santa Eulalia: The Religion of a Cuchumatán Indian Town*. Chicago, Illinois: University of Chicago Press; 1947.

Leslie, Charles M.: *Now We Are Civilized: A Study of the World View of the Zapotec Indians of Mitla, Oaxaca*. Detroit, Michigan: Wayne State University Press; 1960.

Malinowski, Bronislaw: *Coral Gardens and Their Magic*. Two volumes. London: George Allen & Unwin, Ltd.; 1935.

——: *Magic, Science and Religion and Other Essays*. Glencoe, Illinois: The Free Press; 1948.

——: *The Foundations of Faith and Morals*. London: Oxford University Press; 1936.

Mead, Margaret: *The Mountain Arapesh. II. Supernaturalism*. New York: Anthropological Papers of the American Museum of Natural History, Vol. XXXVII, Part III; 1940.

Métraux, Alfred: *Voodoo in Haiti*. New York: Oxford University Press; 1959.

Murphy, Robert F.: *Mundurucú Religion*. Berkeley, California: University of California Publications in American Archaeology and Ethnology, Vol. 49, No. 1; 1958.

Nadel, S. F.: *Nupe Religion*. Glencoe, Illinois: The Free Press; 1954.

Parsons, Elsie Clews: *Pueblo Indian Religion*. Two volumes. Chicago, Illinois: University of Chicago Press; 1939.

Radcliffe-Brown, A. R.: *Structure and Function in Primitive Society*. Glencoe, Illinois: The Free Press; 1952.

——: *The Andaman Islanders*. Glencoe, Illinois: The Free Press; 1948.

Rapaport, Robert N.: *Changing Navaho Religious Values: A Study of Christian Missions to the Rimrock Navahos*. Cambridge, Massachusetts: Harvard University Peabody Museum Papers, Vol. 41, No. 2; 1954.

Redfield, Robert: *The Folk Culture of Yucatan*. Chicago, Illinois: University of Chicago Press; 1941.

Reichard, Gladys A.: *Navaho Religion: A Study of Symbolism.* Two volumes. New York: Bollingen Series XVIII, Pantheon Books; 1950.

Richards, Audrey I.: *Chisungu: A Girl's Initiation Ceremony among the Bemba of Northern Rhodesia.* New York: Grove Press; 1957.

Róheim, Géza: *The Eternal Ones of the Dream.* New York: International Universities Press; 1945.

Schram, Louis M. J.: *The Monquors of the Kansu-Tibetan Border: Part II, Their Religious Life.* Philadelphia: Transactions of the American Philosophical Society, New Series, Vol. 47, Part 1; 1957.

Slotkin, J. S.: *The Peyote Religion: A Study in Indian-White Relations.* Glencoe, Illinois: The Free Press; 1956.

Speck, Frank S.: *Naskapi: The Savage Hunters of the Labrador Peninsula.* Norman, Oklahoma: University of Oklahoma Press; 1935.

Spencer, Dorothy M.: *Disease, Religion and Society in the Fiji Islands.* New York: Monographs of the American Ethnological Society, No. 2, J. J. Augustin; 1941.

Spencer, Katherine: *Mythology and Values: An Analysis of Navaho Chantway Myths.* Philadelphia: American Folklore Society, Memoirs Vol. 48; 1957.

Srinivas, M. N.: *Religion and Society among the Coorgs of South India.* London: Oxford, The Clarendon Press; 1952.

Steiner, Franz: *Taboo.* New York: Philosophical Library; 1956.

Sundkler, B.: *Bantu Prophets in South Africa.* London: Lutterworth Press; 1948.

Tegnaeus, Harry: *Blood Brothers, An Ethno-Sociological Study of the Institutions of Blood-Brotherhood with Special Reference to Africa.* New York: Philosophical Library; 1952.

Underhill, Ruth: *Papago Indian Religion.* New York: Columbia University Press; 1946.

Wagley, Charles: *The Social and Religious Life of a Guatemalan Village.* Menasha, Wisconsin: Memoir of the American Anthropological Association, No. 71; 1949.

Warner, W. Lloyd: *A Black Civilization: A Study of an Australian Tribe.* Revised edition. New York: Harper & Brothers; 1958.

Williamson, Robert W.: *Religion and Social Organization in Central Polynesia.* Ed. Ralph Piddington. Cambridge at the University Press; 1937.

Wilson, Monica: *Communal Rituals of the Nyakyusa.* London: Oxford University Press; 1959.

——: *Rituals of Kinship among the Nyakyusa.* London: Oxford University Press; 1957.

Worsley, Peter: *The Trumpet Shall Sound: A Study of "Cargo" Cults in Melanesia.* London: Macgibbon & Kee; 1957.

JOURNALS

Africa. London: International African Institute, Oxford University Press.

African Studies. Johannesburg: University of the Witwatersrand.

American Anthropologist. Menasha, Wisconsin: American Anthropological Association.

Anthropological Quarterly. Washington, D. C.: The Catholic University of America Press.

Comparative Studies in Society and History. The Hague, Netherlands: Mouton & Co.

Current Anthropology. Chicago, Illinois: University of Chicago Press.

Journal of American Folklore. Philadelphia: American Folklore Society.

Journal of the Royal Anthropological Institute of Great Britain and Ireland. London: Royal Anthropological Institute.

Man. London: Royal Anthropological Institute.

Oceania. Sydney: University of Sydney, Australia.

Southwestern Journal of Anthropology. Albuquerque, New Mexico: Laboratory of Anthropology, University of New Mexico.

INDEX

abhinaya, Indian gesture language, see dance

aesthetic quality: in folk religion, 308–9; in funeral rites, 317

age-set system, 89

ambiguity in Nuer religion, 65, 98

ambivalence: Tallensi father-son relationship, 28–9; in Nuer religion, 98

ancestors: Tallensi worship of, xv, 18–21, 27–8, 37–8, 39–45; West African cults of, 12; Nuer identification of cattle herd with, 82, 84; spears of Nuer, 83; Iatmul totemic, 270, 281; Chinese cult of, 307; spirits of, in Tikopia, 316, 318; in Haiti, 393

Andaman Islands, 304

animism: anthropological usage, 55; and origins of religion, 96; in Haiti, 432

Annam, 304, 307

anthropology: ideas used to analyze religion in, x–xi; human irrationality a theme of, xiii–xiv, xv; judgments of fact and value in, xv–xviii, 55; British school of, 3–4

Apache tribe (North America), 329

art: distinction between arts of delectation and true art, xii–xiii, xvii; compared to science, 261

atheism in India, 112, 132

Austen, Jane, 261

Azande people (Sudan), 54

Badaga tribe (India), 222, 223

ballad form in Indian films, 125

baptism, Voodoo, 436

Barton, Ralph, xvi

Bascom, William R., 12, 13

Bastide, Roger, 421

Bateson, Gregory, viii, xvii, 259–60

Bateson, William, 259

Bay, André, 306

Beals, Alan Robin, 192

belief: variation of, in India, 187–8, 190, 195, 205–6, 208, 210–13, in primitive societies, 303–4, in Yucatan, 353, 361–2; related to practice in Tusik, 349; see also factionalism, sects

Bell, Daniel, 103

Benin (West Africa), 13

Bhāgavata Purāṇa, 120, 122, 192

Bhajans (Hindu ritual), 119–21

Bhakti (path of devotion): in urban culture, 115–17; religious movements, 117–21; in storytelling, 121–3; Hindu classicists' attitude toward, 130; sects in Madras, 130; essence of *harikathā* performance, 132; see also Hinduism

Boas, Franz, 302

Bombay: population of, 108–9; encounter of civilizations in, 109

Brahmans: priestly and worldly, 113; changes in religious orientation among, 115–17; Vedic culture reserved to, 123; cultural role of in Madras, 162–6; in village of Kishan Garhi, 170, 180–1; slight Sanskritization of, 203–4

Brazil, Afro-American cults in, 431

breath, symbol of life, 22

Calcutta, 109

cannibalism, xiv

Carnap, Rudolf, 103

Carroll, Lewis, 306

Cassirer, Ernst, ix

caste system: essential to Hinduism, 165; weakening of, 165; in village of Kishan Garhi, 170, 171; ignored by terms of address, 174; distribution of deities by, 203–5; little communities related to larger Indian society through, 179–83; Kota tribesman punished for violating, 245–6; Kota tribe entering, 252; in Haiti, 392

castration of bulls among Nuer, 74

cathartic effect: in Tallensi religion, 36–8; in Nuer religion, 98

CHARLES LESLIE was born in Lake Village, Arkansas, November 8, 1923. He is a graduate of the University of Chicago, where he received his Ph.B. (1949) from the College, and his M.A. (1950), and Ph.D. (1959) in the Department of Anthropology. He has taught at Southern Methodist University (1950–1), the University of Chicago Downtown College (1951–2), and the University of Minnesota (1954–6). Since 1956 he has been assistant professor of anthropology at Pomona College. Mr. Leslie received a Ford Foundation grant to do field research among the Zapotec-speaking Indians of Oaxaca, Mexico, 1953–4, for the Redfield project in "Comparative Study of Cultures and Civilizations." He is a Fellow of the American Anthropological Association and was director of the annual meeting of the Southwestern Anthropological Association in April 1960. He is the author of *Now We Are Civilized: A Study of the World View of the Zapotec Indians of Mitla, Oaxaca* (1960). With his wife and three children, Professor Leslie lives in Claremont, California.

THIS BOOK is set in *Electra*, a Linotype face designed by W. A. Dwiggins who was responsible for so much that is good in contemporary book design. Electra cannot be classified as either modern or oldstyle. It is not based on any historical model, nor does it echo a particular period or style.

This book was composed, printed, and bound by The Colonial Press Inc., Clinton, Mass. The paper was manufactured by S. D. Warren Co., Boston. Cover design by JOSEPH LOW.

VINTAGE WORKS OF SCIENCE
AND PSYCHOLOGY

A free catalogue of VINTAGE BOOKS, listed by subject matter, will be sent to you at your request. Write to Vintage Books, Inc., 501 Madison Avenue, New York 22, New York.

VINTAGE POLITICAL SCIENCE
AND SOCIAL CRITICISM

VINTAGE HISTORY
EUROPEAN

VINTAGE HISTORY
AMERICAN